Law and Legislation for Social Service Workers

Nora Rock

ADVISORY PANEL

Rebecca Bromwich FANSHAWE COLLEGE

Gary Cassidy ALGONQUIN COLLEGE

David Little LOYALIST COLLEGE

Bonnie Oddie LOYALIST COLLEGE

Judy Overgaard

Neil McMahon MOHAWK COLLEGE

Steven Shadd CONESTOGA COLLEGE

Leo Smits UNIVERSITY OF GUELPH–HUMBER

 2008
Emond Montgomery Publications
Toronto, Canada

Emond Montgomery Publications Limited
60 Shaftesbury Avenue
Toronto ON M4T 1A3
http://www.emp.ca/highered

Printed in Canada.
Reprinted December 2015.

We acknowledge the financial support of the Government of Canada through the Canada Book Fund for our publishing activities.

The events and characters depicted in this book are fictitious. Any similarity to actual persons, living or dead, is purely coincidental.

Acquisitions and developmental editor: Peggy Buchan

Marketing manager: Christine Davidson

Director, sales and marketing, higher education: Kevin Smulan

Copy editor: Christine Purden

Supervising editor: Jim Lyons

Production editor: David Handelsman

Proofreader: Debbie Gervais

Text designer and typesetter: Tara Wells

Indexer: Paula Pike

Cover designer: John Vegter

Library and Archives Canada Cataloguing in Publication

Rock, Nora, 1968-
    Law and legislation for social service workers / Nora Rock.

Includes index.
ISBN 978-1-55239-187-7

    1. Social workers—Legal status, laws, etc.—Canada.   I. Title.

KE450.S6R62 2008   344.7103'2   C2007-906600-3
KF390.S6R62 2008

Contents

PART IV   THE CRIMINAL JUSTICE SYSTEM

CHAPTER 9   The Criminal Justice System

CHAPTER 10   Correctional Services for Adults

CHAPTER 11   The Youth Criminal Justice System

CHAPTER 12   Community Policing

- It enhances your understanding of the limits of your practice—which activities fall within the scope of your duties and which do not.

- It helps you to avoid actions or omissions that might expose you to professional **sanctions**, criminal charges, or civil **liability** (lawsuits).

- It helps you to understand your legal rights and the legal rights of your clients.

- It helps you to understand which benefits and services are available to your clients, as well as the circumstances in which benefits or services may be denied.

- It provides insight into how government works.

The discussion of the legal context presented in this book is organized as follows:

1. *Regulation of the social service profession and legal liability of social service workers*: This opening chapter introduces the system that regulates social service professionals. The consequences of malpractice or professional misconduct are discussed in the final chapter (chapter 23).

2. *How the law works*: This chapter explains why social service workers need to know about the law, and how to work with lawyers. Chapter 2 provides a general overview of the Canadian legal system, including law-making authority, sources of law, and the structure of the court system. Chapters 13 to 16 describe the procedures for resolving legal disputes, including the trial process in the traditional court system; access to legal advice and representation; and mechanisms for resolving disputes without recourse to the courts.

LEGISLATIVE SHORTCUT

Social Work and Social Service Work Act, 1998

SO 1998, c. 31

Objective: To set standards for social workers and social service workers, minimize poor service, and thereby raise the profile of the profession in the public eye by increasing consumers' trust.

Target Population: Social workers, social service workers, and their clients.

Program Administration: The Ontario College of Social Workers and Social Service Workers is governed by a 21-member council equally "representing" social workers, social service workers, and the public.

Administrative Tribunal: Complaints from the public about a member social worker or a social service worker are first heard by the Complaints Committee. If the complaint is pursued, there is a hearing before the Discipline Committee.

Summary: The *Social Work and Social Service Work Act, 1998* provides the framework under which the professions of social work and social service work are self-regulated by the Ontario College of Social Workers and Social Service Workers. Members must obey the college's code of ethics and follow its standards of practice or face sanctions. ◇

CHAPTER 1

Social Services Practice and the Law

CHAPTER OBJECTIVES

After reading this chapter, you should be able to:

- Explain why social service workers need to know about the law.
- Understand the importance of keeping up to date in your legal knowledge.
- Explain what it means to give legal advice, and why social service workers should never do so.
- List some of the situations in which a social service worker might work with a lawyer.
- Describe the advantages of professional self-regulation.
- Describe the role of the Ontario College of Social Workers and Social Service Workers.
- Explain the relationship between professional standards and legal obligations.

INTRODUCTION

This is a book about the law.

Many people give little thought to the law until some event—a divorce, a criminal charge for an offence, or a dispute with an employer—happens to bring them into contact with the legal system. However, the reality is that almost every aspect of our daily lives is regulated, at least to some degree, by laws. For example, if you live in Ontario and drive to work, you are expected to comply with the *Highway Traffic Act*. Your relationship with your employer is regulated by a number of statutes, including the *Employment Standards Act* and the *Occupational Health and Safety Act*. Your professional status as a social service worker is regulated by the *Social Work and Social Service Work Act, 1998*. And finally, your work with your clients is often regulated by laws applicable to specific services such as the *Ontario Disability Support Program Act, 1997*.

This book is designed to raise your awareness of the legal context of social service work. This is important for a number of reasons:

PART I

Overview of the Legal Context

3. *Specific statutory regimes and regulatory systems*: Chapters 3 to 12 and 17 to 22 describe the various statutory regimes and regulatory systems that govern the delivery of services by social service workers in various contexts—for example, child and family services, income assistance, corrections, and housing.

Social service work encompasses a broad and diverse range of services, and social service workers may be employed in a variety of public and private sector settings. The following list is illustrative but by no means exhaustive:

- youth programs
- women's shelters and programs
- children's aid societies
- anger management programs
- addictions counselling
- programs for disabled persons
- immigrant services
- housing and community development
- halfway houses and rehabilitation programs

Each of the service delivery areas in which social service workers are active is subject to legal regulation. In some cases, such as health and long-term care, multiple statutes and regulations (rules made under statutes) are applicable to a social service worker's daily activities. Because of the great diversity in both law and practice, it is impossible for one book to cover every legal detail that every social service worker needs to know. Instead, this text provides an overview of the more important legal issues in particular service areas. This introduction to the statutes that regulate social service delivery and practice is the starting-point for a more detailed study of the legal framework that governs your work in the field.

It is important to keep up to date with changes in the law. Statutes are frequently amended (revised), repealed (rendered no longer applicable), proposed (created), or enacted (passed into law) by consent of the legislature. Regulations are changed more easily because they don't require any action other than legislative approval. If you need to be certain of the exact state of the law on a particular issue, you should check the current official version of the applicable statute and regulations. If you supervise social service workers who frequently need to refer to the law, it may be useful to keep a copy of the applicable statutes and regulations in a location handy to all employees. You may also find it helpful to put one employee in charge of checking, on a regular basis, for changes to the legislation.

WEB LINK

Up-to-date versions of statutes and regulations can be found on the website of the Canadian Legal Information Institute at www.canlii.org.

WORKING WITH THE LAW AND LAWYERS

Legal Advice

Social service workers need to have a basic understanding of the law as it applies to their work. With experience, they may become very familiar with particular laws and how they apply to clients' situations. They may find that they can quite accurately identify the legal implications of a client's situation, or predict how the law will apply to something that a client is proposing to do.

However, social service workers are not lawyers. They are not qualified to provide **legal advice**, and they must not give clients the impression that they can act as a substitute for a lawyer. Understanding the law involves much more than simply referring to the words of a statute. The application and effect of a statute depends on many things, including

- regulations made under the statute;

- policies, both written and unwritten, of the ministry, department, or agency that administers the statute;

- other statutes, such as the constitution, including the *Canadian Charter of Rights and Freedoms*, or human rights legislation; and

- the common law—interpretations of the statute or its predecessors in cases decided by the courts.

Generally, it takes years of legal training and experience to acquire the knowledge needed to provide reliable legal advice. In addition, even if, over time, you acquire detailed knowledge of the law relating to a particular issue, there are other reasons why you must not advise a client on matters of law:

- You may be sued for misrepresentation and **malpractice**. If your advice has resulted in financial loss or other harm, you may be held liable for damages and required to pay the client compensation. Moreover, you will likely face disciplinary action by the governing body that regulates your profession (discussed below), with potentially serious consequences for your professional standing.

- Communications between a lawyer and his client are protected by a rule of confidentiality known as **solicitor–client privilege**. There is no similar rule to protect the confidentiality of communications between a social service worker and her client in the event of litigation. As a result, if your advice to a client leads to or is implicated in a criminal charge or a lawsuit, any written or oral communication between you and your client may be subject to disclosure to the prosecutor or litigants.

It is very important that social service workers restrict their professional practice to the field in which they are trained. This is required by the standards of the profession and by the expectations of employers and clients. When legal services are required, your professional duty to your client compels you to refer him to a lawyer.

Legal Information

While social service workers should never give legal advice, they are often asked to provide **legal information**. The difference between advice and information generally relates to the level of specificity.

For example, if a client asks you how she can obtain legal immigrant status in Canada, you may tell her that there are various categories under which an immigrant may apply, and give her a government brochure explaining the different categories and the application process. However, you should not express an opinion on whether or not the client's application would be successful, since that would constitute legal advice. Other examples of the distinction between legal information and legal advice, in a family services context, are provided in chapter 4.

Another way of thinking about the distinction between legal information and legal advice is to remember that legal information is limited to a description and/or explanation of what the law is, while legal advice is an attempt to apply the law to a particular situation or set of facts.

Social service workers must ensure that the legal information they provide is accurate. If brochures or information sheets are not available from government sources, one strategy is for service agencies to produce their own lawyer-approved handouts for clients. For example, the agency's service personnel, including social service workers, could identify the legal matters that arise frequently for their clients, and work with a lawyer to develop a handout that summarizes the relevant law. The summary would be either prepared or approved by the lawyer and presented in a reader-friendly format. The handout would include a recommendation that the reader obtain legal advice on how the law would apply in his particular situation.

Working with a Client's Lawyer

When a client has retained a lawyer to handle a legal matter, sometimes it is useful for the lawyer and the social service worker to communicate directly. However, the respective obligations of the social service worker and the lawyer to protect the confidentiality of client information pose a challenge regarding communications between them. To address this problem, the client can be asked to sign waivers that release both professionals from their obligations to maintain confidentiality in their communications with each other with respect to certain client information.

Sharing information allows for a multidisciplinary approach to the client's needs. Consider the example of a prison inmate who has applied to the parole board for early release. He is working with a social service worker to develop a plan for addictions counselling after his release, while a lawyer is representing him in his application to the board. If the two professionals share information directly, the lawyer will get complete and accurate information about the counselling and will be better able to present a persuasive case to the parole board. However, the inmate must first give his express consent to the sharing of information—preferably in writing. Consent is always required before a social service worker discloses personal information about a client to the client's lawyer, or to anyone else.

Social service workers may also work with lawyers when acting as a client's support person during a legal proceeding. For example, a social service worker may accompany a victim of spousal abuse to court to offer moral support. In this situation, the social service worker will best serve her client by taking care to establish a good working relationship with the client's lawyer. Here too, boundaries must be respected. When a social service worker accompanies a client to court, hearings, or other formal meetings, she should take care not to answer questions on behalf of the client, express an opinion about the legal advice given, or attempt to influence the client's instructions to the lawyer. The social service worker must act only in her professional capacity and limit her role to providing support to the client.

Working with Your Employer's Lawyer

There are many situations in which a social service agency may need to consult a lawyer, including the following:

- The agency wants to incorporate or seeks charitable status.

- The agency needs advice about service issues.

- The agency needs to defend itself in a lawsuit or wants to sue another party.

- The agency needs advice on the legal implications of a proposed activity.

As an employee of the agency, you may be asked to work with the agency's lawyer on these and other legal matters.

One of the more common situations in which social service workers deal with agency lawyers is in the context of preparing documents that create or limit legal rights—for example, consent forms, releases, or other contracts. These and any other legal documents should be reviewed by a lawyer.

Ideally, a lawyer should also be consulted any time a social service agency proposes to undertake a new activity that may have legal implications. The following are a few typical examples:

- offering access to a sports or fitness program (for example, aquafitness classes for seniors);

- arranging transportation by chartered bus for program participants, if the agency has never done this before;

- extending services to a category of clients who have never been served by the agency before, and who may have special needs (for example, extending a horseback riding program at a summer camp for young clients to include a class for children with developmental disabilities);

- holding a fundraising event such as a distance run, a skip-a-thon, or other such contest; or

- trying a new form of fundraising, such as a telephone appeal campaign.

The agency may ask the lawyer to research the legal risks associated with the new activity, explain any laws that may apply, identify any insurance or tax concerns, and arrange for necessary permits or licences. If the agency is a not-for-profit corporation or a registered charity, the lawyer will also be able to advise whether the activity is consistent with the requirements of the agency's legal status.

If you are asked to work with your employer's lawyer, you should find out whether you have the employer's consent to disclose any requested business information. You must also be careful not to disclose any confidential client information, whether intentionally or not. This includes information contained in a database, such as names and addresses.

Sometimes, in the course of your work, you may find yourself in need of a lawyer's advice about a service issue. When this happens, speak with your supervisor and request that the question be put to the agency's lawyer. It is important, however, to distinguish your own legal interests from the agency's interests. If your question relates to the employer and not to you personally—for example, you notice that young clients and their friends are using the agency's parking lot for skateboarding and you're worried about the agency's liability for any injuries—it is appropriate to raise your concern with the employer's lawyer. However, if the question relates to you personally—for example, you have a violent client whom you don't want to be alone with and the employer is not listening to your concerns—you may need to talk to your own lawyer.

Working with Your Own Lawyer

As suggested above, situations may arise where you need to consult a lawyer on your own behalf in a matter related to your professional practice. For example, you may question the legal basis for a decision made by your employer that affects you directly, or a client may make a formal complaint accusing you of professional misconduct. Whatever the circumstances, you must remember that your duty to the client comes first. That duty requires you to:

- act in the best interests of the client, even when it is against your own interests to do so; and

- maintain the confidentiality of the client's information.

These duties can be onerous indeed. For example, if you are accused of misconduct with respect to a client, you should be honest and straightforward and admit any wrongdoing; in particular, you should avoid "blaming the victim" in order to further your own interests at the expense of the client. Protecting a client's confidentiality while responding to legal or professional charges can also be very difficult. For example, you may have information about your client that undermines his credibility and is relevant in defending charges against you. However, if the information is of a confidential nature, you are duty-bound to keep it that way. The obligation to maintain client confidentiality is discussed in detail in chapter 22.

THE REGULATION OF SOCIAL SERVICE PROFESSIONALS: THE ONTARIO COLLEGE OF SOCIAL WORKERS AND SOCIAL SERVICE WORKERS

The social service professions—social workers and social service workers—became self-regulating in 1998, when the Ontario government enacted the *Social Work and Social Service Work Act, 1998*. Other professions, including medicine, nursing, law, psychiatry, psychology, and engineering, have been self-regulated for many years.

The regulating body is the Ontario College of Social Workers and Social Service Workers. It is governed by a 21-member council equally representing social workers, social service workers, and the public. The college carries out a number of responsibilities or functions on behalf of the membership and the public. These include setting the criteria for membership, establishing a code of ethics, defining standards of practice, and maintaining professional standards through sanctions for non-compliance. Each of these functions is described more fully below.

Membership

To promote high-quality client services, the college encourages individuals who work in the social service sector to obtain professional **accreditation** by becoming members of the college. Professional status is indicated by the designation "social worker," "registered social worker," "social service worker," or "registered social service worker." The use of these titles is restricted to members of the college. Employers rely on these designations in hiring individuals who are qualified to practise in the social service sector.

To be eligible for membership, an applicant must establish that she meets the college's criteria for certification, including educational qualifications. A further condition of membership is that, on acceptance, the applicant agrees to comply with the college's code of ethics and standards of practice. Failure to comply can lead to disciplinary action by the college, including possible revocation of membership and loss of professional status.

The college recognizes that social workers and social service workers represent two distinct professions. As you know, one important difference between the two relates to educational qualifications: social workers typically study at a university, where they obtain a bachelor of social work or master of social work degree; social service workers study at a community college, where they obtain a diploma. The difference in training is reflected in the college's definition of the scope of practice of each profession. In this context, the key difference is that social workers are permitted to provide "diagnostic" services while social service workers are not.

Membership in the college provides important benefits, including

- recognition as an accredited professional;
- clarification of the scope of professional practice;
- recognized standards of professional practice;
- potential coverage of services under insurance and employment benefit plans;
- increased potential for fair remuneration for professional services;
- enhanced public confidence in social service professionals;
- the opportunity to work with colleagues in the profession on matters of common interest; and
- a unified political voice on issues of concern to social service professionals.

Code of Ethics

A **code of ethics** reflects the core values of a profession, defines its commitment to the clients whom it serves, and provides a principled framework to guide individual practice. The college's code of ethics provides as follows:

1. A social worker or social service worker shall maintain the best interest of the client as the primary professional obligation;

2. A social worker or social service worker shall respect the intrinsic worth of the persons she or he serves in her or his professional relationships with them;

POLICY EXCERPT

Scope of Practice of a Social Service Worker

The Ontario College of Social Workers and Social Service Workers defines the scope of practice of a social service worker to include the following:

- The provision of assessment, treatment, and evaluation services within a relationship between a social service worker and client;

- The development, promotion, management, administration, delivery and evaluation of human service programs, including that done in collaboration with other professionals;

- The supervision of another social service worker or a social service work student;

- The provision of consultation services to other social service workers or professionals in relation to assessment, treatment and evaluation;

- The development, promotion, implementation and evaluation of social policies aimed at improving social conditions and equality;

- The conduct of research or provision of education regarding the practice of social service work; and

- Any other activities recognized by the College.

Source: Ontario College of Social Workers and Social Service Workers, *Standards of Practice Handbook*, available online at www.ocswssw.org. ◇

3. A social worker or social service worker shall carry out her or his professional duties and obligations with integrity and objectivity;

4. A social worker or social service worker shall have and maintain competence in the provision of a social work or social service work service to a client;

5. A social worker or social service worker shall not exploit the relationship with a client for personal benefit, gain or gratification;

6. A social worker or social service worker shall protect the confidentiality of all professionally acquired information. He or she shall disclose such information only when required or allowed by law to do so, or when clients have consented to disclosure;

7. A social worker or social service worker who engages in another profession, occupation, affiliation, or calling shall not allow these outside interests to affect the social work or social service work relationship with the client;

8. A social worker or social service worker shall not provide social work or social service work services in a manner that discredits the profession of social work or social service work or diminishes the public's trust in either profession;

9. A social worker or social service worker shall **advocate** for workplace conditions and policies that are consistent with this Code of Ethics and the Standards of Practice of the Ontario College of Social Workers and Social Service Workers;

10. A social worker or social service worker shall promote excellence in his or her respective profession;

11. A social worker or social service worker shall advocate change in the best interest of the client, and for the overall benefit of society, the environment, and the global community.

Standards of Practice

Professional standards are benchmarks against which a professional is expected to measure his or her performance. For members of the profession, they serve as a guide to the development of good practices and the achievement of excellence on an individual level. For clients and the public at large, they facilitate assessment of the quality of services received and identification of problems with services.

The college published its standards of practice for social service professionals in 2000. The current *Standards of Practice Handbook* is divided into eight subject areas, as follows:

    I. Relationship with Clients
   II. Competence and Integrity
  III. Responsibility to Clients
  IV. Social Work and Social Service Work Record
   V. Confidentiality
  VI. Fees
 VII. Advertising
VIII. Sexual Misconduct

Each subject area is defined by a key principle—a brief statement that conveys the profession's philosophy of how social workers and social service workers should manage that particular aspect of their practice. Each principle is supported by a set of interpretation points designed to give more practical guidance, as illustrated by the following example.

Example
The principle for subject area III, "Responsibility to Clients," is expressed as follows:

> Principle III
> College members ensure that professional services are provided responsibly to those persons, groups or organizations seeking their assistance.

Two of the interpretation points provided in support of principle III address the important issue of **dual relationships**:

> 3.7 College members avoid conflicts of interest and/or dual relationships with clients or former clients, or with students, employees and supervisees that could impair members' professional judgement or increase the risk of exploitation or harm to clients.
>
> 3.8 In a situation where a personal relationship does occur between the member and a client or former client, it is the member, not the client or former client, who assumes full responsibility for demonstrating that the client or former client has not been exploited, coerced or manipulated, intentionally or unintentionally.

A dual relationship exists where there is both a personal relationship and a professional relationship between a social service worker and a client. In cases where the initial contact between the social service worker and the client occurs in the context, or as a result, of the delivery of services, the development of a personal relationship during the period of service must be avoided. Sometimes, however, a social relationship exists before the professional relationship, or the parties wish to commence a social relationship after the professional relationship has ended.

It can be hard to avoid a pre-existing social relationship in a very small community, where clients may be acquaintances, neighbours, or even distant relatives. In a larger community, a client can be referred to another social service worker; but in a very small community, the social service worker may be "the only show in town." In such cases, where the existence of a dual relationship is unavoidable, it should not become a barrier to the provision of service to the client. Instead, the social service worker should take special care to discuss with the client such issues as

- the nature of the professional relationship;
- the separation of the personal and professional relationships; and
- the social service worker's obligation to maintain client confidentiality and any limits on that obligation.

Sometimes it is acceptable to have a social relationship after the professional relationship has ended, but social service workers should be cautioned by interpretation 3.8, above.

Non-Compliance

The code of ethics and the principles expressed in the *Standards of Practice Handbook* are guidelines as opposed to laws. A social service worker who violates the code or the standards of practice will not automatically face legal penalties as a result. However, she will likely face disciplinary action by the college. Moreover, a significant lapse from the professional standard may expose the social service worker to civil liability, or even criminal charges, if it results in injury or harm to others.

Depending on the circumstances, the consequences of non-compliance can be severe. A complaint against the social service worker can lead to a disciplinary review by the college and the imposition of sanctions, ranging from a reprimand to revocation of membership. The disciplinary process and the applicable sanctions are discussed further in chapter 23.

Exposure to criminal charges or civil action and the potential consequences are also discussed in chapter 23.

It is clearly very important for a social service worker to be thoroughly familiar with the code of ethics and the standards of practice applied by the profession. Doing your job competently and with integrity is the best protection against both professional and legal penalties. For social service workers in today's world, doing your job competently includes understanding how the law applies to you and your work. This book provides the foundation for building that understanding.

WEB LINK

The code of ethics and standards of practice applicable to social service workers are reproduced on the website of the Ontario College of Social Workers and Social Service Workers, at www.ocswssw.org.

KEY TERMS

accreditation	legal advice	privilege
advocate	legal information	professional standards
code of ethics	liability	sanctions
dual relationship	malpractice	solicitor–client privilege

REFERENCES

Canadian Charter of Rights and Freedoms, part I of the *Constitution Act, 1982*, being schedule B of the *Canada Act 1982* (UK), 1982, c. 11.

Employment Standards Act, 2000, SO 2000, c. 41.

Highway Traffic Act, RSO 1990, c. H.8.

Occupational Health and Safety Act, RSO 1990, c. O.1.

Ontario College of Social Workers and Social Service Workers, Code of Ethics and *Standards of Practice Handbook*, online at www.ocswssw.org.

Ontario Disability Support Program Act, 1997, SO 1997, c. 25.

Social Work and Social Service Work Act, 1998, SO 1998, c. 31.

REVIEW QUESTIONS

1. Name four things, other than the wording of provisions, that affect how a statute operates.

2. Why should a social service worker never provide legal advice? Give three reasons.

3. Explain the difference between legal information and legal advice, and give an example of each.

4. How can cooperation between a social service worker and a lawyer benefit the client? Is a client's permission needed before information is shared?

5. What are some agency activities for which legal advice should be sought in advance?

6. List at least three benefits of membership in the Ontario College of Social Workers and Social Service Workers.

7. What are professional standards?

8. What is a dual relationship, and why is it problematic?

DISCUSSION QUESTIONS

Consider the following dual relationships. Which are problematic, and why?

1. The social service worker, Brenna, works for a centre for pregnant teenagers. She met Marguerite seven years ago, when Marguerite became one of Brenna's clients at the centre. Marguerite "graduated" from the program after three years, went back to school, and has returned to the centre as an employee. Now co-workers, Brenna and Marguerite have begun spending time together socially, as friends.

2. The social service worker, Tonya, worked briefly with an agency that provides alternative schooling for expelled students. Tonya served as a volunteer aide to the person who ran the physical education program. There she met Kyle, a participant in the program who had been expelled from school twice. Tonya left the agency to take a job as an assistant program director at a municipal recreation centre. Eight months later, she runs into Kyle downtown. They stop to talk, but Tonya is on her way to an appointment. She gives Kyle her telephone number and suggests that they should get together for a movie sometime. Tonya is 22 years old and Kyle is 19.

3. The social service worker, Marcus, is the leader of a community-based support group for the family members of alcoholics. Andrea was a member of his group for two years but then moved across town and joined another group. Marcus was both disappointed and relieved to see Andrea go: he was sexually attracted to her, though he never said so or made any advances. Three months after her move, Andrea sends Marcus an e-mail saying that she misses his group, that he was a better leader than her current leader, and that he has a much cuter butt. Marcus responds by e-mail, thanking her for her compliments, and the two develop an e-friendship that includes some sexual innuendo. Marcus is 38 and Andrea is 24. While she belonged to his group, Andrea sometimes discussed her experiences of childhood sexual abuse.

CHAPTER 2

The Canadian Legal System

CHAPTER OBJECTIVES

After reading this chapter, you should be able to:

- Describe Canada's federal system of government and how the law-making authority of governments is established.

- Describe, in general terms, the scope of federal and provincial legislative responsibility.

- Explain the differences between statutes, regulations, and policies, and their respective functions.

- Describe the origins of and differences between common law and statute law.

- Explain how the common law evolves and is applied.

- Understand the role of the *Canadian Charter of Rights and Freedoms*.

- Describe the basic structure of the Canadian court system.

- Explain the nature and function of administrative tribunals.

INTRODUCTION

A multiplicity of laws and policies are relevant to social service work. They can be found in the case law; in federal and provincial statutes and regulations; in municipal bylaws; in the written and unwritten policies of all three levels of government; and in the bylaws and policies of private and quasi-private organizations, such as charities and not-for-profit corporations.

As a social service worker, it's important for you to have a general understanding of all of these sources of law and policy, and how they fit together within the Canadian legal system. You also need to understand the structure of the justice system that applies the law, and the system of administrative tribunals that assists in the administration of myriad government policies.

SOURCES OF LAW

This section provides an overview of four sources of the law in Canada:

- the common law (case law) created by judges;

- statute law (legislation) created by federal and provincial legislatures;

- the constitution; and

- bylaws created by municipal councils.

Laws applicable to social services can be found in all four sources.

Common Law

The **common law** is a body of legal principles, established through court decisions (cases), that govern legal issues or subject areas that are not fully addressed by statutes. Many of these principles have been applied so frequently that they have become widely accepted and well-settled legal rules. Judges try to develop rules that can be applied over and over again in order to create certainty and predictability in the application of the law.

To achieve predictability, our common-law system requires courts to make decisions in accordance with precedent. **Precedent** requires courts to decide like cases alike. Common-law rules created in legal decisions bind the decision makers in future decisions, at least where those decisions turn on the same or similar facts. The decisions of higher-level courts (provincial courts of appeal, or the Supreme Court of Canada) must be respected and followed in lower courts unless the facts of the new case differ substantially.

Common-law rules are sometimes the precursors of legislative provisions; that is, a **legislature** might create a statute that incorporates rules derived from the case law. The federal *Criminal Code*, for example, has generally supplanted the common law with respect to criminal law. It is the statute, created by the elected legislature, that primarily governs.

Statutory provisions, in turn, can be interpreted by common-law rules. For example, a provision in the *Criminal Code* (section 215) that requires parents to provide "necessaries of life" for a child has been interpreted by the courts to include the provision of medical treatment. Even though medical treatment is not mentioned in the statutory provision, the next time a case involving a parent withholding necessary medical care for a child comes up, the court will likely find that, according to the common law, medical care is a necessary of life for the purposes of the legislative provision.

Statute Law and Regulations

STATUTES

Statutes (also called "acts" or "legislation") are written "codes" of law. Statutes typically deal with a particular subject matter, which is often identified in the title of the statute (for example, the *Child and Family Services Act* or the *Mental Health Act*).

Many statutes are accompanied by regulations, which are supplementary rules that fill in the details of how the provisions of the statute are to be implemented.

Statutes are created by a legislature: either the federal Parliament in Ottawa or the legislature of a province or territory. The legislature is the elected arm of government, accountable to the electorate (citizens entitled to vote). In creating statutes, legislatures may refer to the case law and enact provisions that embody, or codify, well-known and settled common-law rules. Sometimes, however, legislatures may choose to override a principle set out in the case law by clearly stating a different rule in the statute, provided that the statutory rule does not violate constitutional principles (as discussed below).

Many statutes affect how social service workers do their job. They will be discussed throughout this text. For an overview, consider the statutes listed in figure 2.1 and the questions they may answer.

As figure 2.1 illustrates, legislatures have been quite active in codifying rules in statutes for different areas of the law. But it must be remembered that statutes are not the only source of law. Where a statute is silent on a particular issue, the common law will still apply. Also, courts may make decisions about the proper interpretation of statutory provisions, and this body of case law becomes part of the law under that statute.

Figure 2.1   Examples of Statutes Applicable in the Social Services Context

Area of law	Statute	Example of application
Child protection	*Child and Family Services Act*	Everyone has a duty to report suspicion of child abuse.
Family law	*Family Law Act*	Parents have an obligation to support their children to the extent that they are able.
	Children's Law Reform Act	Determination of custody and access is based on the best interests of the child.
Income maintenance	*Ontario Works Act, 1997*	Generally, a recipient of benefits under the Act must demonstrate continued efforts to find employment.
Employment	*Employment Standards Act, 2000*	Generally, an employee is entitled to return to his or her job after taking unpaid parental leave.
Immigration	*Immigration and Refugee Protection Act*	Fear of persecution is a ground for claiming refugee status, but famine is not.
Housing	*Residential Tenancies Act, 2006*	Tenants are entitled to a hearing before they may be evicted.
Human rights	*Human Rights Code*	Ontario employers are responsible for ensuring that employees are not sexually harassed in the workplace.
	Canadian Human Rights Act	Federally regulated employers may not discriminate against candidates for employment on the basis of religion.

REGULATIONS

Many statutes authorize the creation of **regulations**, a subordinate form of legislation that clarifies how the statute is to be implemented. Regulations cannot exist on their own without a parent statute. For a regulation to lawfully exist, the statute must include a provision that designates regulation-making authority. Under that authority, regulations are prepared by legal and other administrative staff in the responsible department or ministry. Unlike statutes, regulations do not have to be approved and passed by the legislature.

Regulations tend to be very practical and can include lists, schedules, diagrams, forms, and charts. The information contained in regulations is important in understanding the requirements for compliance with the statute; for example, regulations under the *Child and Family Services Act* establish the housing standards to be met (room sizes, number of children to a room, etc.) for children in care.

Regulations are published separately from the statute and may be revised when changes are made to the statute. If you need to consult a statute in the course of your work, you must also consult the regulations made under that statute.

Canada's Constitution

THE DIVISION OF POWERS

The **constitution** is the supreme law of the land. It is the basic framework under which all other laws are created, and it establishes the basic principles to which all other laws must conform. Canada's *Constitution Act, 1867*, creates a **federal system of government**, according to which law-making powers are divided between the national (or federal) government and the provincial governments according to subject matter. The federal government has **jurisdiction** over matters of national and international interest that affect Canadians from coast to coast. It also has law-making jurisdiction with respect to the territories. The provincial governments have jurisdiction over matters of provincial and local importance, including the creation of municipalities with local governing authority.

The **division of powers** is set out in sections 91 and 92 of the *Constitution Act, 1867*, and summarized in figure 2.2. Federal powers include the authority to regulate defence, currency, and criminal law. The basic rule is that matters that require a

Figure 2.2   Examples of Division of Federal and Provincial Law-Making Powers Under Sections 91 and 92 of the Constitution Act, 1867

Federal powers (section 91)	Provincial powers (section 92)
Interprovincial/international trade	Property
National defence	Civil rights (such as contract, tort)
Immigration	Hospitals
Shipping	Incorporation of companies operating within a province
Currency	Matters of a local nature (such as local trade and public works)
Criminal law	
Postal service	Municipalities
Residual powers: peace, order, and good government	Schools

national standard are within the jurisdiction of the federal government. The federal government also has a residual power to make laws for the peace, order, and good government of Canada in all matters that do not come within a provincial head of power. This means that any matters not specifically delegated to the provinces are matters over which the federal government has jurisdiction. An example is the law applicable to immigrants and refugees. The decision as to who may enter and take up residence in Canada is a matter of national and international significance, and requires a uniform set of legal rules and standards to be applied across the country. Therefore, this responsibility falls within federal jurisdiction.

Provincial powers include authority to make laws governing property, civil rights, and other matters of local concern (such as public works and education).

This division of powers means that the provinces have legislative responsibility over many more aspects of daily life than the federal government. As a result, there are more provincial statutes, and accompanying regulations, than federal statutes and regulations.

Statutes created by both levels of government may be applicable in a particular area of the law. For example, with respect to children's rights, the federal *Youth Criminal Justice Act* will govern rights in the context of criminal offences, while Ontario's *Child and Family Services Act* will govern a child's civil rights. Other examples can be found in figure 2.1.

Law enforcement agencies can be federal (such as the Royal Canadian Mounted Police), provincial (such as the Ontario Provincial Police), or local (such as the Toronto Police Service). While federal agencies tend to enforce federal laws (such as drug and gun laws) and provincial or local agencies tend to enforce provincial laws (such as traffic statutes), in practice enforcement authority is often shared.

Occasionally, one level of government passes a law that appears to intrude on the jurisdiction of the other. Censorship is a good example. Controlling the sale of sexually explicit literature and images can be viewed as either a provincial concern (trade and commerce within a province) or a federal concern (the distribution of obscene matter as a criminal offence).

Where someone alleges that a law is outside the jurisdiction of the government that passed it, courts are often called upon to settle the issue. If a law does not fit squarely into one camp or the other, the federal government takes jurisdiction under the principle of **paramountcy**.

THE CANADIAN CHARTER OF RIGHTS AND FREEDOMS

The *Canadian Charter of Rights and Freedoms* is part of the constitution of Canada, enacted by the *Constitution Act, 1982*. The Charter expresses the fundamental values and principles of our society, centred on Canada's perception of itself as a free and democratic country. Essentially, the Charter provides a mechanism for balancing the rights and freedoms of individuals against the broader need to protect society, including its more vulnerable members.

The enactment of the Charter has had a profound impact on Canadian law. It entrenches specific rights and freedoms, including equality, freedom of religion, and freedom of expression; and it provides that government legislation and actions cannot infringe on those rights and freedoms unless the infringement can be reasonably justified in a free and democratic society.

Therefore, the Charter has two important effects:

- If any law or government policy contravenes the provisions of the Charter, a court or administrative tribunal may declare that law or policy to be unconstitutional and of no force and effect.

- Any action of an agent or representative of any level of government that contravenes any right or freedom protected in the Charter can be challenged.

REASONABLE LIMITS ON RIGHTS AND FREEDOMS

Section 1 of the Charter is a very important provision. It provides that all rights and freedoms are subject to "such reasonable limits prescribed by law as can be demonstrably justified in a free and democratic society." Each time a court is asked to determine whether a law violates the Charter, it must consider whether the law imposes a reasonable limit as described in section 1. A law will be struck down only when both of the following conditions are present:

- the law infringes on a Charter right or freedom; and

- the law cannot be justified as a reasonable limit in the particular circumstances.

For example, consistent with the duty of society to protect children from sexual exploitation, the government has enacted laws prohibiting the production and distribution of child pornography. In cases where these laws are challenged as a violation of the right to freedom of expression under the Charter, the courts have generally concluded that the law does infringe on the Charter right but that the infringement is reasonable and justified.

SCOPE OF APPLICATION

The precise scope of the Charter's application has been a matter of debate and litigation. Although it is clear that the Charter applies to the content and effects of statute law and to the nature and effects of government action, it has sometimes been difficult to define what is meant by "government" action. A multitude of organizations and regulated industries in Canada have some connection to government; many cases have been argued that turn on whether an action of a quasi-governmental organization is a government action.

Unregulated private activity within a province is not intended to be subject to the Charter. For example, if an apartment building owner discriminates against potential renters by refusing to rent to people with children, this is not likely a Charter violation. The Charter would apply only if the discriminatory act resulted from the application of law or government policy. To protect equality rights in situations outside the scope of the Charter, the federal and provincial governments have enacted human rights legislation. The respective roles of the Charter and human rights legislation in Canada's legal system are discussed in chapter 20.

The protections provided by the Charter have an impact on the social service sector, affecting both service providers and their clients. Some examples are shown in figure 2.3. It is important for social service workers to be aware of Charter rights and to be alert to circumstances where they may be infringed. Whether or not such infringement is justified is a matter for the courts to decide.

Figure 2.3   Examples of Social Service Impact of Charter Provisions

Charter provision	Right or freedom	Social service impact
Section 15	*Equality rights:* Freedom from discrimination in the application and protection of the law based on enumerated grounds (age, sex, race, religion, etc.).	Disabled persons are entitled to access to government-mandated services.
Section 2(b)	*Freedom of expression:* The right to express ideas, opinions, beliefs, etc. of one's own or of others.	Freedom of expression does not preclude regulation protecting the confidentiality and privacy rights of clients.
Section 2(d)	*Freedom of association:* The right to establish, maintain, and belong to an organized group, and to engage in lawful collective action.	Clients may not be denied access to services by reason of their participation in a lawful political or activist group.
Section 2(a)	*Freedom of religion:* The right to hold any religious or spiritual belief, and to express such belief by worship, practice, teaching, etc.	Religious rights of clients must be respected by government policies and employees.
Section 6	*Mobility rights:* The right to reside and work anywhere in Canada.	Residency requirements imposed as a qualification for the receipt of publicly provided social services must be reasonable under the Charter.
Section 3	*Right to vote:* The right to vote in elections of legislative representatives.	Inmates of correctional institutions are entitled to vote in federal and provincial elections.
Sections 8, 9, and 10	*Legal rights:* The right not to be detained arbitrarily or searched unreasonably, and the right to be informed of the charges and of the right to a lawyer.	The *Criminal Code* and common-law rules of arrest are interpreted by the courts according to Charter principles.

CASE IN POINT
Scope of Charter Application

In *Eldridge v. BC (AG)*, the court considered whether an infringement of a Charter right arose where the provincial statute governing the provision of medical and health-care services did not include a requirement that sign language interpreters for the deaf be provided at a publicly funded health-care facility. The applicants, who were born deaf, asserted that the absence of a sign language interpreter at the hospital where they were seeking care impaired their ability to communicate with doctors and receive medical and health-care services in accordance with the provincial legislation, and that this was a violation of their right to equality under section 15 of the Charter.

The court held that the failure of the *Medical and Health Care Services Act* to provide expressly for sign language interpretation did not violate section 15(1) of the Charter; however, it also held that governments should not be allowed to evade their constitutional responsibilities by delegating the implementation of their policies and programs to private entities. The hospital was merely the vehicle that the legislature chose to deliver medical and health-care services, and provision of these services was an expression of government policy.

Lesson

The Charter may protect the rights of persons who seek benefits or services from agencies carrying out government policy.

Source: *Eldridge v. BC (AG)*, [1997] 3 SCR 624. ◇

Municipal Bylaws

The fourth source of law under the Canadian legal system is municipal **bylaws**, which are passed by municipal councils. Municipal councils are the government bodies responsible for municipalities (cities, towns, or regions). Provincial governments create municipalities by statute and provide specific designated powers to municipal councils. Municipal councils exercise these powers by making municipal bylaws. Municipalities are responsible for many basic local services, including sewage and water supply, police, public health, public transit, garbage collection and disposal, libraries, and arenas.

Land-use planning is another important function of municipalities. Bylaws passed by the municipality determine the use of land within the municipality's boundaries. For example, an area may be designated as a high-density residential area that includes high-rise apartments and condominiums, or a low-density residential area restricted to houses and low-rise apartments. Other areas may be designated as industrial, commercial, or agricultural. There may also be bylaws restricting the placement of group homes or social assistance housing.

POLICY

Government **policy** is not law; however, it is a very important source of guidance for many social service workers. While legislation often sets basic rules for interactions between individuals and their government, sometimes those laws, and even the regulations made under them, cannot capture all of the details of how a sphere of activity is managed by government. Especially where legislation leaves room for **discretion** in administrative decision making, how the law will be applied in practice often evolves as a matter of government policy.

Policies can be formal or informal, written or unwritten. They can also have a wide range of objectives—for example, promoting fairness to users of a program or service, or setting priorities for the allocation of government resources.

As discussed above, government policy should be guided by the Charter. In addition, it must not have objectives or operate in a way that runs counter to the spirit of any applicable legislation. If policies are found to operate in a way not contemplated by the legislation, courts may choose not to support their enforcement. The text box below provides an example of how this can happen.

CASE IN POINT

Government Policy and Statutes

Section 752.1 of the *Criminal Code* provides that prior to sentencing an offender convicted of certain serious offences, the court may order a mental health assessment (usually by a psychiatrist) to determine whether the offender is a "dangerous offender." If a person is designated as a dangerous offender, his future eligibility for parole will be significantly reduced. Because of a lack of funding for hospital beds for the mentally ill, the Ontario government formulated a policy that dangerous offender assessments were to be performed on an out-patient rather than an in-patient basis.

In *R. v. Burrows*, a convicted offender awaiting sentencing asserted that he should be in a hospital, not in jail (as he would be under the government policy). He argued that a determination as to whether he was treatable, and therefore not a "dangerous offender," could only be made in an appropriate treatment environment, namely, a hospital.

The judge agreed, noting that the findings from a hospital-based assessment would be more useful to her in making her sentencing decision. The judge overrode the government policy and ordered that the client be assessed on an in-patient basis—in the hospital.

Lesson

Government policies do not have the force of law, and when they are in conflict with provisions of a statute, they may be overridden by a court.

Source: *R. v. Burrows* (October 24, 2005) (Ont. SC) [unreported]. ◊

As a social service worker, it is your responsibility to be familiar not only with the legislation that applies to your work, but with the government policies, practices, and guidelines that support that legislation. For example, if you work in the mental health field in Ontario, you should be familiar with the policies of the Ministry of Health and Long-Term Care. If your work involves assisting Ontario clients with obtaining income support, you should familiarize yourself with the policies of the Ministry of Community and Social Services.

Policies are often developed to respond to local needs and circumstances. As a result, the policies of the Ministry of Municipal Affairs and Housing (for example) in one region of the province might be quite different from those just a few counties away. It is important for you to become familiar with how the government does business in your jurisdiction.

Government policy documents are often made available to the public on the website of the relevant ministry, or copies can be picked up at local government offices.

Governments are not the only organizations that create policies. Most private corporations, associations, and charitable organizations have policies (sometimes called bylaws) of their own. If you work for a private organization, such as a nursing home, you will be expected to know and comply with its policies. Also, when you do business with an outside organization in the course of your work, you or your client may be required to comply with that organization's policies.

For example, if one of your duties is to arrange relief child care so that a client can attend job interviews, you may work with an organization that provides child-care services. You will need to know, and help your client to understand, the organization's policies with respect to such matters as reservations, payment, emergency contact forms, special-needs disclosure, and pick-up and drop-off times. Failure to comply—for example, if the client is late picking up the child—may result in an additional charge to the client.

Occasionally, you may find yourself in the position of having to advocate for a client who feels he has been wronged by an organizational policy. For example, if you work in a program that provides income assistance, and you have a client whose financial troubles have led to the loss of electricity in his apartment, you may need to help the client challenge the hydro company's policy governing the cancellation of service. In such situations, it is important to remember that an organization's policies are *only* policies; they are not laws. Where they conflict with the law (for example, a law that prohibits shutting off the supply of electricity during extreme weather), the law overrides.

STATUTES GOVERNING PROCEDURE

As discussed earlier, most statutes deal with a specific and well-defined subject matter, such as long-term care or education. These statutes typically create a self-contained scheme for the regulation of a particular industry, service, program, or activity. A few statutes, however, have a much more general application, providing legal rules that govern procedure.

Procedural laws are generally designed to promote **procedural fairness** or **natural justice**. More particularly, their aim is

- to ensure that **substantive law** is applied equally to everyone;

- to provide any person affected by the law with the opportunity to explain his position or actions to an unbiased decision maker; and

- to create a framework for reconsidering legal decisions.

An example of a general procedural statute is Ontario's *Provincial Offences Act*. Many Ontario statutes create offences as part of their regulatory scheme, but they do not include detailed provisions for charging and prosecuting those offences. Instead, the Ontario legislature has created a general procedural scheme, set out in the *Provincial Offences Act*, to govern the prosecution of most provincial offences. In other words, if you want to know what happens when a person commits an offence under a provincial statute, you often need to consult not only the offence-creating statute but also the *Provincial Offences Act*.

For example, suppose that a social service worker employed by a facility governed by the *Mental Health Act* withholds personal mail from a patient, thereby contravening section 26 of that Act. If the Minister of Health and Long-Term Care decides to prosecute (typically after a complaint on the part of the patient or her family), the employee should first refer to the offence section of the *Mental Health Act* (section 80). That section states:

> Every person who contravenes any provision of this Act or the regulations is guilty of an offence and on conviction is liable to a fine of not more than $25,000.

Next, the employee should consult the *Provincial Offences Act* to determine the details of how the offence will be prosecuted. There are many such details, including how the offender is to be informed of the charge, whether she has a right to disclosure of the minister's evidence against her, how the trial date will be set, which court will hear the trial, and how an appropriate sentence will be determined.

Another example of a general procedural statute is Ontario's *Statutory Powers Procedure Act*. This statute provides a general procedural framework for the decision-making function of administrative tribunals, discussed in the next section.

ADMINISTRATIVE LAW

Administrative law is the body of law that governs how government administrators and employees exercise the decision-making powers granted to them under statute. Generally, these decisions involve conferring some kind of benefit or right on citizens; as a result, administrative decisions may have important consequences to the individuals concerned.

Depending on the provisions of the particular statute, administrative decisions may be made quickly and routinely (as in the case of registration of a driver's licence), or they may be quasi-judicial, involving a hearing and an **impartial** decision maker. Often decisions will start out as routine, but if a person who is denied a right or benefit chooses to challenge the decision, it will be reviewed by a more senior official, and eventually by an independent board or tribunal.

Administrative decisions may also be reviewed by a court; however, it is a principle of administrative law that deference should be given to the government official or tribunal that made the decision, owing to their expertise in the particular regulatory regime. The rights of appeal and judicial review differ depending on the governing statute, so it is important to refer to that statute for the particulars.

Administrative Discretion

An administrator is anyone who makes decisions in the context of a policy scheme, such as a government program. Every decision-making scheme is governed by laws or policies, or a mixture of both. For example, the allocation of not-for-profit housing spaces, or the process of making changes to housing allocations based on the results of reviews, is an administrative function that takes place within a policy scheme. Another example that may be familiar to social service workers is the decision to apprehend a child under section 40(7) of the *Child and Family Services Act*.

The decisions of administrators are made within a defined scope of authority: laws and/or policies place limits on the range of decisions that an administrator can make. Within this range, an administrator's decisions must be guided by **administrative discretion**. The social service workers employed in government departments and agencies must make choices every day in responding to particular circumstances. This exercise of administrative discretion is called discretionary power.

The principles of administrative law require that discretionary power be exercised in a fair and reasonable manner. This includes the following limits on decision makers:

- A decision maker must not exercise discretion beyond the authority delegated to him by statute.

- Decisions must be consistent with the wording and intent of the statute.

- Similar cases must be treated in a similar way.

- There should be no discrimination or bias based on irrelevant factors or the personal feelings of the decision maker.

As a power that is granted to administrators, administrative discretion comes with a responsibility to use it properly. When used properly, discretion has the potential to bring the benefits of informed judgment and practical experience to what would otherwise be a theoretical scheme. Policy and discretion are designed to work together synergistically, but this can happen only if you understand the limits of your decisions, and consider only appropriate factors in deciding within those limits.

Suppose, for example, that you are an administrator with responsibility for recommending placements in a housing assistance program in cases of overhousing. On Monday, you feel energetic, and you are willing to tackle the paperwork needed to recommend most of your review caseload for changes based on overhousing. By Wednesday, you are preoccupied with other work, and you approve the continuation of all of your housing placements until the next review. Doing this is *not* exercising administrative discretion, because your choices are based on factors that are not recognized as valid by the policies that guide your work. When you allow inappropriate factors to affect your decisions, you are not exercising your discretionary power in a principled way.

Many decision-making functions have aspects of procedural fairness built into the policies that guide them. For example, where the decision affects whether an individual will receive benefits (such as social assistance) or services (such as Wheel-Trans), it is common for the agency's policies to require that clients who are denied access to benefits or services be given written reasons for the denial. This requirement makes it easier for a client to challenge the decision. A challenge of an administrative decision may proceed through several stages of review, from the level of the agency to a tribunal and ultimately to a court. The review process is described below.

Administrative Tribunals

Administrative tribunals are created by statutes. Their purpose is to provide a mechanism for resolving disputes over administrative decisions relating to the rights, entitlements, or duties described in the particular statute. A person who disagrees with the decision of an administrator may apply for a review by the appropriate administrative tribunal.

For example, an applicant for Ontario Works benefits whose application is refused by the local Ontario Works office may challenge the decision by submitting a written request to the office for an internal review. The decision will be reviewed by an officer other than the original decision maker. If the decision is confirmed, the applicant may apply to the Social Benefits Tribunal for a further, independent review. The Social Benefits Tribunal is created by the *Ontario Works Act, 1997* and the *Ontario Disability Support Program Act, 1997*, and has authority to review administrative decisions made pursuant to those statutes.

Examples of other administrative tribunals that are often relevant to social service workers and their clients are shown in figure 2.4. Note that this is just a sampling, not a complete list.

Administrative tribunals may also be called "boards," "commissions," or some other name. Their decisions are subject to stricter rules of procedural fairness than is the case for routine decisions made by administrative staff. Tribunals function in a similar manner to courts, with both sides making arguments and providing evidence to the adjudicator (a member or a panel of members of the tribunal). However, there are some important differences between a court and a tribunal.

In the case of a court, the decision maker—the judge—has a law degree and broad knowledge of and experience in the law. In the case of an administrative tribunal, the decision makers typically have expertise in the specific subject matter dealt with by the tribunal. For example, a member of the Social Benefits Tribunal will be an expert on income maintenance, but she need not be a lawyer and may not have experience in many other areas of the law. However, she will have detailed knowledge of the law governing social benefits. This specialization is one advantage of an administrative tribunal over a court.

The other major advantage of an administrative tribunal is that hearing procedures are generally much less formal than trial procedures, and matters can be resolved more quickly. However, tribunals vary widely with respect to the style and level of formality of their proceedings. If you are called upon to assist a client with a submission to an administrative tribunal, it's a good idea to obtain a copy of the tribunal's procedures, so that you can talk to the client about what will happen at the hearing and how he can prepare. (But remember that your role is to provide information, not legal advice.) Information about tribunal procedures is generally available on the particular tribunal's website or at its local office.

Figure 2.4   Examples of Administrative Tribunals That Are Relevant to Social Service Workers and Their Clients

Statute	Administrative tribunal	Function
Ontario Works Act, 1997; Ontario Disability Support Program Act, 1997	Social Benefits Tribunal	Determines eligibility for provincial social assistance and disability benefits
Workplace Safety and Insurance Act, 1997	Workplace Safety and Insurance Board	Grants compensation to injured workers
Human Rights Code	Ontario Human Rights Tribunal	Determines whether or not human rights legislation has been violated
Residential Tenancies Act, 2006	Landlord and Tenant Board	Resolves disputes between landlords and tenants
Social Work and Social Service Work Act, 1998	Ontario College of Social Workers and Social Service Workers	Grants licences to social workers and social service workers to practise their profession
Corrections and Conditional Release Act	National Parole Board	Decides whether prisoners should be released on parole to serve the remainder of their sentences in the community

Standard of Procedural Fairness

As previously stated, the rules for procedural fairness are generally stricter for tribunals than for staff who are making routine decisions. At the least, the person seeking a decision is entitled to know the reasons for the decision and to have an opportunity to respond. However, he does not necessarily have the right to natural justice—that is, the right to a hearing with the submission of evidence and argument similar to a trial. The required standard of procedural fairness depends on the wording of the statute under which the tribunal operates.

Whether a decision is administrative or quasi-judicial (with a hearing before a tribunal), the decision must be fair—based on the applicable criteria and made by an unbiased decision maker.

CASE IN POINT

Procedural Fairness and Administrative Discretion

O.N. (Litigation Guardian) v. Ontario Human Rights Commission involved a complaint made by a parent against a school under Ontario's *Human Rights Code*, alleging violation of her children's right to education services. The school that the two children attended initially treated them as having learning disabilities, but then discarded that approach and began to treat them as having behavioural problems. This ultimately led to the expulsion of one of the children. The children's mother claimed that the school's actions constituted discrimination on the basis of disability.

The matter was investigated by the Ontario Human Rights Commission (OHRC), and the school filed a complaint. The OHRC did not provide the children's mother with a copy of the response. On the basis of the evidence, the OHRC decided that referral to a board of inquiry for a hearing was not warranted. The mother sought reconsideration on the basis of non-disclosure of the response.

The OHRC's reconsideration staff agreed and declared the decision invalid owing to a procedural error: the school's response should have been conveyed to the mother. The matter was returned to the Investigation Branch, and the mother was provided with a seven-page report summarizing the school's response. When the OHRC again decided not to refer the matter to a board of inquiry, the mother applied for judicial review. The issue before the court was whether the OHRC's decision should stand, despite the fact that the mother did not receive full and complete disclosure of the school's response but only a summary.

The court agreed that the mother was owed a duty of fairness—specifically, the right to be informed of the substance of the case against her and to be afforded a full opportunity to respond. However, the court found that the mother was provided with the same material that was available to the OHRC when it made its decision and that the OHRC did not have before it the longer version of the school's response.

The court held that

- the mother received procedural fairness by being provided with all of the materials that were before the OHRC, and she was given full opportunity to respond;

- the power to bar certain complaints from proceeding further, regardless of their merit, reflects the legislature's overriding commitment to considerations of administrative efficiency and to specific policy objectives;

- the OHRC is not obligated to proceed with every complaint but does so at its discretion; and

- the decision of the OHRC was not patently unreasonable and must be respected.

Lesson

Administrative law recognizes that decision makers may be required to balance the principle of procedural fairness with considerations of administrative efficiency.

Source: *O.N. (Litigation Guardian) v. Ontario Human Rights Commission*, 2004 CanLII 9576 (ON SCDC). ◈

Judicial Review and Appeal to Court

A discussion of administrative law would not be complete without mention of **judicial review** and how it differs from appeal.

A party may apply to the Ontario Divisional Court for judicial review of a tribunal's decision where he has reason to question the decision on procedural grounds. Judicial review does not involve consideration of the legal merits of the decision—that is, whether the tribunal arrived at a correct legal result. Instead, the issue before the court is whether the tribunal acted within its jurisdiction, or statutory authority, with respect to the decision-making process. If the court finds that the tribunal did not act within its jurisdiction (for example, if it failed to follow specified rules of procedural fairness), the court may order a rehearing.

Unlike judicial review, an appeal does involve examination of the legal merits of the decision. On appeal, the tribunal's decision may be overturned if the court finds that it was based on an erroneous interpretation or application of the law—in other words, that the decision was "wrong."

Requests for reconsideration of administrative decisions may often be made to higher levels in the ministry hierarchy, or to the relevant tribunal; however, a decision of an administrative tribunal may be appealed to a court only if expressly permitted by the statute that creates and governs the tribunal. The rationale for limiting appeals of tribunal decisions is that essentially an appeal involves replacing a tribunal's decision with a court's decision. This undermines one of the advantages of tribunals—their expertise in their particular subject area.

To summarize the discussion above, figure 2.5 illustrates the review process available to an applicant who is denied social assistance under the Ontario Works program.

Figure 2.5   Challenging a Denial of Ontario Works Benefits

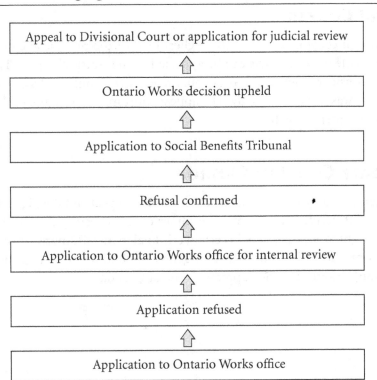

COURT SYSTEM AND HIERARCHY

In broad terms, the hierarchy of Canadian courts consists of three main levels:

- **trial courts**,
- **appeal courts**, and
- the Supreme Court of Canada.

This simplified picture is deceptive, since there are separate federal and provincial court systems that include courts to deal with specific areas of the law. For example, there are federal trial and appeal courts, and special courts (such as the Tax Court of Canada), as well as a military court system. For the purposes of this book, it is the provincial court systems that are most relevant, and particularly the Ontario system. This will be the focus of the discussion here and in the chapters that follow.

Trial Courts

Provincial courts where a dispute is first heard are called trial courts, and these include specialty courts like the Small Claims Court, Family Court, and Youth Court.

In Ontario, and some other provinces, there are two levels of trial courts. Generally, lower provincial courts deal with civil disputes and lesser offences, and more serious offences are tried in a superior court. Also, in some limited situations, a decision of a lower court can be appealed to a superior court; for example, decisions of a judge in the Small Claims Court may be appealed to a judge of the Ontario Superior Court of Justice. The structure of the Ontario court system is described in more detail in chapter 13.

Appeal Courts

The provincial court of appeal is the highest level of the provincial court system. Decisions made by trial courts can be appealed to the court of appeal. The appeal court will consider whether the trial court made any significant legal errors such that the case was decided wrongly. The appeal court may reverse the trial decision, uphold it, or order a new trial.

Supreme Court of Canada

The Supreme Court of Canada is the court of final appeal and the highest court in the country. It decides only a limited number of cases every year, and there is no automatic right to appeal except in certain criminal matters. Otherwise, only parties with cases of national importance and general public interest are granted leave (permission) to appeal to the Supreme Court of Canada.

SOURCES OF LEGAL INFORMATION

It is easy to access statutes and regulations online, but it is important to ensure that you are using a website that maintains official versions, updated regularly. Many government websites contain links to statutes and regulations, such as the federal Department of Justice website and the Ontario government website. Additionally, the Canadian Legal Information Institute (CanLII) website contains statutes and regulations for the federal and provincial governments, as well as case law.

Many cases are accessible from the CanLII website, and you can use key words to search by topic. Case reports in print form can be found at law libraries. They are published in case reporter series, which are organized either by jurisdiction (such as the Supreme Court Reports) or by subject area (such as the Reports of Family Law), and by year.

WEB LINK

For information on federal statutes and regulations, visit the website of the Department of Justice at www.justice.gc.ca. Information on Ontario statutes and regulations is available at www.e-laws.gov.on.ca. Information on federal and provincial statutes and on case law is available from the Canadian Legal Information Institute at www.canlii.org.

KEY TERMS

administrative discretion	division of powers	policy
administrative law	federal system of government	precedent
administrative tribunal	impartial	procedural fairness
appeal court	judicial review	procedural law
bylaws	jurisdiction	regulation
common law	legislature	statute
constitution	natural justice	substantive law
discretion	paramountcy	trial court

REFERENCES

Burrows, R. v. (October 24, 2005) (Ont. SC) [unreported].

Canadian Charter of Rights and Freedoms, part I of the *Constitution Act, 1982*, being schedule B of the *Canada Act 1982* (UK), 1982, c. 11.

Canadian Human Rights Act, RSC 1985, c. H-6.

Child and Family Services Act, RSO 1990, c. C.11.

Children's Law Reform Act, RSO 1990, c. C.12.

Constitution Act, 1867, 30 & 31 Vict., c. 3 (UK).

Corrections and Conditional Release Act, SC 1992, c. 20.

Criminal Code, RSC 1985, c. C-46.

Eldridge v. BC (AG), [1997] 3 SCR 624.

Employment Standards Act, 2000, SO 2000, c. 41.

Family Law Act, RSO 1990, c. F.3.

Human Rights Code, RSO 1990, c. H.19.

Immigration and Refugee Protection Act, SC 2001, c. 27.

Medical and Health Care Services Act, SBC 1992, c. 76 (now the *Medicare Protection Act*, RSBC 1996, c. 286).

O.N. (Litigation Guardian) v. Ontario Human Rights Commission, 2004 CanLII 9576 (ON SCDC).

Ontario Works Act, 1997, SO 1997, c. 25.

Provincial Offences Act, RSO 1990, c. P.33.

Public Authorities Protection Act, RSO 1990, c. P.38.

Residential Tenancies Act, 2006, SO 2006, c. 17.

Social Work and Social Service Work Act, 1998, SO 1998, c. 31.

Statutory Powers Procedure Act, RSO 1990, c. S.22.

Workplace Safety and Insurance Act, 1997, SO 1997, c. 16, Sch. A.

REVIEW QUESTIONS

1. Name four sources of law.

2. What is precedent, and why is it important?

3. What is the difference between a statute and a regulation?

4. Describe Canada's system of government and the division of powers between different levels of government.

5. Name three federal statutes and three provincial statutes.

6. Explain how the Charter protects the rights and freedoms of individuals.

7. Does the Charter apply to the private sector?

8. What is government policy, and why is it important?

9. What is the basic purpose of procedural laws?

10. What is administrative law, and why is it important?

11. What is administrative discretion?

12. What are the advantages of being heard before an administrative tribunal rather than a court?

DISCUSSION QUESTIONS

Should administrative discretion be narrow or broad? What are some of the advantages and disadvantages of allowing broad versus narrow discretion for administrative decision makers?

PART II

Children and Families

CHAPTER 3

Child Protection and the Child and Family Services Act

CHAPTER OBJECTIVES

After reading this chapter, you should be able to:

- Describe the general principles of the *Child and Family Services Act* (CFSA).

- Explain the roles that social service workers may play in working with the CFSA.

- Understand the duty to report neglect and abuse, and describe the triggering circumstances for that duty.

- Understand the general principles of safety and risk assessment.

- Describe the various levels of intervention mandated by the CFSA and understand how a level is chosen.

- Be aware of contemporary issues in child protection, such as using community resources, advocacy on behalf of children, and cultural sensitivity.

INTRODUCTION

Before the 18th century, protecting children was viewed as simply one facet of raising them, and the responsibility of parents. While neglecting or harming one's children was often denounced as morally wrong, parents had the final word over how children were provided for, supervised, and disciplined. In extreme cases of abusive treatment, a relative might intervene, taking a child at risk into his or her own home; but the courts and the government were rarely involved.

Gradually, as the result of pressure from children's advocates—sometimes educators, clergy, or related organizations—the government began to set limits on parental decision-making authority. Nowadays, if a child is at risk from parental harm, the decision to remove the child from the nuclear family is generally made not by extended family members or neighbours, but by government agencies, and these agencies take responsibility for the care of children in need of protection.

In Ontario, the *Child and Family Services Act* (CFSA) governs the process for taking children in need of protection into custody and sets standards for their care. It also creates a duty of care for *all* people to report evidence of suspected abuse or neglect of a child.

Social service workers can be involved with child protection in a variety of ways. For example, those who work in recreation facilities, women's shelters, hospitals, or other centres with child clients may be confronted with evidence of child abuse or neglect, which they will be required to report. Many social service workers also work with children who have already been taken into care, perhaps supporting foster parents or working in children's residences. In these settings, social service workers may be required to support children or parents in accessing and using programs and services in the context of a **plan of care**. They may also help clients to prepare for hearings and other administrative processes.

This chapter provides an introduction to the CFSA, beginning with the purposes and principles that guide its application. For a more detailed discussion, refer to Rock (2005: chapter 8).

PURPOSES AND PRINCIPLES

The most important purpose of the CFSA, as expressed in section 1, is

> to promote the best interests, protection and well being of children.

The requirement that legislation be applied according to the **best interests of the child** is not unique to the CFSA. This phrase is used in family law statutes as well, with respect to issues of custody and access. Best interests do not necessarily mean

---

LEGISLATIVE SHORTCUT

Child and Family Services Act

RSO 1990, c. C.11

Objective: To protect children from child abuse and neglect.

Target Population: Children and families.

Program Administration: The *Child and Family Services Act* permits the government to provide services directly, or to fund service providers to do so. Approved agencies are corporations that work as agents for the government in providing these services. Children's aid societies, of which there are more than 50 in Ontario, are especially designated approved agencies.

Administrative Tribunal: The Child and Family Services Review Board makes decisions regarding residential placements and disclosure of information; however, decisions regarding whether a child is in need of protection and should be apprehended must be made by a court.

Summary: The *Child and Family Services Act* imposes a duty of care on all people to report child abuse and neglect. It governs the process for taking abused children into custody and sets standards for their care. It also provides for counselling and other services for children and their families for the purpose of preventing abuse and neglect. ◇

what the child wants, although a child's wishes may be considered, particularly in the case of older children.

The CFSA also recognizes the following secondary purposes, to be achieved only as long as they are consistent with the best interests of the child:

- While parents may need help in caring for their children, that help should give support to the autonomy and integrity of the family unit and, wherever possible, be provided on the basis of mutual consent.

- The least disruptive course of action that is available and appropriate in a particular case to help a child should be considered.

- Children's services should be provided in a manner that respects children's needs for continuity of care and for stable family relationships, and takes into account differences in physical and mental development among children.

- Services to children and their families should, wherever possible, be provided in a manner that respects cultural, religious, and regional differences.

- First Nations and other native people should be entitled to provide, wherever possible, their own child and family services, and all services to native children and families should be provided in a manner that recognizes their culture, heritage, and traditions and the concept of the extended family.

The secondary purposes of the CFSA reflect strong support for the preservation of the family unit and a commitment to assisting children within the context of family relationships. Choosing the "least disruptive" course of action requires consideration of the child's existing environment, including, in addition to the family unit, the community and educational setting and the physical environment.

The secondary purposes also recognize the importance of culture, religion, heritage, traditions, regional differences, and community values. To the extent possible, a child's ties to these should be preserved even when the child is in need of assistance or protection. For example, a child in care should be given a chance to attend services at a place of worship for his or her own faith. Attempts are often made to place children with foster families who share their culture.

The needs of native children are specifically referenced in recognition of historical inequities and the tragedy of residential schools. Native children should receive, where possible, services from organizations that are managed and operated by their own community with respect for its heritage and traditions. This is a reversal of earlier government policy, which aimed to assimilate native children by taking them out of their homes and communities and placing them in residential schools. In those schools, native children were stripped of their language and culture; many were also subjected to physical, emotional, or sexual abuse. The effects continue to be felt generations later.

APPROVED AGENCIES AND CHILDREN'S AID SOCIETIES

The CFSA permits the government to provide services directly, or to fund service providers to do so. Approved agencies are corporations that work as agents for the government in providing these services.

Children's aid societies are specially designated approved agencies. There are more than 50 children's aid societies in Ontario, most associated with municipalities. Many also receive funding from private sources. Because of its size and diversity, Toronto has four children's aid societies:

- Catholic Children's Aid Society of Toronto,
- Children's Aid Society of Toronto,
- Jewish Family & Child Service of Toronto, and
- Native Child and Family Services of Toronto.

Children's aid societies are mandated to provide protection to children under the age of 16. The specific functions of a children's aid society include the following:

- provide guidance, counselling, and other services to families for protecting children, or for the prevention of child abuse and neglect;
- investigate allegations or evidence that children under 16, or in the society's care or under its supervision, may be in need of protection;
- provide care and supervision for children assigned or committed to the society's care; and
- place children for adoption in appropriate circumstances.

Duties of Service Providers

The duties of service providers set out in section 2(2) of the CFSA emphasize the importance of procedural fairness when making decisions that affect families in such a fundamental way. In particular, children's aid societies must implement procedures for the disclosure of information to parents and, where appropriate, to children, and to provide parents and children with the opportunity to challenge decisions that affect their rights and interests. Section 2(3) requires service providers to ensure

- that children and their parents "have an opportunity where appropriate to be heard and represented when decisions affecting their interests are made and to be heard when they have concerns about the services they are receiving"; and
- that decisions affecting the rights of children and their parents are made "according to clear, consistent criteria and are subject to procedural safeguards."

Respecting and promoting procedural fairness is a critical aspect of social service practice. In order to do your job fully, you need the trust of your clients, and it is difficult to establish and maintain that trust if the client's rights have not always been respected. Failure to follow procedures may also result in administrative decisions being overturned by a court, and even disciplinary action against the decision maker.

VOLUNTARY SERVICES

Services may be provided to children and families on a voluntary basis or pursuant to a court determination that the child is in need of protection. The range of voluntary services available will vary from community to community. Some may be provided by a children's aid society and others by different kinds of agencies. Voluntary services can include parenting classes and programs designed to address developmental problems, disabilities, behavioural problems, addiction, domestic abuse, or divorce.

Temporary Care Agreements

A person who is temporarily unable to care for a young child or children may enter into a written agreement with a children's aid society for temporary care. The time limit for such an arrangement is one year for children under six and two years for children aged six or over.

Some children's aid societies may offer parent relief programs through which an exhausted or ill parent of a young child or children can rely on volunteers or staff to care for the children overnight, in either the parent's home or the caregiver's home. These arrangements are typically very temporary (up to a limited number of nights).

A **temporary care agreement** may also be used where a parent needs to take time in an addiction rehabilitation program. Where a parent recognizes that he or she is unable to cope and that an order for apprehension will likely be ordered by a court, the parent may agree to place the child in the care of a children's aid society and reserve the right to active participation.

How exactly a parent will participate in a child's care during a voluntary placement will vary among different children's aid societies, and will depend on the reasons for the child's placement in care and parental factors. In almost all cases, the children's aid society will, at minimum, provide opportunities for parents and children to visit each other. Social service workers may be called upon to assist parents in remaining involved in their children's care, and in improving their parenting skills with a view to having the children back home.

Special-Needs Agreements

A voluntary temporary placement may also be made where there is no parenting problem, per se, but the child is not thriving at home because he or she has special needs that the parent cannot address. Such special needs may arise, for example, from a disability, a developmental delay, an emotional problem, or a serious behavioural disorder.

DUTY TO REPORT SUSPECTED CHILD ABUSE OR NEGLECT

A report of suspected child abuse or neglect is often the trigger for all further actions under the CFSA. Reports may come from friends, neighbours, teachers, relatives, or even parents. Actions under the CFSA may include apprehension of a child, but more often the children's aid society provides less intrusive programs to support parents, and parents accept assistance voluntarily. All societies encourage parents who are struggling with parenting problems to seek support from a local children's aid society.

When to Report

Section 72 of the CFSA makes it mandatory for anyone to report a reasonable belief that a child—any child—has suffered or is at risk of suffering from abuse or neglect. It is important to familiarize yourself with the actual wording of section 72. Essentially, a person has a duty to report a suspicion, based on reasonable grounds, that a child has suffered or is at risk of suffering

1. physical harm through
   a. abuse or
   b. neglect;

2. sexual molestation or exploitation, either
   a. directly or
   b. by not being protected;

3. deprivation of necessary medical treatment;

4. emotional harm through
   a. abuse or
   b. neglect;

5. deprivation of treatment for an emotional or developmental problem, whatever the cause of the problem;

6. abandonment;

7. deprivation of services or treatment designed to prevent a child (under 12) who has killed or seriously injured someone from doing so again;

8. the risk (for a child under 12) of doing serious harm to a person or property through the encouragement of, or insufficient supervision by, the person in charge of the child.

EXTRA CREDIT
Duty to Report Child Pornography

Should possession of child pornography trigger the duty to report child abuse? Manitoba is the first province to say "yes" and introduce amendments to child and family services legislation that expand the definition of child abuse. The new law will compel anyone who stumbles upon images, or other materials they suspect to be child pornography, to report them.

The duty to report applies to everyone, but it will have particular significance for computer technicians and Internet service providers (ISPs) whose concerns about privacy rights may have inhibited reporting in the past. The new law will make it clear: they must report. ISPs in the United States are already obligated to report child pornography, and face heavy fines for the failure to do so, but until now there were no similar provisions in Canada.

Reports should be made to Cybertip.ca, which receives funding from both the federal Department of Public Safety and from Manitoba Justice. Cybertip.ca has been the national clearing house for all Internet child sexual-abuse reporting in Canada since 2005, and since that time it has received more than 25,000 reports from the public. ◇

The duty to report is triggered as soon as the person making the relevant observations has reasonable grounds to suspect that harm has occurred, is occurring, or is threatened. This is a fairly easy threshold to meet, since it does not require certainty in the mind of the person reporting, but only a reasonable suspicion. For example, a social service worker who observes bruises on a child's body that are not consistent with normal play should make a report, even in the absence of any other evidence and, in some cases, despite an "innocent" explanation by the child.

The low threshold for reporting means that many reports will be baseless. Society employees are trained to assess reports and to conduct investigations in order to make such determinations. The low threshold encourages people to leave it up to the experts. When in doubt, report.

How to Report

Once a person has reasonable grounds to suspect any form of abuse or neglect listed in section 72, the duty to report is triggered. The specifics of that duty, as expressed by the legislation, are the following:

- report without delay;

- report to a children's aid society;

- explain the reasons for your suspicion;

- report directly—do not rely on your supervisor or subordinate; and

- report any new observations that occur after your initial report.

While all reports should be made promptly, the timing of the report will be influenced to some degree by the perceived seriousness of the harm observed or the presence of an ongoing threat. For example, if an adult is observed in the act of beating a child, it will usually be appropriate to call the police immediately, before calling a children's aid society. Note that even when the police are called, you are nevertheless obligated to report to a children's aid society.

Where the circumstances are more ambiguous, it may be acceptable to wait and see whether an observation is simply an isolated incident of inadequate parenting (all parents have the occasional bad moment) or part of a pattern. However, it is never appropriate to ignore signs of abuse or neglect in the hope that they will be resolved on their own, or be reported by someone else.

When calling to make a report, it's useful to be prepared with notes about your observations and suspicions. It is important to be calm, objective, and open, and to refrain from using the reporting process as a personal attack on the suspected abuser. If your report sounds malicious or exaggerated, the credibility of your information will be tainted. Regardless of your feelings about the abuse or neglect you have witnessed, a coherent, impartial, factual report is likely to be most helpful to the child.

The requirement that reports be made directly means exactly that. It is not possible to delegate your duty to report to someone else, even to your supervisor. You must make the call yourself. In many cases, it will be appropriate to advise another person of your suspicions, and in some cases, to consider that person's advice with respect to reporting. However, the duty to report is always yours personally, and if you fail to make a report in circumstances where you should have, you may be charged with an offence.

Special Duty

While everyone has a duty to report, the consequences of failing to report are more severe for people who perform professional or official duties with respect to children. Section 72(4) provides that if a person

- works with children, such as a teacher, youth worker, recreation worker, or employee of service agencies;

- obtains information triggering a duty to report in the course of professional duties; and

- does not make a report,

that person can be charged with an offence and, if convicted, fined up to $1,000.

The list of professionals who are liable to be fined does not specifically include social service workers, but many social service workers are employed in at least one of the listed job categories.

INVESTIGATION

When a report is made to a children's aid society under section 72, the society is obligated to investigate. Usually, the first step is to interview the person who made the report. The investigation may proceed from that point on a **consensual** basis, with the parents giving permission to interview and assess the child, and the suspected abuser consenting to an interview as well. Where the society suspects that a child may be in need of protection, it will typically refer the case to a review team under section 73.

Review Team

A review team must be made up of at least one legally qualified medical practitioner and others qualified to perform psychological, developmental, educational, or social assessments, as appropriate for the particular case. If the child's parents consent, the child may be assessed by the review team without being apprehended by a children's aid society. If a problem is uncovered, the parties involved may agree to the provision of services by the society or another suitable agency. Voluntary services may be provided with the child remaining in the home, or with the child moved to a foster home or other facility.

Of course, the children's aid society will not always have the cooperation of parents. Where a society cannot adequately review a child's case because the parents will not consent to an assessment, the child may need to be apprehended—that is, taken into the custody of the children's aid society.

Homemaker Option

Where a children's aid society has sufficient suspicion to begin the apprehension process, it can elect, instead of actually apprehending the child, to have a **homemaker** remain with the child in his or her home. According to section 78, a homemaker may live with the child for up to 30 days. If the parent is still not able to care for the child after 30 days, the child is typically apprehended. Reliance on a homemaker is not appropriate in situations where a child is suffering abuse. Placement of a homemaker in the home tends to be used in circumstances where, for some extraordinary reason, a good parent is temporarily unable to care for a child and there are no relatives available to help out; for example, a parent may suddenly fall ill, be delayed while travelling out of the country, or be detained in criminal custody pending a bail hearing.

CHILD PROTECTION PROCEEDINGS

As a social service worker, you need to know and understand the various stages in child protection proceedings, including court procedure, so that you can inform and reassure clients who are experiencing this process.

Example
You work in a women's shelter and have a client whose child was apprehended as a result of a domestic assault in the child's presence. The child's mother is shocked that her child was taken, panicked about the situation, and anxious to have the child returned. You can assist by explaining why the child was apprehended—that exposing a child to domestic violence constitutes child abuse, which the mother was unable to prevent—and that there will be a court hearing to determine whether the child needs protection. The client should understand that child protection hearings can be quite lengthy, extending over several days, and that it is unlikely that her child will be returned immediately following the first court appearance. It is also very important, in a case such as this, to advise the client to seek legal representation.

Grounds for Apprehension

As stated earlier, children's aid societies have a mandate to provide protection to children under the age of 16. A child in need of protection is defined in section 37(2), which lists criteria very similar to those listed in section 72, Duty to Report. This makes sense, because the intent of section 72 is to impose a duty on people to report information that suggests that a child is in need of protection. The circumstances in which a child may be in need of protection include the following:

- physical, sexual, and emotional abuse;
- risk of physical, sexual, or emotional harm;
- risk of sexual abuse or molestation;
- denial of necessary medical or psychological treatment; and
- failure to address behaviour of a child that would result in criminal charges if the child were 12 years of age or older.

Additional grounds for apprehension include the following:

- a child already in the care of the children's aid society has left or has been removed from care without authorization (section 41);
- a child under 12 has committed an act that, if the child were 12 or older, could form the basis for a criminal charge (section 42); and

- a child is a "runaway"—that is, a child who is under 16 has "withdrawn from the care and control" of parents, guardians, or agencies approved under the CFSA (section 43).

Situations where children have been apprehended and placed in the care of a children's aid society include, but are not limited to, the following:

- A young teenager with a new-born child does not appear to have appropriate support services available to assist her in caring for the child. The children's aid society considers the child to be in need of protection and has the baby removed from the mother's care at birth.

- A children's aid society has grounds to believe that a parent in a primary care giving role is using illicit drugs.

- A domestic assault occurs within the family home with the child present at the time of the assault.

- A physician has found marks on a child, resulting in concerns by the children's aid society that inappropriate disciplinary measures are being used in the home.

- The home has not been cleaned by the caregiver for a significant period of time, resulting in concerns for the hygiene and health of the child.

EXTRA CREDIT

Justice Suggests Social Service Workers Should Deliver Cautions

Suspects to a crime have the right to be told that any statements that they make may be used against them in court. Therefore, police officers "administer a caution" to a suspect upon arrest: "You have the right to remain silent. Anything you do say may be used against you ..." Failure to respect this right may result in such statements being excluded from evidence.

The right to be told about the potential for having your statements used against you is not restricted to the context of arrest, however. Under the law, any time a person is at risk of making an incriminating statement to a person in authority, this statement has the potential to be treated as a confession by the court.

Can an employee of a children's aid society come under the definition of a "person in authority" for the purpose of the confession rule? Justice Stephen Hunter said yes, at a January 2006 lecture to social service work students at Loyalist College:

> a person in authority is a person who has the power to have an impact on your life. A children's aid society employee can, without a warrant, come into your house and take your child away. I think that amounts to an impact on your life.

Justice Hunter recommended that children's aid society employees take steps to protect the rights of people with whom they come into contact when the circumstances are such that a person may make a confession. This means, for example, upon attendance at a home to apprehend a child, cautioning a parent that his or her statements may be used against him or her in court.

If you work for a children's aid society, ask if it has a policy with respect to cautioning parents. If not, you might suggest that your employer consider developing one. ◇

Apprehension With or Without a Warrant

Generally, a warrant is required before a child may be apprehended. Pursuant to section 40(2), a justice of the peace may issue a warrant authorizing a child protection worker to bring a child to a place of safety if the justice of the peace is satisfied, on the basis of a child protection worker's sworn information, that there are reasonable and probable grounds to believe that the child is in need of protection and that a less restrictive course of action is not available or will not protect the child adequately.

However, if a child protection worker believes, on reasonable and probable grounds, that there is a substantial risk to the child's health or safety during the time necessary to obtain a warrant from the court, the child may be apprehended immediately, according to section 40(7). Although this provision is consistent with the primary purpose of the CFSA—to promote the best interests, protection, and well-being of children—the effect is to give a children's aid society a significant degree of power to apprehend children and remove them from their home, without first having to establish before a justice of the peace or a court that, on a balance of probabilities, there is a need for apprehension.

In some instances, following apprehension, the court has ordered the return of the child to the previous caregiver subject to restrictions imposed on the caregiver. In those circumstances, the least disruptive alternative to apprehension was considered appropriate, in accordance with the other purposes of the CFSA.

When a child is apprehended, he or she is taken to a "place of safety," which is defined under the CFSA as a hospital, a foster home, or another place designated as a place of safety under section 17 (often, a group home established for the temporary care of children awaiting child protection proceedings).

A review team is assigned to every apprehended child. Within five days after the apprehension, one of three options must be chosen under section 46(1):

- return the child to the parent(s) or guardian;

- bring the case before the court for a child protection hearing; or

- have a temporary care agreement put in place.

The purpose of a child protection hearing is to make a legal determination as to whether the child is in need of protection, and to provide for the child's care. Until such a determination is made by a court, the child may not be placed in the care of a children's aid society and the society may not deliver services without parental consent.

It is often difficult to balance the best interests, protection, and well-being of a child with the autonomy and integrity of the family unit and the least disruptive course of action available to assist a child. The apprehension process is extremely disruptive to the family. In the effort to protect a child, and to err on the side of caution in ensuring that a child is protected, the integrity and autonomy of the family is often threatened, as well as the emotional security of the child, who may not be accustomed to being apart from his or her caregiver.

As a social service worker, you may wish to inform a client who is involved in child protection proceedings that, if appropriate, the child may be placed with a family member pending the resolution of the proceedings. Any family member willing to care for the child should present a plan of care to be assessed by the children's aid society.

Participants in the Child Protection Hearing

Parents of the child may be parties to the proceedings; that is, they may present evidence and make arguments. Additionally, any person who has cared for the child continuously for the six months before the hearing, such as a foster parent, may participate in the hearing.

A child aged 12 or over who is the subject of the hearing is generally entitled to attend unless the court thinks that being present would cause the child emotional harm. A child under 12 is generally not entitled to attend the hearing unless the court decides otherwise, on the basis that the child is capable of understanding the hearing and is unlikely to suffer emotional harm as a result.

A child may be represented by a lawyer; however, most children don't have the means to retain a lawyer. In certain cases, the court will decide that the child *should* have legal representation, and will make an order that he or she is to be represented by the Children's Lawyer (discussed in chapter 4). This is generally done where the court thinks that the child's interests as expressed by the child do not coincide with either the society's view or the parent's view of those interests. An example is a case in which an older child expresses a strong desire to remain in the care of an abusive parent.

A social service worker may be called as a witness in a child protection case, particularly if he or she was the one who made the original report. In most cases, giving evidence as a social service worker is a fairly simple matter of truthfully answering the questions asked—without exaggerating, fabricating, or concealing anything, and without making inappropriate or biased judgments about people or facts. How to conduct yourself as a witness in court will be explored further in chapter 13.

Dispositions

The purpose of a child protection hearing, as mentioned above, is to determine whether a child is in need of protection, and to provide for the child's care. In some cases, the court will make a care order based on a plan of care that has been prepared by a children's aid society. A plan of care must include the following:

- a description of the services proposed to be provided to the child;

- an estimate of the time needed to achieve the results hoped for; and

- a description of the criteria the society will use to determine that those results have been achieved.

Social service workers employed by children's aid societies may be involved in the preparation of plans of care and may be required to testify in court about them. In making an order, a court need not endorse or follow a plan of care exactly as proposed, but the plan of care is often a useful starting point in preparing a court order.

BEST INTERESTS OF THE CHILD

The decision to make a child protection order must be based on the best interests of the child. Section 37(3) lists some factors to be considered in determining the child's best interests. These include, among others,

- the child's physical, mental, and emotional needs;

- the child's physical, mental and emotional level of development;

- the child's cultural background;

- the child's religious faith (if any);

- the child's existing family relationships and the importance, for the child's development, of a positive relationship with a parent and a secure place as a member of a family; and

- the child's views and wishes.

Though the court must consider a child's ethnic and cultural background in all cases, the court has a special responsibility with respect to First Nations children. Any person who makes an order with respect to an Aboriginal child in need of protection must "take into consideration the importance, in recognition of the uniqueness of Indian and native culture, heritage and traditions, of preserving the child's cultural identity" (section 37(4)).

If a court is convinced that a child is in need of protection, before it may make an order removing the child from home, the court must be satisfied that less disruptive alternatives would be inadequate to protect the child (section 57(3)). This is consistent with the overall purposes of the CFSA: to promote the best interests, protection, and well-being of children, and to consider the least disruptive course of action that is available and appropriate in a particular case.

Where the children's aid society proposes to keep a child in care, it must explain why adequate protection cannot be assured if the child is returned to his or her home, and what efforts, if any, will be made to maintain the relationship between the child and the parents or guardian. If the society proposes to remove the child permanently, it must inform the court of its plans for a long-term stable placement for the child.

CARE AND PROTECTION ORDERS

In some cases, where a child has been brought before the court with the participation of the parents, or with his or her own consent, the court can make a **consent order**. This is an agreed plan for the child's care, developed with input from the parents and/or the child, and consented to by them.

Most child protection orders are not agreements, but rather are imposed by the court. Under section 57, the court has three choices when making an order for care on behalf of a child without the parents' consent:

- a supervision order,

- an order of society wardship, or

- an order of Crown wardship.

Supervision Order

A **supervision order** allows the child to remain in the care of the parents or guardian. The children's aid society provides supervision for a period of 3 to 12 months, giving guidance to the parents or guardian and making sure that the child is safe and well cared for.

Society Wardship

If the court determines that a child cannot be adequately protected at home, but that it is appropriate for the child to continue to have contact with the parents or guardian, the court will typically make an order of **society wardship**. An order for society wardship provides for a child's placement in residential custody for a maximum of 12 months.

A child who is a ward of a children's aid society has the right to visit his or her parents. If the parents (and sometimes others, such as grandparents) wish to visit the child, they must apply to the court for an access order (section 58). The court will permit access only if it is determined to be in the best interests of the child.

The court can also make a **consecutive order** of society wardship followed by supervision (after the child has been returned to the care of the parents or guardian) for a total period not exceeding 12 months.

In some cases, where a child has been made the ward of a society, the court may subsequently determine that it would not be appropriate to return the child to the care of the parents or guardian. In these circumstances, the court can make an order of Crown wardship in respect of the child.

Crown Wardship

If the court determines that it is unlikely that the parents or guardian will ever be able to care for the child adequately, the court will make an order of **Crown wardship**. When a child becomes a ward of the Crown, it is not expected that the child will ever be returned to the care of the parents or guardian. A child who has been made a Crown ward may subsequently become available for adoption without the consent of the parents or guardian.

In general, access orders are not made for Crown wards. If circumstances were so extreme as to result in Crown wardship, access is unlikely to be in the child's best interests. Access could also jeopardize the child's chances to be placed in a stable home environment.

A Crown wardship order ends on the day the child turns 18. A society wardship or supervision order that has not already expired is also terminated when the child reaches 18.

Critical Perspectives

Raised by the State

While infertile couples desperate for families of their own spend $30,000 or more pursuing overseas adoptions, thousands of Ontario's children languish as "wards of the state." Many children spend most of their childhood bouncing from one foster home or group home to another, only to be expelled from the system, with virtually no family or social support, at age 18.

Many of these children have special needs; others are hard to place through adoption simply because they are no longer babies, or are of mixed race or part of a sibling group. Another major stumbling block has been Ontario's adoption law. Until recently, children could not be adopted if their birth parents retained access rights. This has changed with the passage of Bill 210, which amends the CFSA and allows for children to maintain ties to their birth families after adoption. Despite the obvious potential problems for adoptive families dealing with birth families, adoption advocates assert that this amendment opens doors for many children seeking stability in loving homes. ◇

Restraining Order

In some cases, instead of or in addition to a supervision or wardship order, a court may make a **restraining order** under section 80. A restraining order protects the child from another person by restricting the access of that person to the child. A restraining order can be an appropriate solution where the child has been abused by a person other than the custodial parent, such as a member of the extended family, a family friend, or a neighbour.

Review of Orders

Time-limited disposition orders made by the court (supervision orders, society wardship orders, and consecutive orders) must be reviewed prior to their expiration. The society is required under the CFSA to commence a status review application and to serve it on all parties entitled to **notice** of the proceeding. On status review, the court may terminate the order that was made previously, or make a further order of the same kind or another kind.

Status reviews of Crown wardship orders must be carried out at least once per year. There is one restriction on the making of a further order by the court: a society wardship order cannot be made on a status review of a Crown wardship order.

Kinship Care

An alternative to society wardship, which should be considered if appropriate, is the placement of a child in the care of a relative, friend, or neighbour, or, in the case of First Nations children, a member of the child's First Nations band. This type of placement is made with the consent of the person who will be taking charge of the child.

Kinship care refers to placement of an at-risk child (or children) in the care of grandparents, aunts, uncles, other close relatives, or even non-relatives, such as godparents, with whom the child has a kinship bond. An arrangement to place a child in kinship care can happen at two different stages in a child welfare case. It can happen with the consent of parents—for example, as part of a voluntary intervention by a children's aid society—or after a formal order has been issued to make the child a society ward.

In Ontario, kinship care is currently being explored and has not been formally implemented at the second stage described above (that is, after a wardship order). The infrastructure needed to support this kind of arrangement (for example, a clear legal basis and the availability of adequate economic support for caregiver candidates) is not yet fully in place in the province; however, child protection workers can expect developments in this area over the next few years.

Differential Responses

Child welfare organizations in many US and Canadian jurisdictions are beginning to embrace the benefits of adopting a program of differential responses to child welfare cases, depending on the particular circumstances. The Centre for Excellence for Child Welfare (CECW), an agency funded by Health Canada, describes differential response as follows:

> Differential response models, sometimes referred to as "alternative response models" or "multi-track systems" ... include a range of potential response options

customized to meet the diverse needs of families reported to child welfare. Differential response systems typically use multiple "tracks" or "streams" of service delivery. While some jurisdictions may initiate up to five tracks, as is the case with Michigan, most differential response systems employ two streams with the investigative track handling high-risk cases. High-risk cases include all reports of sexual abuse, serious physical or emotional harm, chronic neglect and cases in which criminal charges may be laid. Less urgent cases are shifted to an alternative "assessment" or "community" track, where the focus of intervention is on brokering and coordinating services to address the short and long-term needs of these children and families.

In Canada, the only province to have formally implemented a differential response model is Alberta. In Ontario, however, research studies and draft papers have been completed on the subject, including a paper by the Ontario Association of Children's Aid Societies (OACAS) entitled "A Differential Service Response for Child Welfare in Ontario." While the OACAS suggests that the CFSA implicitly permits the development of a differential response model, changes to the regulations would likely be required to fully support this initiative.

RESPONSIBILITIES TOWARD CHILDREN IN CARE OR IN RECEIPT OF SERVICES

Once a child has been found to be in need of protection, a duty arises, on the part of the children's aid society and its employees, to actively protect the child. Failure to provide protection and service to a child as required by the CFSA could lead to loss of the designation as a child protection agency or loss of a licence to run a children's residence.

There is also the potential for a civil lawsuit arising out of failure to protect a child. Section 81 of the CFSA specifically permits the Children's Lawyer to bring a civil suit for damages on behalf of a child against his or her abuser. The definition of abuse for the purpose of section 81 is set out in section 79 of the CFSA. Section 79(2) provides:

> No person having charge of a child shall, ...
>> (b) by failing to care and provide for or supervise and protect the child adequately,
>>> (i) permit the child to suffer abuse, or
>>> (ii) permit the child to suffer from a mental, emotional or developmental condition that, if not remedied, could seriously impair the child's development.

Under this section, a civil suit could be brought against an individual social service worker, or against a children's aid society or other child protection agency or residence. In some circumstances, a social worker may even face criminal prosecution for failure to prevent the injury or death of a child.

Child welfare experts have suggested that social workers and social service workers who perform their duties in good faith and to the best of their abilities within the standards of their profession can generally expect to be free from criminal or civil liability. However, it is clear that law enforcement personnel will respond to the human cost of mistakes, and to the public outrage that follows serious harm to a child under agency supervision.

CASE IN POINT

Social Worker Charged with Criminal Negligence

In 1997, Angie Martin, a social worker with the Catholic Children's Aid Society (CCAS) of Toronto, was charged with criminal negligence causing death (*Criminal Code* section 220), an offence that, if proven, carries a maximum penalty of imprisonment for life.

Ms. Martin had been assigned to monitor the case of Jordan Heikamp, who was born on May 18, 1997 to Renee Heikamp, a 19-year-old homeless woman. Jordan was released from hospital into his mother's care on May 29. By June 23, he was dead. An autopsy showed that he had died of starvation while living with his mother at a shelter for abused women.

During the preliminary inquiry into the charges against Ms. Martin, evidence was led with respect to mistakes she had made in her monitoring of the case. The evidence showed that Ms. Heikamp had lied to Ms. Martin about her attendance with Jordan at the doctor, and about the baby's weight gain, and that Ms. Martin had relied on this misinformation in assuming that Jordan was receiving appropriate care. Nevertheless, the court found that this and other mistakes on Ms. Martin's part were not sufficient evidence upon which to sustain a charge under section 220. The presiding judge found that Ms. Martin's care was not a substantial departure from the accepted standard of care for children's aid workers, that she had not demonstrated a wanton disregard for Jordan's life, and that she had not directly contributed to his starvation. The charge was dropped.

A subsequent coroner's inquest into the case was very critical of both the CCAS and Ms. Martin, and the social worker endured substantial negative publicity in the wake of the baby's death. While she escaped criminal sanction, baby Jordan's death and the criminal case had a very significant impact on Ms. Martin from both a personal and a career perspective.

See *R. v. Heikamp and Martin* (3 December 1999), Toronto (Ont. CJ) (judgment on committal). ◇

KEY TERMS

best interests of the child	homemaker	society wardship
consecutive order	kinship care	supervision order
consensual	notice	temporary care agreement
consent order	plan of care	
Crown wardship	restraining order	

REFERENCES

Child and Family Services Act, RSO 1990, c. C.11.

Heikamp and Martin, R. v. (3 December 1999), Toronto (Ont. CJ) (judgment on committal).

Ontario Association of Children's Aid Societies (OACAS), Differential Response Sub-Committee of Ontario Children's Aid Directors of Service, "A Differential Service Response for Child Welfare in Ontario," September 2004.

Rock, Nora, *Child Protection and Canadian Law: A Service Perspective* (Toronto: Emond Montgomery, 2005).

REVIEW QUESTIONS

1. What is the paramount purpose of the CFSA?

2. Which kinds of interventions are designed to minimize disruption to the lives of children?

3. Which organizations are primarily responsible for the administration of the CFSA?

4. Who, according to the CFSA, has a duty to report child abuse or neglect?

5. List four kinds of observations that would trigger a duty to report under the CFSA.

6. List three possible consequences of failing to report suspected child abuse or neglect.

7. What would you do if you observed signs that a child in the care of a children's aid society was being abused or neglected?

8. What happens after a child has been apprehended by a children's aid society?

9. Who decides whether a child is in need of protection?

10. List three possible dispositions that can be made once a child is determined to be in need of protection. How do they differ?

11. Does the child protection system provide services to children who have not been found to be in need of protection?

12. List three kinds of consensual/voluntary interventions contemplated by the CFSA.

DISCUSSION QUESTIONS

Consider the following scenarios and decide whether a duty to report is triggered. Also note whether your observations relate to abuse or the threat of abuse, neglect or the threat of neglect.

1. You are a support worker in a strict-discipline educational program for expelled students. Terry, a grade 10 student, has been reprimanded, along with two of his friends, for a prank played on a maintenance worker: his mop was saturated with shaving cream and his floor wax was replaced with maple syrup. You point out to Terry that he knows he shouldn't enter the maintenance closet without permission and mess with the cleaning equipment. In addition, since this is his second offence of this nature, his parents will be told of his misbehaviour. Terry looks panic-stricken and begs you to reconsider, saying, "My dad is gonna kill me!"

2. You are working a shift in the lunchroom at a school for hearing-impaired children. For the third time this week, seven-year-old Vezna has not brought her lunch. She tells you that her mom forgot to make it. You encourage other students to share their lunches with her. You've noticed that Vezna often looks unkempt; she dresses inappropriately for the weather, her hair is hopelessly tangled, and she smells bad. This freezing January day, Vezna is wearing a pair of cropped pants in a thin summery fabric, and sandals with socks. You ask her if her mother helped her pick out these clothes, and Vezna says, "My mom is never awake in the mornings before school, but I'm old enough to choose my own clothes."

3. You are a passenger on a city bus. You take the same bus every morning, and most mornings, a woman gets on with a boy who looks to be about three years old and a newborn. The boy is fairly well behaved on the bus, but his mother, it seems to you, is impatient with him and responds quite angrily when he "acts up." Before the bus has travelled two blocks, she has

yelled at the boy three times for kicking the seat in front of him. The fourth time he does it, she grabs his foot and shoves it violently downward, causing him to lurch forward and bump his head hard against the armrest on the seat in front. He begins to cry, and his mother immediately says she's sorry and rubs his forehead. However, within 10 minutes, she is yelling at him again, this time for humming.

RESEARCH PROJECT: VOLUNTARY SERVICES IN YOUR COMMUNITY

Using the telephone directory, the Blue Book, the Internet, and any other resources you can think of, research the voluntary services provided or recommended by children's aid societies in your community. Choose one facility to visit (or care provider to interview).

Visit the facility or interview the provider and learn about the program. Here are some examples of the kind of questions you might ask:

- How are children and families referred to the voluntary services program?

- Is the program run by, associated with, or recommended by a children's aid society?

- Is the program staffed by volunteers or by employees of the agency?

- What kind of training/credentials do the staff have?

- Is the program targeted to any particular client group?

- What kinds of problems does the program seek to address?

- Can you give some examples of problems that are beyond the mandate of the program?

- Does the program or facility have a policy for identifying children in need of protection?

Give a presentation to your class about the program and the facility or care provider.

CHAPTER 4
Family Law

CHAPTER OBJECTIVES

After reading this chapter, you should be able to:

- List the federal and provincial statutes that codify family law in Ontario.
- Understand the key principles that govern custody, access, and support in Ontario.
- Explain the legal importance of the best interests of the child.
- Explain the role of the Children's Lawyer.
- Describe the role of a family support worker with respect to access to Ontario Works benefits.
- Understand the work of the Family Responsibility Office.

INTRODUCTION

Divorce, family property, and child custody and access are among the most common types of litigation undertaken by Canadians. The Canadian divorce rate has hovered near the 50 percent mark in recent decades, and most research suggests that common-law partnerships break up at least as often as marriages.

Divorce and separation affect many families in the peak child-raising years. Family breakdown has significant negative economic, practical, and emotional consequences for all members of the family.

Social service workers may be involved with separating families in a variety of ways. They may work in shelters for the victims of family violence, as employees of children's aid societies, in the office of the Children's Lawyer (in an investigative capacity), or in any of a myriad of other roles supporting children. In these settings, clients may need basic information about a range of legal issues that arise early in a separation, such as the right to live in the matrimonial home.

Social service workers may also encounter clients (in various recreational or support settings) who have begun to adjust to a separation but need help with parenting skills. An example of a social service worker's role at this stage might be supporting **supervised access** by a parent to his or her children at a special access and exchange centre.

While social service workers may be called on to provide basic legal information to their clients, it is very important for them to avoid providing any kind of legal advice. Each case of separation and divorce has its own individual circumstances, and most social service workers lack the training to determine the best course of action for their clients. Even advice that might seem, to the social service worker, to be a matter of common sense may ultimately be detrimental to a client's case.

For example, a social service worker who is concerned about the safety of a separating wife in her home may think that the wife should wait until the husband goes to work and then have the locks changed. However, the law provides that both spouses have an equal right to live in the matrimonial home unless a court order has been obtained granting one spouse the right of exclusive possession.

Likewise, where there are children involved, advising a client to leave the matrimonial home, with or without the children, may also have significant legal consequences. Before a parent leaves with the children, a court order for interim custody should be obtained. If the parent leaves without the children, this may be viewed under the law as abandonment.

A person contemplating separation should review the options carefully with a lawyer before taking any action. Any improper action that a party takes has the potential to be raised by the other party as an issue in the course of subsequent proceedings.

"Commonsense" advice can have serious legal ramifications with respect to access as well. For example, it might seem reasonable to recommend that a child with a cold should stay at home instead of going out on a scheduled visit with her father. But this could be interpreted as impeding the father's access, and could influence a court to determine that the mother is uncooperative and not a good candidate for custody.

In short, it is essential that a social service worker make no recommendations that could be perceived as legal advice to a client in a family law matter. A social service worker who oversteps these boundaries risks being sued if the client follows her advice and suffers economic or other harm as a result.

Figure 4.1 provides some examples of the difference between legal information (which, if accurate, is acceptable to give) and legal advice, which must be avoided. Social service agencies can help their staff to avoid giving legal advice by preparing

FIGURE 4.1   Examples of the Differences Between Legal Information and Legal Advice

Legal information	Legal advice
◆ Explaining the importance of obtaining legal advice and providing referral to lawyers	◆ Recommending that a client leave the home
◆ Providing contact information for local Legal Aid offices	◆ Recommending that a client change the locks in the home
◆ Advising clients of the range of issues they may encounter, such as custody and access, support, division of property, occupancy of the matrimonial home, and personal safety	◆ Recommending that a client refuse to relinquish the children
	◆ Suggesting that a client pay less support
◆ Explaining the services provided by supervised access and exchange centres	◆ Recommending that a client withdraw money from a joint account to keep it from the other spouse

a standard handout with basic legal information. The agency can ask a family lawyer to review and approve the handout, so that social service workers can feel comfortable providing it to their clients.

FAMILY LAW ISSUES

Family law has evolved to address the wide range of needs of separating parties and their children:

- Divorce law addresses the "status" issue of whether or not (and when) the parties can consider themselves single again (and remarry, if they wish).

- Family property law determines the appropriate division of assets and **real property** brought into and accumulated during the union.

- Family support law is designed to ensure that economically dependent family members who are unable to fully support themselves after family breakdown receive economic help from those who supported them during the union.

- Custody and access law is designed to ensure that the day-to-day care of children, and the children's ongoing relationships with parents, are arranged in a manner that reflects the children's best interests.

- Family law also addresses the issue of the personal safety of spouses and children.

Like most other areas of law, family legislation evolved from the common law, and many of the directions it has taken reflect common-law court decisions. Most modern family law, however, is statute-based. While court decisions dictate the *application* of statutory provisions, our federal and provincial legislation forms what is intended to be a complete and exhaustive code for dealing with the issues families face after the partners separate.

Family law issues are not resolved only by courts; in fact, handling family matters without going to court is encouraged under our family law. While a court order is needed for a divorce to be final, many couples, whether they were legally married or simply living together, resolve all or most of their family law issues outside court. This can happen by direct negotiation between the parties, who (sometimes with the help of lawyers) draft an agreement, or contract, to manage their post-separation relations. It can also happen through **mediation**, when a trained, neutral professional supports the parties in working out their issues and achieving an acceptable agreement. Mediation and other forms of alternative dispute resolution are discussed in greater detail in chapter 13.

Mediation is sometimes said to take place "in the shadow of the law." This means that parties enter into mediation knowing that if their negotiations break down, they will have no choice but to go to court, where resolving problems is more expensive and the parties lose some control over the process (because a judge makes the final decisions). The threat of court can encourage mediated solutions, and the state of the law (for example, the child support formulas used in the court) can serve as guideposts to help the parties know "what's fair," even if this law is never directly applied to their own situation by a court.

FAMILY LEGISLATION

Family law in Canada is complicated somewhat by the historical division of constitutional powers between the federal government and the provinces. While the property aspects of family law fall squarely within provincial jurisdiction, marriage and divorce were assigned to federal jurisdiction under the *Constitution Act, 1867*.

This means that when a married couple separate and want the marriage to be legally dissolved, the ensuing divorce is governed by the federal *Divorce Act*, but property issues are resolved under provincial family law legislation. When an unmarried cohabiting ("common-law") couple separate, however, the legal consequences of the separation are governed by provincial family law statutes.

DIVORCE

The *Divorce Act*, a federal statute, governs the dissolution of formal marriages in Canada. Unless an existing marriage is dissolved, marriage partners are not eligible to be married again. **Marriage breakdown** is the only ground for divorce in Canada. Marriage breakdown can be proven using evidence of

- one year's separation,

- adultery, or

- cruelty.

The great majority of Canadian divorces are granted on proof of one year's separation. A couple seeking a divorce can apply for a divorce order before the year of separation is up, but the divorce cannot be granted until the one-year mark. The *Divorce Act* requires couples (at least in the absence of cruelty or abuse) to consider reconciling, and failing that, to attempt to come to an agreement about issues of

---

LEGISLATIVE SHORTCUT

Divorce Act

RSC 1985, c.3 (2d Supp.)

Objective: To govern the dissolution of formal marriages in Canada, including child support, spousal support, and custody and access.

Target Population: Married couples seeking divorce.

Program Administration: Not applicable

Administrative Tribunal: Not applicable—decisions are made by the court

Summary: The *Divorce Act*, a federal statute, provides for divorce where the marriage has broken down. Generally, the parties must be separated for a year before a divorce is granted. Divorce is granted on a "no-fault" basis, which means that the court is generally not interested in the conduct of the parties. The *Divorce Act* includes provisions governing spousal support, child support, and custody and access, all of which are determined based on the best interests of the children. ◇

EXTRA CREDIT

Same-Sex Marriage

Today, in Ontario, partners of the same sex can be formally married. For a few years before same-sex marriage was recognized, cohabiting (living together) arrangements between same-sex partners were recognized under the *Family Law Act* for the purpose of some post-separation legal issues, but formal marriage was unavailable to lesbian and gay (male) couples.

Beginning in the late 1980s, a number of gay and lesbian couples in Ontario brought lawsuits challenging their exclusion from access to formal marriage. These legal challenges were usually raised on the basis of discrimination or violation of rights under the *Canadian Charter of Rights and Freedoms*. The Ontario Court of Appeal ultimately ruled that it is against the law to prohibit gay and lesbian couples from marrying, and same-sex marriages became legal in Ontario. The first such marriage, which was performed on January 14, 2001, was registered (accepted as a legal marriage) in June 2003.

Around the same time, similar legal challenges were being brought in other provinces. Finally, in July 2005, the federal parliament clarified the law by enacting legislation that makes it legal for same-sex couples to marry anywhere in Canada. Same-sex married couples can also obtain a divorce under the *Divorce Act*.

It is important to note that the change to the law does not compel any religious group to endorse or perform same-sex marriages. For example, a Catholic priest cannot be required to officiate at such a ceremony. ◇

---

support and custody through a mediated process before entering into litigation (going to court).

It is important to understand that divorce based on separation of at least a year is considered to be "no-fault." This means that it is not relevant for the court to know how the parties treated (or mistreated) each other, or who left, and why. This may be a difficult concept for some marriage partners to grasp, particularly when they are struggling with feelings of anger or loss. Social service workers can help these clients to express and deal with their emotions in a clinical setting, and encourage them to approach legal issues dispassionately.

DISTRIBUTION OF FAMILY PROPERTY UPON SEPARATION

When a married couple separates, there is legislation in place in every province to govern the division of their **net family property**.

In Ontario, the *Family Law Act* establishes rules for the calculation and division of family property, so that the couple's property can be divided equitably between them upon separation. Under the Act, a spouse does not acquire an ownership interest in property owned by the other spouse, but does have a right to an **equalization payment** if the parties separate. The equalization payment equals one-half of the difference between the net family property of each spouse, calculated as follows:

1. Start with the value of the property owned by each spouse at the time the parties separate, including land, vehicles, bank accounts, and business interests; then

Family Law Act

RSO 1990, c.F.3

Objective: To provide for the equitable resolution of issues between separated parties including property division, support, and financial responsibility for children.

Target Population: Separated couples.

Program Administration: Not applicable.

Administrative Tribunal: Not applicable—decisions are made by the court.

Summary: The *Family Law Act* governs the division of the couple's property upon separation by providing for a payment from one spouse to the other in order to equalize the value of their assets. The Act also provides for equal interests in the matrimonial home, regardless of ownership, and for spousal and child support. ◇

2. Subtract from this amount

    a. debts and liabilities on the date of separation;

    b. the net value of property owned on the date of marriage (property owned minus debts and liabilities); and

    c. excluded property (gifts and inheritances, damage awards for personal injury, and property excluded by a spousal agreement).

Once this calculation is completed for each spouse, the equalization payment is determined by subtracting the smaller net family property amount from the larger. The spouse with the larger net family property amount must pay half the difference to the other spouse, thereby "equalizing" the net family property.

MATRIMONIAL HOME

The *Family Law Act* creates special rules for deciding what happens to the matrimonial home. The legislation defines a **matrimonial home** as property that the spouses ordinarily occupied as their family residence at the time of separation. Unless and until a court orders otherwise, both spouses have an equal right of possession of a matrimonial home, and neither spouse may sell the matrimonial home without the consent of the other. Depending on the circumstances, one party may be temporarily granted the exclusive right to live in the matrimonial home (**exclusive possession**), one party may buy out the other, or the home may be sold and the proceeds divided equally.

CUSTODY AND ACCESS

Custody generally refers to the legal arrangement for the day-to-day care of and decision making with respect to a child. Having custody of a child means having the authority to make decisions about matters such as education, medical treatment, and religious observance. **Access** generally refers to the arrangement by which the parent who does not have custody is permitted to spend time with the child. Although these terms are still used in family law statutes, their meaning is elastic.

Similarly, expressions like "sole custody" and "joint custody" do not have rigid definitions. Sole custody generally refers to a situation where one parent has decision-making power, and joint custody generally refers to shared decision making. However, involvement in decision making need not be all or nothing. Instead of describing an arrangement as sole or joint custody, better terminology may be "parenting plan." In a parenting plan, the rights and responsibilities of each parent may be mixed and matched, according to the family's particular needs. For example, one parent might make decisions about day-to-day medical concerns, and the other parent might make decisions regarding religious observance.

Shared decision making requires considerable contact between the separated parents. For joint custody to work properly, the parents must be able to negotiate contentious issues, and also accommodate each other's schedules. If the parents have joint custody but are incapable of calm and rational discussion, a parenting coordinator may be used as a mediator or arbitrator, to assist the parents in making decisions.

Parenting coordinators are sometimes social workers and are trained to assess what is in the best interests of the child. If the parenting coordinator is unable to facilitate a compromise between the parents, he or she is empowered, either by the court or by agreement between the parties, to make a binding decision. This helps to diminish conflict and reduce expenses by keeping the parties out of court.

Social service workers may also be involved in exchange programs, which provide a neutral location where parents can drop off and pick up their children. These programs can help to minimize conflict that might arise if one parent had to go to the other parent's residence (for example, if a parent did not get along with the other parent's new spouse), or if the dropping-off parent has a history of entering the other parent's home uninvited.

Both custody and access are governed by legislation: the federal *Divorce Act* and, in Ontario, the *Children's Law Reform Act* (CLRA). Under the *Divorce Act*, either (previously married) parent can automatically apply for custody or access, and other

LEGISLATIVE SHORTCUT

Children's Law Reform Act

RSO 1990, c. C.12

Objective: To ensure that custody and access issues are determined in the best interests of children.

Target Population: Children with separated parents (formally married or common law) who have not applied for divorce.

Program Administration: Not applicable.

Administrative Tribunal: Not applicable—decisions are made by the court.

Summary: The *Children's Law Reform Act* governs custody and access on the basis of the best interests of the children. "Custody" generally means the authority to make decisions about things like education, medical treatment, and religious observance. Where parents share decision-making, custody is "joint." "Access" generally describes the arrangement by which the parent who does not live with the child spends time with the child. ◇

individuals can apply if they have the permission of the court. Under the CLRA, a parent (whether previously married or a former common-law partner) "or any other person" can apply.

Best Interests of the Child

According to both statutes, custody and access arrangements are to be based on the best interests of the child. Where both parents want custody, the court is required to decide the issue not on the basis of which parent is more "deserving," but on the basis of what will be best for the child.

There are many factors to be taken into account in making custody decisions, and it is very important that clients have the benefit of a lawyer's advice when shaping a parenting plan to be negotiated or litigated between the parties. The court will generally favour an arrangement that fosters stability in the child's life, and it will give weight to historical caregiving patterns. For example, if the child has been cared for by a full-time stay-at-home mother who intimately knows the child's needs, habits, schedules, and preferences, the court will be more likely to award custody to the mother, even if the divorce means that both parents will have to go out to work.

The court will also consider the will and ability of each parent to support and foster a good relationship between the child and the other parent. For example, if

Critical Perspectives

The Voice of the Child in Family Law

It is more or less settled in Canadian law that the opinion of children with respect to custody and access is a factor that can properly be considered by the courts in making decisions. However, the extent to which children should be directly involved in the legal process is much more controversial.

Allowing or encouraging children to testify in court raises a number of concerns. In many cases, children are quite hesitant to express any opinions at all, for fear of displeasing one parent or the other. Where a child who is unwilling to express an opinion reports feeling pressured to do so, a social service worker may have sufficient reason (ideally, after consulting with a lawyer) to advocate for the child's right not to comment.

Where one parent seems to be placing undue pressure on a child to take part in a family law dispute, the court (and/or a mediator) will typically address this concern from the perspective of the best interests of the child; that is, it will allow participation by the child only to the extent that this seems to be in the child's best interests. In extreme cases, a parent's attempts to pressure a child might be viewed as evidence of the parent's unwillingness to further the child's best interests (thus going against an award of custody).

However, where a child is willing, or even eager, to participate in the legal process as a witness, many experts now believe that it is not necessarily damaging, and it may in fact be beneficial, to allow the child to do so. In a recent report for Canada's Department of Justice (*The Voice of the Child in Divorce, Custody and Access Proceedings*), Ronda Bessner noted:

- Many children of divorce have witnessed arguments at home that are at least as bitter and confrontational as divorce proceedings.

- Allowing a child to appear as a witness gives the child the assurance that his point of view has been put before the court in his own words, without being filtered through the bias of any well-meaning adult.

- Excluding a child who is eager to participate in the legal process that will determine her future may be much more damaging than exposing her to the process. ◇

one parent obstructs the other parent's access to the child, or speaks negatively to the child about the other parent, the court may try to address this by limiting the time the obstructive parent spends with the child.

Finally, in some situations, the court will consider the emotional ties and the preferences of the child. Particularly in the case of an older child, the child's own wishes about living arrangements will often influence the court's decision. The older and more mature the child is, the more influence his or her preferences are likely to have in the court's determination.

With respect to access arrangements, in the great majority of cases, it is considered to be in the child's best interests to maintain a relationship with both parents. The court will even go so far, in some cases, as to award access to a parent against the child's own expressed wishes. Such a decision is always controversial. It is usually made where the court believes that the child's current attitude toward the parent is probably temporary, perhaps coloured by negative feelings arising out of the separation process. If there is no apparent risk of child abuse or neglect, courts are generally very supportive of access.

Custody and Access Assessment

If custody and access issues are contentious and there are "clinical issues," meaning mental health concerns regarding one or both parents and/or the child or children, the court may appoint an assessor to provide it with expert advice. An assessor is a person with "technical or professional skill," such as a psychologist or social worker, who will interview the parents, children, teachers, and mental health professionals involved with the family, and submit a report with recommendations to the court. The parties will be required to pay for the assessment.

If the parties do not have the resources to pay for an assessment, the court may recommend involvement by the Children's Lawyer.

The Children's Lawyer

The provision of a court-ordered or government-funded lawyer for children in Ontario dates back to 1826, when a private lawyer was appointed to serve as guardian *ad litem* (at law) for children who needed legal representation. That role is now filled by the **Children's Lawyer**, an office within the Ontario Ministry of the Attorney General.

The Children's Lawyer represents children in a range of cases, such as contested wills and personal injury lawsuits. In custody and access cases, the Office of the Children's Lawyer may appoint a lawyer to represent the child, or in cases involving young children, appoint a social worker to undertake an investigation and make recommendations based on the child's best interests.

A child may become a client of the Children's Lawyer only by court order; however, the Children's Lawyer may decline to take the case where it determines that the issues are minor or that the parties can afford to pay for a private custody and access assessment.

In some cases, before the Children's Lawyer is appointed, the child will be accompanied to court by a social worker, a social service worker, or a family support worker from a family support program (created in support of the Ontario Works program, discussed at the end of this chapter).

Supervised Access

Where the court has concerns about the child's safety in the care of a parent, it can award supervised access. The supervision is often provided by a social welfare agency and involves the presence of a social worker or social service worker during the parent's visits with a child. Examples of reasons for ordering supervised access include

- substantiated suspicions that the access parent will abduct the child;

- believable allegations of prior child abuse, whether emotional, physical, or sexual, or evidence of such abuse;

- believable allegations or evidence of child neglect, or a belief on the part of the court that the parent is not fully capable (for example, by reason of substance addiction or mental illness) of caring for the child; and

- the child's expressed fears or reservations about the access.

When supervised access goes well, the parent under supervision may eventually be successful in having the access order changed to allow unsupervised visits.

EXTRA CREDIT
Supervised Access and Exchange Centres

The Ontario Ministry of the Attorney General, in partnership with a range of community service agencies, runs a program that provides supervised access and exchange at designated centres across the province. These centres provide a place for divorced or separated parents to either drop off and pick up their children or participate in supervised visits. Parents can obtain the services of one of these centres by getting a court order for supervised access or exchange, or by signing an agreement in writing to use the centre's services.

As described by Marion Hunter, the program director at the Durham Supervised Access Program in Ajax, Ontario, the staff of a supervised access centre may play a role in court hearings. Ms. Hunter notes that her staff includes social service workers. Although supervised access centres do not make custody and access recommendations to the court, summary notes prepared by staff members are sometimes reviewed by assessors (typically social workers with a master's degree who work with the courts) in the context of an assessment; and in some cases, a staff person may be called as a witness in court to testify about his or her observations. The Durham program has no specific guidelines in place for staff who are called as witnesses, but supervisors in the program usually provide staff members with general information about what to expect after being subpoenaed (ordered to appear in court) as a witness.

Government-sponsored centres charge a modest fee, typically less than $200 per year, or a maximum of $25 per supervised visit. Some cities have privately owned and operated centres that offer similar services. These private centres are not subject to the same policies and guidelines that the government-sponsored centres are required to follow.

For more information about supervised access, see Ontario, Ministry of the Attorney General at www.attorneygeneral.jus.gov.on.ca. ◇

Enforcement of Custody and Access Orders

Where one or both parties are not following the terms of a custody or access agreement or order, the CLRA provides mechanisms for enforcement. In some cases, social service workers may need to bring the relevant provisions of the CLRA to the attention of separated or divorced clients who are having problems working with the other spouse. For example:

- Where one party, contrary to the terms of a custody or access order, is withholding a child from the other party, the court can make an order under section 36 allowing the person from whom the child is being withheld (or his or her representative) to "locate and apprehend" the child.

- The court can also issue an order under section 37 restricting removal of the child from the jurisdiction. This order can be enforced by requiring the uncooperative party to place property in trust or post a bond, pending the return of the child at the end of an access visit, or by requiring surrender of the child's passport to the court for safekeeping.

- Finally, under section 38, the court has a broad power to punish those who exhibit "wilful contempt of or resistance to its process or orders in respect of custody of or access to a child." Disregard for the court's orders can result in a fine of up to $5,000 and/or 90 days' imprisonment.

SPOUSAL SUPPORT

A spouse who was economically dependent during the marriage or common-law relationship may be able to claim **spousal support**. Spousal support is separate and distinct from child support, discussed below.

A spouse can claim support under the *Divorce Act* provided that the couple was legally married. In Ontario, a common-law partner can claim support under the *Family Law Act* provided that the couple

- cohabited continuously for three years or more, or

- had a child together while cohabiting with some degree of permanence.

Eligibility to claim spousal support does not mean that support will automatically be granted. Both spouses have a duty to be self-sufficient. If self-sufficiency is not possible, in determining whether an award should be made, and the amount of any award, the court will consider factors such as a disability, the needs and means of each spouse, and any economic disadvantage attributable to the marriage, such as primary responsibility for child-rearing. Generally, spousal support awards tend to be smaller, or denied, for spouses who are employed or readily employable, and support may be time-limited.

Other factors affecting spousal support awards include the age of each spouse and the duration and nature of the union. If the partners are young, childless, and lived together for only a few years while both worked, it is unlikely that one party will be awarded significant support from the other. On the other hand, in the case of a breakup of a long marriage, in which the spouses assumed traditional breadwinner–homemaker roles, the likelihood that support will be awarded is high. When a couple with young children separate during or just after a period in which one parent bore a disproportionate share of child-care responsibilities, the caregiving parent may be entitled to support in order to prepare for entering or re-entering the workforce.

Where a person has a viable claim for support but has not pursued that claim, access to social security benefits (such as Ontario Works benefits) may be denied until he or she has attempted to collect support. In some jurisdictions, local social service workers and provincial government offices can help the individual to pursue an application for support (for example, in Ontario, through a local family support program, discussed below). Similar assistance may also be available where a former spouse has been awarded support and the other party defaults on the agreement and is in arrears (behind in making payments). In Ontario, the former spouse can pursue arrears of support through the Family Responsibility Office (also discussed below).

CHILD SUPPORT

Both the *Divorce Act* and the *Family Law Act* provide for **child support** orders. Under the *Divorce Act*, both parents are required to contribute to the support of a "child of the marriage." This term includes not only the biological children of the two partners, but also adopted children, stepchildren to whom one of the partners has stood *in loco parentis* (in place of a parent), and children born outside the marriage union (once called "illegitimate children").

The *Divorce Act* requires parents to pay support until a child is 16 years old, and beyond that age if the child is incapable of supporting himself or herself (for example, because of an intellectual deficit).

The *Family Law Act* requires both parents to support a child up to the age of 18, and beyond if the child is enrolled in a full-time program of study. However, where a child is 16 or older and has withdrawn from parental control (a factual determination, proven through evidence), parents are no longer required to provide support.

Child support is paid by one parent to the other, and is an issue separate from custody and access. Child support is the right of the child, and a parent can be ordered to pay it even if that parent has not been given legal access to the child, or if access has been given and later suspended. By the same token, access rights are not affected by a failure to pay support. This means that a parent is not permitted to restrict the access of the other parent in retaliation for refusal to pay arrears of child support.

Because support is the right of the child, children are permitted to take their parents to court to obtain it. While most children's family law rights are pursued by one parent or the other, the *Family Law Act* (section 33(2)) allows a child to bring an application for support in his or her own right (through a **litigation guardian**). Where there is no litigation guardian available to do this, the child can sometimes seek representation by the Children's Lawyer.

An application for support for a child may also be brought by Ontario's Ministry of Community and Social Services, or by any of the following agencies:

- a municipal corporation, including a metropolitan, district, or regional municipality, but not including an area municipality (an example would be a subsidized housing corporation);

- a district social services administration board under the *District Social Services Administration Boards Act*; or

- a delivery agent under the *Ontario Works Act, 1997*.

All of these agencies provide services to individuals in need, and may pursue support to recover some of their costs. The Ministry of Community and Social Services may pursue support to recover some of the living expenses of children in its care.

The amount of child support ordered by the court used to be calculated from scratch on a case-by-case basis, factoring in such issues as the child's needs and the supporting parent's ability to pay. In recent years, however, Ontario moved to a system of guidelines that set out what is essentially a mathematical formula for calculating a particular support payment based on the payer's income. The guidelines were designed to simplify the process of quantifying child support, and reduce litigation.

DOMESTIC CONTRACTS

Married and common-law couples may avoid the application of family law rules on breakup of the relationship by means of a **domestic contract**. Where a couple have negotiated a valid contract that provides for different rights on separation than those that are described in legislation, the contract may take precedence over the legislation. Part IV of the *Family Law Act* provides that domestic contracts and agreements to amend domestic contracts must be in writing, signed by the parties, and witnessed. There are three kinds of domestic contracts:

- A **marriage contract** may be made by a couple who are married or who intend to marry. The contract can address ownership or division of property other than the matrimonial home, support obligations, and the right to direct the education of children, but not the right to custody of or access to children.

- A **cohabitation agreement** is similar to a marriage contract, but made by a couple who are cohabiting or who intend to cohabit. If the parties to a cohabitation agreement marry, the agreement is deemed to be a marriage contract.

- A **separation agreement**, made between a couple who are married or cohabiting with the intention of separating, or who are already separated, may include provisions governing each party's rights and obligations after separation, including ownership or division of property, support obligations, the right to direct the education of children, and the right to child custody and access.

Domestic contracts are important because they can allow each partner in the relationship to maintain a measure of control over his or her life, and valid contracts are generally respected by the courts. However, a child's right to support cannot be bargained away, and a court will not enforce a provision regarding custody and access that it considers contrary to a child's best interests. In addition, a court may rule that a domestic contract signed under duress or without independent legal advice is unenforceable.

FAMILY VIOLENCE

Spousal Abuse

Spousal abuse (whether physical or emotional) can precede a breakup or be precipitated by the departure of a spouse. In general, the point of separation and the months following are the most dangerous time in terms of potential for violence. Social service workers who encourage victims of domestic abuse to leave the relationship must recognize the heightened risk that separation presents. The *Family Law Act* recognizes this reality and provides for police involvement in certain situations.

The police will generally not become involved in the enforcement of an order or settlement agreement, unless the order specifically provides otherwise. For example, an order providing for pick-up and drop-off times will not be enforceable by the police unless the order actually states that it is. If a child is not delivered according to the order, the normal recourse is to go to court. The court will hear such a case immediately, and the non-compliant party may be charged with contempt of court. If the police are called, they will talk to the parties and try to calm everyone down, but they are not generally authorized to enforce a civil order.

If an order does provide for police enforcement, or if there is a concern about possible violence or harm to a child, the police will intervene. The *Family Law Act* also provides for the arrest without warrant of a spouse who has violated a restraining order issued under the legislation.

Child Abuse

Child abuse is discussed in detail in chapter 3, but it is useful to understand how child abuse allegations are addressed in the context of a couple's separation.

Often, when a couple separates, at least one ex-spouse is plunged into a state of emotional distress and insecurity. Coping with separation is difficult for anyone, but having to deal, at the same time, with a child's distress is a significant complicating factor. Separation can trigger a wide range of reactions, including a deep sense of betrayal, intense anger, and an instinct to protect the children from the other spouse (whether or not they are actually at risk).

Where child custody is a contentious issue between the parents, criticism of the other partner's fitness to be a parent is almost par for the course. Sometimes criticism escalates into allegations of child neglect, or of physical, emotional, or sexual abuse.

Child abuse allegations made in the context of a separation create an enormous challenge for all concerned. Allegations of abuse that appear to have some foundation automatically require the involvement of child protection agencies in what is no longer a routine divorce.

Where a parent makes an allegation of abuse involving the other parent, the person to whom the allegation is made—including the complainant's lawyer—has a duty to report to a children's aid society under section 72 of the *Child and Family Services Act*. The children's aid society will then investigate the allegation.

THE FAMILY RESPONSIBILITY OFFICE

Ontario's Family Responsibility Office is part of the Ministry of Community and Social Services. It was created under the provincial *Family Responsibility and Support Arrears Enforcement Act, 1996*.

The Family Responsibility Office (FRO) receives and registers a copy of every family support (spousal and/or child support) order made by Ontario courts, and assists in the enforcement of those orders in cases of non-compliance (that is, where the full amount of support has not been paid as required by the order). It is possible to opt out of the services of the FRO, but both parties (the payer and the payee) must agree to do this.

POLICY EXCERPT

First Steps for New FRO Users

The following is an excerpt from the website of the Family Responsibility Office, explaining the first steps a new user should take once support has been ordered:

I am a support recipient (person who receives payment) and the support order was made yesterday. What should I do now?

Step 1: Obtain court order and support deduction order
If you were represented by a lawyer in court, your lawyer should have prepared the court order and the court will prepare the support deduction order. If a lawyer did not represent you, you should speak to the court staff.

The court order and support deduction order are sent to the Family Responsibility Office (FRO).

Step 2: Obtain FRO case number and registration package
When the FRO receives your support deduction order, you are assigned a FRO case number. You will receive a letter from the FRO with your case number and a registration package. Please complete the registration package and return it to the FRO as soon as possible.

Step 3: Support deduction notice is sent to employer
If the name of the payor's (person who owes support) employer or income source was provided on the support deduction order or your filing package, the FRO will send a support deduction order to the employer to notify them they are obligated to deduct your support payments from the payor's wages or salary and forward these deductions to the FRO. A support deduction notice is automatically sent when there is a known employer.

Step 4: Payment
The FRO will send you the payment when it is received. Whenever possible direct deposit is the preferred method of payment. It is more efficient and secure. To arrange for Direct Deposit, fill out the Registration for Direct Deposit for Recipients form in your registration package, or print it off of the website and return to the FRO.

Source: Ontario, Ministry of Community, Family and Children's Services at www .mcss.gov.on.ca. ◇

The FRO charges administrative fees for some of its services and uses various mechanisms to enforce support orders. The most prevalent method is to arrange for support to be deducted from the payer's wages or salary by his or her employer, forwarded to the FRO, and then transferred to the payee.

Social service workers should be familiar with the function and procedures of the FRO, because they may be asked to assist clients in ensuring compliance with a support order. For example, a client may need help in contacting the office, filling out forms, and gathering the documents necessary to support a request for enforcement of support.

WEB LINK

Contact the FRO at:
www.cfcs.gov.on.ca.

LEGISLATIVE SHORTCUT

Family Responsibility and Support Arrears Enforcement Act, 1996

SO 1996, c.31

Objective: To facilitate payment of support obligations.

Target Population: Children and spouses who are owed support under an agreement or court order.

Program Administration: The Family Responsibility Office is an Ontario government office within the Ministry of Community and Social Services. It receives and registers a copy of every spousal and child support order made by an Ontario court and assists with enforcement.

Administrative Tribunal: Not applicable—applications to vary support must be made to the court.

Summary: The *Family Responsibility and Support Arrears Enforcement Act, 1996* provides for the enforcement of spousal and child support orders using a variety of methods, the most common being a deduction from a payer's wages by his or her employer, which is forwarded to the Family Responsibility Office and distributed to the payee. ◇

FAMILY SUPPORT AND ONTARIO WORKS BENEFITS

The Ontario Works social security program provides financial and other assistance to Ontario residents who, because of unemployment, disability, or other difficulties, lack sufficient income to support themselves and their dependants. The program is discussed in greater detail in chapter 8. However, it is worth pointing out here that a person's application for Ontario Works benefits may be denied, or benefits may be reduced, if program administrators determine that the applicant is entitled to claim financial support from other sources, including family support (child support, spousal support, or both) from a former spouse. In a case like this, it is generally necessary for the applicant to pursue his or her right to family support in court before qualifying for Ontario Works benefits.

In some locations, there are programs in place to assist people in this process. One example is the City of Ottawa's Family Support Program. This program employs family support workers (including social service workers) who can assist people in pursuing their legal rights. Assistance includes providing information about support rights and family law, helping to fill out court forms, and helping to secure legal aid representation. Social service workers who work for family support programs require special training in family law and social benefits issues.

KEY TERMS

access	equalization payment	mediation
child support	exclusive possession	net family property
Children's Lawyer	litigation guardian	real property
cohabitation agreement	marriage breakdown	separation agreement
custody	marriage contract	spousal support
domestic contract	matrimonial home	supervised access

REFERENCES

Bessner, Ronda, *The Voice of the Child in Divorce, Custody and Access Proceedings*, background paper 2002-FCY-1E.

Canadian Charter of Rights and Freedoms, part I of the *Constitution Act, 1982*, being schedule B of the *Canada Act 1982* (UK), 1982, c. 11.

Child and Family Services Act, RSO 1990, c. C.11.

Children's Law Reform Act, RSO 1990, c. C.12.

Constitution Act, 1867, 30 & 31 Vict., c. 3 (UK).

District Social Services Administration Boards Act, RSO 1990, c. D.15.

Divorce Act, RSC 1985, c. 3 (2d Supp.).

Family Law Act, RSO 1990, c. F.3.

Family Responsibility and Support Arrears Enforcement Act, 1996, SO 1996, c. 31.

Ontario Works Act, 1997, SO 1997, c. 25, Sch. A.

REVIEW QUESTIONS

1. Does family law legislation apply to couples who were never legally married?

2. Which level of government (federal or provincial) has jurisdiction over the division of family property after separation?

3. What is the overriding principle that guides a court's decisions on custody and access?

4. Do all separating couples go to court to resolve their separation issues? If not, what are the alternatives?

5. Are all spouses entitled to spousal support? Are all children entitled to child support? Explain.

6. What is the matrimonial home, and how does the law treat it differently from other property?

7. In what kinds of cases may a child be represented by the Children's Lawyer?

8. What is the difference between sole and joint custody?

9. What is a domestic contract? Describe the different kinds of domestic contracts.

10. List three contexts in which a social service worker may work with family members who are going through separation or divorce.

DISCUSSION QUESTION

When 16-year-old Gary's parents separated, the breakup was acrimonious and sometimes violent. Before the separation, Gary himself had some serious conflicts with his father, and ran away twice, both times returning to the family home within the month. During the separation, Gary couldn't stand to be in the same house as his parents, so he moved in with his friend Hugh's family. Hugh's mother said he could stay until the end of the school year, or until things settled down.

Now that his parents are officially living apart, Gary has learned that his father has convinced his mother to sign a "negotiated" separation agreement, which contains a statement that Gary has withdrawn from parental control and his father is not obligated to support him. His mother can't afford to support him on her own.

Gary speaks with a social service worker. What guidance and advice should she give him?

CHAPTER 5
Education

CHAPTER OBJECTIVES

After reading this chapter, you should be able to:

- Identify at least two statutes that deal with education.
- Understand the key principles of the *Education Act*.
- Describe the government's approach to violence and harassment in schools, and the relevance of this approach to social service workers who work with students.
- Describe the process by which a student is deemed eligible to access special-needs programs and resources.

INTRODUCTION

School boards and individual schools may employ social service workers and youth workers to provide counselling to students. Other social service workers may find themselves dealing with aspects of the education system in the course of providing services to homeless youth or families in crisis. Finally, social service workers may work with students who have been expelled from school and who require counselling and other support so that they can continue their education.

Ontario statutes that govern education include the *Education Act* and its "safe schools" amendments, and the *Education Quality and Accountability Office Act*.

The duty to report suspected child abuse or neglect, created by the *Child and Family Services Act*, is also important to anyone working in schools. This was discussed in chapter 3.

Ontario's *Immunization of School Pupils Act* and the *Health Protection and Promotion Act* require schools to take measures to avoid outbreaks of disease, by, for example, requiring proof of student immunization status, reporting outbreaks, and taking steps to prevent the transmission of communicable diseases within the school population.

PUBLIC AND PRIVATE SCHOOL SYSTEMS

Like most developed countries, Canada funds public education. Each province administers its own education system, and many responsibilities are further delegated to regional school boards. The Ontario *Education Act* and the regulations made under it set out the legal framework for the education of Ontario's children.

The Ontario public school system is divided into two streams: secular public schools and Catholic schools (run by "separate" school boards). The funding of Catholic schools is largely a historical practice and is provided for under Canada's *Constitution Act, 1867*.

The government's funding of Catholic schools and not other religious schools has long been a controversial issue. Section 2 of the *Canadian Charter of Rights and Freedoms* provides that everyone has the freedom of conscience and religion. Many parents, if given the choice, would prefer that their children receive a government-paid education in a school of their own religious denomination, such as a Protestant, Jewish, or Muslim school. The unfairness of funding only Catholic schools has attracted attention at the international level: in 1996, the United Nations Human Rights Committee ruled that Canada was in violation of the International Covenant on Civil and Political Rights because of government funding of Roman Catholic schools and not those of other faiths. In response to the ruling, some Canadian provincial governments implemented partial funding to certain non-Catholic religious schools. Ontario has no such system.

THE EDUCATION ACT

The *Education Act* creates a framework for the administration of public education in Ontario and covers the following topics:

- responsibilities of parents and students within the education system;

- consequences of a student's violation of the safe schools provisions; and

- means by which parents and students can seek access to special-needs services.

LEGISLATIVE SHORTCUT

Education Act

RSO 1990, c.E.2

Objective: To ensure that all children in Ontario are educated.

Target Population: Children in Ontario, their parents, and their teachers.

Program Administration: Ontario's Ministry of Education.

Administrative Tribunal: Ontario Special Education Tribunal.

Summary: The *Education Act* sets up school boards and creates a framework for the administration of public education in Ontario, including the responsibilities of parents and students, teacher training, the consequences of a student's violation of the safe schools provisions, and the means by which parents and students can seek access to special-needs services. ◇

Compulsory Attendance

Under the *Education Act*, parents are required to ensure that their children between the ages of 6 and 16 attend school. Failure to enrol a child in school or to take reasonable steps to ensure his or her daily attendance is an offence punishable by a fine under section 30 of the Act.

There are exceptions to compulsory attendance at a public school, such as illness, religious holiday, attendance at a private school, and **home-schooling**. The home-schooling exemption under section 21(2)(a) allows absence from school for children who are "receiving satisfactory instruction at home or elsewhere." Private schools and home-schooling must comply with basic curriculum standards set by the province.

HOME-SCHOOLING

Home-schooling has always been a controversial subject, probably because a parent's decision to home-school children is a rejection of the public school system. Parents who are critical of the public system are unlikely to provide instruction closely consistent with that system's curriculum. Home-schoolers tend to focus on different educational values and priorities than those of public schools. The instruction provided by parents who home-school their children is subject to review by the Provincial School Attendance Counsellor. To confirm that a home-schooled child is eligible for exemption from school attendance under section 21(2) of the *Education Act*, the counsellor can launch an inquiry into the parent's home-schooling program under section 24 of the Act.

Social service workers may have clients who are home-schooling their children and who need assistance in obtaining the ministry's approval of their home-schooling program. Some information on the evaluation of home-schooling is available through the government's "Policy/Program Memorandum No. 131—Home Schooling." Additional information is available from the Ontario Federation of Teaching Parents, a provincial non-profit home-school group providing support and information to home-schooling families.

WEB LINK

Visit the Ontario Federation of Teaching Parents, a support, information and advocacy group for homeschoolers in Ontario, at www.ontariohomeschool.org.

ABSENCE AND CHILDREN AT RISK

A child's non-attendance at school can sometimes be a warning sign that something is not right at home. In some cases, children who are subject to neglect may not make it to school because there is simply no parent taking charge of waking, dressing, and feeding them, and getting them onto the bus. In more serious cases, abused children may be kept at home so that teachers and others in the community will not be alerted to the situation. Absence from school may even be a warning that a child has been abducted (whether by a parent defying a custody/access order or by a person with criminal intent).

If a social service worker has a child client who is missing school and the reason isn't apparent, the parent or guardian should be asked to explain the child's absence. If the explanation raises a suspicion of child abuse or neglect, the social service worker must report to the children's aid society. In extreme cases, it may also be appropriate to contact the police.

> ## CASES IN POINT
> ## Non-Attendance at School as a Red Flag for Abuse
> ### *Randal Dooley*
>
> Randal Dooley, aged 7, died on September 25, 1998 of head injuries suffered in the course of a pattern of physical abuse by his stepmother and birth father. Randal's parents had not enrolled the boy in school for the 1998 school year because he had visible injuries from an August 30 whipping and the parents feared that school personnel would inform the children's aid society (CAS). The previous spring, Randal's grade 1 teacher had noticed welts on the child's arm and had called both the police and the CAS. The father and stepmother were eventually convicted of second-degree murder.
>
> ### *Gavin Hollett*
>
> Gavin Hollett was removed from Ontario by his mother in December 1994, contrary to a custody/access order. He was 4 years old at the time. His father spent the next eight years searching for Gavin with the aid of missing children's agencies. During that period, Gavin's mother changed their residence several times and used various pseudonyms to conceal Gavin's identity. In the spring of 2003, she and Gavin (who was then 12 years old and called Leaf) were living on a herb farm—a women's commune—on Vancouver Island, and Gavin/Leaf was not enrolled in school. His absence from school was one of the factors that led a missing children's agency to investigate his identity. His mother was charged with parental abduction. ◇

Safety

Schools are responsible for the safety of children on their premises during the school day. This responsibility requires measures such as maintaining school buildings and property in safe condition, monitoring systems such as water quality and ventilation, providing safe transportation to and from school, and planning for emergencies such as fires and bomb threats.

Schools are also responsible for protecting children against interpersonal threats from school personnel or other children. For example, school boards must carefully screen teachers, special-needs education specialists, coaches, counsellors, social workers, social service workers, and other individuals who will have contact with children, to ensure that they do not pose a risk to the safety of those children. Schools must also monitor and control situations such as bullying and fights, where children might harm each other.

In addition, schools must try to protect their personnel from the risk of harm from children (for example, threats or physical aggression against teachers, or various forms of harassment).

In 2000, the Ontario government enacted an extensive set of amendments to the *Education Act*, known as "the safe schools amendments." This legislation provided for the creation of a code of conduct to address bullying and other worrisome behaviours in schools.

The safe schools amendments provide that schools can create policies for enforcing the code of conduct. These policies generally include automatic penalties for violation of the code of conduct. In recent years, many schools have adopted a policy of "zero tolerance," which mandates immediate suspension or expulsion for prohibited behaviours, especially acts of violence.

In April 2007, the education minister announced plans to replace the zero tolerance policy with a progressive disciplinary approach. The government hopes that this will change behaviour while keeping students in school. A prohibition against **cyber-bullying** is also expected to be included in the legislation. Cyber-bullying is harassment or abuse of other students or of teachers via electronic media, such as e-mail, text messaging, or posting comments or pictures on the Internet.

Social service workers who work with schools, with expelled or suspended students, or with early leavers (students who have not returned to school after expulsion) should familiarize themselves with issues of and responses to violence and harassment in the school environment, so that they can better assist their clients.

STRICT-DISCIPLINE PROGRAMS

The Ministry of Education has a policy that expelled students be given both "academic support and non-academic support" to address their educational and behavioural needs. School boards are required to provide programs that deliver this support, unless they are already providing these services through a formal **strict-discipline program**. Strict-discipline programs are only available in a limited number of boards, and most of them have a waiting list.

Strict-discipline programs include counselling, typically by a social worker or a psychiatrist, but may employ social service workers for additional client support.

If no strict-discipline program is available through an expelled child's school board, the services offered to the child must comply with ministry policies. These policies require that the student undergo a needs assessment and be given both academic and behavioural support, either by school board staff or by an outside agency. Social service workers may be involved in providing support via an outside agency.

Special Education

About 10 percent of Canadian school children struggle, at some point in their education, with some kind of learning problem. Learning and behavioural problems are often closely related and difficult to distinguish, especially in younger children.

Accommodating learning problems often requires support beyond the capacity (in terms of both time and expertise) of classroom teachers. This means that in order to guarantee access to education for children with learning problems, schools must devote human, material, and physical resources specifically to the needs of these children.

The *Education Act* requires school boards to provide special education programs and services for students who require them, and to implement procedures to identify such students. Pressure on public budgets is often particularly threatening to the allocation of resources to special-needs children. Many Ontario educators believe that the system is in a state of economic crisis. With schools experiencing cuts to programs once taken for granted—for example, physical education, music, and library programs—the provision of special-needs programs has been reduced to minimal levels.

WEB LINK

For information on addressing bullying and harassment, and resources to assist schools, visit the Ministry of Education website at www.edu.gov.on.ca.

Critical Perspectives

Consequences of Zero Tolerance

The zero tolerance approach to violence in schools is not uncontroversial. A recent five-year review of Ontario's safe schools rules revealed that while the rate of expulsions has risen considerably since the passage of the legislation, zero tolerance policies and school discipline have been applied unevenly across the province. Rates of suspension and expulsions vary widely from school board to school board. These study results suggest that zero tolerance is not generally well understood or consistently applied in Ontario. It appears that many school boards have yet to achieve a satisfactory balance between the need to prevent violence in schools and the province's commitment to ensure access to education for all of Ontario's children.

Figure 5.1 shows the rate of expulsions for one district school board (Durham) compared to the provincial average in the 2000-1 school year (before the safe schools amendments) and in the three years following (when the new rules were being applied). These statistics show an increase of almost 500 percent in expulsions for this school board from 2000-1 to 2003-4.

Children expelled from school as a result of zero tolerance policies need support to further their education, and in some cases, to find new schools and become integrated into the new school community. Children who have committed violent acts are often emotionally vulnerable to begin with, and placement in a new school can exacerbate this vulnerability. While zero tolerance policies in school may make education safer for the majority of students, it appears that these policies will lead to an increased demand for social services support of the students affected by the policies.

The April 2007 announcement to abolish the zero tolerance policy of the safe schools amendments came after the ministry settled some of the hundreds of legal cases launched by parents in response to actions taken under the legislation. Studies of the application of the safe schools amendments have shown that the legislation operates especially unfairly against black youth, youth vulnerable to the allure of gang violence (earning the legislation the nickname "The Gang Recruitment Act"), and youth and children with special needs. Many critics of the legislation have suggested that youth do not need a zero-tolerance policy, but rather a policy that emphasizes relationship skills and empathy. Interestingly, one of the recommendations made by a prominent critic of the legislation (lawyer Selwyn Pieters) is that schools renew their investment in in-school social work and counselling professionals. ◇

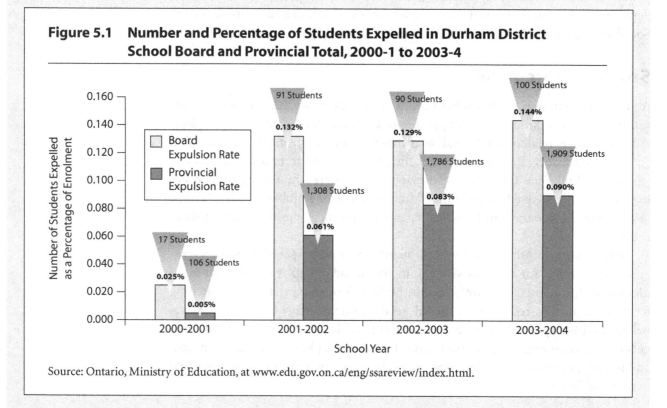

Figure 5.1   Number and Percentage of Students Expelled in Durham District School Board and Provincial Total, 2000-1 to 2003-4

Source: Ontario, Ministry of Education, at www.edu.gov.on.ca/eng/ssareview/index.html.

CASES IN POINT

Funding for Autism

Ontario

In 2005, a group of Ontario parents of autistic children were successful in their lawsuit against the province. The court held that cutting off funding for autism treatment at age 6 was discrimination based on age and disability, and violated the *Canadian Charter of Rights and Freedoms*. The cost of treatment can be about $60,000 per child.

Premier Dalton McGuinty responded to the ruling with concern that the court was mandating the expenditure of money, without identifying a source for the money, and launched an appeal to the Ontario Court of Appeal.

See *Wynberg v. Ontario*, 2005 CanLII 8749 (ONSC).

British Columbia

A similar case in British Columbia was eventually heard by the Supreme Court of Canada in 2004. The court determined that the province had the right to set its own priorities for health-care funding and could not be forced to pay. With increasing pressures on government to address a wide variety of growing health-care needs, how should priorities be set? Should these decisions be made by courts or by elected politicians? Autism may affect approximately 1 in 250 Canadian children.

See *Auton (Guardian ad litem of) v. British Columbia (Attorney General)*, [2004] 3 SCR 657. ◇

The result is that many children who would once have been identified as in need of special support are being left to fend for themselves in regular classrooms. This practice undermines the right to quality education, not only for these children but for other children as well, by putting unrealistic demands on regular classroom teachers.

When it becomes apparent to school staff that a student may have special educational needs, the student's case may be reviewed (following notice to the parents) by an identification, placement and review committee (IPRC). These committees are established within the Ministry of Education to assist in determining which students require and are eligible for special services. Parents and students can also request referral to an IPRC if the school does not initiate the process.

If an IPRC decides that a student has special needs, there are several options available for meeting those needs. The regulation governing IPRCs requires the committee to consider whether the student's needs can be met in a regular classroom, because this may be preferable for the student from the perspective of normal socialization. Service delivery options for special-needs students can include special education for the whole school day, attendance for part of the day in a class designed to support certain skills (such as reading), or special attention in the regular classroom, either from the regular teacher or from an additional trained staff member. Students with severe hearing or vision disabilities may be referred to a school for the hearing or visually impaired.

Language Barriers

For some children, the ability to benefit from quality public education is a challenge because of language barriers. Especially in urban centres, the Canadian student population enjoys considerable diversity with respect to culture and language.

Canada is a popular destination for new immigrants from all over the world. For many such immigrants, access to quality public education is a high family priority. However, children entering Canadian public schools who are not fluent speakers of English (or, in francophone communities, French) are at a significant disadvantage in the classroom.

In areas where there is a high percentage of children for whom English (or French) is not a first language, remedial programs exist to ease the transition of both children and their parents into English (or French) education. Schools tend to do a good job of identifying children who need this assistance, because struggling students put an increased demand on the time of classroom teachers.

Often, a school's efforts on behalf of a child end up assisting the whole family. In smaller centres, however, or in times of cuts to public funding of education, access to language programs is more limited, and social workers, social service workers, and other children's advocates may need to become more active on behalf of children facing language barriers to education.

THE EDUCATION QUALITY AND ACCOUNTABILITY OFFICE

The quality and effectiveness of elementary and secondary education in Ontario are evaluated by the Education Quality and Accountability Office (EQAO), established by the *Education Quality and Accountability Office Act, 1996*. The EQAO tests students in grades 3, 6, 9, and 10 to assess levels of literacy and competence in mathematics.

Testing has been promoted as a means to ensure government accountability in the provision of public education, and to increase public confidence in education standards in the public school system. Parent reaction to the testing has been mixed. Some parents believe that the intensive testing is stressful for children, and that it is of limited value in identifying specific problems in the education system. Other critics question both the value and the cost of testing in the context of cuts to education, particularly where there is no follow-up funding to remedy problems.

LEGISLATIVE SHORTCUT

Education Quality and Accountability Office Act, 1996

SO 1996, c. 11

Objective: To evaluate the quality and effectiveness of primary and secondary school education in order to ensure government accountability in the provision of public education and to increase public confidence in educational standards.

Target Population: Children in grades 3, 6, 9, and 10.

Program Administration: The Education Quality and Accountability Office.

Administrative Tribunal: Not applicable.

Summary: The Education Quality and Accountability Office administers province-wide testing of students in grades 3, 6, 9, and 10 to assess levels of literacy and competency in mathematics. ◇

KEY TERMS

cyber-bullying

home-schooling

strict-discipline program

REFERENCES

Canadian Charter of Rights and Freedoms, part I of the *Constitution Act, 1982*, being schedule B of the *Canada Act 1982* (UK), 1982, c. 11.

Child and Family Services Act, RSO 1990, c. C.11.

Constitution Act, 1867, 30 & 31 Vict., c. 3 (UK).

Education Act, RSO 1990, c. E.2.

Education Quality and Accountability Office Act, 1996, SO 1996, c. 11.

Health Protection and Promotion Act, RSO 1990, c. H.7.

Immunization of School Pupils Act, RSO 1990, c. I.1.

Ontario Ministry of Education. (2002). "Policy/Program Memorandum No. 131: Home Schooling." Available online at www.edu.gov.on.ca.

REVIEW QUESTIONS

1. List at least three capacities in which social workers or social service workers may have dealings with the school system.

2. Which children are subject to compulsory school attendance, and what are the major exceptions?

3. Who decides whether a child is being adequately home-schooled?

4. Why is it important for a social service worker with a child client to pay attention to recurrent or unexplained absence from school?

5. Why do the Safe Schools amendments to the *Education Act* have the potential to increase the demand for social services for children?

6. What is the most significant challenge facing children with special needs in the public school system, and how can social service workers respond to this challenge?

7. How can efforts to obtain English or French language assistance for immigrant students benefit the family as a whole?

8. What is the purpose of Education Quality and Accountability Office testing?

DISCUSSION QUESTION

Why is it important for social workers and social service workers (especially those who work with child clients) to stay informed about the state of education (funding, politics, curriculum trends) in Ontario?

PART III

Health and Welfare

CHAPTER 6

Mental Health

CHAPTER OBJECTIVES

After reading this chapter, you should be able to:

- List the statutes that define the mental health system in Ontario.

- Describe the circumstances under which a person can be admitted into hospital voluntarily for a mental health crisis.

- Understand the mechanisms by which a person can be detained in hospital involuntarily for a mental health crisis.

- Explain the rights of a mentally ill hospital patient.

- Describe the role of a substitute decision maker in representing an incapable patient.

- Understand the use of powers of attorney within the mental health system.

- Explain the nature and function of community treatment orders.

INTRODUCTION

According to the Canadian Mental Health Association (Toronto branch), one in five Canadians will be affected by a mental illness at some time in their lives. Mental illness is disproportionately common in certain populations who are heavy users of social services: youth, homeless people, and the poor.

All social service workers will, at some point in their career, be called upon to support clients who are struggling with mental illness. For this reason, it is essential that social service workers be familiar not only with the facts about mental illness itself (these you will learn in other courses), but also with the legal framework for mental health service delivery in Ontario.

Mental health legislation is very complex, and an entire textbook could be dedicated to explaining it. This chapter will provide only the basics. While it will cover some key issues, it will not attempt to discuss every possible point of contact between social service workers and the mental health system. Specifically, the focus will be on supporting mentally ill clients in their efforts to navigate the health-care delivery system, and not on working within mental health settings (hospitals, long-term care facilities, etc.). If you work within the mental health system itself, or with client populations with very specific needs (children with behavioural problems, for instance),

WEB LINK

For information about mental health services, education, advocacy, and research, visit the Canadian Mental Health Association at www.cmha.ca, or the Ontario or Toronto branches at www.ontario.cmha.ca and www.toronto.cmha.ca.

you will have to supplement the basic legal information provided in this chapter with more detailed information relevant to your role. However, the overview provided here will serve as a solid foundation for that future learning.

EXTRA CREDIT

How Common Is Mental Illness?

The Canadian Mental Health Association provides some striking statistics about the prevalence of mental illness:

■ Over 10 percent of adult Canadians suffer from a depressive disorder.

■ Almost 20 percent of children and youth have a diagnosable psychiatric disorder.

■ Two-thirds of the clients of homeless shelters have some form of mental illness.

■ "Of the ten leading causes of disability worldwide, five are mental disorders: major depression, schizophrenia, bipolar disorder, alcohol use disorder and obsessive compulsive disorder."

Source: Canadian Mental Health Association (Toronto) at www.toronto.cmha.ca. ◇

THE LEGISLATIVE FRAMEWORK

Three statutes form the legal framework for mental health service delivery in Ontario:

■ the *Mental Health Act* (MHA),

■ the *Health Care Consent Act* (HCCA), and

■ the *Substitute Decisions Act* (SDA).

The HCCA and the SDA are also relevant for purposes of health-care access and delivery for individuals who are not diagnosed as mentally ill. Therefore, you should keep in mind the discussion presented in this chapter when you are reading chapter 7 (which deals with issues of access to health care and the care of elderly people).

For a good understanding of the mental health delivery system, the MHA, HCCA, and SDA need to be considered together; considering each in isolation provides only a piece of the total picture. For this reason, the discussion in this chapter

WEB LINK

The Community Mental Health Evaluation Initiative (CMHEI) was created in 1997 by the Ontario Mental Health Foundation, the Centre for Addiction and Mental Health, and the Canadian Mental Health Association (Ontario branch), with funding from the Ontario Ministry of Health and Long-Term Care. The objective of the CMHEI is to evaluate community mental health programs in Canada by identifying program activity, monitoring progress, and evaluating cost-effectiveness. The results of the CMHEI's ongoing evaluations can be viewed at www.ontario.cmha.ca.

is organized by issue, and the relevant provisions of each statute are examined in that context.

The focus of Ontario's mental health legislation is on hospital-based treatment. The MHA explains, among other things, how a person is identified as an appropriate candidate for hospital care; how a decision to detain a person without his or her consent is made; how the use of restraints and other intrusive measures is to be managed; how hospital placements are extended, reviewed, and terminated; and what happens if a person does not cope well with release. The HCCA and SDA fill in the details of consent-to-treatment issues, and what happens when a patient is deemed unable to consent to or guide his or her own care.

SUBSTITUTE DECISION MAKING

When a person suffering from a serious physical or mental illness seems unable to manage his care competently, or to make reasonable care decisions, health-care providers are required to obtain consent for his treatment or admission to care from another person who has the power to speak on his behalf. The general term used for this representative is **substitute decision maker**.

Substitute decision makers can step forward or be chosen in a variety of ways, including informal selection of a relative at the health-care facility, appointment by a government tribunal (the Consent and Capacity Board) under the HCCA, appointment by power of attorney, and appointment of a guardian under the SDA.

Informal Choice of Decision Maker

When a health practitioner determines that a patient is not capable of giving or refusing consent to treatment or admission to hospital, the HCCA provides for the appointment of a representative of the patient to make those decisions on his behalf. The most informal method of appointment involves a health practitioner requesting consent from a relative listed in section 20 of the HCCA—a spouse, adult child, parent, or other relative—in that order. This method of choosing a decision maker may save time and often works well if the patient is only temporarily incapable (for example, if he is unconscious and undergoing surgery). On the other hand, the choice of decision maker in these circumstances may be arbitrary—whoever happens to be accompanying the patient—and not necessarily the person whom the patient would have chosen. If the patient is not satisfied with the informal appointment of a relative by the health practitioner, he or she may apply for a review of the appointment by the Consent and Capacity Board, as discussed below.

In cases where the patient is likely to be incapable for longer periods, or where a complex or lengthy regimen of treatments is contemplated, it is prudent to choose a decision maker in a more formal way and, ideally, with the input of the patient.

Appointments by the Consent and Capacity Board

If an informal appointment cannot be made, or if the patient disagrees with the attending practitioner's choice, a substitute decision maker may be appointed by the Consent and Capacity Board under the HCCA.

Mental Health Act

RSO 1990, c. M. 7

Objective: To facilitate care for psychiatric patients.

Target Population: Psychiatric patients, their families, and others who may be closely involved with patients.

Program Administration: Psychiatrists assess their patients.

Administrative Tribunal: Consent and Capacity Board

Summary: The *Mental Health Act* explains how to identify those in need of hospitalization for psychiatric care; how a decision to detain a person without his or her consent is made; how the use of restraints and other intrusive measures is to be managed; how hospital placements are extended, reviewed and terminated; and what happens if a person does not cope well following discharge. ◇

Health Care Consent Act, 1996

SO 1996, c. 2, Sch. A

Objective: To provide consistent rules with respect to consent for treatment, to facilitate treatment, and to enhance the autonomy of patients.

Target Population: All recipients of health care, their families, and persons who may act as substitute decision makers.

Program Administration: Health practitioners make the initial determination as to whether a patient is capable of giving or refusing consent to treatment or admission to hospital. If the patient disagrees with the doctor's choice, the patient may apply for a Consent and Capacity Board hearing in which the decision of ability of the patient to consent to treatment is reviewed.

Administrative Tribunal: Consent and Capacity Board.

Summary: The *Health Care Consent Act, 1996* fills in the details of consent to treatment issues and what happens when a patient is deemed unable to consent to or guide her own care. The Consent and Capacity Board may appoint a representative to act as a substitute decision maker for patients who are incapable of consenting to treatment. ◇

The board has the power to appoint a representative to act as a substitute decision maker for patients who are incapable. Alternatively, the patient himself can apply for a representative to be appointed; often this is the person who has helped the patient make the application. An individual can also apply to the board to be appointed as the representative of an incapable patient; however, if that individual is not the patient's preferred choice, the patient may dispute the finding of incapacity.

Social service workers may be involved in helping clients to make an application for appointment of a representative, or to challenge appointments with which they disagree. However, it's a good idea for the client to have legal representation for a hearing before the board.

The role, composition, and procedures of the board are discussed later in this chapter, in the context of involuntary admission and treatment.

Attorneys

The terms "attorney" and "power of attorney" may sometimes seem confusing because "attorney" is used in other contexts (for example, in the American courts) to refer to a lawyer or legal adviser. In the context of substitute decision making, **attorney** means a representative formally appointed by a person to make decisions on his or her behalf. The attorney need not be, and usually is not, a lawyer. Usually, a friend or relative is appointed.

There are two kinds of attorneys. One, an **attorney for property**, makes decisions regarding property, such as bank accounts, real estate, and investments. The other, an **attorney for personal care**, makes decisions regarding personal care, such as health-care and treatment decisions. One person may be appointed for both purposes, a different person may be appointed for each, and sometimes two people share the decision making.

The main advantage of appointing an attorney, rather than choosing a different form of representation, is that the individual's preferences are more fully taken into account:

- she chooses the representative; and

- she can communicate her actual wishes to the representative, in advance.

Appointment of an attorney requires advance planning; however, people in the early stages of an illness that may lead to incapacity can often benefit greatly by choosing a trusted person to act as their attorney and formalizing the relationship while they still can.

The first step in appointing an attorney is to obtain the consent of the person chosen to act as substitute decision maker. Then the person making the appointment ("the grantor") must prepare a legal document, usually with a lawyer's help, and sign it in the presence of two witnesses. The legal document—the **power of attorney**—will describe the extent of the powers granted to the attorney to act on the grantor's behalf. The grantor can give the attorney some powers and specifically exclude others. She can also include a provision that requires a second person to confirm that she is incapable before the attorney takes over decision-making authority, or another provision naming a second person (an "alternate") in case the attorney cannot act for her at some future time. Again, the grantor must first obtain the alternate's consent. Once the power of attorney has been signed, the grantor can communicate her specific wishes to the attorney, either in writing or orally. The grantor and the attorney should each keep a copy of the power of attorney. The original should be kept by the lawyer or in some other secure place.

Social service workers can explain the advantages of a power of attorney to their clients and can assist clients in finding a lawyer to complete the necessary documents. Social service workers who work with mentally ill clients should ask for and keep on file the contact information of the client's attorney(s) for property and/or personal care. A social service worker may occasionally be asked to serve as a client's attorney for personal care. However, section 46(3)(b) of the *Substitute Decisions Act* prohibits this in most circumstances.

LEGISLATIVE SHORTCUT

Substitute Decisions Act, 1992

SO 1992, c. 30

Objective: To provide a procedure for appointing substitute decision makers.

Target Population: Anyone who is or could become incapable of making decisions with respect to personal care or property.

Program Administration: Not applicable.

Administrative Tribunal: Consent and Capacity Board.

Summary: The *Substitute Decisions Act, 1992* provides a process for appointing powers of attorney over personal care and property and for court-ordered guardianship. ◈

Guardians

The law that governs substitute decision making, including power of attorney, is codified in the SDA. It covers such issues as the following:

- how legal incapacity is determined;

- how to confer, continue, or revoke a power of attorney;

- how an attorney can resign from the role;

- how an attorney's actions can be challenged, or how to remove the person from the role; and

- how a guardian of property and/or a guardian of the person can be chosen for a person who has no attorney in place to carry out these roles.

For more information about the Office of the Public Guardian and Trustee, or to report a situation involving an adult who you believe is mentally incapable and who is suffering, or at risk of suffering, serious harm, visit the website of Ontario's Ministry of the Attorney General at www.attorneygeneral.jus .gov.on.ca.

The SDA stipulates that where a person who has no attorney is found incapable of managing his property, or of making decisions with respect to his own care and treatment, the Public Guardian and Trustee (PGT) becomes his guardian of property or guardian of the person, as the case may be.

The Office of the Public Guardian and Trustee is part of the Family Justice Services Division of Ontario's Ministry of the Attorney General. The PGT has various responsibilities, including protecting mentally incapable people. Section 62 of the SDA allows the PGT to apply for an order designating itself as temporary guardian of the person where a person's inability to handle his or her personal care threatens to cause "serious adverse effects." A guardianship ordered under this section lasts a maximum of 90 days.

Guardianship by the PGT is often used as a stop-gap measure to address a crisis, until a family member or trusted friend can be appointed. The PGT cannot offer truly personalized and responsive representation to every Ontarian who needs it.

Section 55 of the SDA provides that a court can appoint a person to be an incapable person's attorney for personal care. The court will not make such an appointment if it believes that there is an alternative method to handle personal-care decision making that is "less restrictive of the person's decision-making rights." A typical less restrictive method would be for a caregiver to obtain consent to care or treatment from a family member under section 20 of the HCCA (as discussed above), without having a formal guardian appointed.

An order appointing a guardian of the person includes, as part of its application, a finding that the person is incapable of consent or refusal of treatment and of managing his or her own care.

Section 59 sets out the powers of a guardian of a person who has full rights of guardianship. These include the right, on behalf of the incapable person, to make decisions in relation to the following matters:

- living arrangements;
- litigation;
- disclosure of medical records;
- decisions under the HCCA, including consent to treatment, personal care, and moving into a care facility;
- health care, nutrition, and hygiene;
- employment, education, training, clothing, and recreation; and
- any social services provided to the person.

A guardian can be given partial guardianship for certain things and not others, if the court determines that the person is incapable only with respect to certain aspects of his own care.

Social service workers are generally ineligible to be appointed as a guardian of the person for a client, according to section 57 of the SDA. This is similar to the restriction against choosing a social service worker to act as power of attorney for personal care.

Besides caring for clients with a mental illness, social service workers may find themselves in the position of supporting clients who have family members in need of guardianship. In cases like these, the social service worker can (1) provide basic information about the substitute decision-making options available (power of attorney; applying for guardianship under the SDA), (2) refer the client to the Ministry of the Attorney General as a source of information about these issues, and (3) assist the client in finding a lawyer. Specific advice on decisions relating to guardianship and power of attorney should be provided by a lawyer.

ADMISSION TO A MENTAL HEALTH FACILITY

A person may be considered for admission to a hospital or other mental health facility via a number of different routes. Many patients make their way to hospital on their own after deciding that they cannot cope with a mental health crisis. Other patients are escorted to hospital, either voluntarily or not, by relatives, friends, or helping professionals such as counsellors, therapists, social workers, or social service workers. Some people arrive at hospital after being apprehended by the police.

Under the MHA, a hospital is not required to admit a person simply because the person arrives in the emergency room. In general, because of the limited number of beds available for mentally ill patients, hospitals admit only those patients who are suffering a serious crisis and/or who may be at risk of harming themselves or others.

Voluntary or Informal Admission

Under section 12 of the MHA, doctors have the discretion to admit patients whom they believe to be "in need of the observation, care and treatment provided in a psychiatric facility." Doctors may admit patients who do not necessarily meet the criteria for involuntary admission, described in the next section. Typically, these voluntary or "informal" patients are admitted for a brief period only, to allow for observation for signs of the need for a further stay, or to see how the patient responds to an adjustment in medication. Voluntary or informal patients cannot be detained or restrained, and may leave the hospital at any time if they wish to do so.

In some cases, children may be admitted as informal patients for a longer stay than would apply to an adult. The MHA contains provisions allowing children between the ages of 12 and 16 to challenge their admission.

Involuntary Admission

Any person who is examined by a doctor may be deemed in need of an assessment to determine whether **involuntary admission** to a mental health facility is appropriate. In practical terms, this means that any time a patient with mental health concerns goes to the doctor or to a hospital emergency room, there is at least a possibility that the patient may be admitted involuntarily to a hospital or other mental health facility, and prevented from leaving.

Because of the shortage of hospital beds and the MHA's formalized process for evaluating hospital candidates, in most cases where a doctor concludes that hospitalization is warranted, it really is. However, social service workers must be frank with clients about the possibility that seeking treatment during a mental health crisis could lead to a hospital stay.

CONSIDERATIONS BEFORE GOING TO HOSPITAL

A social service worker working with a mentally ill client can help prepare for a trip to the hospital. This may involve planning for the possibility of involuntary admission. The kind of assistance provided can range from arranging for someone to collect the mail or look after the cat, to exploring the issue of appointing a substitute decision maker in the event that the client is found to be incapable of consenting to treatment.

If there is time available, the social service worker can suggest that the client retain a lawyer to prepare a power of attorney for personal care. In more urgent circumstances, the client might get in touch with the person he would like to have as a representative and communicate his general wishes; then, if the need arose, that person could be declared a guardian under the SDA or a representative under the HCCA.

A social service worker who has a good understanding of the law related to substitute decision makers will be able to support the client in ensuring that his wishes are respected.

THE "FORM 1" PROCESS

Upon examining a patient, a doctor may apply for a psychiatric assessment under section 15 of the MHA in the following circumstances.

The doctor reasonably believes that the patient has been or is currently

- threatening or attempting to cause bodily harm to himself,

- behaving violently toward another person,

- causing another person to fear bodily harm, or

- showing a lack of competence to care for himself;

and the doctor is also of the opinion that the person is apparently suffering from a mental disorder that likely will result in

- serious bodily harm or serious physical impairment to the patient, or

- serious bodily harm to another person.

Where a patient has previously received treatment for a chronic or recurring mental disorder that poses a risk when not treated, and for which treatment has shown clinical improvement in the past, the test for a psychiatric assessment is less stringent. Behaviour typical of the illness may be considered when considering the risk to the patient and others, even if the patient is not currently behaving in such a manner.

In 2000, the Ontario government passed amendments (known as "Brian's Law") that expanded the criteria for a psychiatric (form 1) assessment. Brian's Law (named after an Ottawa man, Brian Smith, whose killing by a mentally ill person in 1995 led to a critical review of the existing legislation) changed some provisions in the MHA and the HCCA, and made it easier to commit a psychiatric patient. Before Brian's Law, it was necessary for a physician to find that a person was an "imminent" threat to himself or herself or others before he or she was eligible for an assessment. This wording proved to be confusing and, as critics pointed out, it excluded certain people who clearly ought to be assessed (such as Smith's killer). Brian's Law removed the word "imminent" from MHA section 15.

It also listed additional criteria for ordering a form 1 assessment, making it easier for a person with a chronic mental disorder who poses a risk to be admitted involuntarily for assessment and to receive treatment before a crisis occurs.

Another important change made by Brian's Law was the introduction of a community treatment option pursuant to a "community treatment order," discussed in a later section of this chapter.

When an application for a psychiatric assessment is made, the patient is said to be "placed on a form 1" (referring to the application form). A patient who is subject to a form 1 application has the right to consult a lawyer.

When a patient is placed on a form 1, she will be detained in hospital for up to 72 hours. During that period, she will be observed by a psychiatrist, who will decide whether she is well enough to be released during or at the end of the 72-hour period, or whether she should be detained as an involuntary patient—often called "committed to hospital" or "placed on a form 3."

RIGHTS ARISING ON FORM 3 ADMISSION

If, as a result of a form 1 assessment, a person is found to be in need of admission to a mental health facility, he becomes an involuntary patient—"placed on a form 3." As soon as possible after a patient is placed on a form 3, he must be visited by a **rights**

Critical Perspectives

Brian's Law

After Brian Smith, an Ottawa sportscaster, was shot and killed in the parking lot of his workplace by a mentally ill attacker, his wife, Alana Kainz, vowed to make sure that no one else would suffer the same fate. She was the driving force behind Brian's Law, amendments to the MHA and the HCCA, passed in 2000, that make it easier to commit dangerous patients to hospital and ensure that they receive treatment, either in hospital or in the community under a community treatment order.

Many family members of the mentally ill welcome the change. Previously, their hands were largely tied with respect to getting their loved ones into treatment. A common characteristic of mental illnesses involving delusional thinking, such as schizophrenia, is the inability to recognize the illness in oneself; refusal of treatment can be considered a symptom of the illness. According to the Ontario Ministry of Health and Long-Term Care, "the legislative changes remove barriers to families, police and social workers by ensuring that people posing a risk to themselves or others get the care and treatment they need."

Not everyone agrees that Brian's Law is a good idea. Many psychiatric patient advocacy groups, poverty groups, and even the Canadian Mental Health Association have raised concerns that the law swings the pendulum back too far, reminiscent of human rights abuses in the days of insane asylums.

Critics of the law argue that community treatment orders criminalize the mentally ill, and that forcing patients to take medication violates their human rights and dignity. Some argue that more emphasis should be placed on community and social supports and housing, rather than quick-fix pharmaceuticals. ◇

adviser. The rights adviser will advise the patient of his right to apply for a review of the decision to place him on a form 3.

A rights adviser is a helping professional who has completed a government training course to qualify for this special designation. The rights adviser is not involved in the patient's clinical care. A rights adviser may, but need not, be a lawyer; a social service worker can apply to be designated in this role.

A form 3 placement lasts up to two weeks; patients can be released earlier if they improve. When a form 3 expires, a doctor who believes that the patient should remain admitted will apply for a form 4 extension.

When the initial form 3 is issued, and each time a physician applies to extend a patient's admission via a form 4, the patient has a right to challenge the decision before the Consent and Capacity Board. The board must hear the application within seven days. The rights adviser must visit each time a new form is ordered, to assist the patient in applying for a review if he so chooses, and in finding a lawyer to represent him. The procedures for applying to the board for a review and the hearing process are discussed in more detail below under the heading "Treatment and Release."

A patient who is in hospital on a form 3 or form 4 may not leave unless he is discharged and may be physically restrained, if necessary, to prevent him from leaving. The MHA and the HCCA contain rules for the use of restraints and the administration of intrusive treatments such as sterilization, shock therapy, and surgery. Social service workers who regularly work with hospitalized mental health patients should familiarize themselves with these rules. Further discussion here is beyond the scope of this book.

ADMISSION TO A CARE FACILITY

The HCCA defines certain non-hospital facilities as "care facilities." These facilities include homes for the aged, rest homes, and nursing homes. In most cases, people decide on their own, or in collaboration with family members, to move into care facilities. However, if a person is not in agreement about moving, family members or an "evaluator" (a social worker employed by the facility) may seek to have him moved without his consent.

In the event that a person is incapable of giving consent to move into a care facility, the situation is analogous to consent to treatment, and it is addressed by the HCCA in a similar way. The same procedures for appointing a substitute decision maker apply.

TREATMENT AND RELEASE

Once admitted to hospital, a patient's treatment raises a number of legal issues, most of which revolve around the concept of consent. The HCCA is intended to achieve the following objectives regarding consent to treatment, admission to care facilities, and personal assistance services:

- provide rules that apply consistently in all settings;
- facilitate decision making for persons lacking the **capacity** to make their own decisions;
- enhance the autonomy of the patient;
- allow those found incapable to have the finding reviewed by a tribunal;
- ensure a significant role for supportive family members; and
- permit intervention by the PGT only as a last resort on behalf of incapable persons.

Capacity, Consent, and the Health Care Consent Act

Under the HCCA, before a treatment is administered, and before a person is admitted to hospital for treatment or to a care facility for care, a health practitioner must determine whether the patient is capable of giving or refusing consent to the treatment or admission.

A person is capable if able to understand the information required for making a treatment or admission decision and able to understand the consequences of the decision (section 4(1) of the HCCA). Patients should be presumed to be capable unless there is evidence to the contrary. This evidence will vary from case to case. In some cases, a person may appear unable to understand a treatment that is being proposed—for example, if she refuses to listen to information or asks questions that suggest a lack of comprehension. In other cases, a person may express wishes that are clearly irrational, such as refusing a treatment that has a high success rate, few risks, and few side effects.

WEB LINK

The Psychiatric Patient Advocate Office (PPAO) provides advocacy services to individual patients, addresses facility-based or provincial systemic issues affecting patients' rights, and provides public and health-care professional education through speaking engagements, published reports, and media releases. For further details, visit the PPAO website at www.ppao.gov.on.ca.

If the health practitioner believes the patient to be incapable, the practitioner must obtain consent for the treatment from someone who is authorized to provide it on the patient's behalf. Section 20 of the HCCA lists the people able to consent on behalf of an incapable patient:

- a guardian of the person, if the guardian has authority to consent to treatment;

- an attorney for personal care, if the power of attorney confers authority to consent to treatment;

- a representative appointed by the Consent and Capacity Board under section 33 of the HCCA, if the representative has authority to give consent to treatment;

- the person's spouse or partner (but not if separated);

- an adult child (aged 18 or over) or parent of the person, or a children's aid society or other person who is lawfully entitled to give consent to treatment in the place of the parent (but not a parent who has only a right of access);

- a parent who has only a right of access;

- a brother or sister;

- any other relative.

When seeking consent to treat a patient, the health professional must work his way down this list, in the sequence shown, to determine who is authorized to act on the patient's behalf. This process is facilitated if the patient, or a person accompanying the patient (such as a social service worker), can identify the person who has authority to give consent and can provide the necessary contact information.

A person who consents on behalf of an incapable person must do so in accordance with that person's best interests, and after receiving full information about the treatment.

A social service worker with a client who suffers from a mental disorder (or other serious illness) should address the subject of treatment decisions at a time when the client is mentally capable. This is important because a person who is incapable cannot execute a valid power of attorney. Once a person is incapable of consenting to treatment, it is also too late to appoint an attorney. Therefore, it is essential to plan ahead and anticipate the client's future needs.

Where a health professional has reasonable grounds to believe that a patient, when capable, expressed a wish to refuse a certain treatment, the health practitioner cannot give the treatment later if the person becomes incapable (section 26). For example, if there is a notation in a chronically ill patient's medical records that the patient, when capable (and over the age of 16), mentioned that he did not want to receive a particular treatment, that wish must be respected.

If the patient disagrees with the health practitioner's finding that she is incapable of giving consent, she can apply for a review of that finding. This application is made to the Consent and Capacity Board.

APPLICATION TO THE CONSENT AND CAPACITY BOARD

The Consent and Capacity Board is an independent tribunal created under the HCCA. It conducts hearings of issues arising under the MHA, the HCCA, the SDA, and the *Personal Health Information Protection Act.* Board members include psychiatrists, lawyers, and laypeople appointed by the Lieutenant Governor in Council. To avoid bias, members who are employees of a hospital may not participate in decisions relating to that hospital. Decisions may be made by a single member or by panels of three or five members.

The HCCA and the board's rules of practice contemplate (but do not require) that parties appearing before the board will be represented by a lawyer. The board has the power under section 81 of the HCCA to arrange for legal representation for a party, or to serve notice of the hearing on the Children's Lawyer in the case of a patient under the age of 16. The social service worker should strongly encourage the client to retain a lawyer or, if this is difficult, to ask the board for help in arranging for legal representation.

If the review is urgent, the social service worker may need to assist the client in preparing application documents before a lawyer's services can be secured. If at all possible, a lawyer should review the application before it is delivered to the board. However, if this is impossible, the board will assist the patient in correcting any deficiencies in the application.

Once the board has received a patient's application for a review, it must hold a hearing within seven days and issue its decision within one day of the hearing. If the patient has applied for a review of a finding of incapacity, treatment cannot proceed until the board has completed its review, except in the case of an emergency.

A patient who disagrees with the results of a review can appeal the result to Ontario's Superior Court of Justice. The patient will need expert legal assistance to do this. A social service worker can help by providing contact information for a legal aid office or lawyer referral service.

A patient who has been found incapable by a health practitioner and is willing to accept that finding can request that the board appoint someone to be her representative for the purpose of consenting to or refusing treatment. Alternatively, a person can apply to be the representative of the patient. In practice, there is not much difference, because at this stage it is likely that another person will already be involved, at least informally, in the patient's care. The board's involvement in appointing a substitute decision maker helps to ensure that the patient's wishes and best interests are taken into account in the choice of a representative.

Community Treatment Orders

As discussed above, the legislative amendments known as Brian's Law introduced **community treatment orders** (CTOs), in addition to a lower assessment threshold. The purpose of a CTO is to address the revolving-door situation where a patient is admitted to hospital, stabilized, and released, only to stop treatment and again require hospitalization. CTOs are designed to allow patients to be treated in the community even though they meet the criteria for being involuntarily admitted to a mental health facility. A patient can be put on a CTO to avoid a new hospital admission, or in order to be released from hospital despite meeting the criteria for a form 3 or 4 placement. Treatment and monitoring that are part of a typical CTO include medication, therapy, and regular medical appointments.

A patient who is mentally ill can enter into a CTO only if the criteria set out in section 33.1(4) of the MHA are met. In general terms, these criteria are as follows:

WEB LINK

For more information about the Consent and Capacity Board, and a complete list of its rules of practice, visit www.ccboard.on.ca.

- The patient has a prior history of hospitalization.

- A community treatment plan for the person has been completed and approved.

- The patient has been examined by a physician within the 72-hour period immediately preceding his entry entering into the CTO plan.

- The patient is considered to be capable of complying with the CTO.

- The patient and, if applicable, his substitute decision maker have consulted a rights adviser.

- The patient or his substitute decision maker consent to the CTO.

In preparation for seeking a CTO, the health-care professionals, helping professionals, relatives, and other supporters of a mentally ill person must collaborate in developing a plan of care for the ill person, and the plan must be approved before the CTO is ordered. A social service worker may be one of the professionals named in a client's plan of care and may be in a position to contribute to the plan.

Once in place, a CTO lasts six months, but it can be renewed. To ensure that the rights of the patient are respected, the patient is entitled to challenge the making of the CTO (or CTO renewal) before the Consent and Capacity Board, much as he might challenge a form 3 or a finding that he is incapable, as discussed above.

Critical Perspectives

Medication Versus Psychosocial Therapy

In a March 2002 article in the *New York Times*, Courtenay Harding, then a senior director at Boston University's Center for Psychiatric Rehabilitation, criticized the current North American focus on medication as the primary treatment for mental illness. Harding was also very critical of the "self-fulfilling prophecy of a downward course" that seems to characterize the modern approach to mental illness.

Harding cited a Vermont study from the 1950s involving mentally ill patients, including chronic schizophrenics, who participated in a psychosocial rehabilitation-focused program that challenged the notion of mental illness as incurable. He noted that these patients were often well enough to leave the hospital, while others who were treated by medication alone were not. Thirty years later, when a followup study was done, 62 to 68 percent of the patients were enjoying better mental health than they had when originally diagnosed, and 45 percent showed no signs of mental illness at all.

These numbers seem to challenge the current pessimistic view of schizophrenia as essentially incurable, and bring into question an approach that relies heavily on medication alone. In fact, a 1980 World Health Organization study noted that people in developing countries recover more quickly and fully from mental illness than their peers in developed countries with sophisticated health-care systems.

Harding urged a radical change in the medical system's approach to mental illness—away from medication, institutionalization, and pessimism, and toward a rehabilitative approach:

> Although there are many pathways to recovery, several factors stand out. They include a home, a job, friends and integration in the community. They also include hope, relearned optimism and self-sufficiency.

Adapted from Courtenay M. Harding, "Beautiful Minds Can Be Recovered," *New York Times*, March 10, 2002. ◇

A patient who fails to comply with a CTO may be admitted to hospital as an involuntary patient, if warranted, pursuant to a form 1 application.

In support of the use of CTOs, the Ontario government has cited research in other jurisdictions suggesting that CTOs can reduce hospitalization, increase treatment compliance, decrease the victimization of mentally ill persons in the community, and decrease violence against members of the general public. However, a CTO will be ineffective if the treatment resources needed to support it do not exist in the community or are underfunded.

Social service workers may be employed by agencies that provide treatment services under CTOs. In those roles, social service workers can serve their clients not only directly, but also by advocating for the proper funding of these services and the development of new, high-quality treatment resources designed to meet the needs of individual communities.

Appropriate conflict and crisis management training should be a part of any position that involves working with a client who is on a CTO. The social service worker should have the contact information for caregivers named in the client's plan of care, so that appropriate referrals can be made and any issues adequately communicated and followed up. The MHA provides for sharing of records between those caregivers under certain circumstances; thus, privacy rules may differ, in this context, from the usual **norms** of client–service provider confidentiality.

Release

A patient is typically released from hospital when he or she is deemed to no longer meet the criteria for a form 3 or 4 placement. A release can be made at any time within the period of a placement; there is no need to wait until the placement expires. When a patient continues to meet the form 3 criteria but an adequate support system exists, he may be released on a CTO, as discussed above.

When a patient who is the subject of a CTO improves or recovers to the point where he no longer meets the form 3 criteria, the CTO can be terminated.

KEY TERMS

attorney	involuntary admission
attorney for personal care	norm
attorney for property	power of attorney
capacity	rights adviser
community treatment order	substitute decision maker

REFERENCES

Health Care Consent Act, 1996, SO 1996, c. 2.

Mental Health Act, RSO 1990, c. M.7.

Personal Health Information Protection Act, 2004, SO 2004, c. 3, Sch. A.

Substitute Decisions Act, 1992, SO 1992, c. 30.

REVIEW QUESTIONS

1. Why do social service workers need to understand the legislative framework of Ontario's mental health system?

2. Name three context in which social service workers might encounter mentally ill clients.

3. Explain how a person who arrives voluntarily at a hospital emergency room might find himself admitted to hospital for mental health treatment even if this is not his wish.

4. What is Brian's Law and how did it change the criteria for ordering a form 1 assessment?

5. Explain the role of rights advisers in the mental health system.

6. If a patient disagrees with a physician's finding that she needs to remain in hospital as an involuntary patient, what can she do? List some appropriate steps.

7. If a health practitioner believes that a patient is incapable of consenting to or refusing a treatment, who should the health practitioner approach to seek consent? What is the legal basis (statute? section number?) for your answer?

8. List three kinds of rulings that the Consent and Capacity Board can make, and describe what they mean or their function.

9. What is a community treatment order? Under what circumstances might one be made?

10. What is a power of attorney for personal care? Why might a client consider executing one?

11. Describe the circumstances under which the court might appoint a guardian of the person for someone as provided in the SDA.

DISCUSSION QUESTIONS

1. You are a social service worker working in a group home for residents with various mental disorders. One of your residents, a 46-year-old man named Kevin who is receiving treatment under a CTO, has become increasingly difficult to deal with. In particular, he complains that other residents are helping themselves to some of the food treats that his sister brings him when she visits. On several occasions, Kevin has refused to retire to his bedroom at lights-out, arguing that he has to remain in the common area to guard against kitchen raiders. Getting Kevin to go to bed and stay there has become an exhausting nightly battle for staff members.

   One night, you're in charge at lights-out time. All of the residents go to their rooms without incident. Once they are in bed, you go to the washroom. When you come out, Kevin is sitting quietly on the living-room couch, but as soon as he sees you, he appears to shove something between two of the cushions. You argue with him about going back to bed. When he finally agrees and gets to his feet to go, you reach between the couch cushions and find a metal fork hidden there.

   What should you do? What are the likely consequences of any steps that you might take?

2. You work for a community centre that provides recreational daytime supervision for elderly people and younger adults in the community who require special care. As part of your work, you counsel the participants on how to manage aspects of their own care outside the hours of the program.

   One of your clients is a 62-year-old divorced woman, Patricia, who lives alone. She is driven to the program every day by her best friend and neighbour, Kathy. Patricia has been diagnosed with Alzheimer's disease, and, like many such patients, has good days and bad days. On good days, she functions quite normally and manages her affairs very well; on bad days, she needs special care, and lately these have become more frequent. Since Patricia lives alone and has nobody at home to help her, she knows that she may need to move to some kind of care facility in the near future. She is worried that her preferences regarding the choice of facility and the kinds of services she will receive will not be respected, especially if she is incapable of communicating her wishes when it comes time to do so.

   How might you help Patricia to put these fears to rest?

CHAPTER 7

Health-Care Issues: Access, Aging, and Privacy

CHAPTER OBJECTIVES

After reading this chapter, you should be able to:

- Describe the public health-care system in Ontario, and discuss issues relating to access to care.

- Describe the regulation of nursing homes and other residences for the aged.

- Understand how the privacy of patients and the confidentiality of health records are protected.

INTRODUCTION

Perhaps the highest-profile aspect of Canada's social welfare program is our public health-care system. Each province offers public health insurance covering the cost of a wide range of health-care services and treatments. Social service workers who work with the elderly or other populations with high health-care needs should familiarize themselves with the general workings of the health-care system so that they can offer meaningful support to their clients. It is very common, for example, for social service workers to be employed by agencies that deliver home and community support services to seniors. Social service workers should be aware of the legal issues that will arise in these environments.

This chapter will focus on the health-care delivery system, access to health-care services, care for the aged, and issues of confidentiality with respect to health records. A fuller discussion of privacy and access to records is provided in chapter 22. The legal issues relating to consent to treatment, personal-care services, and hospitalization, and substitute decision making, are also relevant, but since they are discussed at length in chapter 6, they will not be repeated here.

PUBLIC HEALTH CARE

Ontario Health Insurance Plan

The Ontario Health Insurance Plan (OHIP) is administered by the Ministry of Health and Long-Term Care (in this chapter, referred to as "the ministry"). OHIP offers coverage to Ontario residents who are Canadian citizens, landed immigrants, permanent residents, persons granted refugee status, or First Nations people on reserves. To qualify as a "resident," an individual must live in Ontario for at least 153 of the first 183 days after applying for coverage and, generally, 153 days or more in each subsequent year. Premiums are payable by taxpayers above a specified income threshold.

Most children born in Ontario hospitals are registered under the plan before they leave the hospital. Home-birthed children and new residents must be registered at an OHIP office.

OHIP covers general health care provided by a physician and some services provided by specialists and other health professionals. Coverage of certain services may vary depending on the patient's particular circumstances; for example, certain chiropody (foot-care) services are covered for diabetics, but not for people without this underlying health condition. Other services, such as naturopathy, are not covered for anyone. Since the limits of coverage are complicated, the ministry suggests that people with questions about coverage contact a local OHIP office for advice.

OHIP does not generally cover drugs (over-the-counter or prescription) or other health supplies, such as nutritional supplements or health-care aids and devices. Some Ontarians enjoy full or partial insurance coverage for drugs and otherwise uninsured services through an employer.

When the cost of medications, special nutritional supplements, or health-care equipment for an individual is high, that person may be able to claim an income

WEB LINK

For more information about OHIP, including how to obtain coverage, visit the government website at www.health.gov.on.ca.

WEB LINK

Information about private and public reimbursement plans is posted by Plasmid Biocommunications Inc., a company specializing in prescription drug reimbursement, at www.drugcoverage.ca.

LEGISLATIVE SHORTCUT

Health Insurance Act

RSO 1990, c.H.6

Objective: To provide health care to the residents of Ontario.

Target Population: Ontario residents who are citizens, landed immigrants, permanent residents, Convention refugees, or Indians pursuant to the *Indian Act*, and who have lived in Ontario for at least 153 of the first 183 days after applying for coverage and for 153 days of each year thereafter.

Program Administration: The Ministry of Health and Long-Term Care administers the Ontario Health Insurance Plan.

Administrative Tribunal: Health Services Appeal and Review Board.

Summary: The Ontario Health Insurance Plan offers general and most specialized health-care coverage to Ontario residents without the payment of premiums. It does not generally cover drugs. ◇

tax deduction to help defray the cost. There is also a patchwork of other assistance programs for which patients in financial need may qualify. Some are publicly funded, such as the Trillium Drug Program and the Assistive Devices Program; others are funded by charities or other private organizations, such as the Easter Seals Society.

Local Health Integration Networks

Ontario has recently made structural changes to the way health care is delivered. The *Local Health System Integration Act, 2006* delegates more control over the delivery of health services to the local level (for example, to municipalities).

Ontario is divided into 14 Local Health Integration Networks (LHINs), each responsible for managing local health services and integrating local health systems. This includes local health system planning and community engagement, and providing funding to a wide range of health service providers. The Ontario government continues to set direction, strategic policy, and system standards.

The goal is to redesign the system with a greater emphasis on prevention, wellness maintenance, and responsiveness to local care demands. Theoretically at least, the changes will also save money.

WEB LINK

Access information about your Local Health Integration Network at www.lhins.on.ca.

LEGISLATIVE SHORTCUT

Local Health System Integration Act, 2006

SO 2006, c.4

Objective: To provide for an integrated and coordinated health system with efficient management at the local level by local health integration networks.

Target Population: All users of health care and also all health-care providers.

Program Administration: Ontario is divided into 14 Local Health Integration Networks (LHINs), each responsible for managing local health services and integrating local health systems. The Ontario government continues to set direction, strategic policy, and system standards.

Administrative Tribunal: Not applicable.

Summary: The *Local Health System Integration Act, 2006* delegates more control over the delivery of health services to the local level (for example, municipalities) and emphasizes prevention, wellness maintenance, and responsiveness to local care demands. ◇

Barriers to Access

The effectiveness of a universal public health-care system depends on accessibility. There are a number of barriers that may impede access to health services for some people, including the following:

■ ineligibility for OHIP coverage owing to immigration status

■ language and cultural barriers

- living in an isolated area with minimal health services

- living in a heavily populated area with high demand for health care

- issues related to consent (where a substitute decision maker fails to facilitate access to health care)

- mental illness

- addiction

- poverty

- homelessness

A client's limited access to health care, or receipt of poor quality care, may come to the attention of a social service worker. Occasionally, a social service worker may observe a symptom, such as an early sign of vision or hearing loss, which has developed so gradually that it has escaped the notice of the client or others. A social service worker may also form the opinion that the client has a chronic health problem (for example, a persistent cough) that is not being addressed through medical care. In such situations, where the client is an adult and capable of handling her own care, the normal course of action is for the social service worker to encourage the client to see a doctor. If the client has a substitute decision maker involved with her care, the social service worker should also speak with this person about any health concerns.

Children under school age may be particularly at risk if health-care issues are not adequately addressed by the child's parent or guardian. When a child is not attending

Critical Perspectives

Public Versus Private Health Care

Canada is defined in part by its public health-care system. As Canadians, we proudly differentiate ourselves from our neighbours across the border, many of whom live without health insurance. Most of us are also well aware of the high cost of public health care (which we pay for through our taxes), and the frustration of the long wait times that result when the high demand for services exceeds the supply. Hospital emergency rooms are seriously understaffed, leading to long delays in treatment. For patients who must wait months for cancer treatments or years for hip replacements or cataract surgery, the shortage of services is much more than just an inconvenience.

Some argue that more money should be pumped into the public system, to ensure that high-quality and timely health care is available equally for all. Proponents of the public system insist that permitting a broad spectrum of private health-care services will result in a two-tiered system, and those who cannot afford to pay will receive inferior care. They argue that health care is too important to leave to the vagaries of the market. Others argue that sole reliance on the public system is a recipe for waste and that it won't measurably improve either quality or wait times.

Those who want to expand private medicine point out that we already have private care in Canada for many medical services—including optional or non-essential procedures such as cosmetic surgery—and that this has not undermined the public system. Why, some ask, should a person be free to choose to spend money on liposuction, but be prevented from buying potentially life-saving treatments? ◇

school or day care, his health problems may go unnoticed. General measures undertaken to protect children—for example, parent education, new-immigrant support programs, and income support programs—often tend to improve access to health care by extension. However, potentially serious health problems are sometimes difficult to detect, even by community workers in contact with a child. For example, in the *Heikamp* case, discussed in chapter 3, the social worker assigned to supervise the mother's care of baby Jordan did not recognize that the child was suffering from severe dehydration and malnutrition (which ultimately led to his death).

Health and safety concerns may also be hard to detect in elderly clients. There is a general assumption, in our society, that health declines with age. However, this should not influence a social service worker in responding to signs of problems with a client's health or comfort. Clients may not themselves realize that their health complaints (for example, chronic pain, or side effects from medication) can be relieved or remedied with proper care. It's quite appropriate for a social service worker to inquire tactfully about how a client is feeling, to suggest that the client visit a doctor, or to ask permission to discuss an apparent health concern with other people in the client's support network (family and friends).

Sometimes social service workers can also provide practical help in overcoming barriers to access. For example:

- *Immigration-related barriers*. A social service worker can refer a client to a lawyer and provide basic information about how to obtain status as a legal immigrant. (Immigration matters are discussed in chapter 18.)

- *Language barriers*. A social worker can help the client to find health information in his own language, or to find a health-care provider who speaks the client's language. If the social worker also speaks the client's language, she might offer to accompany the client to health-care appointments and help with communication.

- *Location-related barriers*. A social service worker can help the client to arrange for transportation to another community where the required health-care services are available, and also help the client to find overnight accommodation if necessary.

- *Consent-related barriers*. A social service worker can monitor the client's capacity to manage his own treatment and, if necessary, can provide information to help the client put a power of attorney in place (as discussed in chapter 6). If the social service worker observes problems with the assistance being provided by a substitute decision maker, she can—subject to the restrictions of privacy law—communicate those concerns to people who might take action, such as relatives of the client.

- *Mental illness or addiction*. A social service worker can assist clients with organizing their medications, and accessing services and programs.

- *Poverty-related barriers*. A social service worker can research information about programs that provide financial assistance with health-care expenses, and can assist the client in making any necessary applications. A social service worker can assist a homeless client with finding shelter and direct the client to an appropriate health clinic.

Community Care Access Centres

Community Care Access Centres (CCACs) were introduced in 1996 to serve as a gateway to the range of government-sponsored health and personal-care services available. The local CCAC is the point of contact to determine a client's eligibility for financial subsidies and government services, and for finding service providers and applying for care. Services such as in-home care and support are available on a short-term basis for those recovering from an illness or surgery, and long-term home and residential care are available for the disabled and elderly.

The first step is for the senior, or a family member, or other support person, to arrange for a consultation with a CCAC case worker. The case worker can

1. provide information about the services available;

2. assess the client's need (and eligibility) for particular kinds of care or services;

3. help with filling out application forms for residential care and other services; and, where necessary,

4. place the client's name on any waiting lists.

WEB LINK

To find the CCAC closest to you, visit the website of the Ontario Association of Community Care Access Centres at www.oaccac.on.ca.

Note that before a person can receive government-sponsored care and support services, he must be assessed by a CCAC. However, CCAC assessment is not required if the person wants to access regular OHIP-covered medical services, wishes to purchase in-home support services from a private supplier, or chooses to move into a retirement home (which is a private facility).

Social service workers can help direct clients to a local CCAC office; they may also work as employees in those offices, though not in a diagnostic capacity (unless qualified to do so).

HEALTH CARE AND THE ELDERLY

With the "baby boom" generation moving into its senior years, and a low provincial birthrate, Ontario's population is steadily aging. This trend has important implications for health-care and social services in Ontario. The elderly population has widely varying needs, depending upon the individual's particular circumstances, including general health, disabilities, financial situation, housing, and support network (family and friends). In recognition of this diversity of needs, Ontario has developed a complex framework of community health support and residential care options available to seniors. The CCAC is the first point of contact for many seniors to assess the services available and formulate a plan for care.

Care in the Community

Seniors and disabled adults who are in good general health and who can manage most daily activities without assistance usually prefer to remain in their own home. For these individuals, four different kinds of in-home care are available through a CCAC: visiting health professional services, personal care and support, homemaking, and community support services (collectively referred to as "home and community support services"). Which of these services are appropriate for a particular client is determined by a CCAC assessment. Each type of in-home care is described briefly below.

The agencies that deliver home and community support services often employ social service workers.

VISITING HEALTH PROFESSIONAL SERVICES

Professionals such as nurses, physiotherapists, occupational therapists, and social workers may provide health care and support in the client's home. Services include assessment of needs, planning, providing care, and teaching the client how to manage the health condition. Services may be provided temporarily (for example, during recovery from surgery) or on an ongoing basis.

PERSONAL CARE AND SUPPORT

Personal care and support workers may offer assistance with everyday activities such as eating, bathing, dressing, and using the toilet. They may also assist with escorting clients to health-care appointments.

HOMEMAKING

Homemaking services may assist with routine household activities and chores such as shopping, preparing meals, laundry, cleaning, and banking.

COMMUNITY SUPPORT SERVICES

Community support services are many and varied. They include meal delivery, transportation, caregiver relief, adult day programs, social and recreational services, and safety and security checks. Providers may be either non-profit organizations or for-profit businesses. A few of the many community support services available are described below.

- *Safety and security checks.* Security checks may involve regular check-in phone calls or visits by a volunteer, to ensure that the client is not in distress. Some for-profit businesses also offer emergency response system technologies, which include in-home monitoring devices and transmitters worn by the client.

- *Transportation.* Many communities provide assisted transportation through various organizations such as Wheel-Trans (in Toronto), service clubs, and religious organizations.

- *Meal services.* Meal services may deliver a meal per day for a few days or every day of the week, depending on need and availability. There are also organizations that provide transportation to a dining facility, where a meal is served to many clients.

- *Caregiver respite and counselling.* Caregiver respite provides a break to the regular caregiver (often a family member) by providing either a replacement person for a brief period, or an activity outside the home to occupy the client. Caregiver counselling attends to the social and emotional needs of caregivers. Caregiver services are important to encourage family members

WEB LINK

For more information on the community care programs available, visit the website of the Ontario Community Support Association (OCSA) (which represents 360 not-for-profit home and community care agencies in Ontario) at www.ocsa.on.ca.

to take on what can be a crushing responsibility, and to reduce the risk of elder abuse by caregivers who become unable to cope.

Residential Care

Many seniors eventually move from their own home into some form of accommodation where support services are offered. The kinds of specialized housing available to seniors vary enormously. The choices include government-sponsored housing, private housing paid for by the residents, and resident-ownership housing. There are also different levels of care. At one end of the spectrum, there is apartment-style housing where residents occupy self-contained units and handle much of their own care, while living in a community of seniors with benefits such as recreational activities. At the opposite end of the spectrum are long-term care facilities, which accommodate residents in private or shared rooms or wards, and provide different levels of nursing and personal care, depending on individual needs. These facilities often provide recreational activities and special events for residents as well.

Figure 7.1 illustrates the numerous residential care options available to seniors. Each is discussed in more detail below.

Figure 7.1   Residential Care Available to Ontario Seniors

Type of residence	Ownership and public funding	CCAC referral/ assessment	Level of care/ assistance	Ministry regulation and inspection	Governing statute
Retirement home/ residence	Private for-profit, no government subsidy; residents are tenants of a private landlord	No	Low to moderate	No	*Residential Tenancies Act, 2006*
Life lease housing	Owned by non-profit corporation, no government subsidy; residents have an ownership interest in units	No	Low or none	No	*Condominium Act*
Supportive housing	Private for-profit or non-profit with government subsidy; residents are tenants	Yes	Low to moderate	No, except for certain subsidized services	*Residential Tenancies Act, 2006* *Long-Term Care Act, 1994**
Nursing homes	Private for-profit or non-profit with government subsidy	Yes	Moderate to heavy	Yes	*Nursing Homes Act***
Homes for the aged and rest homes	Non-profit with government subsidy; owned and run by the municipality	Yes	Moderate to heavy	Yes	*Homes for the Aged and Rest Homes Act***
Charitable institutions/ residences	Non-profit with government subsidy; owned and run by a charitable organization	Yes	Moderate to heavy	Yes	*Charitable Institutions Act***

  * On proclamation, this Act will be renamed the *Home Care and Community Services Act.*
** On proclamation, to be repealed and replaced by the *Long-Term Care Homes Act, 2007.*

RETIREMENT HOMES

Retirement homes or "communities" provide rental accommodation for seniors. They are owned by private landlords with no government funding of accommodation or on-site services. Prospective residents apply directly to the landlord without prior consultation with or referral from a CCAC.

Because they don't receive provincial funding, retirement homes are not regulated by the ministry, though some municipalities have passed bylaws establishing standards of care in for these residences. Some aspects of their operations, such as food service standards and occupational health and safety, may also be subject to inspection and regulation by the province or municipality. In addition, membership in the Ontario Retirement Communities Association (ORCA) requires ongoing compliance with ORCA standards for retirement home operations and services.

Landlord–tenant issues are governed by the *Residential Tenancies Act, 2006* (discussed in chapter 19).

LIFE LEASE HOUSING

"Life lease housing" is similar, in many respects, to a condominium. The residential units are apartments, with fees similar to condo fees. The complex is owned by a non-profit corporation; no government funding is provided. Residents purchase from the non-profit corporation the exclusive right to occupy a particular suite and to use the common facilities. When the resident moves out, she receives market value for the apartment.

Many of these projects offer light support services, such as housekeeping, hair care, and personal care, for which residents pay a user fee.

These facilities fall within the *Condominium Act*. They are not subject to ministry inspection or regulation.

SUPPORTIVE HOUSING

"Supportive housing" facilities provide rental accommodation and limited on-site or in-home support services. Residents must be assessed and referred by a CCAC.

These facilities are generally owned and operated by municipal governments or other non-profit organizations, such as religious or cultural groups, service clubs, and seniors' organizations. While they may receive some government funding, they are not fully regulated by the ministry. The form of accommodation, on-site services, costs, and the availability of government subsidies vary, and the particulars are set out in a contract between the service provider and the tenant.

Supportive housing is sometimes located on the same property as a long-term care (LTC) home, to give residents access to additional services, such as personal care, daily visits, meals, and assisted transportation. Residents may also apply for visiting health professional services through the local CCAC.

Providers and residents of supportive housing facilities are subject to the *Residential Tenancies Act, 2006*. Where the service portion is funded by the ministry, inspection and regulation are governed by the *Long-Term Care Act, 1994*.

LONG-TERM CARE HOMES

People seeking admission to long-term care must apply through a local CCAC. Following assessment and confirmation of eligibility, the CCAC will make a referral

WEB LINK

For information about retirement homes in Ontario, visit the website of the Ontario Retirement Communities Association (ORCA) at www.orca-homes.com.

on behalf of the applicant to one or more facilities of his choice. Often the applicant's name is placed on a waiting list until the requested accommodation becomes available.

All LTC homes receive government funding through the ministry. Because of the vulnerability of individuals who require long-term care, and the complexity of the services provided to them, these residential care facilities are the most closely regulated by the government. Classified by service provider, there are three kinds of LTC homes, each governed by a different provincial statute:

- Nursing homes (*Nursing Homes Act*) can be non-profit or for-profit, and are usually owned by private corporations.

- Homes for the aged (*Homes for the Aged and Rest Homes Act*) are required to be established by each municipality, are run by the municipality, and are always non-profit.

- Charitable institutions (*Charitable Institutions Act*) are usually owned by charitable organizations and are always non-profit.

The ministry is responsible for regulating all LTC homes. Regulation includes

- defining eligibility (who can access each level of care);

- managing wait-lists;

LEGISLATIVE SHORTCUT

Long-Term Care Act, 1994

SO 1994, c. 26

On proclamation of the Lieutenant Governor, to be renamed the *Home Care and Community Services Act, 1994* (2007, c. 8, ss. 215(1), 232(2)).

Objective: To reduce reliance on institutional care, by ensuring that health care and related support services are available to people in their own homes and community.

Target Population: People in need of long-term health care and related support services, who can have their needs met while continuing to living in their own homes.

Program Administration: The Ministry of Health and Long-Term Care administers long-term health care in Ontario.

Administrative Tribunal: Health Services Appeal and Review Board.

Summary: The *Long-Term Care Act, 1994* provides a framework for the provision of in-home and community health care and related services from various sources, according to the particular needs of each user. ◇

Long-Term Care Homes Act, 2007

SO 2007, c. 8

This Act is not yet in force and awaits proclamation.

Objective: To govern the operation of long-term care homes so that residents may live with dignity, safety, and comfort and have their physical, psychological, social, spiritual, and cultural needs adequately met.

Target Population: Residents of long-term care homes, and their service providers.

Program Administration: The Ministry of Health and Long-Term Care administers long-term residential health care in Ontario.

Administrative Tribunal: Health Services Appeal and Review Board.

Summary: When it is proclaimed, the *Long-Term Care Homes Act, 2007* will replace the *Homes for the Aged and Rest Homes Act* and *Charitable Institutions Act*. It will set standards to protect the rights of residents and ensure their health-care needs are met. ◇

- setting standards for all aspects of residence operations and delivery of care;

- ensuring the promotion and protection of residents' rights; and

- conducting inspections, including the imposition of sanctions for unmet standards.

In regulating LTC homes, the ministry refers to the statutes cited above and the regulations made under those statutes, and to general health policy guidelines. A detailed description of the legislation and regulations is well beyond the scope of this book; however, social service workers who work in an LTC home will need to be familiar with the applicable standards.

It is also important to note that a new statute, the *Long-Term Care Homes Act, 2007*, has been passed by the Ontario legislature and awaits **proclamation**. On proclamation, this new statute will govern all three kinds of LTC homes (nursing homes, homes for the aged, and charitable institutions) and the three separate statutes (*Nursing Homes Act*, *Homes for the Aged and Rest Homes Act*, and *Charitable Institutions Act*) will be repealed.

Some LTC homes are accredited by the Canadian Council on Health Services Accreditation (CCHSA). The CCHSA accredits facilities that meet and maintain its standards for care. The government encourages LTC homes to become accredited by providing extra funding for accredited homes.

LEGISLATIVE SHORTCUT

Homes for the Aged and Rest Homes Act

RSO 1990, c. H.13

To be repealed when the *Long-Term Care Homes Act, 2007* is proclaimed in force.

Objective: To govern the operation of homes for the aged and rest homes so that residents may live with dignity, safety, and comfort and have their physical, psychological, social, spiritual, and cultural needs adequately met.

Target Population: Residents of homes for the aged and rest homes, and their service providers.

Program Administration: The Ministry of Health administers long-term residential health care in Ontario.

Administrative Tribunal: Health Services Appeal and Review Board.

Summary: The *Homes for the Aged and Rest Homes Act* sets standards to protect the rights of residents and ensure their health-care needs are met. This Act will be repealed when the *Long-Term Care Homes Act, 2007* is proclaimed in force. ◇

Charitable Institutions Act

RSO 1990, c. C.9

To be repealed when the *Long-Term Care Homes Act, 2007* is proclaimed in force.

Objective: To govern the operation of charitable homes for the aged, so that residents may live with dignity, safety, and comfort and have their physical, psychological, social, spiritual, and cultural needs adequately met.

Target Population: Residents of charitable homes for the aged, and their service providers.

Program Administration: The Ministry of Health administers matters concerning approved charitable homes for the aged.

Administrative Tribunal: Health Services Appeal and Review Board.

Summary: The *Charitable Institutions Act* sets standards to protect the rights of residents and ensures their health-care needs are met. This Act will be repealed when the *Long-Term Care Homes Act, 2007* is proclaimed in force.

◇

Inspections

All LTC homes are inspected by ministry-appointed inspectors at least annually, to determine whether they are in compliance with relevant legislation and standards. Inspectors issue a finding of "unmet" when they determine that a standard is not being met, and a "citation" when the LTC is found not to be in compliance with legislation. Inspection findings must be posted in a public area on the premises for viewing by residents and family.

LTC homes subject to a citation must respond with a plan of corrective action, which is filed with the ministry. The ministry then monitors whether the plan is being carried out. If no plan is filed or the changes are not made within a specified period of time, the ministry can impose sanctions. Available sanctions vary depending on the circumstances and the type of home, but in general, they can include suspending the home's right to accept new patients. In certain serious cases, the ministry can take over the operation of the home.

The ministry also plays a role in investigating complaints by residents or their family members. Every LTC home operator must have an internal complaints review process posted in the home where it can be easily seen by residents and visitors. Anyone may make a complaint to the ministry by mail or by phone using the long-term care action line at 1-866-434-0144. Information about complaints and the results of ministry investigations is tracked on a database.

WEB LINK

For more information on long-term care facilities, visit the website of the Ontario Long Term Care Association (OLTCA) at www.oltca.com. For more information about non-profit residential facilities and services, visit the website of the Ontario Association of Non-Profit Homes and Services for Seniors (OANHSS), an organization representing long-term care facilities, seniors' housing, and community agencies, at www.oanhss.org.

Addressing Elder Abuse

The elderly are vulnerable to abuse at the hands of caregivers, whether these are family members or staff of a residential facility or other residents, and they may conceal an abusive situation, believing that it will worsen if they complain or report it. Legislative amendments to the *Long-Term Care Homes Act, 2007* propose to address this concern by

- promoting zero tolerance of abuse and neglect of residents in long-term care;
- protecting whistle-blowers (including staff, residents, and volunteers) who report abuse or neglect;
- requiring that a registered nurse be on duty in the LTC home 24 hours a day, seven days a week; and
- restricting the use of restraints to limited circumstances where it is absolutely necessary and only with appropriate safeguards.

It is already a requirement under the *Homes for the Aged and Rest Homes Act* that all homes post and follow a Residents' Bill of Rights. This practice has been adopted by other LTC facilities as well. The Bill of Rights serves as a reminder to residents,

Legislative Excerpt

Residents' Bill of Rights

A municipality maintaining and operating a home, the municipalities maintaining and operating a joint home and the board of management of a home shall ensure that the following rights of residents of the home are fully respected and promoted:

1. Every resident has the right to be treated with courtesy and respect and in a way that fully recognizes the resident's dignity and individuality and to be free from mental and physical abuse.

2. Every resident has the right to be properly sheltered, fed, clothed, groomed and cared for in a manner consistent with his or her needs.

3. Every resident has the right to be told who is responsible for and who is providing the resident's direct care.

4. Every resident has the right to be afforded privacy in treatment and in caring for his or her personal needs.

5. Every resident has the right to keep in his or her room and display personal possessions, pictures and furnishings in keeping with safety requirements and rights of other residents of the home.

6. Every resident has the right,

   i. to be informed of his or her medical condition, treatment and proposed course of treatment,

   ii. to give or refuse consent to treatment, including medication, in accordance with the law and to be informed of the consequences of giving or refusing consent,

   iii. to have the opportunity to participate fully in making any decision and obtaining an independent medical opinion concerning any aspect of his or her care, including any decision concerning his or her admission, discharge or transfer to or from a home, and

   iv. to have his or her records of personal health information within the meaning of the *Personal Health Information Protection Act, 2004* kept confidential in accordance with the law.

7. Every resident has the right to receive reactivation and assistance toward independence consistent with his or her requirements.

8. Every resident who is being considered for restraints has the right to be fully informed about the procedures and the consequences of receiving or refusing them.

9. Every resident has the right to communicate in confidence, to receive visitors of his or her choice and to consult in private with any person without interference.

10. Every resident whose death is likely to be imminent has the right to have members of the resident's family present twenty-four hours per day.

11. Every resident has the right to designate a person to receive information concerning any transfer or emergency hospitalization of the resident and, if a person is so designated, to have that person so informed forthwith.

12. Every resident has the right to exercise the rights of a citizen and to raise concerns or recommend changes in policies and services on behalf of himself or herself or others to the residents' council, staff of the home, government officials or any other person inside or outside the home, without fear of restraint, interference, coercion, discrimination or reprisal.

13. Every resident has the right to form friendships, to enjoy relationships and to participate in the residents' council.

14. Every resident has the right to meet privately with his or her spouse in a room that assures privacy and, if both spouses are residents in the same home, they have a right to share a room according to their wishes, if an appropriate room is available.

15. Every resident has a right to pursue social, cultural, religious and other interests, to develop his or her potential and to be given reasonable provisions by the home to accommodate these pursuits.

16. Every resident has the right to be informed in writing of any law, rule or policy affecting the operation of the home and of the procedures for initiating complaints.

17. Every resident has the right to manage his or her own financial affairs if the resident is able to do so and, if the resident's financial affairs are managed by the home, to receive a quarterly accounting of any transactions undertaken on his or her behalf and to be assured that the resident's property is managed solely on the resident's behalf.

18. Every resident has the right to live in a safe and clean environment.

19. Every resident has the right to be given access to protected areas outside the home in order to enjoy outdoor activity, unless the physical setting makes this impossible.

Source: *Homes for the Aged and Rest Homes Act*, section 1.1(2). ◈

WEB LINK

For more information on issues concerning the rights and protection of seniors generally, visit the website of the Advocacy Centre for the Elderly (ACE) at www .advocacycentreelderly.org.

staff, and families that the physical, psychological, social, cultural, and spiritual needs of every resident must be adequately met.

Many LTC homes have a residents' council, and some have a family council. These councils provide a forum in which clients can discuss issues of importance to them, including concerns about the quality of care and human rights issues. Concerns based on violation of a home's Residents' Bill of Rights can form the basis of a complaint to the ministry, which it must investigate (see above). Social service workers working in an LTC home are expected to be aware of, and to uphold, the rights of the residents.

PRIVACY AND THE CONFIDENTIALITY OF HEALTH RECORDS

Privacy and confidentiality are discussed more generally in chapter 22; however, it is worth touching on the subject in the health context, particularly since patients suffering from health problems sometimes become incapable of managing their own care. When this happens, special rules must be followed to facilitate decision making by others, while protecting, as much as possible, the privacy interests of patients.

Privacy Legislation Applicable in Ontario

Ontario has enacted legislation—the *Personal Health Information Protection Act, 2004* (PHIPA)—that specifically governs access to private health records. This statute is discussed in detail in the next section. In addition, there is general privacy and access to information legislation that may govern some non-health-related information

Critical Perspectives
Privacy and Technology at Odds

Canada Health Infoway, a $400 million plan to convert paper health records to electronic, was unveiled as part of the federal government's 2007 spring budget. The benefits of such a system—efficient storage and sharing of information—are also raising concerns. The ability to use e-mail to send a patient's records to specialists, lab reports to doctors, or even prescriptions to pharmacists, could no doubt speed up the process of communicating information. However, unless these messages are encrypted, they are vulnerable to interception and unauthorized use.

Consider the case heard in Alberta's Provincial Court in April 2007. A clerk in a medical office was fined $10,000 after pleading guilty to illegally accessing the medical records of her lover's wife, who was being treated for cancer. This invasion of privacy was characterized as a "death watch" by the prosecution.

There are also increasing concerns about the ability of businesses and other institutions to protect personal information against theft by computer hackers or individuals who obtain unauthorized access to electronic files. In one widely reported incident, a hacker stole credit card and other personal data on millions of customers of Winners and Home Sense stores. Other recent cases have involved the theft of personal tax files and medical records. ◇

about hospital patients or residents of facilities for seniors' care. These statutes, including the federal *Personal Information Protection and Electronic Documents Act* and *Privacy Act*, and Ontario's *Freedom of Information and Protection of Privacy Act* and *Municipal Freedom of Information and Protection of Privacy Act*, are discussed in chapter 22.

Personal Health Information Protection Act, 2004

The purposes of the PHIPA are stated in section 1, and can be summarized as follows:

- to establish rules for the collection, use, and disclosure of personal health information about individuals, which protect the confidentiality of that information and the privacy of individuals with respect to the information, while facilitating the effective provision of health care;

- to provide individuals with a right of access to personal health information about themselves, subject to limited and specific exceptions set out in the Act;

- to provide individuals with a right to require the correction or amendment of personal health information about themselves, subject to limited and specific exceptions set out in the Act;

- to provide for independent review and resolution of complaints with respect to personal health information; and

- to provide effective remedies for contraventions of the Act.

The measures contained in the legislation to achieve these purposes are briefly described below.

LEGISLATIVE SHORTCUT

Personal Health Information Protection Act, 2004

SO 2004, c.3, Sch.A

Objective: Establish rules for the collection, use, and disclosure of personal health information.

Target Population: Everyone with health-care records and the "custodians" of personal health information.

Program Administration: The *Personal Health Information Protection Act, 2004* is administered by the Information and Privacy Commissioner for Ontario.

Administrative Tribunal: An individual who is denied access to a record of personal health information may make a complaint to the Information and Privacy Commissioner.

Summary: The PHIPA requires the patient's consent before personal health information may be collected, used, or disclosed for purposes such as treatment, research, fee collection, quality assurance, and education. ◇

COLLECTION, USE, AND DISCLOSURE

The PHIPA regulates persons who are authorized to collect, use, and disclose personal health information, referred to as "**custodians**." Custodians include a wide range of organizations, including (the "officers in charge" of) medical practices, hospitals, LTC residences, pharmacies, ambulance services, boards of health, and more.

Personal health information is broadly defined in the PHIPA. In addition to factual details of a person's physical health, it includes

- the person's OHIP number;

- a plan of service, as defined under the *Long-Term Care Act, 1994*;

- details of the person's eligibility for health-care services, and of payments made in relation to those services; and

- the identity of the person's substitute decision maker, if any.

In general, the PHIPA does not regulate information that is regulated by the *Freedom of Information and Protection of Privacy Act* or the *Municipal Freedom of Information and Protection of Privacy Act*. The two privacy-protection regimes are designed to operate separately, and information is governed by either one or the other.

Under the PHIPA, a custodian cannot collect, use, or disclose personal health information about an individual unless the collection, use, or disclosure is necessary and permitted by the legislation, and unless the individual consents. The appropriate purposes for collection of personal health information are listed in the legislation, and include not only treatment, but also certain research, fee collection, quality assurance, and education purposes.

From a practical perspective, consent to collection, use, and disclosure of personal health information is usually managed by providing the individual patient with a **waiver** form that explains the issue of consent. The patient's signature on the form constitutes **consent** provided that it is reasonable to believe that the patient understands the content of the form and the legal effect of the waiver. Each time there is the potential for collection or use of new information, the patient should be provided with a new form; for example, each time he or she visits a new health practitioner.

The PHIPA requires collectors and custodians of personal health information to protect that information. This requirement relates to both paper and electronic records. The details of how information is to be protected (for example, from theft, destruction, tampering, hackers, etc.) may eventually be covered in a regulation made under the PHIPA; at the present, there are no specific guidelines for how protection is to be guaranteed. If information is lost, illegally accessed, illegally disclosed, or tampered with, the person whose information it is must be notified promptly.

Each custodian of personal health information is required to appoint a contact person. The contact person handles requests for disclosure of information and inquiries about the handling of information, and receives complaints under the PHIPA. Custodians must prepare and distribute to the interested public a written policy with respect to the handling of personal health information.

The PHIPA creates rules with respect to consent to disclosure and use of personal health information. It defines consent, and provides that an individual, or the

CASES IN POINT

Why Should Social Service Workers Know About the PHIPA?

Social service workers can be involved with personal health information in a variety of ways.

From the Custodian's Perspective

A social service worker who works for a custodian of personal health records (for example, an LTC residence), and has access to personal health information about residents, must understand how to manage requests for access to that information. Consider the following scenarios.

- There is a major fire at a nursing home and several ambulances are called to the scene. A social service worker who has been helping to evacuate residents is approached by a reporter and asked whether anyone was injured.

In this situation, it is probably safe to make a very general statement; for example, "While three residents were taken to hospital for evaluation and observation, we are aware of no serious injuries." No names should be given and, particularly if the residence is small, no details provided about the gender and age of the residents. In addition, the name of the hospital to which the residents were taken should not be divulged (assuming that there is more than one hospital in the community). A senior manager at the nursing home should be assigned as the contact for families who may call to inquire about the condition of loved ones. This manager should be trained in handling privacy issues and should be prepared to tactfully confirm the identity of people who make inquiries.

- A social service worker is employed in a hospital-based physiotherapy program for disabled adults. The wife of one of the program participants is concerned that another participant has a persistent cough and should be excluded from the program. She asks the social service worker for details of the other participant's health.

It would be completely inappropriate, in this scenario, to disclose any information about the coughing participant. However, the social service worker may reasonably accommodate a request by the wife to allow her husband to exercise at a distance from the coughing participant.

From the Individual's Perspective

A social service worker may work outside the health-care field with clients who have health problems, and may be called upon to assist clients with privacy-related issues. Consider the following scenarios.

- A social service worker who works in a prison may be approached by an inmate who claims that he requires a special diet because of food intolerances. To assist him in making his case with the dietary staff, the inmate asks the social service worker to help him obtain a note from his family doctor detailing his dietary needs.

In this case, the social service worker can act as the inmate's intermediary in making the request. It is unlikely that the inmate (or the social service worker acting on his behalf) will need to seek access to his health records under the PHIPA; family physicians will generally provide such information on confirmation of the source of the request by the office receptionist. However, if the request is denied and the inmate encounters problems gaining access to his records, the next step is for him, or the social service worker, to ask to speak with the privacy inquiry contact person in the doctor's office. If this approach is fruitless, the inmate will need to make a request to the office of the Ontario Information and Privacy Commissioner, for a ruling ordering access to the necessary information.

- A social service worker who works in a resource centre for single parents is approached by a client who was denied a job because she failed a physical examination that was part of the job qualification process. The client asks the social service worker to help her in obtaining access to the examination results so that she can challenge the employer's decision.

Similarly, the social service worker can assist the client in making a request for information from the doctor who carried out the examination and, if this is unsuccessful, assist with a request to the Ontario Information and Privacy Commissioner. ◇

individual's substitute decision maker, has the right to consent, to withhold consent, to give conditional or limited consent, and to **revoke** consent to the disclosure and use of personal health information. In order to be able to make meaningful health-care decisions on behalf of a person, a substitute decision maker must often have access to personal health information, and the PHIPA provides a statutory mechanism for that access.

Where a custodian makes a finding that a person is incapable of consenting to actions in respect of her personal health information, the custodian must communicate that finding to the person. If the person disagrees that she is incapable, she can apply for a review of the incapacity finding by the Consent and Capacity Board. (The functions and procedure of the Consent and Capacity Board are discussed in chapter 6.)

A custodian can also apply for a hearing by the Consent and Capacity Board. Section 24 of the PHIPA provides "considerations" that substitute decision makers should apply when deciding to give or withhold consent. If the custodian feels that the substitute decision maker has not made his decision with these considerations in mind, the custodian can bring the matter before the Consent and Capacity Board.

THE INDIVIDUAL'S RIGHT OF ACCESS

Under the PHIPA, individuals are entitled to access their own health records except under certain special circumstances, including the following:

- the records are subject to legal privilege or were collected primarily for use in a legal proceeding that has not been completed;

- the records relate to an investigation of an attempt by the individual to obtain health services by fraud; or

- allowing the individual access to the record would put him at risk of serious bodily harm, or would jeopardize his treatment or recovery, or risk of serious bodily harm to another person.

An individual who is denied access to a record of personal health information can make a complaint to the Information and Privacy Commissioner (the commissioner) appointed under the *Freedom of Information and Protection of Privacy Act*. The custodian has the **onus** of proving that access to the record is legally denied; that is, the custodian must demonstrate to the commissioner's satisfaction that the custodian has legal grounds for withholding the record.

CORRECTION OF INFORMATION

An individual who finds an error in a record of personal health information can request that the custodian correct the error. The custodian must respond, advising whether or not the correction will be made. If the individual objects to a correction not being made, he or she can make a complaint to the commissioner.

COMPLAINTS AND REMEDIES

Complaints may be brought before the commissioner, and in appropriate cases, a custodian or another person may be found guilty of an offence in relation to private records. In general, an offence can only be charged if the custodian or other person "willfully" violated the provisions of the PHIPA. Individuals found guilty of a PHIPA offence can be fined up to $50,000, and corporations found guilty can be fined up to $250,000.

Where an individual has suffered an invasion of privacy or mental anguish because of disclosure of personal health information that the commissioner has found to be improper, and all appeals of the order have been completed, the individual can seek compensation in court (the Ontario Superior Court of Justice). As a practical matter, this kind of lawsuit will be costly and difficult to pursue, and the individual should weigh the costs of litigation, in terms of both money and time, against the likelihood and the amount of compensation.

KEY TERMS

consent

custodian

onus

proclamation

revoke

waiver

REFERENCES

Charitable Institutions Act, RSO 1990, c. C.9.

Freedom of Information and Protection of Privacy Act, RSO 1990, c. F.31.

Health Insurance Act, RSO 1990, c. H.6.

Homes for the Aged and Rest Homes Act, RSO 1990, c. H.13.

Local Health System Integration Act, 2006, SO 2006, c. 4.

Long-Term Care Act, 1994, SO 1994, c. 26.

Long-Term Care Homes Act, 2007, SO 2007, c. 8.

Municipal Freedom of Information and Protection of Privacy Act, RSO 1990, c. M.56.

Nursing Homes Act, RSO 1990, c. N.7.

Personal Health Information Protection Act, 2004, SO 2004, c. 3, Sch. A.

Personal Information Protection and Electronic Documents Act, SC 2000, c. 5.

Privacy Act, RSC 1985, c. P-21.

Residential Tenancies Act, 2006, SO 2006, c. 17.

REVIEW QUESTIONS

1. Are new residents of Ontario automatically entitled to claim OHIP benefits? Do different rules apply in different circumstances?

2. How can an Ontario resident obtain coverage for or reimbursement of the costs of prescription drugs and medical aids and devices?

3. List at least three barriers to accessing health care that a client might face.

4. If, as a social service worker, you determine that an elderly client who has been living independently now needs more supportive care, what first steps might you take?

5. List a few of the differences between a nursing home and a retirement home.

6. What should a resident of a long-term care facility do if she has concerns about the living conditions in the home?

7. List at least three statutes that offer protection for a person's private information.

8. Why should social service workers know about the application of privacy laws?

DISCUSSION QUESTION

You are a social service worker in a mid-size Ontario community, employed in a support program for people caring for family members with terminal illnesses. One of your clients is Spiro, who is 71 and the sole caregiver for his wife, Sofia. Sofia has inoperable cancer and is living at home, but confined to her bed. Her doctor has prescribed morphine to relieve her pain.

One afternoon you receive a call from Spiro's son, Al. He is worried about his parents. He tells you that two nights ago, Sofia placed a call to 911 in the middle of the night. She had been awakened by severe pain and could not get her morphine pump to work; although she had called out several times for Spiro (who sleeps on a couch in the same room), she could not wake him. The paramedics who were sent to the house had to take the door off the hinges to get in, and even then had difficulty waking Spiro. It turned out that he had mistakenly taken a double dose of his own pain medicine, Tylenol with codeine. He uses this medication daily to manage his chronic back pain, which is aggravated every time he has to turn Sofia to change her or her bedding.

Al is concerned that Spiro may no longer be competent to care for Sofia. Al lives too far away and has too many responsibilities with his own young family to take over the care giver role. What advice should you give him?

CHAPTER 8

Income Maintenance

CHAPTER OBJECTIVES

After reading this chapter, you should be able to:

- Explain the role of income maintenance programs in the context of the social support system

- List three general kinds of income maintenance programs.

- Understand the general eligibility criteria for each kind of income maintenance program.

- Suggest strategies for improving clients' access to income maintenance programs.

- Understand the value of advocacy on behalf of economically disadvantaged clients.

INTRODUCTION

Two important components of Ontario's social security system—public health-care systems—have been discussed in the preceding chapters. Here we will consider a third major component, income maintenance (also known as "income support," "poverty relief," "welfare," "workfare," or "social assistance").

Most people pay for their living expenses out of personal income or savings. Where circumstances such as age, poor health or disability, or the lack of available employment make it difficult to earn a living, poverty may be the result. When people with young families cannot earn an adequate income, their children suffer as well.

In an effort to respond to poverty, all three levels of government support a framework of programs providing income maintenance or social assistance to Ontario residents. Federal programs include Employment Insurance (EI), which provides temporary relief for people who have lost their jobs; Old Age Security (OAS), which provides a modest pension to Canadians who have reached 65 years of age; and the Canada Pension Plan (CPP), which provides an additional pension based on years of employment. Provincial programs include Ontario Works and the Ontario Disability Support Program (ODSP), both of which provide income assistance, and Workplace Health and Safety Insurance (WHSI), which provides compensation to individuals who have suffered a job-related injury or illness. Ontario municipalities also contribute by providing administrative support for certain programs.

Some programs, such as CPP, EI, and WHSI, are fully or partially funded by premiums paid by employees and their employers. Other programs, such as Ontario Works and programs for the disabled, are funded solely from the general tax base.

Income maintenance programs are only useful when they are accessed successfully by those who need them. Sometimes this can be a complicated and frustrating endeavour for unsophisticated and marginalized people. Social service workers can be an important resource to clients by providing information about programs and eligibility, by supporting clients in the application process, and by advocating on behalf of clients for access to benefits.

Social service workers may also work in the administration of income maintenance programs. For example, they may be employed at an Ontario Works resource centre, providing referrals to training, helping with resumé preparation, and coaching benefit recipients in interview skills. While these individuals will benefit from knowing about other government-funded income assistance programs, the information in this chapter is directed mainly at those who are working in settings in which they support clients' access to such programs.

Programs designed to directly replace lost working income, such as WHSI and EI, will be discussed in chapter 17. This chapter will focus mainly on the Ontario Works, ODSP, and CPP programs.

ONTARIO WORKS

Ontario Works is Ontario's primary last-resort income relief program. It is managed by the Ministry of Community and Social Services (MCSS) and provides very modest subsistence-level benefits to Ontario residents who lack adequate means of support.

The province chose the name "Ontario Works" as a reminder that the benefits are intended to support Ontarians temporarily while they seek economic independence through employment. The purposes of the program are set out in the *Ontario Works Act, 1997*:

- to recognize individual responsibility and promote self-reliance through employment;

- to provide temporary financial assistance to those most in need while they satisfy obligations to become and stay employed;

- to effectively serve people needing assistance; and

- to be accountable to the taxpayers of Ontario.

Ontario Works benefits are **needs- and means-tested**. Before a person can gain access to the benefits, he must prove that he does not have the means (any other source of money) to provide for his basic needs. The needs that the program is designed to pay for are basic **subsistence needs**, such as food and housing. In considering an application for Ontario Works benefits, the program administrators will investigate whether the applicant has any assets, such as a registered retirement savings plan (RRSP), or access to other sources of help, such as spousal support **entitlements** or housing **subsidies**. If he has, these sources must be exhausted first; otherwise, the

LEGISLATIVE SHORTCUT

Ontario Works Act, 1997

SO 1997, c. 25, Sch. A

Objective: To provide last resort minimum income to cover basic needs after all other resources are exhausted and to promote self-sufficiency through employment.

Target Population: Able-bodied Ontario residents who are unable to meet the basic needs of themselves and their families.

Program Administration: Ontario Works is a provincial program and costs are shared by the federal government; however, municipal governments administer it.

Administrative Tribunal: The first step when disputing a finding of ineligibility is to seek an internal review. If this is unsuccessful, the case may be heard by the Social Benefits Tribunal.

Summary: Ontario Works provides benefits to cover basic subsistence needs for those without the means to provide for themselves. Benefits, also called social assistance, welfare, and workfare, are meager and intended to be temporary and to provide primarily for shelter, food and clothing. Recipients are expected to achieve self-sufficiency as soon as possible and must participate in employment-seeking activities as specified in "participation agreements." Non-compliance may result in ineligibility and cessation of benefits. ◇

applicant may be ineligible for Ontario Works benefits, or benefits paid under the program may be reduced.

Ontario Works was created by the *Ontario Works Act, 1997* and the five regulations made under it, replacing the previous income support program provided under the *General Welfare Act* (now repealed). The administration of the program is also guided by more than 50 provincial policy directives.

Although Ontario Works is a provincial program, it is partially funded by the federal government and administered by municipal governments. Municipal administration means that although the same set of rules is applied across the province, there are minor differences in how benefits are administered by different municipalities.

WEB LINK

You can access the current Ontario Works policy directives at www.css.gov.on.ca.

Eligibility

Because government funding for income assistance is limited, fairness demands that applicants for Ontario Works benefits meet strict eligibility criteria. The first requirement is that the applicant must be an Ontario resident. An application for benefits must be made to the Ontario Works office in the municipality (or municipal area) where the applicant lives.

Once Ontario residency is confirmed, to determine whether the applicant is eligible for benefits, the local program administrator assesses all sources of support available to the applicant. These include employment income, business income, compensation settlements (for example, an award of damages for injury in a motor vehicle accident, or workers' compensation benefits), spousal and child support payments, savings, and other assets.

The program provides benefits to "benefit units"—that is, to families living together. For that reason, total family income and assets are taken into account when eligibility is considered. This means, for example, that an applicant may be denied benefits (or may receive reduced benefits) if her spouse receives a pension.

An applicant may qualify for Ontario Works benefits even if she (or a family member) is currently earning employment income. This can happen, for example, where the applicant is employed part-time, works full-time but at a very low wage, or has child-care costs that offset a large portion of her earned income. If the applicant (or a family member) has employment income, Ontario Works benefits are reduced to reflect the availability of that income.

Cutoff levels for income and assets, which vary depending upon the size of the family, determine whether a person is eligible for benefits, and if so, for how much. For example, the amount of benefits may vary depending on whether a parent is a sole-support parent or is in a spousal (married or common-law) relationship. Where two adults live in the same residence and one of them is seeking to apply as a sole-support parent, program administrators will investigate the nature of the relationship between the adults to determine whether it is a spousal relationship or not.

If an adult applicant lives with his (or her) parents, it can be difficult (though not impossible) for him to obtain benefits. The applicant can qualify if he is financially independent and in need. In some cases, an adult living with parents who are also in need of income assistance will be treated as part of the parents' benefit unit; that is, he will receive benefits, but they will be included in the payment to his parents rather than paid separately.

In general, children under the age of 18 must be supported by their parents. A financially independent teen living at home will not be paid benefits if Ontario Works views such payments as providing an incentive to the teen to leave home. However, a teen who is 16 or 17, living on her own, and not being supported by parents can, in some cases, have herself declared independent of her parents. This situation could arise, for example, for a teen who has left home because of abuse. A recipient under 18 cannot receive benefits directly; the payments will be managed by an agency, or by an adult trustee or guardian. Teens under 18 must be attending high school in order to qualify for benefits, and their attendance at school is verified monthly.

EXTRA CREDIT
Temporary Care Assistance

"Temporary care assistance" is a benefit payable to a person who is providing a home for a child for whom he or she has no legal support responsibility. For example, a woman who takes in her brother's child for a few months while he is hospitalized might apply for this type of assistance. Although called "temporary," benefits may be available for an extended period, until the child reaches 18.

To qualify, the caregiver must make reasonable efforts to pursue support from the child's parents and must not be receiving any compensation for caring for the child under the *Child and Family Services Act*. Eligibility is based on the income and assets of the child, not those of the adult caregiver. ◇

Benefit Rates

Benefit rates under the Ontario Works program are based on a number of factors, including family size, age of dependants, housing costs, location, and whether the applicant requires a special diet because of health problems. The calculation of benefits to pay for basic monthly needs other than shelter is illustrated in figure 8.1. Benefits may be higher for recipients who live north of the 50th parallel and do not have year-round road access, and for those who require a special diet.

Added to this basic needs amount is another amount for shelter. The calculation of the shelter benefit takes into account the applicant's actual shelter costs. These include (as applicable) rent, mortgage payments, taxes, insurance premiums, and the cost of heating, electricity, and water/sewage service, including hot water. However, a limit is set on the amount of the shelter benefit paid under the program. This maximum monthly shelter allowance is adjusted upward as the size of the benefit unit increases (as shown in figure 8.2). For this purpose, the size of the benefit unit means the number of people in the family for whom benefits are paid.

In determining the amount that will be paid to the recipient, the general rule is that the shelter benefit is the lesser of the actual shelter expenses and the maximum benefit. However, the maximum benefit is so low that, in practice, it would be rare for the actual cost of shelter to be lower. Consider the benefit amounts shown in figure 8.2 in relation to the current cost of housing in Ontario. Even allowing for variations between communities, there has been a steep and steady increase in the price of owner-occupied housing in recent years, and the cost of rental accommodation, particularly in larger urban centres, is well above the maximum benefit threshold. Therefore, for many recipients of Ontario Works benefits, there will be a significant gap between actual shelter costs and the monthly shelter allowance.

The total benefits payable under the Ontario Works program are calculated by adding the basic benefit, the shelter benefit (the maximum allowance, or the actual shelter cost if it is less than the maximum), and an amount for special diet or northern residence, if applicable.

Figure 8.1   Ontario Works Benefit: Monthly Amount for Basic Needs Other than Shelter, by Number and Age of Dependants in Benefit Unit

			Monthly basic needs amount	
No. of dependants other than a spouse	Dependants 13 years and over	Dependants 0-12 years	Recipient	Recipient and spouse
0	0	0	$211	$420
1	0	1	480	512
	1	0	523	550
2	0	2	571	619
	1	1	615	657
	2	0	653	696

* For each additional dependant, add $147 if the dependant is 13 years of age or over or $109 if the dependant is less than 13 years of age.

Source: O. Reg. 134/98 (effective December 1, 2007).

Figure 8.2   Ontario Works Benefit: Amount of Maximum Monthly Shelter Allowance by Benefit Unit Size

Benefit unit size	Maximum monthly shelter allowance
1	$349
2	549
3	595
4	647
5	697
6 or more	723

Source: O. Reg. 134/98 (effective December 1, 2007).

Example

A family living in Sarnia, Ontario consists of a sole-support mother and three children, aged 14, 12, and 8. None of them requires a special diet. The mother has no income from employment or other sources and qualifies for full benefits under the Ontario Works program. The family's actual shelter costs are $900 a month. The total benefit paid is $1,274 ($572 for the mother and the two older children; $100 for the third child; and $602 for housing). Therefore, after paying the actual cost of housing, the family will be left with $374 to pay for food, clothing, and all other household expenses. It is clear from this example (which is by no means unusual) that where a family has no other source of support, Ontario Works benefits sustain an extremely meagre existence.

The benefits payable are different in certain circumstances—for example, where the recipient lives in a women's shelter or a homeless shelter, or where housing and food expenses are paid through a room-and-board arrangement. Also, the benefits are subject to change over time to reflect the cost of inflation. For accurate information about current benefits, it is advisable to consult the statute and the relevant policy directives.

WEB LINK

For more information about Ontario Works and to access the policy directives, visit the website of the MCSS at www.mcss.gov.on.ca.

Employment Assistance

Because the purpose of Ontario Works is to provide last-resort assistance while recipients of benefits work toward employed self-sufficiency, the program incorporates a number of initiatives designed to support the back-to-work journey. These include

- resource centres where participants can work with counsellors to develop resumés and cover letters;

- advice and coaching in interview skills;

- referrals to basic education and job retraining programs at no cost to the participant (these typically focus on basic and general skills, such as literacy);

EXTRA CREDIT
Working in an Ontario Works Resource Centre

Policy Directive No. 36 describes the skills and training necessary for the staff of an Ontario Works resource centre. Social service workers who would like to work in such a centre should be aware of the following training requirements:

- knowledge of the local labour market and available resources and services to support participants including other income support programs;

- knowledge of community resources;

- ability to accurately link the participant's skills and resources to appropriate employment assistance activity;

- ability to communicate correct information to respond to written and verbal requests;

- ability to communicate with participants, sponsoring organizations, and the public about employment measures, community participation, and employment placement; and

- knowledge of other federal and provincial employment measures.

The delivery agent is responsible for ensuring that staff have the required knowledge and skills. ◇

- the Community Placement program, which places Ontario Works recipients in unpaid positions in community agencies or programs, to assist them in gaining skills, working experience, and confidence;

- the LEAP (Learning, Earning, And Parenting) Program for young parents (aged 16 to 21) who are attending or who wish to return to high school; and

- the Employment Placement program, which identifies employers willing to take on employees who are "less job-ready" and require retraining in order to make the transition from welfare to work.

Ontario Works strives to assist participants in taking the shortest path to re-entry into the job market. This means that even while the participants are retraining, they must be actively searching for work. Participation in job search activities is closely monitored by the program administrators, and failure to participate may be grounds for the discontinuation of benefits (as discussed below).

LEAP PROGRAM

The LEAP Program is compulsory for all teen parents aged 16 and 17 who are recipients of Ontario Works benefits and have not completed high school. It is recommended, but not compulsory, for recipient parents aged 18 to 21 who have not completed high school. LEAP provides supports such as child care and alternative education options to allow teens with dependants to complete their education.

The "learning" portion of LEAP involves education, either at a regular school or at a special facility for teen parents. The "earning" portion involves taking part in activities such as school co-op programs, apprenticeship and job shadowing programs, and summer employment (depending on availability). The "parenting" portion of LEAP refers to participation in a minimum of 35 hours of parenting training.

EARNINGS EXEMPTION

As noted above, an applicant may qualify for Ontario Works benefits even though he receives income from another source, such as employment income or WHSI benefits. In general, every dollar of income received from other sources is subtracted from the benefit amount for which the applicant would otherwise be eligible.

However, to support a participant's efforts at finding gainful employment and becoming independent, modest earnings received from a job found *while on benefits* are counted on a 50 percent basis. Returning to the example considered earlier, suppose that the mother of three living in Sarnia (who is entitled to monthly benefits of $1,274) starts a dog-walking business from which she earns $250 per month. Her Ontario Works benefits will be reduced by $125, leaving her with a benefit level of $1,149 (and a total monthly income, including her business income, of $1,399).

Application Process

Applying for Ontario Works benefits involves a number of steps. Policy Directive No. 4 describes the process in detail and provides a list of the documentation required to support an application. Social service workers often assist clients in applying for Ontario Works benefits and should be thoroughly familiar with this directive.

Critical Perspectives

Is Workfare Failing Families?

Deb Matthews, a London, Ontario MPP, released a report in December 2004 of her review of the Ontario Works program. Her findings suggested that the program was not effectively meeting its goal of returning Ontarians to work, even though the study showed that most recipients of Ontario Works benefits want to return to the workforce.

A key conclusion of the report was that benefit recipients need individualized support in getting retrained and finding work, instead of being required to participate in standardized programs or risk losing benefits. As reported in an MCSS news release,

> Matthews' discussions looked at what kind of supports people on social assistance need to permanently move back into the workforce, and where things are not working currently. Overall, the findings demonstrate that clients need a wider range of individual supports as they transition to employment and that program rules need to be simplified and punitive policies eliminated.
>
> > "The bottom line is that a one-size-fits-all approach to getting people working simply doesn't cut it anymore," said Matthews. "We cannot continue to invest taxpayer dollars in programs and services that don't deliver the kind of results we want to see. It's time we all admit that the system needs to change and we need to find new, innovative ways to helping people on social assistance fulfil their potential."

Source: Ministry of Community and Social Services, *News Release*, December 1, 2004. ◇

FIRST STAGE: TELEPHONE SCREENING

As noted earlier, an application for benefits is made through the municipality where the applicant lives. At the initial contact with the program office (which is usually by telephone), the prospective applicant typically receives information from an intake officer about the program, the application process, and the supporting documents that will be required. He is also pre-screened for possible eligibility. After obtaining the applicant's oral consent to disclose personal information, the intake officer asks a series of questions designed to determine whether eligibility is likely. If the answers indicate that the applicant may be eligible, an in-person interview is scheduled.

If the answers elicited on the telephone indicate that the applicant is not eligible for benefits, the intake officer must communicate this conclusion, with reasons, to the applicant while still on the telephone, and must then mail a written copy of the conclusion to the applicant. Within 10 days of receiving the reasons, the applicant may submit a written objection and demand an appointment to continue the application process through an in-person interview. A different intake officer must conduct the interview.

SECOND STAGE: IN-PERSON INTERVIEW

Once an interview is scheduled, the applicant should begin gathering the documentation needed to support the application (described below). Since this may take some time, emergency assistance is available in appropriate cases, until the application can be decided. A municipality may also arrange emergency shelter and board under Policy Directive No. 10, "Emergency Assistance" (available on the MCSS website).

Applicants can bring a support person, including, if appropriate, a social service worker, to the interview. Policy Directive No. 4 provides as follows:

> Any person, either applying for or in receipt of financial assistance, has the right to be accompanied by an advocate of his/her choice, and must be advised of this right, at the initial contact. This advocate could be a relative, friend or a person from a community group or local legal clinic.

There are a number of components to a second-stage interview. Policy Directive No. 4 describes these as follows:

- an employment information session;

- completion of a participation agreement;

- completion of the rest of the application;

- verification of information gathered at both stages;

- a request for additional information related to the first stage, as appropriate; and

- signing of all forms.

The information session includes communication, by the municipal staff, of the principles of the program. These include a statement that social assistance is a last-resort benefit, that people are better off working and being self-reliant, and that the conditions of assistance require that the applicant pursue activities in support of returning to the workforce.

The intake worker will discuss return-to-work programs and strategies available to the applicant, and together they will make a plan for the applicant to undertake these activities while receiving assistance.

The plan will then be incorporated into a participation agreement. The participation agreement puts the applicant's commitment to specific back-to-work strategies in writing. If at any time while the applicant is receiving benefits he fails to meet the terms of the participation agreement (for example, he stops participating in a community placement), Ontario Works can begin to take steps to withhold benefits.

The second-stage interview must take place within four business days of the initial application. More than one interview may be required, especially if the applicant does not have all the necessary documentation available when he first comes in. Once the entire process is complete, the applicant, if successful, will complete all the necessary forms.

DOCUMENTATION

Numerous documents are required for the application, and gathering them can be onerous for many applicants. Social service workers can help their clients with completing forms and organizing documents.

The applicant should be prepared to complete the following Ontario Works forms provided by the Intake Screening Unit:

- Application for Assistance, Part I: Financial Assistance (Form 0983), to determine the financial circumstances or budgetary needs of the applicant

- Application for Assistance, Part II: Participation Agreement (Form 2845), to determine participation requirements and employment activities for the applicant and all adult members of the benefit unit

- Consent to Disclose and Verify Information (Form 0985)

- Rights and Responsibilities Form (Form 1107)

- Declaration of Support and Maintenance (Form 2212), where applicable

- Application for Temporary Care Assistance (Form 0984), where applicable

The applicant must also bring the following supporting documents to the interview:

- birth verification: birth certificates or passports for the applicant and all other members of the benefit unit ("beneficiaries")

- marital status: divorce or separation documents

- spousal and/or child support: support order or agreement

- immigration status: immigration documents, sponsorship documents, Canadian citizenship card, or certificate

- pension and social assistance income: eligibility for benefits under other programs (for example, EI, WHSI, ODSP, or CPP), with assignment forms where appropriate

- property: copies of deeds and/or mortgages for any property owned by the applicant or beneficiaries

- debts: verification of all debts over $500

- social insurance numbers: identity cards or tax returns

- health cards

- bank account statements

- receivables: details of monies owing to the applicant or beneficiaries and their efforts to recover them

- year and make of vehicles

- funds held in trust

- rental income: payments received from a roomer or boarder (including a family member)

- proof of current income

- accommodation costs: lease/rental agreements (including number of occupants where applicable); verificiation of insurance and condominium fees

WEB LINK

For information on benefits available to Ontario residents, visit Canada Benefits (a website maintained by the federal government) at www.canadabenefits.gc.ca and follow the links for "I am a parent in Ontario."

Disputes over Eligibility

If an applicant goes through the second stage of the process and is then informed, in writing, that she is ineligible for benefits, or is only entitled to a reduced level of benefits, she can request an **internal review** of the decision. While she waits for the review and any subsequent **appeal** to be completed, she can request interim financial assistance; however, if she is eventually found not to be eligible for equivalent program benefits, she will have to repay the full amount of any support received to which she is not entitled.

The internal review process is designed to provide an informal, open, and efficient means of addressing disputes over eligibility, and to reduce the number of times applicants seek recourse to the Social Benefits Tribunal (SBT). Internal reviews are intended to provide the applicant with as much information as possible to help her understand why she has been found ineligible for program support. The policy directives also reinforce the fact that eligibility decisions that go against an applicant may sometimes be reversed, once all of the relevant circumstances have been assessed in the course of a review.

INTERNAL REVIEW

An applicant can request an internal review by submitting a written, signed request (form 2280) to the municipal administrator. The request must be delivered to the program office within 10 calendar days of receipt of written notice of the administrator's decision. In exceptional circumstances, this time period can be extended (see Policy Directive No. 33).

On receiving the request, the administrator decides whether a review is warranted. If he decides that it is, he has 10 days to complete the review and report the results to the applicant. The person conducting the review cannot be the person who made the original eligibility decision and must be of equal rank or senior to the original decision maker. If the administrator chooses not to conduct a review, the applicant has a right to appeal the decision directly to the SBT.

The review process is described in Policy Directive No. 33. The case file and the original decision are examined to determine whether the decision was

- consistent with the Ontario Works legislation, regulations, and policy;

- based on correct application of the legislation, regulations, and/or policy;

- reasonable;

- based on information that was factual and comprehensive;

- based on a correct interpretation of the facts;

- the result of appropriate use of discretionary power; and

- not the result of administrative error.

The person conducting the review must also consider any additional information available at that time. The policy directive notes that internal reviews are an informal process, and that legal representation is not required as a part of that process. However, if the applicant goes on to appeal the review decision, he may wish to engage a legal representative at that stage.

From the perspective of social service workers who may be involved in the administration of the Ontario Works program, the legislation and policy directives establish important internal standards for tracking and documenting reviews. Notably, Policy Directive No. 33 requires program administrators to keep track of certain statistics with respect to reviews and report them to MCSS in accordance with a regular schedule.

To avoid appeals based on a municipality's failure to handle reviews appropriately, municipal staff, particularly officers charged with conducting reviews, should take special care to keep on file all relevant correspondence and other documents (for example, the letter giving notice of the decision). They should also note any oral request for a review; while an oral request must be followed by a written request, in certain circumstances it may permit a time extension. In addition, staff should document the specific procedural safeguards employed, such as ensuring that a different decision maker handles the review.

Municipal staff should also ensure that the review process is consistent with the principles established by the legislation—namely, that it is informal, open, and informative.

APPEAL TO THE SOCIAL BENEFITS TRIBUNAL

If an applicant is not satisfied with the review decision, or if the 10-day time period following the request has elapsed and the administrator has not conducted a review, the applicant can appeal the original eligibility or quantum decision to the SBT. The applicant has 30 days from the date of completion of the internal review (or 40 days from the date of his request for a review that does not take place) to file an appeal. Appeal forms are available from the Ontario Works office or the municipality.

Before the hearing, both parties (the applicant and the administrator) can make **written submissions** to the SBT. The SBT encourages this, because a written submission provides a useful reference to the issues in dispute. In some cases, the SBT can make a ruling based on written submissions alone, without holding a hearing.

If a hearing is scheduled, it is very important that the applicant attend. Failure to do so without a good reason will result in automatic denial of the appeal, and the applicant will not be able to make another SBT appeal for two years.

At the appeal hearing, the onus of proof is on the applicant: that is, it is up to the person seeking benefits to show why he is eligible. In general, the applicant is the first to state his side of the case at the hearing. However, if the applicant has no lawyer, the SBT may ask the Ontario Works administrator to make his presentation first, so that the applicant can see how the process works and understand what questions need to be answered to prove the case.

The timing of hearings varies. The SBT is required to schedule a hearing within 60 days of receiving notice of the appeal, but the actual date of the hearing could be more than 60 days after filing. The policy directives suggest a range of wait times between about 6 weeks and 3 months from the time of filing; however, the current reality is that it may be as much as 8 to 10 months before a hearing is held. This has the unfortunate effect of discouraging some applicants from making an appeal, either because it is too long to wait for a resolution, or because the applicant is worried that he or his family would be required to pay back months of interim assistance if he lost the appeal.

After the hearing, or after the SBT decides to proceed on the basis of written submissions, the SBT has 60 days to issue a written decision to the parties. If the decision orders that the applicant is entitled to benefits, Ontario Works must comply and provide those benefits. If the applicant's appeal is denied, he has a right to request reconsideration by the SBT. (The administrator can also request reconsideration.) The procedures for reconsideration are discussed in Policy Directive No. 34.

After a request for reconsideration is made and addressed by the SBT, if either party is still not satisfied with the result and believes that the SBT has misinterpreted the legislation or regulations in making its decision, that party can appeal the decision to the Ontario Divisional Court. The facts of the case are not reconsidered by the Divisional Court, but only matters of law. A party who chooses to proceed to court will need legal representation.

Monitoring Eligibility and Discontinuation of Benefits

Ontario Works participants are monitored on a regular basis to ensure that they are complying with the terms of their participation agreement. A participant who leaves Ontario and is away for more than seven days without notifying the program office, or who acquires assets or earns income over eligibility thresholds, or who stops complying with program requirements, will become ineligible for benefits.

Participants are required to report any changes in circumstances, such as getting a new job, about once a month. The participation agreement is updated every three months, and the effectiveness of employment assistance activities is reviewed at that time. Sometimes it is more efficient to conduct these reviews upon achievement of an employment assistance milestone, such as completion of a training program. A complete review of the participant's financial situation, called the consolidated

Critical Perspectives

Questioning the Tie Between Employment and Financial Security

The *Ontario Works Act, 1997* is firmly anchored in the philosophy that the key to financial security is employment. And certainly, for many people, it seems to be a reflexive reaction, particularly in moments of frustration, to respond to the plight of the poor by thinking, "Just get a job."

Finding and keeping a job is the explicit goal prescribed by Ontario Works, but it's also more subtly communicated in other statutes, like the *Canada Pension Plan*, that tie future benefits to past contributions from employment.

But is full employment really the cure for poverty? And is full employment even achievable in our society?

A book by economist Jeremy Rifkin, *The End of Work: The Decline of the Global Labor Force and the Dawn of the Post-Market Era*, questions our reliance on the market's ability to sustain our continued employment. Rifkin explains that technological advances have led to a world in which less and less labour is required to produce the resources and goods society needs. He expects that this trend will lead to the death of the blue-collar working class, a phenomenon that is already beginning to show in the enormous disparity in wages between well-paid jobs—which are typically tied in some way to technology—and poorly paid work, which is vulnerable to phasing out. Rifkin also points out that, because of the rise in temporary and part-time work relative to full-time employment, having a job no longer means the same thing as making a living, because the pay is often insufficient to meet the worker's basic needs.

Other economists have also long believed that full employment is an unrealistic expectation for a modern society. In the 1950s, New Zealand's A.W. Phillips developed a theory (known as the Phillips Curve) that suggests that as employment increases, so does inflation, lowering the overall standard of living in a society. While this theory has been eclipsed by more sophisticated models, most economists still believe that full employment is neither achievable nor sustainable, a view that clearly clashes with social programs that prescribe employment as the surefire answer to poverty.

But what's the alternative? Rifkin suggests that the most likely consequences of the death of work will be increasing crime and political instability, *unless* a concerted effort is made to support people pushed out of the world of employment in their efforts to contribute in other ways. He suggests that people for whom there is no work could devote

their time instead to "rebuilding communities" through the volunteer sector.

Rifkin describes the volunteer sector as "the realm in which fiduciary arrangements give way to community bonds, and where the giving of one's time to others takes the place of artificially-imposed market relationships based on selling oneself and one's services to others." He defines the volunteer sector broadly to include, for example, people who contribute to their community through the arts, through religion, and through advocacy. Rifkin maintains that participation in this sector could heal the psychological damage wrought by the elimination of the working class, by offering "a place where personal relationships can be nurtured, status can be achieved, and a sense of community can be created."

The challenge, of course, is in figuring out how to put supper on the table for this "third sector" (distinguished from the public and private sectors). Because volunteers and charitable organizations are already forced to pick up the slack when governments cut back their social spending, Rifkin urges governments to forge a new alliance with this sector. He notes that the US charitable sector has considerable potential economic clout, with assets that exceed the gross national product of many nations. Together, governments and the third sector may be able to rebuild the social economy, so that those who serve each other can have access to the resources to meet their own needs.

How would this work? One example suggested by Rifkin involves the concept of a "shadow wage"—a tax deduction, offered by the government to individuals, for every hour of time donated to recognized charitable organizations. Offering this kind of incentive to do unpaid work would theoretically support people in their choice to reduce their working hours (which creates more jobs) in order to free up time for volunteer work. The result would be a society in which the limited amount of paid work would be spread more equitably across the population, with many more people contributing to the third sector and reaping benefits from it, which, in turn, would reduce their dependence on employment.

Although putting theories like Rifkin's into practice is challenging, it's worth keeping them in mind while we take a critical look at the employment-centric philosophies that underlie programs like Ontario Works. ◇

verification process (CVP), is performed once a year. A CVP review consists of an examination of the budgetary needs of the recipient and benefit unit, including any changes in family size, accommodation arrangements, income sources, asset levels, residence in or absences from Ontario, and any other factors that affect eligibility.

If a recipient of benefits fails to comply with Ontario Works requirements (for example, if he does not participate in return-to-work activities, or drops out of school), the terms of the participation agreement can sometimes be renegotiated to take extenuating circumstances into account. If the participant fails to comply with the renegotiated participation agreement, he becomes ineligible for the benefits originally awarded, and any future benefits are reduced or cancelled. Reduction or cancellation of benefits may be applied either to the primary recipient alone, or to other members of the benefit unit as well. Policy Directive No. 43 provides guidelines for making a determination that a participant is not complying.

When an Ontario Works administrator determines that a participant is no longer eligible for benefits because of non-compliance, the participant's benefits may be suspended for three months for a first occurrence and six months for a subsequent occurrence. The reason for the non-compliance is important: circumstances beyond the person's control, such as illness, child-care responsibilities, addiction, mental health, homelessness, and other personal circumstances, are considered before making a decision to cancel benefits. The consequences of applying this penalty are potentially severe—there is a real possibility that the family will be unable to meet their basic needs if they cannot find other income through employment or personal supports. What is demanded of participants is a reasonable effort, and those who are unable to achieve self-sufficiency should not be cut off from benefits.

It is possible for an adult's benefits to be cancelled while those of a dependant child are continued, because children under 16 are not themselves subject to participation requirements.

If a participant objects to a decision to suspend benefits, he can request an internal review and/or appeal to the SBT, as described above.

ONTARIO DISABILITY SUPPORT PROGRAM

ODSP was created by the *Ontario Disability Support Program Act, 1997*. It is designed to provide income assistance to adult Ontario residents who, because of long-term health problems or disabilities, are unable to earn enough income from employment to cover their basic living needs. The program is both regulated and administered by MCSS (in contrast to Ontario Works, for which program delivery has been delegated to municipalities).

Eligibility

In order to qualify for ODSP benefits, a person must

- be 18 or older and an Ontario resident;

- meet the threshold for financial need; and

- suffer from a substantial physical or mental impairment that is either continuous or recurrent and expected to last for a year or more.

Benefits and Employment Assistance

The level of benefits available under ODSP varies with the recipient's family circumstances. Additional health benefits, such as drug subsidies, are also available (see chapter 7).

Ontario Disability Support Program Act, 1997

SO 1997, c. 25, Sch. B

Objective: To provide last resort minimum income to disabled people and their families, to cover basic needs after all other resources are exhausted, and to provide employment supports to those who are employable.

Target Population: Disabled people whose income is insufficient to meet their own and their families' daily needs (addictions are not considered disabilities under this Act).

Program Administration: The cost of the Ontario Disability Support Program is shared by the federal government and it is administered by Ontario's Ministry of Community and Social Services.

Administrative Tribunal: The first step when disputing a finding of ineligibility is to seek an internal review. If this is unsuccessful, the case may be heard by the Social Benefits Tribunal.

Summary: The Ontario Disability Support Program provides a minimum income to cover basic needs for disabled people who are unable to provide for themselves. It also offers employment supports, such as special equipment, child care, and transportation, to facilitate employment for those recipients who are able to work. ◇

While some benefit recipients will be completely unable to work owing to their disabilities, others may be able to do certain kinds of work, especially if job modifications or **accommodations** are made for them. ODSP provides employment assistance services designed to support participants' efforts to enter the workforce.

Unlike the Ontario Works program, the employment program for disabled clients under ODSP is voluntary; there is no obligation for the recipient of benefits to achieve self-sufficiency. However, able-bodied spouses and adult dependants in the same household are required to participate in employment activities through Ontario Works.

While participation in employment assistance services is voluntary, reporting on status is compulsory. Recipients of benefits are required to report once a month on their current status, advising of any changes in employment, home address, accommodation, income, and financial situation.

Recipients are encouraged to earn income if they are able to do so. Income earned is deducted from the benefits otherwise provided on a 50 percent basis; however, the calculation of the deduction takes into account certain expenses related to employment. Specifically, the recipient may claim the cost of child care up to $600 per month per child for unlicensed care, and the full amount for licensed care, and up to $300 per month for disability-related equipment or services needed for work. If the calculation of the deduction leaves the recipient with a net income below the threshold for eligibility, she will receive the full amount of the monthly benefit. She may also be entitled to a separate benefit, up to $100 a month, to assist with work-related transportation or clothing expenses. The calculation of the benefit is illustrated in the following example:

Example

Assume that, in a particular month, a disabled person has

employment income of $1,500,
child-care costs of $500 at a licensed centre,
personal assistance expenses of $400, and
transportation costs of $90.

The full $500 of child-care costs and $300 of the disability-related personal assistance costs are first deducted from the employment income, leaving a balance of $700. Fifty percent of this amount is deducted from the full amount of the employment income ($1,500 – $350), leaving $1,150 of employment income. Since this is below the eligibility threshold, the recipient will receive her full disability benefit and an additional $90 for transportation costs.

In the spring of 2006, the Ontario government announced plans to enhance the provision of employment assistance services to the disabled, including ODSP participants. The planned improvements include, for example, the continuation of health benefits for people who, through employment, have become ineligible for financial assistance but do not yet have employer-sponsored health benefits.

ODSP also offers a "community start-up and maintenance benefit" (CSUMB), a one-time payment, to assist ODSP recipients with a move, or to preserve existing housing. This benefit can be used to pay expenses associated with moving out of an institution, moving out of a home where the recipient is at risk of abuse, moving to accept a job, or moving as a result of eviction for non-payment of rent or utilities. The payment can also be used to pay arrears of rent and prevent an eviction, if necessary. The CSUMB benefit can generally only be claimed once in a 24-month period.

Young disabled people under the age of 18 may also be eligible for benefits under the Assistance for Children with Severe Disabilities Program, also administered by the Ministry of Children and Youth Services.

> **WEB LINK**
>
> For more information about Ontario's support programs for the disabled, visit the MCSS website at www.css.gov.on.ca. For information on other government-funded benefits available to Ontario residents with disabilities, visit Canada Benefits at www.canadabenefits.gc.ca and follow the links for "I am a person with a disability in Ontario." For information about the Assistance for Children with Severe Disabilities Program, visit the Ministry of Children and Youth Services at www.children.gov.on.ca.

Application Process

Applicants for ODSP benefits follow a procedure that is similar to, though typically slightly less formal than, the Ontario Works application procedure. The initial contact and screening are usually conducted by telephone, and if the applicant appears to qualify, he is invited to schedule an appointment for a full screening at an ODSP office. As under the Ontario Works program, there are upper limits on the assets and income that an applicant may have in order to qualify for benefits. Income from other adults in the household, such as a spouse, may reduce benefits.

If the applicant qualifies on the basis of financial need, he will receive a "disability determination package," consisting of several forms, which must be completed and returned to the Disability Adjudication Unit (DAU) within 90 days of the date of issue. The package includes a "Health Status Report and Activities of Daily Living Index," which describes the applicant's health, capabilities, skills, and limitations, and must be completed by a medical professional. There is a second form authorizing the release of medical information, and a third, discretionary (optional) form in which the applicant is asked to describe what it is like to live with his disability. On receipt of the completed forms, the DAU determines whether the applicant is eligible for program benefits. If the applicant fails to meet the 90-day deadline for submitting the package, he will be found ineligible. A one-time request for an extension is permitted.

Disputes over Eligibility

An applicant who is found to be ineligible can request an internal review of the decision. If the basis for the finding is the applicant's financial standing, the request for the review is directed to the local ODSP office. If the applicant is found to be ineligible on the basis of his disability status, the request is directed to the DAU.

As in the case with the Ontario Works program, an applicant who disagrees with the outcome of an internal review can appeal the decision to the Social Benefits Tribunal.

FEDERAL INCOME ASSISTANCE PROGRAMS FOR OLDER CANADIANS

Many people rely on government-funded programs to support an acceptable standard of living after they reach retirement age. There is a trend among Canadian employers to eliminate once-common pension plans for employees. Sometimes these plans are replaced with matched or partially matched contribution savings plans and RRSPs, but in many cases, employers make no provision at all for employees' post-retirement financial needs—apart from their obligation to match employee contributions to the Canada Pension Plan (discussed below). CPP is just one component of the federal system of income assistance for older Canadians; the other programs—Old Age Security (OAS), the Guaranteed Income Supplement (GIS), and the Allowance—are discussed in a later section.

Canada Pension Plan

CPP is a federal government-run savings plan created under and governed by federal legislation, the *Canada Pension Plan*. It is designed to provide seniors who have worked in their lifetime with a basic income upon retirement. Eligibility for pension benefits and payments to recipients under the plan are administered by Social Development Canada (SDC).

Throughout their working years, individuals make contributions to the plan, either through paycheque deductions or, if self-employed, through an annual payment. Employers also contribute by matching the payments made by employees. The government collects and invests the money, to fund distributions from the plan to participants during their retirement years.

WEB LINK

Information about the Canada Pension Plan is available on the SDC website at www.sdc.gc.ca.

CONTRIBUTIONS

Employees earning salary or wages above a minimum threshold must make CPP contributions. The amount of the contribution is calculated as a percentage of income earned (up to a maximum income threshold), and is deducted by the employer from

Canada Pension Plan

RSC 1985, c. C-8

Objective: To establish a comprehensive program of old age pensions and supplementary benefits in Canada payable to contributors.

Target Population: Retired workers in Canada.

Program Administration: The Canada Pension Plan is a federal program managed by Human Resources and Social Development Canada.

Administrative Tribunal: The Office of the Commissioner of Review Tribunals hears appeals from Reconsideration decisions made by Social Development Canada about Canada Pension Plan or Old Age Security benefits.

Summary: The Canada Pension Plan is a government-run savings program designed to provide seniors who have worked in their lifetimes with a basic income upon retirement. While participants work they make contributions to the plan, either through paycheque deductions, or in the case of the self-employed, through an annual payment. Employers also contribute by matching the payments made by employees. ◇

the employee's pay. These employee contributions are matched dollar-for-dollar by the employer.

Self-employed people must pay both the employee and employer portions.

BENEFITS

There are three kinds of benefits available through CPP:

- retirement benefits: a monthly benefit payable to the retired person until death;

- survivor benefits: benefits payable after the pension holder's death to his estate, spouse, or dependent children; and

- disability benefits: benefits payable to someone who once worked but can work no longer because of a disability.

Recipients do not receive CPP benefits automatically, but must apply. To ensure that pension benefits are received as soon as the pensioner becomes eligible, it is wise to apply at least six months before the planned retirement date. Individuals who are eligible for survivor benefits and disability benefits also should apply at the earliest opportunity.

Retirement Benefits

The retirement benefits payable under the plan are modest: they are designed to replace about 25 percent of the earnings upon which the contributions were based. As a result, CPP alone will not generally sustain the lifestyle that the pensioner enjoyed while working.

Anyone who has made a valid contribution to CPP is eligible for CPP benefits upon reaching age 65, whether or not living in Canada at that time. People aged 60 to 64 are sometimes eligible to receive benefits if they stop working or their income drops considerably, but eligibility for early retirement benefits depends upon compliance with minimum contribution requirements.

The level of benefits is generally based on the individual's earnings and contributions to the plan and his age at retirement. Benefits are indexed to reflect changes in the cost of living over the duration of the pension.

Survivor Benefits

Survivor benefits are benefits paid after a pensioner's death to her estate, or to a surviving spouse and/or dependent children. Additionally, a one-time death benefit is payable when a pensioner dies, provided that the pensioner had paid into the plan for at least three years. This benefit is paid either to the person's estate, or to the person who is handling the funeral expenses, or to the pensioner's spouse or children (in that order). The amount of the death benefit is based on the value of the pension, and is equal to six months of benefits to a maximum of $2,500.

CPP spousal survivor benefits are payable to the pensioner's legal spouse or common-law partner at the time of death. A spouse or partner can receive survivor benefits in addition to his or her own CPP pension. However, the amount of survivor benefits may be reduced where the survivor is already receiving benefits. In 2002-3, the average survivor benefit paid out was $280.49 per month. The calculation of survivor benefits is complex. A social service worker with a client who is eligible for the survivor benefit may need to assist the client in providing information to SDC in order to access the benefit.

Children's benefits are payable to children who are either under 18 when their parent becomes disabled or dies, or between 18 and 25 and enrolled in a full-time program of study at a university or college. Children's benefits are calculated at a flat rate and are currently approximately $200 per month.

Disability Benefits

People who contribute to CPP may be eligible for disability benefits if they have a disability that prevents them from working regularly. The disability must be long-term or permanent, or likely to result in death. Those who are eligible for other income support programs, such as ODSP, are not eligible for a CPP disability benefit.

SDC reviews the health and work status of recipients periodically, to ensure continued eligibility.

DISPUTES OVER ELIGIBILITY OR BENEFITS

If a pensioner disagrees with a CPP decision, such as a decision that he is not eligible for disability benefits, he may request reconsideration within 90 days. A request for reconsideration is made to Human Resources and Social Development Canada (HRSDC) and must be in writing, stating why the applicant disagrees with the decision. When the request is received, a ministry officer reconsiders the decision and either affirms it or makes a new decision.

If the pensioner still disagrees, he has another 90 days to submit a written request for an appeal to the Office of the Commissioner of Review Tribunals (OCRT). This office creates three-person independent panels (the members do not work for HRSDC) who review decisions made by ministry staff. The OCRT has a detailed brochure, available in paper or electronic form, that helps to explain the process.

Pensioners who make an appeal to the OCRT can represent themselves, or can be represented by a lawyer or any other person (such as a family member, friend, or member of a community organization). A social service worker could potentially act as an advocate for a client before an OCRT panel.

If either the pensioner or HRSDC disagrees with the outcome of an appeal to the OCRT, a further appeal may be available to the Pension Appeals Board. These appeals are heard by a panel of judges (usually three judges) from either a provincial court or the Federal Court. For this level of appeal, there is a formal hearing and the parties should be represented by lawyers.

Old Age Security, Guaranteed Income Supplement, and the Allowance

OLD AGE SECURITY

SDC describes OAS as the cornerstone of Canada's income support system for seniors. This is because, (in contrast to CPP) a person does not need to have contributed to the system in order to receive a benefit.

The basic qualification for OAS is residence in Canada for at least 10 years at any time between the ages of 18 and 65. People who have lived in Canada for at least 20 years in this period can qualify to receive OAS while living outside Canada. The amount of OAS benefits is dependent on length of residency in Canada. A person who has lived in Canada for 40 years between the ages of 18 and 65 is eligible for the maximum benefit level, while people who have lived here for less than 40 years receive a smaller pension based on length of residency. (Some people born before 1952 who have lived in Canada for less than 40 years are entitled to the maximum.)

The full OAS pension in 2007 is approximately $500 per month. Every three months, the pension amounts are reviewed and adjusted to the cost of living, if appropriate. The pension may be reduced or eliminated for people with a substantial annual income; however, SDC reports that only about 5 percent of Canadian seniors have their OAS reduced for this reason.

GUARANTEED INCOME SUPPLEMENT

GIS is a pension benefit paid in addition to OAS in order to assure a minimum standard of living for low-income seniors. Seniors with less than about $14,000 in annual income from other sources (such as CPP, a private pension, or an RRSP) may apply for GIS.

The amount of the benefit varies, with a monthly maximum in 2007 of about $400-600 and a monthly average payment of about $250-400 per pensioner, depending upon spousal status and other factors. The SDC has benefit calculation tables available on its website, which can be accessed in order to estimate the amount for which a pensioner might be eligible.

THE ALLOWANCE

Another benefit available to some seniors is called the Allowance. This benefit is designed to provide income to low-income people aged 60 to 64 (that is, those who are not yet eligible to receive OAS) who have a spouse or partner who is eligible for OAS/GIS. This benefit takes into account the situation where an older couple's

WEB LINK

For more information about review tribunals and how to make an appeal, and to download forms, visit the OCRT at www.ocrt-bctr.gc.ca. For more information about the Pension Appeals Board, visit the PAB at www.pab-cap.gc.ca.

Old Age Security Act

RSC 1985, c. O-9

Objective: To provide security in old age.

Target Population: Seniors who have lived in Canada for at least 10 years.

Program Administration: Human Resources and Social Development Canada administers Old Age Security, the Guaranteed Income Supplement, and the Allowance.

Administrative Tribunal: The Office of the Commissioner of Review Tribunals hears appeals from Reconsideration decisions made by Human Resources and Social Development Canada about the Canada Pension Plan or Old Age Security benefits.

Summary: Unlike the Canada Pension Plan, a person does not need to have contributed to the system to receive Old Age Security. The amount of benefits is dependent on how long the person lived in Canada. Low-income seniors may also be eligible for the Guaranteed Income Supplement, and if they are between the ages of 60 and 64, they may be eligible for the Allowance. ◇

WEB LINK

For more information on OAS, GIS, and the Allowance, visit the website of Service Canada at www.servicecanada.gc.ca.

income is low after the retirement of at least one of them, but only one is old enough to access OAS/GIS. If the spouse of a person who is eligible for the Allowance dies, the benefit is increased. This increased benefit is called the Allowance for the survivor.

OAS, GIS, and Allowance decisions can be reconsidered and appealed through a process that is similar to that used for reviewing CPP decisions—that is, by internal reconsideration, followed by an appeal to the OCRT.

PROMOTING ACCESS TO INCOME SUPPORT

Social service workers may encounter clients in financial need in a variety of ways. For example:

- Clients who have recently become disabled may rely on social service workers through health-care support agencies.

- Clients may encounter social service workers at shelters for abused women and children, where they may be fleeing a person who supported them financially.

- Clients may be in financial need as a result of a life crisis (job loss, divorce, death of parents, fire, natural disasters, etc.).

- Clients may be elderly people in various settings, such as nursing homes, who have used up their savings.

In general, Canadians are reasonably well informed about the existence of the "social safety net" and the fact that there are benefits available to them. In many cases, a social service worker may be asked to help clients inquire about the details of the various programs—how to apply, how to appeal a decision, etc. Social service workers can be of particular assistance in helping clients to fill out forms and track down supporting documents.

Social service workers can also play an important role in helping clients to access emergency assistance—for example, temporary lodging in a shelter, interim Ontario Works benefits, or groceries from a food bank. By maintaining a thorough knowledge of the emergency services available in your community, you can buy time for a client while he applies for benefits and awaits the processing of his application.

If there are no emergency services or inadequate emergency services available in the community, social service workers can have an important role in advocating for the development and funding of these services. Clients can even be encouraged to participate in this process (by participating in a clothing/toy exchange, a babysitting co-op, or a ride-sharing program, for example).

In some cases, social service workers will encounter clients who face unusual barriers to accessing income support. For example:

- *Clients who cannot legally work in Canada.* Clients whose immigration status excludes them from access to legal jobs in Canada are also not eligible to participate in programs such as Ontario Works, or to contribute to the Canada Pension Plan. For these clients, you may need to arrange emergency shelter and living support via charitable organizations designed to support refugee claimants or those whose immigration status is unsettled. Once emergency assistance is in place, the first step is to assist the client in obtaining official refugee or landed immigrant status so that he can work in Canada.

- *Clients with communication/comprehension problems.* Some clients may have trouble accessing benefits because of a communication problem. Clients who face a language barrier may need translation services. Clients with a cognitive impairment may need help arranging for a substitute decision maker (an attorney for personal care or other appointee).

- *Clients with interpersonal/family problems.* Some clients may come from families in crisis, where there is abuse or neglect. These clients may be adults (for example, a battered woman who is part of her husband's Ontario Works benefit unit but who is having her benefits withheld by him), or children (children who are living in poverty but whose parents have not applied for benefits or have had benefits cut off because of lack of compliance with program requirements). These clients may need other kinds of help—for example, assistance leaving the family home and moving into a shelter, or a referral to a children's aid society—before effective steps can be taken to support their access to social benefits.

In these special cases, social service workers will need to draw on their experience with other aspects of client service—first, in eliminating barriers to income assistance; and then, once barriers are overcome, in supporting clients in accessing that assistance. Note that overcoming barriers may require the social service worker to refer a client to organizations and services outside the local community.

As a social service worker, you will often be expected to act as an advocate for your clients. This may mean supporting them in their attempts to access benefits even after a decision has gone against them. For this reason, you will need to have a basic understanding of the processes available to challenge administrative decisions (mentioned throughout this chapter). You will also need to know how to assist a client in obtaining legal assistance where legal representation is necessary to protect or establish an entitlement to benefits.

KEY TERMS

accommodation	internal review	subsistence needs
appeal	needs- and means-tested	survivor benefit
entitlement	subsidy	written submissions

REFERENCES

Canada Pension Plan, RSC 1985, c. C-8.

Old Age Security Act, RSC 1985, c. O-9.

Ontario Disability Support Program Act, 1997, SO 1997, c. 25, Sch. B.

Ontario, Ministry of Community and Social Services, *News Release*, December 1, 2004.

Ontario Works Act, 1997, SO 1997, c. 25, Sch. A.

Ontario Works Policy Directive No. 4, Application Process.

Ontario Works Policy Directive No. 29, Calculating Assistance.

Ontario Works Policy Directive No. 33, Notice and Internal Review Process.

Ontario Works Policy Directive No. 34, Appeal Process.

Ontario Works Policy Directive No. 43, Reviewing Eligibility.

Rifkin, Jeremy, *The End of Work: The Decline of the Global Labor Force and the Dawn of the Post-Market Era* (New York: Tarcher/Putnam, 1995).

REVIEW QUESTIONS

1. List at least two federal income assistance programs and two Ontario income assistance programs.

2. Why is the Ontario Works program described as an income maintenance program "of last resort"?

3. What does the name of the Ontario Works program mean, and what values does it reflect?

4. Who funds Ontario Works? Who administers it?

5. What happens if a person who is receiving Ontario Works benefits begins receiving an income, but one that is not enough to live on (for example, income from a low-paying part-time job)?

6. Can children receive Ontario Works benefits? What about teens living on their own?

7. What is the purpose of the participation agreement that an Ontario Works recipient must sign before he can receive benefits?

8. If an Ontario Works recipient has his benefits cut off (for example, for failing to meet the terms of his participation agreement) and he wishes to challenge the decision to suspend or terminate his benefits, what must he do?

9. Assume that you work in Peterborough, Ontario, in a group home for adults with disabilities. One of your residents (a recipient of benefits under the Ontario Disability Support Program) has been making a great deal of progress in developing his employment and independent living skills, and has been offered a job in Toronto. The resident would like to move to accept the job, but the wheelchair-accessible apartment he has located in Toronto requires that he pay first and last months' rent. He can't afford it, but taking the job will help his financial situation in the long term. What would you do to help him?

10. To which office should a disabled person apply to request a review of a decision that she is ineligible to receive ODSP benefits on the basis of financial need? What if benefits are denied because she is deemed not to meet the definition of "disabled"?

11. Who is eligible to receive retirement benefits under the Canada Pension Plan?

12. Who is eligible for Old Age Security?

13. Who is eligible for the Guaranteed Income Supplement? Who is entitled to receive the Allowance?

14. List some of the barriers that can prevent certain individuals from accessing income maintenance programs. How can you help clients who face these barriers?

DISCUSSION QUESTION

You are a social service worker in a shelter for homeless youth. One of your functions is to provide information to shelter visitors about the availability of income assistance, and to help interested visitors to access that assistance.

One of your regular customers is 22-year-old Terry. Terry is homeless because he has had his Ontario Works benefits suspended. This is his second suspension due to non-compliance with the program requirements. While you have helped Terry in various ways (arranged for transportation to an Ontario Works employment resource centre, helped him find an apartment nearer work—from which he was later evicted), he simply doesn't seem capable of making a sustained effort to look for work.

Terry was once examined by a psychiatrist and was found not to have a mental illness. (He had sought the assessment in the course of applying for ODSP benefits, for which he was found ineligible.) However, you know that he has serious problems with initiative, concentration, and taking responsibility for himself. You suspect that Terry may suffer from fetal alcohol syndrome, and that he should be receiving ODSP benefits. He lacks the initiative or the organizational skills to make another application for those benefits. What can, and what should, you do to help Terry?

PART IV

The Criminal Justice System

CHAPTER 9

The Criminal Justice System

CHAPTER OBJECTIVES

After reading this chapter, you should be able to:

- Identify the main statute in Canadian criminal law and other criminal and quasi-criminal statutes (federal and provincial).

- Understand the concepts of *actus reus* (act or conduct) and *mens rea* (intent).

- Understand the differences between summary conviction, indictable, and hybrid offences, and the trial options available for each.

- Understand the general purpose, objectives, and principles of sentencing.

- Explain what is meant by aggravating and mitigating circumstances and list some examples of each.

- Identify different kinds of sentences and describe the main differences among them.

INTRODUCTION

This chapter is intended to serve as a broad and basic overview of the general principles of criminal law. Criminal law comprises both substantive law (what constitutes a crime) and procedural law and evidence (the process for bringing an accused to justice).

Social service workers perform several important roles in the criminal justice system. For example, they may work with youth in programs designed as an alternative to traditional criminal procedure. (The criminal law with respect to young offenders is discussed in chapter 11.) They may work in the corrections system, within prisons, or in community support programs for convicts, discussed in chapter 10. More commonly, social service workers will find that many of their clients are in some way involved with the criminal justice system, either as victims or as offenders. Working with clients who are dealing with issues such as drug abuse, domestic violence, homelessness, gambling, or prostitution requires some basic knowledge of the legal environment affecting those clients.

Regardless of the work setting and the clientele, it is useful for a social service worker to have a general understanding of the criminal justice system. This chapter describes how criminal justice is administered; how the rights of individuals are protected in dealing with the police and the courts; and how convicted criminals are punished, rehabilitated (where possible), and prepared for a new start. An overview of criminal court procedure is presented in chapter 13. The objective in this text is to provide an introduction to the criminal justice system. You can find a more detailed discussion of this area of the law in Rock and Hoag, *Foundations of Criminal and Civil Law in Canada*, 2nd ed. (2006).

CRIMINAL LAW AND THE CONSTITUTIONAL DIVISION OF POWERS

As discussed in chapter 2, Canada's constitution divides the power to make laws between the federal and provincial governments. The federal government has jurisdiction over the creation of criminal law, while the provinces have jurisdiction over its administration and enforcement. All criminal laws are enacted by the Parliament of Canada and codified in a small body of federal statutes. The best-known of these statutes and the one of broadest application is the *Criminal Code*. The Code

- defines a wide range of offences,
- sets the rules of procedure,
- establishes the penalties that may apply to each specific offence, and
- provides guidelines for sentencing.

The provincial courts administer the criminal procedure according to the rules contained in the Code.

In addition to the *Criminal Code*, there are several federal criminal-law statutes that govern subject areas for which the federal government has a discrete enforcement mission, strategy, scheme, or philosophy. Examples of such subject-specific statutes

---

LEGISLATIVE SHORTCUT

Criminal Code
RSC 1985, c. C-46

Objective: To make certain acts illegal and punishable by the state and to provide a fair procedure for trying individuals accused of crimes.

Target Population: All residents of Canada who engage in crimes or are victims of crimes.

Program Administration: The police enforce the laws and the provincial attorneys general prosecute those accused of crimes.

Administrative Tribunal: Not applicable—criminal matters are heard by courts.

Summary: The *Criminal Code* includes many different substantive offences, such as theft, assault, murder and fraud, and provides for a range of sentences appropriate for each offence. The Code also outlines the procedure for a fair trial, emphasizing that the accused is innocent until proven guilty beyond a reasonable doubt. ◇

include the *Controlled Drugs and Substances Act* and the *Crimes Against Humanity and War Crimes Act.*

Legislatures of both levels of government can create laws that impose penalties for certain acts or forms of behaviour that are considered illegal, but not criminal (provided that the subject matter of the statute falls within the government's jurisdiction). In other words, illegality is not synonymous with criminality. This distinction makes practical sense. For example, the licensing of pets is typically regulated by municipalities and there is currently a bylaw in the Durham region that prohibits cat owners from allowing their cats to roam free outside. Since roaming cats are considered to be a nuisance, rather than a safety and security risk, it wouldn't be appropriate to bring the full range of criminal justice system procedures and penalties to bear on a roaming-cat owner. As a result, letting a cat out in that region is illegal but not criminal, and the penalty is minor: the owner (if found) must pay a small fine.

Illegal (or "quasi-criminal") offences are contained in a very wide range of provincial statutes and municipal bylaws. At the provincial level, these statutes are designed to support the enforcement of activities that fall within provincial responsibility under the constitution. An example is Ontario's *Highway Traffic Act.*

FIRST NATIONS AND THE CRIMINAL JUSTICE SYSTEM

Canada's Aboriginal, or First Nations, peoples have a complicated constitutional relationship with the federal and provincial governments. As descendants of the original occupants of Canada, predating the arrival of Europeans, Aboriginals have traditionally characterized their relationship with government as that of two independent nations engaged in negotiating the details of their coexistence in this land. In the last half-century, First Nations have successfully negotiated jurisdiction over a number of aspects of government formerly under federal or provincial authority; for example, many First Nations communities now run their own schools, police forces, and other services.

Many people believe that Aboriginals have the right to self-government and that this includes the right to administer criminal justice within their own communities. The relationship between members of the First Nations and the Canadian justice system has always been fairly rocky. Statistics continue to demonstrate that Aboriginals are overrepresented in the prison population (individuals charged, convicted, and imprisoned for crimes). This means that the percentage of Aboriginal convicts or inmates in Canada's prisons is higher than one would expect on the basis of the percentage of Aboriginal people in our society as a whole. The reasons for this overrepresentation are complex. Many commentators suggest that the poverty and isolation resulting from the marginalization of Aboriginal people have led to a higher crime rate. In addition, systemic discrimination and unfairness in the treatment of Aboriginal people within the justice system results in more Aboriginal people being charged, convicted, and incarcerated compared to non-Aboriginals engaging in the same conduct.

But these factors aside, many commentators suggest that the Canadian justice system, in theory and in structure, is not compatible with Aboriginal cultural ideas about justice. New initiatives designed to remedy problems that Aboriginals face within the justice system have tended to focus on creating alternative approaches to justice that better reflect the cultural values of First Nations peoples.

For example, section 718.2(e) of the *Criminal Code* requires judges, when sentencing Aboriginal offenders, to give particular consideration to "all available sanctions other than imprisonment that are reasonable in the circumstances." **Restorative justice** as a sentencing principle reflects important Aboriginal cultural values: rather than seeking to punish the offender, it focuses on making **reparation** to the victim and to the community in general, for the purposes of healing, rehabilitation, and reconciliation.

In some Aboriginal communities, the principle of restorative justice is applied through the use of a **sentencing circle**, a process that involves an open dialogue in a public forum between the offender, the victim, and other members of the community. One of the key purposes of a sentencing circle is to reinforce the expectation that the offender will assume responsibility for his actions within the community as a condition of receiving its support.

Social service workers who serve Aboriginal clients may be involved in developing or administering alternatives to the traditional criminal procedure that better

Critical Perspectives
Sentencing Circles and Violent Crimes

The role of sentencing circles in the sentencing decisions of the courts can be controversial when the offender has committed a violent crime. Consider the following cases involving Aboriginal offenders.

A Newfoundland court found the accused guilty of a brutal sexual assault and sentenced him to two years' house arrest. This sentence had been recommended by the Innu community sentencing circle. The prosecutor appealed the sentence, arguing that a six-year jail term was more appropriate in this case: the assailant was a repeat violent offender with 16 previous convictions for assault against the same victim.

The Newfoundland Court of Appeal agreed that the offence was serious enough to warrant a prison term and acknowledged concerns that the victim had been pressured by family members to agree to the sentencing circle; nevertheless, the court upheld the sentence.

In an Alberta case, the 18-year-old offender had attacked a 55-year-old man while he was in his truck in a campground. The man was struck with a wrench, resulting in memory loss, visual impairment, loss of balance, loss of intellectual skills, and paralysis to the left side of his body.

After a sentencing circle, the trial judge imposed a suspended sentence with two years' probation, counselling, and 50 hours' community service. The prosecution appealed the sentence. The Alberta Court of Appeal agreed that a prison term was appropriate for such a violent offence and noted that the disabled victim was not supported or represented at the sentencing circle; nevertheless, the court upheld the sentence.

In deciding these cases, the appeal courts raised important questions about process and fairness. Does the community have a stake, and is it prepared to play a role? Does the victim agree to participate? Is there a power imbalance between the victim and the offender? The courts also raised concerns about lenient sentences for violent crimes. However, both courts were reluctant to impose rigid ground rules for sentencing circle procedures and preferred a flexible approach.

Sources: *R. v. J.J.*, 2004 NCCA 81 (CanLII), 192 CCC (3d) 30; *R. v. B.L.*, 2002 ABCA 44 (CanLII), 163 CCC (3d) 404. ◇

serve the interests of Aboriginal people, or in advocating for the development of such alternatives.

THE BASICS OF OFFENCES: ELEMENTS OF AN OFFENCE AND DEFENCES

Elements of an Offence

The *Criminal Code* sets out in every offence provision the specific elements of the **offence** that must exist in order for a **suspect** to be charged with a crime. For the **accused** to be found guilty, the charge must be proven in court through oral **testimony** or **physical evidence**, or both.

The **elements of an offence**, or its substantive part, fall into two categories: the actions or omissions that constitute the offence (the objective component) and any required mental state, such as intent, recklessness, or negligence (the subjective component). These are known respectively as the *actus reus*, the physical act or omission involved in committing the offence, and the *mens rea*, the state of mind or the level of intent attributed to the accused that establishes his or her fault in so acting or failing to act. For example, the offence of assault consists of an action—applying force to another person without that person's consent—and a mental state—applying the force "intentionally." Both of these conditions must be present for an action to constitute an assault.

Perhaps the easiest way to understand the proof of an offence is to think of it as a math equation: *actus reus* + *mens rea* = offence. However, where the *actus reus* or the *mens rea* involves more than one element, the equation will be more complex.

For example, using the example of attempted murder, the *actus reus* of the offence involves an effort to end another person's life that fails: effort + failure = *actus reus*. The *actus reus* may also include the means of the attempt—say, the use of a firearm—since this will affect the penalty imposed under the *Criminal Code* if the accused is found guilty. In this case, the elements of the *actus reus* component will be: effort + failure + firearm.

The *mens rea* of the offence of attempted murder is the intention to end another person's life. If the offender simply wanted to injure the victim, there is no basis for alleging that she had the required mental state to be guilty of attempted murder (though she may be charged with a lesser offence, such as assault). It must be established that the offender intended to kill the victim for a charge of attempted murder to be proven.

Therefore, to secure a conviction of a person accused of attempted murder with a firearm under section 239 of the *Criminal Code*, the Crown must provide convincing proof supporting each element of the offence equation: effort + failure + firearm + intention to end the life of the victim = attempted murder.

ACTUS REUS

The *actus reus* of an offence can be an act, a state of being, or an omission.

Most of the offences in the *Criminal Code* are action offences: offences that require the accused to commit a certain act, such as striking, stealing, counterfeiting, and so on. An action offence may also include a requirement that the action of the accused caused a certain result (for example, the offence of assault causing bodily harm).

Most state-of-being offences are offences of possession: of weapons, of controlled drugs, of break-in tools, and so on. The *actus reus* for such an offence is simply the fact of being in possession and control of the particular item. Another example of a state-of-being offence is drunkenness where the offender causes a disturbance in a public place.

In some cases, the law requires a person to take a particular action in a particular circumstance, and it becomes an offence of omission to *not* take the required action. Examples are refusals to obey police orders, such as stopping at a road block or refusing to provide a breath sample when asked to do so. There is also a class of criminal negligence offences (discussed below), in which the failure to act (whether with intent or otherwise) endangers or causes harm to another person.

MENS REA

Under our law, the availability of criminal sanctions almost always depends upon a legal finding of moral guilt. To determine guilt, the court examines evidence of the accused's state of mind at the time of committing the alleged offence. To be found guilty of a criminal offence, the accused person must have

- made a choice to do something wrong,

- made the choice voluntarily or with free will, and

- known that the act was wrong.

If all of these elements are proven, then the accused is said to have the requisite *mens rea*, or "guilty mind."

Many offences under the *Criminal Code* describe not only physical acts but also the mindset of the accused at the time of committing the act, using modifying words to define the criminal behaviour. Offences may depend not only on the action committed but also on how it is committed—for example, "wilfully," "recklessly," or "with intent to injure."

Intent is a key to *mens rea*. The law recognizes degrees of intent, which range from direct intent (the most serious in a criminal offence) to negligence (the least serious). In general, offences that carry more serious penalties require a higher level of intent: one form of first-degree murder, for example, requires not only a specific intent to kill but also evidence of planning and **deliberation** on the part of the accused. Second-degree murder requires only the specific intent to kill, while the lesser charge of manslaughter requires a general intent to injure the victim, without any particular thought as to whether the victim would die as a result.

At the lower end of the range of intent are recklessness, **wilful blindness**, carelessness, and negligence. These lower levels of *mens rea* may be said to describe unjustifiable risk taking.

Criminal negligence differs from ordinary or civil negligence in that it requires some level of *mens rea*, such as wanton and reckless disregard for the lives and safety of others. A motorist who engages in drag racing on a public road may be criminally negligent even if at the time there is no other traffic and no apparent danger to others. Criminal negligence does not require proof of intention or deliberation; indifference to the possible consequences is enough.

Defences

When a person is charged with an offence and the case is brought to trial, it is the prosecution's responsibility to prove every element of the charge beyond a reasonable doubt. The accused is not required to present a **defence**. However, it is rare for an accused to pass up the opportunity to challenge the prosecution's case. The defence usually presents evidence that casts doubt on one or more elements of the charge. For example, the defence may argue that the accused couldn't have committed the crime because he was somewhere else at the time. By presenting evidence such as an alibi, the defence may raise a reasonable doubt about the validity of the charge.

Most specific defences are designed to prove that the accused did not have the required intent, or *mens rea*, to commit the offence. Recognized defences include self-defence, mental incapacity, consent (especially with respect to sexual assault), and entrapment. If the accused is being tried by a judge and jury, and he presents evidence in support of a recognized defence, the judge will need to explain the legal effect of the specific defence to the jury, so that they can take it into account in their decision to convict or acquit the accused.

Critical Perspectives
The Battered Woman Defence

In a 1990 case before the Supreme Court of Canada, *R. v. Lavallee* ([1990] 1 SCR 852), a woman who had killed her husband succeeded in arguing self-defence under section 34(2) of the *Criminal Code* even though she was not actually being assaulted by her husband at the time. The woman's husband had beaten her regularly, and on the occasion in question, he had handed her a loaded gun, taunting her that if she didn't kill him first, he would kill her. She shot him in the back.

Before this case, the law required an accused to prove an imminent threat to his or her life for a successful claim of self-defence under section 34(2). In *Lavallee*, the Supreme Court accepted the defence of the accused on the basis of expert evidence about "battered wife syndrome," the grounds for the woman's fear, and the lack of options available to her to protect herself. Waiting for him to attack was not considered a viable option, since the woman was convinced that her husband meant to kill her.

The court's decision has proved controversial. Some critics argue that acceptance of the battered wife (or woman) defence gives women a licence to kill, and they should simply leave the relationship. However, others argue that leaving is not a safe option for many women, since domestic violence often escalates when women assert their rights. The battered woman syndrome argument has also been criticized because it generally depicts battered women as psychologically defective by focusing on their learned helplessness, low self-esteem, and victim mentality, rather than emphasizing that in some instances women who kill are acting very rationally—taking the only action that could reasonably save their own lives. ◇

THE INVESTIGATION

The police investigate circumstances in which it appears that someone may have committed an offence. When they have identified a suspect and the information they have collected appears to be sufficient to prove that the suspect committed the *actus reus* and had the *mens rea* on which the specific offence is based, they will generally proceed to lay a criminal charge. Once that has been done, police provide evidence to the **prosecution** (Crown attorney) that supports the case against the accused person. The prosecution later uses this evidence at trial.

Rights of the Individual

To protect the privacy and security rights of individuals, police investigations are conducted according to strict procedural rules. Most people are aware, for example, of the concept of a **search warrant**, and the fact that, at least in non-emergency situations, police must have either a person's permission or an order from a justice of the peace before they can conduct a search.

The rules governing investigations extend beyond search rights and cover issues such as the following: when it is acceptable to detain a suspect without charge (and for how long); when it is acceptable to use some level of force to move or control a person; and what techniques are acceptable for use during questioning of a suspect or **witness**.

Describing all of the rules that govern investigations is well beyond the scope of this book, but there are a few key things that social service workers should know:

- The *Canadian Charter of Rights and Freedoms* has codified a range of rights (for example, right to counsel, right to be free of unreasonable search and seizure, right to trial within a reasonable time) that relate to the criminal law context. Because the Charter forms part of the constitution, its provisions supersede all other laws.

- In general, before the police can engage in any investigative action (searches, detentions, collection of samples, etc.) that invades a person's privacy, they must have reasonable and probable grounds to suspect that an offence has been committed, that the actions that they propose will uncover evidence in support of that suspicion;

- When evidence is collected in a manner that violates the Charter rights of a person accused of a crime, that evidence is sometimes excluded (upon a judge's order) from use in the subsequent trial of that person. This can make it difficult for the prosecution to prove its case. Exclusion rules provide an incentive for law enforcement personnel to do their work fairly and with respect for the privacy and security rights of individuals.

These three points seem simple, but the law of evidence and the rules governing police action are complex and finely nuanced. Any individual who is being treated as a suspect in a criminal matter and who believes that his or her rights have been or are being infringed should obtain immediate legal assistance. The consequences of a criminal conviction are serious; even if there is little likelihood of imprisonment, a criminal record can affect many aspects of a person's life. If, as a social service worker, you take a call from a client who is in trouble with the law, you should suggest that the client contact a lawyer and, if appropriate, you should help the client to do so by putting him in touch with legal aid or a lawyer referral service.

Disclosure Requirements

While the police have extensive investigation powers and resources to collect information related to a suspected crime, an accused person does not have the same resources to help him to prepare a defence. Because our criminal justice system is based on the presumption of innocence, and because an accused person has the right to know the case that will be made against him, there is a system of disclosure that requires the police and the Crown prosecutor to provide to the accused person and his lawyer all **evidence** in their possession related to the particular offence. Before the trial begins, the accused is entitled to disclosure of both **inculpatory evidence** (evidence that tends to suggest that the accused is guilty) and **exculpatory evidence** (evidence that tends to suggest that the accused is not guilty) so that he can adequately prepare his defence.

The initial disclosure should be provided before the accused is asked to choose a mode of trial (by judge or by judge and **jury**) or to enter a **plea** (guilty or not guilty). There is also a continuing obligation on the Crown to disclose new information and evidence to the accused as it is uncovered or discovered.

The disclosure requirement extends through the Crown prosecutor to the investigating police officers themselves. The police have both a statutory and a common-law duty to disclose to the Crown prosecutor all relevant information that has been collected during an investigation, even if that evidence could be used to prove the innocence of the person accused of the offence.

If the police fail to do this, the accused is entitled to a remedy. If evidence has been lost or destroyed either by the police or by the prosecution, and this loss affects the ability of the accused to make a full answer and defence, the judge may issue a **stay of proceedings**. This is a ruling that stops further prosecution of the case; that is, the charge against the accused is dropped. To be granted a stay, the defence must establish that the accused's right to a fair trial has been denied or irreparably harmed, or that the non-disclosure was in bad faith (motivated by improper reasons) or constitutes an **abuse of process**—an improper action or series of actions on the part of the police that undermines the fairness of the criminal procedure.

CHARGES AND ELECTIONS

Types of Charging Documents

The charging document sets out the criminal charges against the accused and begins the process toward trial. It identifies the specific charges or offences (known as counts) that the accused is alleged to have committed. There are two types of charging documents:

- An **information** is the charging document used for offences tried in a provincial court or youth court and is usually sworn by a police officer.

- An **indictment** is the charging document used for offences tried in a superior court of criminal jurisdiction (the provincial Superior Court of Justice) and is usually signed by the prosecutor.

The *Criminal Code* prescribes the forms that are to be used and the procedures for completing and delivering charging documents. It is essential that the charging document be made out correctly for the charge to proceed to trial. For a more detailed discussion of charging documents, you can consult Rock and Hoag (2006).

Classification of Offences

Our criminal justice system classifies *Criminal Code* offences into three categories, according to their seriousness and the procedure used to deal with the charge in court:

- summary conviction offences,

- hybrid offences, and

- indictable offences.

In general, **summary conviction offences** are less serious offences and carry light penalties. Any charge tried by summary conviction is tried in the provincial court before a provincial court judge alone (that is, without a jury). No **preliminary hearing** is held.

Indictable offences are more serious crimes that usually carry stiffer penalties. The court and mode of trial varies according to the offence. Offences listed in section 469 of the Code are to be tried in the Superior Court of a province, with a judge and jury. Offences listed in section 553 are within the absolute jurisdiction of the provincial court. However, most indictable offences are tried according to the **election** (choice) of the accused: in the provincial court before a provincial court judge alone; in the Superior Court of the province before a judge alone; or in the Superior Court of the province before a judge and a jury. In most cases, the accused has the right to a preliminary hearing as well.

Hybrid offences may be tried as a summary conviction offence (and thus subject to lesser penalties) or as an indictable offence (and thus subject to stiffer penalties), at the election of the prosecutor. Hybrid offences reflect the fact that the seriousness of an offence can vary greatly. For example, the hybrid offence of assault may involve a slight nudge or a violent punch. The prosecutor will consider the facts of the case before determining whether to proceed by summary conviction or indictment. That decision will determine the court and the mode of trial, according to the rules outlined above for each type of offence.

Figure 9.1 summarizes the differences in procedure depending on the type of offence.

Applying these rules of procedure under the Ontario court system, all summary conviction offences are tried in the Ontario Court of Justice (the provincial court). Indictable offences may be tried in the Ontario Court of Justice or in the Superior Court of Justice, usually at the election of the accused. The court in which a hybrid offence is tried will depend on whether it is treated as a summary conviction or an indictable offence, and on the election of the accused where available.

Choosing the Court and Mode of Trial

Not all charges proceed to trial: the accused may plead guilty, or may negotiate a plea bargain with the prosecutor. (Pleas and plea bargains are discussed in more detail in Rock and Hoag (2006).) However, if the accused pleads not guilty, he may have the option of choosing (electing) the court and mode of trial to decide the case.

Figure 9.1   Classification of Offences

	Summary conviction	Indictable	Hybrid
Court	Provincial court	Accused chooses provincial court or Superior Court	Prosecutor chooses whether to proceed by summary conviction (lighter penalties) or indictment (harsher penalties)
Preliminary hearing	No	Accused has right to preliminary hearing if he elects to be tried in Superior Court	
Jury	No	Accused has right to have a jury if he elects to be tried in Superior Court	
Charging document	Information	Indictment	

There are various factors that an accused will take into account when electing the court and the mode of trial (by judge alone or by judge and jury). The procedures in provincial court are generally simpler and trials there tend to be shorter; however, the availability of a preliminary hearing may make a Superior Court trial an attractive option. If an accused believes that a jury of his peers may be more likely to empathize with him, or that he can convince at least some jury members that he is not guilty as charged, he may choose a jury trial. (Keep in mind that a jury's decisions must be unanimous, and that "a reasonable doubt" will be sufficient to defeat the Crown's case.) However, if the accused is relying on a complicated or highly technical defence, he may want the matter to be adjudicated by a judge with legal expertise and the training required to apply the law objectively.

If the prosecution is proposing to introduce certain kinds of evidence that may cast the accused in a poor light, the accused and his lawyers may feel that a judge alone will be less inclined than a jury to be swayed by such evidence. For example, a judge who is used to hearing the evidence of young children may be better able to focus on the significance of the evidence rather than on her feelings of sympathy for a child witness. Or, where the prosecution will be introducing evidence of past behaviour (called "similar fact evidence") that is admissible only to prove or disprove one aspect of the offence, an experienced judge may be better able to avoid drawing spurious conclusions, such as "Once a violent drunk, always a violent drunk." The general belief is that members of a jury are more likely to be improperly influenced against the accused upon hearing sensitive evidence, and therefore less likely to accept technical defences in such cases, than a judge might be.

THE CRIMINAL TRIAL

The procedures followed in a criminal trial are described in chapter 13, and also discussed in detail in Rock and Hoag (2006).

SENTENCING

If the accused is found guilty, either after a trial or after entering a guilty plea, the next step is sentencing. The *Criminal Code* provides courts with a range of sentencing options for each offence, including maximum and minimum thresholds. To determine what is an appropriate sentence within the given range, judges consider the sentences imposed in other cases with similar facts. **Precedent** helps to ensure that sentences are consistent and that offenders are treated fairly as compared with others who have committed similar crimes. The court will also apply certain sentencing principles, described below.

Purpose and Principles

PURPOSE

Section 718 of the *Criminal Code* states that the fundamental purpose of sentencing is "to contribute to respect for the law and the maintenance of a just, peaceful and safe society." In particular, the sentence that is imposed should aim to achieve one or more of the following objectives:

(a) to denounce unlawful conduct;

(b) to deter the offender and other persons from committing offences;

(c) to separate offenders from society, where necessary;

(d) to assist in rehabilitating offenders;

(e) to provide reparations for harm done to victims or to the community; and

(f) to promote a sense of responsibility in offenders, and acknowledgment of the harm done to victims and to the community.

In deciding what sentence is appropriate in a particular case, a judge may have to choose between conflicting objectives. For example, a long prison term may satisfy the objectives of **denunciation** and separating the offender from society; however, depriving the offender of the opportunity for employment, cutting her off from family relationships, and placing her within the criminal subculture of the prison may interfere with or frustrate the objective of **rehabilitation**.

In addition, questions arise about how realistic some of these objectives may be. For example, with respect to general **deterrence**, some studies suggest that the probability of imprisonment—even a life sentence—does not deter individuals from committing violent crimes. Repeat offenders appear to prove this argument. There is also considerable debate over the limitations of the rehabilitation objective, particular for those who commit certain types of offences, such as sexual assault or sexual exploitation of children. The necessary resources are often not available, and some offenders do not respond to rehabilitation programs. Confining some repeat offenders for life may be the only sure way to protect society. The dangerous offender provisions in part XXIV of the *Criminal Code* address this issue, in part, by permitting judges to impose indefinite sentences on some repeat, violent offenders (section 753).

PRINCIPLES

To assist judges in making sentencing decisions consistent with the purpose and objectives in section 718, the *Criminal Code* sets out several principles to be applied in choosing among the available sentencing options. The fundamental principle, in section 718.1, is that the sentence must be proportionate to the seriousness of the crime and the degree of responsibility of the offender.

Section 718.2 sets out additional sentencing principles. These include the requirement that the court consider any "aggravating or mitigating circumstances" when imposing a sentence. **Aggravating circumstances** are circumstances that make the crime more serious, such as use of a weapon or the vulnerability of the victim. Where these are found to have been present, the court may choose to impose a heavier sentence in the range of available options. **Mitigating circumstances** are circumstances that indicate a decreased degree of responsibility for the crime or speak to the rehabilitation of the offender, and they may lead the court to impose a lighter sentence. Examples of aggravating and mitigating circumstances are provided in figure 9.2.

The other principles to be applied in sentencing, as specified in section 718.2, include consistency (similar sentences for similar crimes in similar circumstances) and consideration of an alternative to imprisonment in appropriate circumstances.

While the purpose, objectives, and principles set out in the *Criminal Code* are the foundation for sentencing decisions, in practice our sentencing law reflects a compromise between, on the one hand, various theories of the appropriate response to those who commit crimes and, on the other hand, the broad and shifting spectrum of public opinion. This can be a source of frustration for anyone who works within the criminal justice system, including judges, prosecutors, police, defence lawyers, and social service workers, as well as those who are directly affected—offenders, their families, and the victims of crime.

Types of Sentences

The most common sentences imposed are the following:

- imprisonment in a custodial facility
- conditional sentence of imprisonment
- a suspended sentence
- a fine
- discharge, with or without probation.

Figure 9.2   Examples of Aggravating and Mitigating Circumstances

Aggravating circumstances — heavier sentence	Mitigating circumstances — lighter sentence
Hate crime against an identifiable group	Provocation by the victim
Breach of trust with respect to the victim	Public humiliation and ruin, loss of professional status as a result of the crime
Use of violence	Remorse and positive changes to the offender's lifestyle since the offence occurred
History of similar crimes	First-time offender

IMPRISONMENT

Where an offender is sentenced to imprisonment, she may be held in a federally run penitentiary or a provincially run detention centre, depending on the length of the sentence. Sentences of less than two years are served in provincial institutions; longer sentences are served in federal institutions. This is the reason for the popularity of the sentence of "two years less a day"—it keeps the offender in a provincial institution nearer to home. Depending on the risk of violence or escape, the appropriate institution, either federal or provincial, may be maximum, medium, or minimum security. Sometimes short sentences are served only on weekends, permitting the offender to continue living and working in the community during the week.

Offenders who are convicted of a serious offence causing bodily harm, for which the punishment is at least 10 years' imprisonment, may be declared dangerous offenders and kept in prison for life. Offences that qualify include manslaughter, murder, attempted murder, aggravated assault, and aggravated sexual assault. Dangerous offenders are eligible for parole every seven years, but there is no mandatory release. (Parole and statutory release are discussed in chapter 10.)

Currently the prosecution must make a special application for dangerous offender designation within six months after the conviction, and must prove that the offender is a serious threat to the safety of others. Dangerous offenders have a history of violent crime and indifference to the consequences. Most dangerous offenders have convictions for sexual assaults. Proposed amendments to the *Criminal Code* would reverse the onus in cases where there were three convictions for specified crimes—that is, the burden would be placed on the offender to prove that he or she should not be designated a dangerous offender.

CONDITIONAL SENTENCE OF IMPRISONMENT

In some circumstances, a court may impose a **conditional sentence of imprisonment** to be served in the community instead of a prison (section 742.1 of the *Criminal Code*). The offender usually lives in his own home or the home of a relative. The conditions may place the offender under house arrest but permit him to leave home to go to work, attend medical appointments, or shop for necessities; however, his whereabouts will be carefully monitored. This type of sentence is an inexpensive and humane alternative to jail where the offence does not carry a minimum sentence, the sentence imposed is less than two years, and the offender is unlikely to leave the jurisdiction or otherwise violate the conditions. If the conditions are breached, the offender may be imprisoned for the remainder of his sentence.

SUSPENDED SENTENCE

A judge can impose a **suspended sentence** for an offence that does not carry a minimum sentence (section 731 of the *Criminal Code*). A suspended sentence means that the offender is released back into society subject to certain conditions set out in a **probation** order. If the offender breaches the conditions of the probation order before it expires (three years after it is issued), she faces being sentenced on the original offence and forced to serve the sentence. Several possible conditions can be included in a probation order, such as a prohibition against carrying firearms, an order not to approach or associate with certain people, or an order to stay away from certain places. Probation may be ordered on its own, or with either a fine or a term of imprisonment, but not both.

FINE

A fine may be imposed instead of or in addition to another punishment such as probation, a conditional sentence, or imprisonment, provided that the offence does not carry a minimum term of imprisonment. Fines are often imposed for statutory or quasi-criminal offences, such as minor traffic or environmental offences, and for certain summary conviction (including hybrid) offences under the *Criminal Code*. Before imposing a fine, the court must consider the ability of the offender to pay it. Failure to pay a fine can result in imprisonment.

DISCHARGE

In some cases, a person convicted of a less serious offence may be discharged on either an absolute or a conditional basis—that is, without having to serve a sentence or pay a fine (section 730 of the *Criminal Code*). An **absolute discharge** has no conditions attached to it and takes effect right away. An accused who receives an absolute discharge is deemed not to have been convicted and has no criminal record in connection with the offence. A **conditional discharge** includes a probation order with conditions that can be in effect for up to three years. After the probation period has passed without violation of the conditions, the discharge becomes absolute. Violation of the conditions can result in a formal conviction and a sentence.

Pre-Sentence Report

In deciding the type and length of the sentence to be imposed in a particular case, the judge may hear submissions from both the prosecution and the defence. These take place at a sentencing hearing before the judge.

Sometimes the judge orders a pre-sentence report to assist in the sentencing decision. If ordered, the report is prepared by a probation officer before sentencing and is filed with the court. The report usually contains information on the background and character of the offender, separate from the offence. The report gives the judge insight into the offender so that the sentence can be effective both in punishing her for the offence and in promoting rehabilitation. Social service workers who have worked with the offender may be asked to help in preparing a pre-sentence report.

In preparing a pre-sentence report, the probation officer typically begins by reviewing police and correctional files to gain information about the accused's criminal and incarceration history. These details provide clues to the likelihood that the accused will reoffend and information about the kinds of penalties that have been tried in the past, and whether or not they have been successful.

Next, the probation officer will generally interview the accused, and also other individuals who have had contact with her, including family members, employers, and teachers. The purpose of these interviews is to obtain qualitative information about the offender and insights into her behaviour. These insights can help to predict the risk that the offender will reoffend.

Armed with this information, the probation officer will prepare a report for the sentencing judge. Information may be provided in narrative form: for example,

EXTRA CREDIT

Coming Clean in Drug Court

If anyone needs proof that the use of cocaine or heroin is criminogenic (leads to crime), that proof can be found every day in Toronto's Old City Hall. The busy courthouse hears a huge number of summary conviction criminal cases each week. Lawyers and judges working there get to know certain repeat offenders: those whose substance dependencies force them to steal, commit fraud, or engage in prostitution to pay for drugs.

Besides having long offence records, these offenders also tend to have problems in their personal lives: they may be jobless, homeless, and estranged from family and friends.

In 1998, Toronto launched a pilot program aimed at breaking the cycle of addiction and crime. The program, which began as a pilot project and has been extended, is known as Drug Treatment Court. In order to be admitted to the program, participants must be addicted to cocaine, crack cocaine, or heroin, have a history of non-violent drug-related convictions, be willing to accept moral responsibility for their crimes, and be committed to addictions treatment.

The program, which now has counterparts in Vancouver, Edmonton, Regina, Winnipeg, and Ottawa, allows participants to avoid jail time by submitting to treatment, supervision, and weekly urinalysis. (Urinalysis day varies every week, to make it difficult for participants to conceal drug use.) At the beginning of the treatment, participants are expected to show up in court twice a week to report on their progress. Participants who are doing well are permitted to go longer between court appointments. Failure to meet program requirements can lead to discharge from the program, followed by sentencing, and often to a jail term. Participants who graduate from the program (those who are drug-free for a minimum of four months) and reoffend are usually sentenced to probation only.

Kofi Barnes, the first Canadian prosecutor to lead a drug treatment court, had the following to say about the program:

> [W]e have developed a system of frequent court appearances, treatment appointments, urinalysis, and community supervision which makes the drug treatment court participant the most-supervised non-incarcerated participant in the criminal justice system. Such close supervision ensures public safety.

There are about 600 drug treatment courts in operation in the United States. Statistics from those programs suggest that drug treatment court can produce recidivism (reoffending) rates as low as 4 percent, a dramatic improvement on the estimated 45 percent recidivism rate for non-participants.

Social service workers whose clients include people addicted to cocaine, crack, or heroin should be aware of the program so that they can explain it to their clients, and suggest that clients participate, if eligible. An easy-to-read "Pocket Guide" to the program can be downloaded at www.torontodrugtreatmentcourt.ca. ◈

"Despite his history of minor assaults, the defendant is well connected to the community through family ties and steady employment." Or it may be provided through the use of statistical predictions: for example, "The offender's estimated chance of reoffending in the next 12 months is 50 percent."

Research about pre-sentencing reports (described in a 2005 report, *Presentence Reports in Canada*) suggests that judges find pre-sentence reports very useful: 87 percent of judges reported being satisfied with them. Statistics show that custodial sentences are less likely to be imposed in cases for which a pre-sentence report has been prepared, a sign that the report can make it easier for a judge to consider a wider range of sentencing possibilities.

However, the same study suggested that only 40 percent of probation officers were satisfied with the pre-sentence report system. Many probation officers felt that they were not adequately trained in deciding what information to include in a pre-sentence report. They also reported not having enough resources (time, staff, etc.) to do a good job in preparing the reports.

KEY TERMS

absolute discharge	exculpatory evidence	probation
abuse of process	hybrid offence	prosecution
accused	inculpatory evidence	rehabilitation
actus reus	indictable offence	reparation
aggravating circumstances	indictment	restorative justice
conditional discharge	information	search warrant
conditional sentence of imprisonment	jury	sentencing circle
defence	*mens rea*	stay of proceedings
deliberation	mitigating circumstances	summary conviction offence
denunciation	offence	suspect
deterrence	physical evidence	suspended sentence
election	plea	testimony
elements of an offence	precedent	wilful blindness
evidence	preliminary hearing	witness

REFERENCES

B.L., R. v., 2002 ABCA 44 (CanLII), 163 CCC (3d) 404.

Bonta, James, Guy Bourgon, Rebecca Jesseman, and Annie K. Yessine, *Presentence Reports in Canada 2005-03*, report prepared for Public Safety and Emergency Preparedness Canada (Ottawa: Public Safety and Emergency Preparedness Canada, 2005).

Canadian Charter of Rights and Freedoms, part I of the *Constitution Act, 1982*, being schedule B of the *Canada Act 1982* (UK), 1982, c. 11.

Constitution Act, 1867, 30 & 31 Vict., c. 3 (UK).

Controlled Drugs and Substances Act, SC 1996, c. 19.

Crimes Against Humanity and War Crimes Act, SC 2000, c. 24.

Criminal Code, RSC 1985, c. C-46.

Highway Traffic Act, RSO 1990, c. H.8.

J.J., R. v., 2004 NCCA 81 (CanLII), 192 CCC (3d) 30.

Lavallee, R. v., [1990] 1 SCR 852 (1990 CanLII 95).

REVIEW QUESTIONS

1. Where, other than the federal *Criminal Code*, can you find legal definitions of offences?

2. Why are Aboriginal people overrepresented in Canada's prison population?

3. What is meant by an "element" of an offence?

4. Why is the concept of *mens rea* (intent) so central to the imposition of criminal penalties?

5. Why might an accused call evidence of his own even if he is not raising a specific defence (for example, self-defence)?

6. How did the recognition of the battered woman syndrome defence change the law?

7. Can the police search an individual on a hunch—for example, if, when they pull someone over for speeding, the person appears nervous?

8. What can happen if a court determines that police collected evidence in violation of an accused's rights under the *Canadian Charter of Rights and Freedoms*?

9. Why should social service workers who encounter clients in conflict with the law encourage or assist those clients in seeking legal advice?

10. What is a hybrid offence?

11. List the most common types of sentences that can be imposed by a criminal court.

12. What is the purpose of a pre-sentence report, and how might a social service worker be involved in the preparation of one?

CHAPTER 10

Correctional Services for Adults

CHAPTER OBJECTIVES

After reading this chapter, you should be able to:

- Explain the difference between provincial prisons and federal penitentiaries, and what governs the choice of facility for an adult offender.

- Describe the various types of detention facilities and detention programs at each level.

- Understand the general rules governing prison life and the rights of inmates.

- Explain the rules with respect to early release (parole).

- Describe community alternatives and programs.

INTRODUCTION

Compared to the United States, Canada's prison population is small relative to the population as a whole. According to prison data for 2004, shown in figure 10.1, the United States ranked first in the world with 737 prisoners per 100,000 in the general population, while Canada was near the middle with 107 per 100,000. Canada's criminal law treats prison as a last resort, although the prison population is steadily growing. Placing an offender in prison is the ultimate limit on personal freedom, and there are many critics who suggest that isolation from society—and placement within a community of other offenders—impedes, rather than assists, rehabilitation. It is also very expensive to house prisoners.

While rehabilitation is a central goal of our criminal justice system, as discussed in chapter 9, in some cases imprisonment is warranted because it supports other worthy goals, such as deterrence (discouraging other potential offenders from offending by demonstrating the consequences of conviction) and the protection of society (by keeping the offender away from potential victims).

The corrections system is designed to provide the required level of security to protect society and those working and living in correctional facilities. At the time of admission to a facility, the prisoner is classified according to the security risk he presents and assigned to a facility or unit designated as maximum security, medium

Figure 10.1   Prison Population Rates by Country, 2004

Rank	Country	No. of prisoners per 100,000 of national population
1	United States of America	737
2	French Guiana	630
3	Russian Federation	613
28	South Africa	336
52	Iran	214
53	Israel	209
60	Mexico	197
106	Australia	125
113	China	118
114	Nicaragua	114
123	Canada	107
128	Italy	104
137	Germany	94
181	Pakistan	57
196	Iceland	40
214	Congo	22

Source: Data obtained from the International Centre for Prison Studies at www.prisonstudies.org (updated to 2004).

WEB LINK

For information comparing how different countries address prison issues, visit the website of the International Centre for Prison Studies at www.prisonstudies.org.

security, or minimum security. However, the classification is not fixed but may change as the prisoner demonstrates progress in meeting his rehabilitation goals. An offender in a maximum security facility or wing who complies with the rules and makes a strong commitment to rehabilitation may apply for a move to a medium or minimum security placement, and eventually back into the community on parole. Conversely, an offender may be sentenced to a facility with a low or moderate level of security, but if he commits an act of violence while in prison, he may be moved to a medium or maximum security facility. This flexibility in the system exists to allow responsiveness to individual offender circumstances.

Social service workers may work with inmates and former inmates in a variety of settings and circumstances. Some work as probation officers, monitoring offenders who are sentenced to a period of probation rather than incarceration. Some work as parole officers, helping offenders released from prison on conditional release to adjust to community life while monitoring them for compliance with their release conditions.

Other social service workers may work inside prisons as part of a team. They may take social histories and help with assessing offenders, in order to determine the appropriate level of security and to choose programs to meet the individual's needs. They may also help to administer such programs as addictions counselling and anger management. These programs can be offered by prisons themselves or by outside provider agencies, such as the John Howard Society or the Elizabeth Fry Society (discussed in a later section of this chapter). Social service workers may work for any kind of program provider.

Finally, social service workers may work in halfway houses and in the community, helping paroled prisoners to reintegrate into the activities of normal life, for example by obtaining employment or re-establishing a relationship with children or other relatives. Social service workers can be an invaluable information resource, referring clients to many programs and benefits provided by government and non-profit agencies.

This chapter provides an overview of the prison system in Canada, discusses the important issue of prisoners' rights, and describes important features of the federal and Ontario corrections systems. The discussion focuses on adult offenders; corrections services for young offenders are discussed in chapter 11.

WEB LINK

For a list of links to information about many aspects of corrections, visit the Canadian government's Safe Canada website at www.safecanada.ca.

THE PRISON SYSTEM IN CANADA

Responsibility for corrections policies and programs is shared by the federal and provincial governments. The reasons for this are largely historical: when the *Constitution Act, 1867* was passed, there were already correctional facilities at both levels. Section 91(28) of the constitution provides for federal jurisdiction over "the Establishment, Maintenance, and Management of Penitentiaries," and section 92(6) provides for provincial jurisdiction over "the Establishment, Maintenance, and Management of Public and Reformatory Prisons in and for the Province."

Both federal penitentiaries and provincial prisons house inmates who have been convicted of offences under the *Criminal Code.* In general, however, offenders sentenced to two years or more serve their sentences in penitentiaries, while those sentenced to less than two years serve in provincial prisons. This is why the sentence of "two years less a day" is often ordered: it is the maximum sentence that can be served in a provincial prison.

A court that sentences a person to a penitentiary is required to provide reasons for the sentence to the Correctional Service of Canada (CSC), the federal government ministry responsible for the penitentiary system.

INMATES' RIGHTS

Inmates of correctional facilities are entitled to respect for their rights. These include rights set out in federal and provincial human rights statutes and in the *Canadian Charter of Rights and Freedoms* (the Charter), with the obvious exception of rights associated with personal freedom. In addition, for security reasons, the personal privacy rights of inmates may be curtailed; for example, all inmates must undergo a body search on admission to a correctional facility, and may be required to do so on other occasions, as discussed in the next section.

Inmates also have rights and privileges under other statutes and regulations. The rights of offenders serving time in provincial facilities in Ontario are described in the *Ministry of Correctional Services Act* (MCSA) and the General Regulation under the Act. The rights of inmates serving time in federal penitentiaries are described in the *Corrections and Conditional Release Act* (CCRA). Rights specific to young offenders are described in Ontario's *Child and Family Services Act* (CFSA) and the federal *Youth Criminal Justice Act* (YCJA), discussed in chapter 11.

It is important for social service workers to have a basic understanding of prisoners' rights, in order to recognize a violation of a client's rights when it arises, and to participate meaningfully in policy debate and advocacy on behalf of prisoners.

LEGISLATIVE SHORTCUT

Corrections and Conditional Release Act

SC 1992, c. 20

Objective: To protect society by carrying out sentences safely and humanely, and by rehabilitating and reintegrating offenders.

Target Population: Prisoners and parolees in Canada sentenced to incarceration for two years or more (in federal penitentiaries).

Program Administration: Correctional Service of Canada.

Administrative Tribunal: The National Parole Board makes decisions about parole.

Summary: To contribute to the maintenance of a just, peaceful, and safe society by carrying out sentences through the safe and humane custody and supervision of offenders. Assisting in the rehabilitation of offenders and their reintegration into the community as law-abiding citizens through the provision of programs in penitentiaries and in the community. ◇

Ministry of Correctional Services Act

RSO 1990, c. M.22

Objective: To operate provincial prisons and rehabilitate offenders.

Target Population: Prisoners and parolees in Ontario sentenced for less than two years (in provincial correctional centres).

Program Administration: The Ministry of Correctional Services may subcontract corrections services to municipalities or other agencies and corporations.

Administrative Tribunal: The Ontario Parole and Earned Release Board makes decisions about parole.

Summary: The *Ministry of Correctional Services Act* requires that the ministry operate provincial prisons; supervise the detention and release of inmates, parolees, probationers and young persons; and provide training, treatment, and services for the rehabilitation of inmates. ◇

Those who work in correctional facilities should actively support and encourage respect for the rights and privileges of inmates, thereby reducing the likelihood of infringement, and contributing to a humane living environment for individuals in custody. Sometimes social service workers may be required to act as intermediaries between inmates and prison staff, communicating inmate requests, concerns, and complaints to management; or they may be called upon to facilitate inmate access to other helping professionals such as lawyers, counsellors, and politicians.

Social service workers may also work with or for various charitable organizations whose mission is to advocate for offenders both during their incarceration and following release. The best known are the John Howard Society, the Elizabeth Fry Society, and the St. Leonard's Society. The activities of these three organizations—their aims, programs, and services—are described in a later section of this chapter.

Figure 10.2 lists some of the rights of inmates in correctional facilities (including young offenders), and the statutory basis for each of those rights.

Figure 10.2   Statutory Authority for Inmate Rights

Inmate right	Legal authority/source
• The right to be kept in the degree of custody and control that incorporates the lowest level of restrictions on freedom consistent with the protection of society	CCRA, s. 28
• The right to be housed in a penitentiary that is accessible to the prisoner's family, community, and a compatible cultural and linguistic environment	CCRA, s. 28
• The right to take part in programming designed to assist in rehabilitation and reintegration of the offender into the community	CCRA and MCSA (general principles)
• The right to participate in the electoral process (vote)	Charter, s. 3
• The right to medical care for physical or mental illness	MCSA, s. 24 and General Regulation under the MCSA, ss. 2-7; CCRA, s. 86
• The right not to be subject to excessive force	General Regulation under the MCSA, s. 7; Charter, s. 7; *Criminal Code*, s. 25
• The right to appeal most important administrative decisions made about the inmate (for example, a decision to change the inmate's security designation, or move the inmate to a higher security wing or facility)	CCRA, MCSA, YCJA, and CFSA (various provisions)
• The right to have any property confiscated at the time of admission returned upon release	General Regulation under the MCSA, ss. 10-12; Regulation under the CCRA, s. 59
• The right to have visitors	General Regulation under the MCSA, ss. 13-15; CCRA, s. 71
• The right to send and receive correspondence, subject to some rights of review of that correspondence, in the inmate's presence, by facility staff	General Regulation under the MCSA, ss. 16 and 17; CCRA, s. 71
• Limited rights to communicate with others by telephone (in some cases, subject to the monitoring of calls by prison staff)	General Regulation under the MCSA, ss. 17.1 and 17.2; CCRA, s. 71
• Limited rights to assemble and associate with other inmates	CCRA, s. 73
• The right to participate in decisions affecting inmates, except with respect to security	CCRA, s. 74
• Limited rights to participate in religious observance and/or express belief in a religion or spirituality	CCRA, s. 75

Both the MCSA and the CCRA (and/or the regulations made under those statutes) create standards for the living conditions in prison. Section 70 of the CCRA codifies a commitment to a humane environment for penitentiary inmates and staff; it states:

> The Service shall take all reasonable steps to ensure that penitentiaries, the penitentiary environment, the living and working conditions of inmates and the working conditions of staff members are safe, healthful and free of practices that undermine a person's sense of personal dignity.

Sections 68 and 69 of the CCRA provide that no inmate may be placed in restraints as a form of punishment, and that "[n]o person shall administer, instigate, consent to or acquiesce in any cruel, inhumane or degrading treatment or punishment of an offender."

The CCRA requires the corrections service to provide a range of programs designed to address offenders' needs and to support their reintegration into the community. This obligation extends to providing programs specifically tailored to the needs of female inmates.

To encourage offenders to participate in programs (and to help them earn money in preparation for reintegration), the service is permitted to offer payment for participation in these programs. Money earned by offenders is held in trust for them, and in some cases, payments may be made from earnings to an offender's dependants.

Under both the federal and the provincial legislation, offenders are entitled to access to essential health and dental care. Essential health care includes, where appropriate, treatment for mental health problems. Under the CCRA, inmates are entitled to reasonable access to non-essential health care where that care will contribute to rehabilitation and reintegration.

The General Regulation under the MCSA provides rules for the holding of inmates' money in trust for them and, in some cases, the making of payments to dependants. It provides that searches must be conducted only as prescribed by the legislation, that body cavity searches be conducted by a same-sex guard or a medical professional of either sex, and that searches not be conducted in a way that tends to humiliate the inmate.

The General Regulation provides that inmates can make a complaint, in writing, to the superintendent of a prison where they feel that their rights have been infringed.

To address concerns about **systemic discrimination** against Aboriginal offenders (discussed in chapter 9), the CCRA requires the correctional service to provide programs designed to meet the specific needs of Aboriginal offenders. The Minister of Public Safety and Emergency Preparedness has the power to contract out these services to Aboriginal agencies and communities. To assist in planning programs and in determining the particular needs of Aboriginal offenders, the CCRA provides for the maintenance of a National Aboriginal Advisory Committee; in addition (though this is not a specific requirement under the legislation), in Ontario a regional Aboriginal subcommittee has been constituted for each corrections region in the province. The chairs of these subcommittees serve on the national committee.

When an offender expresses a desire to be released into an Aboriginal community, the CCRA requires the corrections service to give notice of the offender's plans to the

Critical Perspectives

Aboriginal Offenders

Statistics consistently suggest that Canada's Aboriginal population is overrepresented in the prison and penitentiary communities. This means that the percentage of inmates who are of Aboriginal heritage or descent is higher than would be expected, given the proportion of Aboriginal people in the general population.

According to the Elizabeth Fry Society, a charitable agency that provides programs and advocacy for incarcerated women, Aboriginal women are even more markedly overrepresented in the corrections system than men. While Aboriginal women represent only about 2 percent of Canada's population, they account for 20 to 25 percent of the total female prison population and as much as 27 percent of women in federal penitentiaries (50 percent in the prairie provinces).

Aboriginal women in penitentiaries are more than five times more likely than non-Aboriginal women to be designated maximum security offenders, and are almost 50 percent more likely to serve a federal sentence in the penitentiary rather than in the community.

The Elizabeth Fry Society interprets these statistics as clear evidence of systemic discrimination against all Aboriginal people in the corrections system, and against Aboriginal women in particular. While the reasons for the overrepresentation of Aboriginal people in the corrections system are undoubtedly complex, the society suggests that

the criminal justice system is discriminatory in its treatment of Aboriginal people and Aboriginal people commit disproportionately more offences because of their marginalized status in Canadian society.

The society also suggests that

[t]he marginalization of Aboriginal people is rooted in their historical exclusion from full participation in the dominant society and, more importantly, the interference with and suppression of their own culture.

The justice and corrections systems have an important role to play in addressing the overrepresentation of Aboriginal people in Canadian prisons. Fairness in sentencing and in post-sentencing treatment of Aboriginal offenders is the first step that must be taken. The second step must be the development and delivery of programs designed in partnership with First Nations communities to address the specific needs of Aboriginal offenders in a culturally sensitive fashion.

Source: Canadian Association of Elizabeth Fry Societies, *Special Report on the Discrimination on the Basis of Sex, Race and Disability Faced by Federally Sentenced Women*, submissions to the Canadian Human Rights Commission, May 2003. ◇

relevant community leaders, so that a plan can be put in place for the offender's successful reintegration.

THE FEDERAL CORRECTIONS SYSTEM

Purpose and Principles

The federal corrections system is governed primarily by the CCRA. Section 3 of the CCRA provides that the purpose of the federal corrections system is "to contribute to the maintenance of a just, peaceful and safe society" by

- carrying out sentences through the safe and humane custody and supervision of offenders; and

- assisting the rehabilitation of offenders and their reintegration into the community as law-abiding citizens through the provision of programs in penitentiaries and in the community.

These purposes are to be carried out with reference to the following principles, set out in section 4 of the legislation

- The protection of society is paramount.

- All relevant available information shall be utilized in carrying out the sentence, including the reasons and recommendations of the court, release policies of the National Parole Board, and information from victims and offenders.

- Correctional Services shall exchange relevant information with other components of the criminal justice system in a timely manner, and communicate its policies and programs to offenders, victims, and the public.

- The least restrictive measures consistent with the protection of the public, staff members, and offenders shall be used.

- Offenders retain the rights and privileges accorded to all members of society, except as necessary as a consequence of the sentence.

- Correctional Services shall facilitate the involvement of members of the public in matters relating to corrections operations.

- Correctional decisions shall be made fairly, and the offender shall have access to an effective grievance procedure.

- Correctional policies, programs, and practices shall respect gender, ethnic, cultural, and linguistic differences, and be responsive to the special needs of women, aboriginal peoples, and other groups.

- Offenders are expected to obey penitentiary rules and conditions governing temporary absence, work release, parole, and statutory release, and to actively participate in rehabilitation and reintegration programs.

- Staff members shall be properly selected and trained and given appropriate career development opportunities, good working conditions, and opportunities to participate in the development of policies and programs.

In applying these principles, administrators of the corrections system must balance the primary goal—the protection of society—against other important objectives, including, in particular, preservation (to the extent possible) of the dignity, human rights, and personal freedoms of individuals in custody, and responsiveness to their special needs and cultural differences. The principles also place a high value on openness, consultation with other participants in the criminal justice system (for example, sentencing judges, the National Parole Board, victims, and offenders themselves), and opportunities for public input and involvement.

Inmate Behaviour: Controls and Privileges

DISCIPLINARY OFFENCES

Most penitentiaries have rules governing inmate behaviour; these rules are developed by the Commissioner of Corrections in accordance with section 97 of the CCRA. While the legislation expresses a preference for dealing with breaches of the rules informally, where serious or recurrent breaches occur and informal means cannot adequately address the issue, an inmate is charged with a **disciplinary of-fence** and a hearing is held.

An inmate who is found guilty of a disciplinary offence may be subject to a variety of sanctions, including a warning or reprimand, a loss of privileges, a fine, and/or extra duties. Disciplinary offences may also affect the inmate's security designation and opportunities for early release (parole).

The Commissioner of Corrections reports directly to the Minister of Public Safety and Emergency Preparedness and may designate any staff person a peace officer (section 10 of the CCRA). This designation, which is typically made for guards and administrators, gives the staff person certain law enforcement powers, such as the right to use force to suppress a riot and the right to carry out searches.

SEARCHES

One of the most important infringements of a person's human rights that results from incarceration is being subjected to searches, including searches of belongings, frisk searches, strip searches, and body cavity searches. Subjecting prisoners to searches is a routine security measure, regardless of an individual's actual behaviour. In this respect, the search powers of corrections staff are very different from those of police officers in the case of a suspected offence: police may search a suspect only when there are reasonable grounds to believe that a law has been broken. While much broader search powers exist behind prison walls, the CCRA nevertheless sets limits on the conduct of searches because they are such an infringement on personal dignity.

Inmates are subject to non-intrusive or frisk searches as a part of prison routine where such searches are reasonably necessary for security. Inmates are also subject to strip searches by a same-sex guard in certain circumstances, such as when they may have had access to contraband, such as drugs or weapons.

As you would expect, the rules for body cavity searches are narrower, because this kind of search is very intrusive. Three ways of searching body cavities are allowed, in certain circumstances: (1) the use of X-ray; (2) isolation of the inmate in a "dry cell" (that is, with no plumbing, "on the expectation that the contraband will be expelled"); and (3) where neither of the first two methods is expected to work, a body cavity search conducted by a qualified medical practitioner. In the last case, the search must be authorized by the head of the correctional institution.

The legislation also provides rules for **demand urinalysis** (used to monitor for drug use), searches of cells, and searches of prison staff members and visitors. Searches (including strip searches) of visitors are voluntary in that a visitor can choose to leave the penitentiary instead of submitting to a search.

ADMINISTRATIVE SEGREGATION

The practice commonly known as "solitary confinement" is described in the CCRA as **administrative segregation**. Inmates can be placed in administrative segregation by recommendation from facility staff (for example, because they are considered dangerous to others), but they can also request such segregation on their own behalf (for example, if they feel that they are at risk from other inmates). There are detailed rules for administrative segregation, both under sections 31 to 37 of the CCRA and in the regulations made under it.

Critical Perspectives

Lessons from the 1994 Riot in Kingston's Prison for Women

By 1990, the Prison for Women in Kingston, Ontario had developed a reputation as a very unpleasant place to be. The prison was noisy and poorly ventilated, and it lacked space for the provision of community interaction and re-habilitation programs. A solid wall, built around the prison in 1981, made the prison look like a fortress; in fact, the outdated construction and layout of the building meant that a large percentage of the women housed there were being held in higher-security surroundings than was ap-propriate for them. Many of the inmates were socially isolated. Of the 130 inmates of the facility in 1990, only 60 were from Ontario. The rest were separated from their families by distances that made frequent visits difficult.

A task force report released in 1990 recommended the closure of the prison.

By April 1994, the prison had still not closed, and ten-sions were running high. Violence broke out between a group of inmates and some of the prison guards. Two days later, inmates took a hostage and there was an attempted suicide. Staff responded by moving some of the prisoners into a segregation unit, but violence continued there, and correctional workers launched a protest outside the prison. On April 26, the warden called in an all-male institutional emergency response team (IERT) from Kingston Peniten-tiary. In their efforts to address the disruptions at the Prison for Women, members of this team strip-searched eight inmates, leaving them in segregation cells wearing paper gowns and leg irons. Video footage of the search was released to the media provoking outrage among many viewers.

In response to the incident, the government appointed Madam Justice Louise Arbour to conduct an investigation of the events. Her eventual report included a list of 16 recommendations, many of which have prompted changes not only to women's corrections, but to the correctional service as a whole.

Examples of Madam Justice Arbour's recommendations are as follows:

1. That the position of deputy commissioner for women be created within the Correctional Service of Canada, at a rank equivalent to that of regional deputy commissioner

2. That the deputy commissioner for women be given the discretion to implement family contact programs, including financially assisted telephone calls or family visits, even if such programs are not available to in-carcerated men, to recognize the different circum-stances and needs of women, particularly—but not restricted to—their child-care responsibilities.

3. That the sexual harassment policy of the Correctional Service of Canada be extended to apply to inmates.

4. That the Correctional Service of Canada acknowledge that the following is a correct interpretation of the existing law, or that it seek modification of the exist-ing law to accord with the following:

    a. Men may not strip search women. The only excep-tion is where the delay in locating women to con-duct the search would be dangerous to human life or safety, or might result in the loss of evidence. No man may witness the strip search of a woman, except as above.

5. That inmates be given the right to counsel before expressing their consent to a body cavity search, and that inmates be advised of that right at the time their consent is sought.

6. That body cavity searches only be performed in sur-roundings that are appropriate for consensual, non-emergency medical examination or intervention.

7. That a body cavity search be performed only by a female physician, if the inmate so requests, and that the physician ensure, to her satisfaction, that the consent was not obtained as a result of inducement or coercion.

8. That body cavity searches and strip searches per-formed in contravention of these recommendations be treated as having rendered the conditions of imprison-ment harsher than that contemplated by the sen-tence, for the purposes of the remedies contemplated in the recommendation dealing with sanctions.

9. That under the supervision of the deputy commis-sioner for women, all regional facilities draw on the resources of the healing lodge for the development of programs and correctional approaches relevant to the particular needs and circumstances of Aboriginal women.

10. That the practice of long-term confinement in admin-istrative segregation be brought to an end.

11. That the women who were the subject of the cell ex-tractions conducted by the male IERT on April 26/27, 1994 and who were kept in prolonged segregation afterwards, be properly compensated by the Correc-tional Service of Canada for the infringement of all their legal rights as found in this report, commencing on April 22, 1994.

Source: *Commission of Inquiry into Certain Events at the Prison for Women in Kingston* (Ottawa: Public Works and Government Services Canada, 1996). ◇

TEMPORARY ABSENCES

As discussed earlier, each inmate of a penitentiary is assigned a security classification. Temporary absences are permitted for low-risk inmates in a variety of circumstances, including the following:

- for medical or dental treatment;

- for reasons of community service or personal development;

- for "family contact";

- to attend rehabilitation programs;

- for compassionate reasons (for example, to attend the funeral of a family member); and

- for "work release"—to allow the offender to work at a job outside the facility.

Except for medical absences, eligibility for a temporary absence generally requires that

1. the offender be assessed as low risk to the community;

2. there is a plan for the temporary release;

3. the offender is supervised on the release; and

4. the offender is subject to having the release cut short and further temporary releases denied for breach of the release conditions.

Many inmates are eligible for unescorted absences halfway through the period preceding the full parole eligibility date, or six months after entering the facility, whichever is longer. However, this varies depending on factors such as whether the inmate is serving an indefinite sentence.

PRISONER INFORMATION

The CCRA has detailed provisions about the handling of information. Penitentiaries are expected to gather accurate information about inmates, their offences, and any other relevant information (for example, a history of violence while serving other sentences). There are rules requiring facilities to provide offenders with information about themselves and the opportunity to challenge the accuracy of the information; and there are rules for providing victims, upon request, with limited information about offenders (for example, a victim can request to be advised if the offender is permitted to be out of the prison on work release).

Conditional Release and Long-Term Supervision

CONDITIONAL RELEASE

Conditional release means any release before the last day of an offender's full sentence. Any time that an offender is released before serving the entire sentence imposed by the court, the release is conditional, which means that it can be revoked for breach of conditions. When this happens, the offender is taken back into custody and returned to the penitentiary.

Consistent with the purpose of the CCRA (set out earlier in this discussion), decisions on the timing and conditions of release should both support the goal of maintaining a just, peaceful, and safe society, and facilitate the rehabilitation of offenders and their reintegration into the community as law-abiding citizens.

There are two types of conditional release:

■ statutory release, which in most cases is available automatically after the offender has served two-thirds of the sentence; and

■ parole, which is discretionary.

Statutory Release

Offenders who are sentenced to imprisonment for life or for an indeterminate term are not eligible for statutory release because these sentences do not have a fixed termination date. However, most offenders are entitled to **statutory release** on completion of two-thirds of their sentence unless the National Parole Board believes that the inmate is likely, while on statutory release,

■ to cause death or serious harm to another person;

■ to commit a sexual offence against a child; or

■ to commit a serious drug offence.

If the board considers that the offender is likely to commit any of these offences, it may refuse to release the inmate before the full sentence is served. However, once the sentence is served, the inmate must be released even if one or more of the above conditions exist and there are serious concerns about reoffending. There is no authority to maintain supervision or monitoring of an offender who has served her full sentence. Therefore, while keeping high-risk offenders behind bars for the duration of their sentence temporarily protects the public, it also has a downside: it does not allow for a gradual, supervised release back to the community.

Parole

Unlike statutory release, **parole** is not automatic—it is discretionary. Parole is granted to an offender who is deemed not to pose an undue risk of reoffending within the term of his full sentence. It generally occurs when one-third to two-thirds of the sentence has been served, depending on the offence, the circumstances, and the offender's behaviour while in prison. Parole is not available for young offenders.

While on parole, the offender (the parolee) is monitored by a parole officer, who ensures compliance with the conditions of parole. Parole conditions may be very similar to the conditions of probation, but their purpose is to ease the parolee back into society. A parolee is required to report to the parole officer and the police department immediately after release, and must report to the parole officer regularly thereafter. If a parolee violates a parole condition, parole may be suspended and the offender returned immediately to prison.

The parole eligibility rules differ somewhat between the federal system (sentences of two years or longer), which is administered by the National Parole Board, and the Ontario system (sentences of less than two years), which is administered by the Ontario Parole and Earned Release Board. Parole hearings are held in the institution where the offender is incarcerated, and interested parties (such as victims) may make submissions regarding the appropriateness of granting parole.

Offenders who would like to be released before their statutory release date may apply for parole, if and when they are eligible as provided by statute. In most cases, a person may apply for parole after serving 7 years or one-third of the sentence, whichever is less. For example, generally a person with a 21-year or longer sentence may apply for parole after serving 7 years.

There are additional rules governing the parole eligibility date in certain circumstances. For example, offenders who have been convicted of certain crimes under the *Crimes Against Humanity and War Crimes Act* are not eligible for parole until they have served at least 25 years. Also, offenders who have been sentenced "without possibility of parole" for a specified number of years are excluded from the general parole formula.

Despite the general parole rules, all but the most serious offenders may be granted parole in certain exceptional circumstances. These exceptions include

- an offender who has a terminal illness;

- an offender who is likely to suffer serious damage to his physical or mental health from continued confinement;

- an offender "for whom continued confinement would constitute an excessive hardship that was not reasonably foreseeable at the time the offender was sentenced" (section 121(1)(c) of the CCRA); or,

- in some cases, a person who is being held for **extradition** purposes.

If an offender sentenced to life or an indeterminate term is released on parole, he continues to be on parole for life. This means that he is required, for example, to report on a regular basis to a parole officer and to inform authorities of any change in his living, employment, or financial situation.

To assist in the reintegration of offenders into society, the CCRA allows some federal inmates to be released on **day parole**. Day parole is normally granted as a stepping stone to full parole: offenders on day parole can go to work or attend rehabilitation/work-readiness programs in the daytime and enjoy a certain degree of daytime freedom, but must return to the penitentiary at night. Day parole is granted after a review similar to the review performed for full parole. Day parole is for a maximum six-month term, though the term can be renewed if the offender is not yet ready for full parole.

WEB LINK

For information about the policies and procedures of the National Parole Board, including the board's policy manual, visit the website at www.npb-cnlc.gc.ca.

LONG-TERM SUPERVISION

Some offenders may be subject to an additional period of community supervision of up to 10 years, if the sentence is at least two years and the court determines that there is both

- a substantial risk that the offender will reoffend and

- a reasonable possibility of eventual control of the risk in the community.

These long-term offenders serve their original sentence normally, including eligibility for all types of early release. However, once this sentence expires, they begin their additional term of long-term supervision.

COMMUNITY PROGRAMS AND SERVICES

The federal and provincial correctional services agencies are responsible for offenders until the completion of their full sentence, both in prison and out on parole. The parole officer (who may be a social service worker) refers the offender to appropriate community services to assist reintegration into the community. These may include public assistance, housing, and community support groups like Alcoholics Anonymous.

Residential Services

Some offenders may return to private homes immediately upon their release. This depends on whether there is a suitable home, supportive of the changes the offender is making to his life. Many offenders are released to halfway houses, such as community correctional centres or community residential facilities.

Community correctional centres are operated by CSC and provide residential services to offenders on conditional release or released under a long-term supervision order who require the structure of a residential program. These centres are technically minimum security penitentiaries; however, residents are all on release programs and are not considered incarcerated offenders.

Community residential facilities provide similar services as community correctional centres but are operated by private agencies. These facilities set their own admission criteria and, unlike community correctional centres, may reject applicants.

Community Programs

The first few months are the most critical in the reintegration process. Many offenders struggle as they return to the environment that fostered the criminal behaviour that led to incarceration. They require the support of ongoing programs, positive relationships, and controls on their behaviour.

There are many community programs that target issues such as substance abuse, mental health, sexual violence and pedophilia, and anger management, or otherwise focus on community reintegration skills. The parole officer monitors the offender's progress in programs, as well as overall compliance with the conditions of release.

Employment Services

CORCAN, an agency of CSC, operates employment services in institutions and the community. Its purpose is to help offenders to obtain suitable and satisfactory employment upon their release. It assists offenders with the preparation of resumés, job searches, and obtaining training.

ONTARIO'S CORRECTIONS SYSTEM

Ministry Mandate

As discussed earlier, the operation of Ontario's prisons is governed by the MCSA. The responsible ministry is the Ministry of Community Safety and Correctional Services (referred to in this discussion as "the ministry"). The statute makes it clear that corrections services include more than just keeping inmates behind bars. Section 5 of the MCSA requires the ministry

EXTRA CREDIT

Advocates for Inmates: The John Howard Society, the Elizabeth Fry Society, and the St. Leonard's Society

Inmates of federal and provincial correctional institutions are isolated from society and often have poor social and political support networks. As a group, they have significant advocacy needs. Three important charitable organizations—the John Howard Society, the Elizabeth Fry Society, and the St. Leonard's Society—have emerged to champion the interests of incarcerated offenders. While there are other charitable organizations that also work to help individuals who have been charged with or convicted of criminal offences, these societies are the most prominent, and so their history, missions, and goals are presented here by way of introduction to advocacy on behalf of inmates.

The John Howard Society

The John Howard Society is the successor to the Prisoner's Aid Association, later called the Citizens' Service Association. A Toronto police chief, General Draper, worked to revitalize the association in 1929, because he believed that the unfavourable circumstances into which prisoners were being discharged were driving inmates to reoffend. Renamed the John Howard Society (after a famous British advocate for prison reform) in 1946, the Ontario group was joined by other groups across the country between 1931 and 1960. The national society is actually an association of independent local societies, which do most of the actual service delivery.

The John Howard Society performs a range of functions; specifically, the society

- works with people who have come into conflict with the law,

- reviews, evaluates, and advocates for changes in the criminal justice process,

- engages in public education on matters relating to criminal law and its application, and

- promotes crime prevention through community and social development activities.

Local societies have small staffs but depend heavily on the involvement of volunteers to deliver programs. These programs include addictions counselling, anger management, relationships management, communication training, housing support, discharge planning, and crime prevention.

The Elizabeth Fry Society

The Elizabeth Fry Society was named after a Quaker who initiated reforms in the treatment of women and children in prisons in the early 1800s. The first Canadian Elizabeth Fry Society was established in 1939, and today, there are 25 societies across Canada.

The Canadian Association of Elizabeth Fry Societies supports the principle that all individuals are equal before the law and deserve to be treated equally, without prejudice on the basis of individual attributes, including gender. The association strives to ensure that women have equal access to advocacy (including legal counsel) and justice (including due process).

The association's goals include the provision of advocacy to draw attention to the situation of women in the corrections system, and the promotion and support of programs to meet their needs. Programs include, for example, the following services provided by the Elizabeth Fry Society of Ottawa:

- Individual Counselling;

- Group Counselling;

- Shoplifting Prevention Program;

- Healthy Choices (communication and relationship management program);

- Anger Solutions (anger management program);

- Conflict Resolution (for youth);

- Hooked-Up (for sex trade workers);

- Gateway (supper club program for sex trade workers);

- Family Support Program (peer network for parents and youth);

- Housing Retention and Support Program;

- J.F. Norwood House (housing);

- Discharge Planning; and

- Court Support and Accompaniment.

The St. Leonard's Society

The St. Leonard's Society began its advocacy work on behalf of people in conflict with the law with the opening of a first "halfway house" in Windsor, Ontario in 1962. It has since grown into a national advocacy organization with the following goals:

- to prevent recidivism (reoffending) by providing educational programs, industrial workshops, community residential centres, and other supportive programs;

- to prevent crime by promoting, developing, and implementing improved policies, procedures, and service delivery within the criminal justice system;

- to promote acceptance of responsibility and accountability by persons in conflict with the law, in order to change behaviour that contributes to crime; and

- to help the community to understand its responsibility regarding the incidence of crime and the community's response to crime.

Further information about advocacy programs and services provided by each of these organizations is available from the John Howard Society at www.johnhoward.ca; the Canadian Association of Elizabeth Fry Societies at www.elizabethfry.ca; and the St. Leonard's Society of Canada at www.stleonards.ca. ◈

- to supervise the detention and release of inmates, parolees, probationers, and young persons; and

- to create a social environment in which inmates may achieve changes in attitude by providing training, treatment, and services designed to afford them opportunities for successful personal and social adjustment in the community

The MCSA allows the ministry to subcontract corrections services to municipalities or other agencies and corporations, and the ministry does in fact delegate many functions to outside agencies. Organizations like the John Howard Society, the Elizabeth Fry Society, and the St. Leonard's Society provide support and educational/ rehabilitation services to inmates and parolees. In addition, non-profit corporations often manage transitional housing for offenders who have been released from correctional institutions but who are not yet ready for independent living and full integration into the community.

Types of Detention Facilities

There are three types of detention facilities operated by the province:

- correction centres,
- jails and detention centres, and
- youth custody facilities.

Correction centres are used to hold offenders serving longer sentences, up to two years less a day. A court cannot sentence an offender to a specific provincial institution; the decision about placement of the offender is made by the ministry.

Jails and detention centres are used primarily to hold people who have been accused but not yet convicted of an offence, while they await trial. However, they may also house convicts who have been given short sentences. Typically, jails are smaller, older centres, often run by individual municipalities, whereas detention centres are typically larger, with a regional service base.

Youth custody facilities can be either stand-alone facilities or youth "wings" of adult prisons (provided that the population of young offenders is kept separate from the adult offenders. The administration of correctional facilities for youth is governed by the federal *Youth Criminal Justice Act* and Ontario's *Child and Family Services Act*, and is discussed in more detail in chapter 11.

Correction and detention centres have different kinds of corrections programs and apply different designations for the level of security. Temporary detention centres have **secure custody** (strict control/restriction) and **open custody** (less strict/restricted) programs. Non-temporary detention facilities identify two levels of security: maximum security and medium security.

Prison Staff

As in the federal system, prison guards and other staff are designated as peace officers and therefore have law enforcement powers. For example, they can search inmates and seize **contraband** items such as weapons and drugs.

Volunteers working in provincial corrections are required to work under the supervision of an employee of the ministry, a contractor, or an employee of a contractor. This provides accountability for the actions of volunteers, who may not be as well trained or as knowledgeable about legal standards and procedures as paid staff.

Prison staff who act in good faith in carrying out or attempting to carry out their duties are protected from lawsuits for damages under section 12 of the MCSA. This protection extends to the acts of inmates, young people, probationers, or parolees in staff care. In practical terms, this means that prison staff cannot be held vicariously liable for the act of an inmate when that inmate commits a tort or a crime while under staff supervision. For example, consider a prison guard responsible for supervising an inmate while outside the prison doing groundskeeping for a library as community service work. If the inmate overpowered the guard, stole the riding lawn mower, and drove away, the prison guard could not be sued by the library or the municipality for the cost of the lawn mower. The guard would also be protected from liability for any harm, such as assault, inflicted on members of the public by the escaped inmate.

It is important to recognize that this protection extends to employees only where the employees are doing or attempting to do their jobs in good faith. As soon as an employee does something that is outside her duties, neglects to perform her duties, or acts in a way that is not in good faith, she is no longer protected from legal liability. For example, if the prison guard turned a blind eye while the prisoner escaped on the mower, the guard could be held liable for harm consequently caused to the public by the prisoner.

Absences

Inmates are sometimes allowed to leave the facility temporarily, in order to work or to participate in rehabilitation programs. In some cases, they can leave to attend academic programs; some youth in custody, for example, attend regular public schools under programs of supervision.

The MCSA contains provisions regulating inmates' absences from the facility for rehabilitation, education, and work purposes. Being absent from prison with or without supervision is a privilege that is extended only to those inmates whose history suggests that they pose no undue risk to the people with whom they will come into contact. Misbehaviour, such as violation of a release condition, will usually lead to revocation of the inmate's absence privileges.

Inmates who would not normally be eligible to be absent from prison can be granted this privilege in certain situations—for example, to receive medical or dental treatment, or for "humanitarian reasons." Not returning to the prison as scheduled, however, can lead to a new conviction with a sentence of one additional year of imprisonment.

Remission and Release

Inmates who obey the rules while in prison and actively participate in rehabilitation programs earn **remission,** which is a system of good-behaviour-time credits that accumulate for **earned release** (parole). The formula for calculating remission is provided in the (federal) *Prisons and Reformatories Act.*

As in the federal corrections system, inmates must apply for parole. Provincial parole decisions are made by the Ontario Parole and Earned Release Board. In considering an application for parole, the board must decide whether the inmate has earned remission, and how much. The amount of remission earned determines the timing of release.

Victims may take part in parole hearings, with permission. A social service worker who works in a victim support program may accompany a victim to a parole hearings.

Parole decisions cannot be appealed to or reviewed by any court. The only recourse for an inmate whose parole is denied is to wait until the next opportunity to request a parole review.

As in the case of federal parole, an early release is a conditional release: the parolee must comply with certain conditions. If he violates any of those conditions at any time before his full sentence expires, he will be apprehended and returned to prison. The board also has the power to suspend the parole of a parolee who has not yet breached a condition where the board is satisfied that suspending parole is necessary to *prevent* the breach of a condition or to protect the public. When the board suspends parole and brings an offender back into custody, it must hold a hearing as soon as possible to consider whether the parole should be revoked.

WEB LINK

For more information about Ontario's parole program, visit the website of the Ontario Parole and Earned Release Board at www.operb.gov.on.ca.

ALTERNATIVE SENTENCES

As discussed in chapter 9, the *Criminal Code* provides the courts with a range of sentencing options, consistent with the objective of imposing imprisonment as a punishment of last resort. Two forms of conditional sentences are reviewed briefly below.

Conditional Sentence of Imprisonment

In appropriate cases, a court may order that a sentence of imprisonment is to be served in the community. Generally, this means house arrest. A conditional sentence of imprisonment cannot be ordered for a crime that carries a minimum sentence or a sentence of two years or longer (section 742.1 of the *Criminal Code*).

When a court orders a sentence to be served in the community, the offender must comply with the terms imposed by the court. Non-compliance can lead to an order that the offender serve the rest of the sentence in custody.

Cases decided under section 742.1 have established, as a matter of precedent, that community sentences are meant to serve both rehabilitative and punitive purposes; that is, they should be designed so as to incorporate elements that remind the offender that she is serving a criminal sentence, such as restriction of freedom during off-work hours.

Release Subject to a Probation Order

Again in appropriate circumstances, a court may impose a suspended sentence (section 731 of the *Criminal Code*) or a conditional discharge (section 730). In both of these cases, the offender must comply with the conditions contained in a probation order. As discussed in chapter 9, probation may be ordered alone, or with either a fine or a prison term, but not both. Thus, a person convicted of assault could be sentenced to one year in prison and two years of probation, subject to the conditions in the probation order. Alternatively, the sentence could be a fine of $1,000 plus two years of probation, subject to the conditions in the probation order.

KEY TERMS

administrative segregation	disciplinary offence	remission
conditional release	earned release	secure custody
contraband	extradition	statutory release
day parole	open custody	systemic discrimination
demand urinalysis	parole	

REFERENCES

Canadian Charter of Rights and Freedoms, part I of the *Constitution Act, 1982*, being schedule B of the *Canada Act 1982* (UK), 1982, c. 11.

Child and Family Services Act, RSO 1990, c. C.11.

Constitution Act, 1867, 30 & 31 Vict., c. 3 (UK).

Corrections and Conditional Release Act, SC 1992, c. 20.

Crimes Against Humanity and War Crimes Act, SC 2000, c. 24.

Criminal Code, RSC 1985, c. C-46.

Ministry of Correctional Services Act, RSO 1990, c. M.22, and General Regulation, RRO 1990, Reg. 778.

Prisons and Reformatories Act, RSC 1985, c. P-20.

Youth Criminal Justice Act, SC 2002, c. 1.

REVIEW QUESTIONS

1. List the two most important justifications for incarceration of people convicted of crimes.

2. Why does Canada's justice system view incarceration as a penalty of last resort?

3. Why is "two years less a day" a fairly common sentence for less serious crimes?

4. List three statutes that describe the rights of incarcerated people.

5. List at least six rights of incarcerated offenders.

6. Identify the paramount principle of the *Corrections and Conditional Release Act*, and describe the other important objectives that corrections authorities must balance against that goal.

7. Explain how the legal basis of searches of people in custody differs from the legal basis of police searches of individuals in the community.

8. For what kinds of reasons might a federal offender be allowed to be absent from custody, and on what condition(s)?

9. What are the two kinds of early release and how do they differ?

10. Where do federal inmates live immediately after their release?

11. Explain how the liability of provincial corrections staff for damages lawsuits is limited by law.

12. How is inmates' eligibility for parole determined in the provincial prison system?

13. What is meant by serving a sentence "in the community"?

CHAPTER 11

The Youth Criminal Justice System

CHAPTER OBJECTIVES

After reading this chapter, you should be able to:

- Summarize the evolution in our society's approaches to youth criminal responsibility and justice.

- Describe the general principles of the *Youth Criminal Justice Act*.

- Explain what is meant by extrajudicial measures and how law enforcement officers decide when it is appropriate to divert certain youths from the traditional criminal justice process.

- List some of the differences in how our criminal justice system treats youths who are accused of offences, as compared with adults.

- Understand how sentencing principles for young offenders differ from those that apply to adults.

- Describe the general rules that govern the treatment of youths in custody.

INTRODUCTION

The Canadian justice system recognizes that young people who commit criminal offences are different, in important ways, from adult offenders.

Research has shown the following:

- Young people (children and teenagers) are not mature, either intellectually, behaviourally, or emotionally; as a result, they may not be capable of understanding the subtleties of right and wrong conduct or the full consequences of their actions.

- **Young offenders** often have motivations for their criminal actions that differ from those of adults for similar crimes, such as peer pressure or thrill seeking.

- Despite media suggestions to the contrary, teenagers commit fewer crimes than adults, and teenage offenders are less likely than adults to use serious violence in committing their crimes.

- Young people who commit a first offence while in their teens are less likely to reoffend than first-time adult offenders.

- Sentences based on deterrence tend to be less effective for teenagers than for adults, but rehabilitation-focused approaches are more effective for teenagers.

- In general, teen offenders are more sensitive to being labelled as criminals (in the sense that **labelling** provokes reoffending), and they are also more worried than adult repeat offenders about the effect that a criminal record may have on their future.

Because of these and other factors, Canada's criminal justice system provides for different treatment of young offenders through two statutes, the *Criminal Code* and the *Youth Criminal Justice Act* (YCJA). The starting point is the codification of an age threshold for criminal responsibility with respect to crimes committed by children. Section 13 of the *Criminal Code* provides:

> No person shall be convicted of an offence in respect of an act or omission on his part while that person was under the age of twelve years.

While young people aged 12 and older are subject to the offence provisions of the *Criminal Code*, the YCJA applies an additional "protective" layer of interpretation and procedure to the way the justice system manages teenage offenders. For example:

- The principles for sentencing young offenders are different from those for adult offenders.

- There is greater protection for the privacy of younger offenders; and there are special rules for certain aspects of the investigation and trial of young offenders (such as the admissibility of confessions).

Ontario provides additional protection to young offenders in custody through the children's rights provisions of the *Child and Family Services Act*, as well as part V of the *Ministry of Correctional Services Act* (discussed in chapter 10).

Social service workers may work with young offenders in various ways. Some offenders, instead of being charged or tried, are referred to programs designed to circumvent the court process and assist them in not reoffending. These **extrajudicial sanctions** may include community service, counselling, and writing an essay about the behaviour. Social service workers may be involved in designing, administering, or supervising these programs. Within the corrections system, social service workers may work with youth in prison or in transitional facilities (halfway houses). Those who work in Aboriginal communities may also be involved with alternative justice initiatives such as sentencing circles (discussed in chapter 9).

HISTORY OF YOUTH JUSTICE

Our society's view of children was once very different from what it is today. Most of us now understand childhood, adolescence, and adulthood to be distinct life stages, and we generally accept the idea that children and youth are more vulnerable than adults, and therefore in need of special protection. However, these views have not always seemed so self-evident. Like most other social constructs, they are the product of certain historical developments and a corresponding evolution of ideas and values.

Until the late 17th century, children as young as six or seven were expected to begin contributing to the support and prosperity of the family and the community. They worked on farms, practised trades (sometimes as apprentices), and participated in commerce. A child's work was not understood, as it often is today, as "doing her chores" or "helping his mom." Instead, the child was depended upon to contribute to the family's survival.

Around the beginning of the 18th century, things began to change. First, new scholarly thinking and writing about psychosocial development introduced the idea that children and adolescents were less than full grown, not only in the physical sense, but also in the emotional, intellectual, and moral senses.

The emergence of these ideas led to increased separation of children and adolescents from adult responsibilities and activities. Upper-class children were kept in school longer than ever before. Working-class children, for the first time, were denied access to certain kinds of employment. This happened for three reasons:

- The great technological leaps of the 18th century meant that many trades and types of work were becoming more complicated. Longer and longer periods of apprenticeship were required to master the new skills and absorb the new knowledge.

- As some kinds of work, such as manufacturing, became increasingly mechanized, the number of jobs decreased. Youth jobs were often the first to be eliminated.

- A workers' rights movement emerged, raising awareness of the dangers and health risks of factory and mining work. Social reformers argued for the need to protect children from these dangers by prohibiting their employment in dangerous work and abolishing long workdays.

As a result of these changes, many working-class teenage children whose families couldn't afford schooling were shut out of the workforce. Without a clear role to play in society, little to do, and no way to earn money, some became involved in (usually petty) crime. With the rise of urban youth crime, the term **juvenile delinquent** was coined, and society began paying attention to the unique developmental stage that we now recognize as adolescence. People began to understand that children behaved, or misbehaved, as they did not simply because of flaws in character, but because their character and abilities were still developing.

Before these shifts in the perception of childhood, the law typically applied equally to children and adults. While a few legal rules—notably those relating to property ownership—suspended certain rights until adulthood, most statutes that were designed either to punish offenders or to protect society applied regardless of age. Thus, children of all ages were held responsible for crimes they had committed.

As the uniqueness of childhood and adolescence became recognized, the idea of **legal capacity**—the right and ability of a person to exercise legal rights—also evolved. Children, once full participants in adult society, were deemed to lack legal capacity until they had achieved the level of physical, intellectual, emotional, and moral development that marked adulthood.

A principle closely related to legal capacity is **criminal responsibility**. As the criminal law has evolved, so has the idea that not all people who commit criminal acts should be made to bear the full legal consequences normally attached to those acts. In certain special cases, some circumstance of the act or some characteristic of the person who committed it warrants different treatment under the law. For example, as most people are aware, in appropriate cases, a court may find an accused "not criminally responsible on account of mental disorder," or an accused may seek to avoid conviction by "pleading insanity" and relying on an "insanity defence."

Proving insanity is actually quite complicated. A much simpler and clearer measure of criminal responsibility is an age threshold, as provided for in the existing *Criminal Code*. The relevance of age as a factor in determining criminal responsibility was recognized in Canada's statutory law early in the last century, and it has helped to shape changes in our approach to the treatment of young offenders, as reflected in subsequent legal reforms.

The first statute designed to address the criminal responsibility of young offenders was the *Juvenile Delinquents Act* (JDA). This statute was introduced in 1908 and remained in effect, with various amendments, until 1984. The JDA had a welfare focus, in the sense that it characterized youth criminality as an "affliction" that could be remedied through appropriate help and guidance. Children aged 7 to 17 who were offered assistance under the JDA were often removed from the care of their parents and "parented" by the government, under a doctrine known as **parens patriae**. This doctrine emphasized the state's duty to protect vulnerable members of society and assumed a connection between poor parenting and youth criminality.

The JDA system was closely connected to social services, and recognized very few legal rights or procedural protections for the children managed under it. In the decades leading up to the mid-1980s, criticisms of the JDA began to emerge. Committing young offenders to institutions was declared to be useless, and even harmful from the perspective of rehabilitation, and the lack of due process in the JDA system came under fire as children's rights became more widely recognized. In 1965, the government created a committee to study legislative reform in the area of youth justice. That reform initiative eventually led to the replacement of the JDA with the *Young Offenders Act* (YOA), which was enacted in 1984.

The YOA abandoned the JDA notion that youth criminality was a "condition," but maintained the view that young children lack full criminal responsibility. The YOA was designed to apply to offenders over the age threshold for criminal responsibility (12 years) but under the age of 18.

The YOA rejected the wholesale institutionalization of young people who committed criminal acts and embraced the notion of diverting youth from the normal process of the criminal justice system in appropriate cases. However, it also introduced a more punitive approach to youth justice, in an attempt to reduce **recidivism** (repeat offending). At the same time, the YOA (in contrast to the JDA) gave formal recognition to the substantial rights of young offenders in contact with the criminal justice system.

The YOA was a controversial statute and seemed incapable of satisfying anyone. While it sought to de-institutionalize the treatment of young offenders, it resulted in a substantial increase in custodial sentences, drawing fire from advocates of alternative solutions. More conservative critics thought that the due process rights provided in the YOA were too broad, notably in the areas of protection of identity and provision of legal representation. Other critics argued that the YOA did not place sufficient emphasis on rehabilitation. The statute had only been in effect for a few years when pressure began to mount for a new round of reforms. This pressure soon led to the drafting of the YCJA, which was passed into law in 2002.

Like the YOA, the YCJA applies to youth between the ages of 12 and 18. When an offence is committed by a person within this age range, the **disposition** of the matter—whether through prosecution or through alternative, extrajudicial measures or sanctions—is governed by the YCJA's comprehensive system for the management of young offenders.

THE YOUTH CRIMINAL JUSTICE ACT: AN OVERVIEW

General Principles

The YCJA incorporates four general principles, expressed in section 3(1). These can be summarized as follows:

- the prevention of crime and protection of the public;

- a criminal justice system for young persons that is separate from the system for adults and emphasizes rehabilitation and reintegration;

- a culturally sensitive response to the offence that promotes respect for societal values and reparations to victims "within the limits of fair and proportionate accountability"; and

- special protections including enhanced civil rights and a role for parents.

LEGISLATIVE SHORTCUT

Youth Criminal Justice Act

SC 2002, c.1

Objective: To protect the public, and to protect youth in trouble with the law, by providing a separate system and procedures that emphasize rehabilitation.

Target Population: Young people, between the ages of 12 and 17, their parents, and their communities.

Program Administration: The police enforce the laws with the involvement of community agencies, and where extrajudicial measures (alternatives to court) are insufficient, provincial Crown attorneys prosecute offenders in youth court.

Administrative Tribunal: Not applicable—criminal matters are heard by courts.

Summary: The *Youth Criminal Justice Act* provides for special treatment of young offenders, including the use of extrajudicial measures, such as cautioning the suspect, referring him or her to a social welfare agency, or requiring the performance of community service. The Act sets up a separate youth court with special rules to protect youth, such as notice to parents, and outlines principles of sentencing that emphasize non-custodial sentences and rehabilitation. The Act also prohibits the publication of identifying information about young offenders in most cases. ◇

The YCJA was introduced in an unsettled socio-political climate. Criminologists and sociologists were beginning to recognize that widespread incarceration has a fairly poor track record as a means of reducing youth crime. At the same time, there was a public perception (mostly unsupported by statistical evidence) that violent crime committed by youths was on the rise. The resulting principles of the YCJA (and the way they have been applied by judges) reflect a tension between these competing values within the law enforcement system.

Structure

The YCJA is divided into numerous parts, the most important of which are as follows:

- *Part 1—Extrajudicial Measures.* Extrajudicial measures provide an alternative to prosecution of an offence through the court system. The use of such measures is often referred to as **diversion**. The measures described in part 1 include issuing a warning or a caution to the offender, referring the offender to a community program or agency, and referring the offender to a sanctions program (in effect, imposing an extrajudicial penalty for the offence).

- *Part 2—Organization of Youth Criminal Justice System.* Part 2 provides for special courts and judges (youth courts) with jurisdiction over young suspects. Provided that the young person was at least 12 years old when the offence was committed and that he is under 18 when the charge is laid, he can be tried in a youth court.

- *Part 3—Judicial Measures.* Part 3 sets out the basic rules of youth court procedure. Where an aspect of procedure is not specifically described, regular criminal court procedure (as specified in the *Criminal Code*) applies. Matters covered in part 3 include the young person's right to counsel; the requirement for notice to parents of certain steps taken against the young person (for example, the laying of a charge); the rules for detention before sentencing; and the ordering and uses of medical or psychological assessments of the young person.

- *Part 4—Sentencing.* The YCJA reflects a strong bias against custodial sentences (incarceration) for young people. Part 4 includes the rationale for this approach (reflected in specific sentencing principles to be applied by the court), as well as detailed provisions describing sentencing options and procedures.

- *Part 5—Custody and Supervision.* Part 5 deals with custody (incarceration) and supervision (commonly known as probation).

- *Part 6—Publication, Records and Information.* Part 6 of the YCJA prohibits the publication of identifying information about young offenders in certain cases, and creates rules for the protection and management of youth criminal justice records.

WEB LINK

For a module-by-module explanation of YCJA procedures, including checklists, visit the federal Department of Justice ("Justice Canada") website at www.justice-canada.net.

SPECIAL PROTECTIONS IN THE YOUTH CRIMINAL JUSTICE SYSTEM

In recognition of the fact that young suspects are not fully mature, the youth criminal justice system incorporates special protections for youth in addition to the protections created by the *Criminal Code* and the *Canadian Charter of Rights and Freedoms*. These protections are designed to utilize a young offender's potential for rehabilitation and for overcoming criminal behaviour, so that she can go on to play a productive role in society.

To support the purpose of these protections, social service workers who frequently work with young offenders should be knowledgeable enough to explain these rights to their clients in a general way. Of course, if a client has been charged with an offence, or if she reveals involvement in criminal activity to the social service worker, she should be immediately referred to a lawyer. The following offers a very general overview of the special rules relating to youth.

Legal Representation

As in the case of adults, any young person suspected or accused of committing an offence is entitled to representation by a lawyer. This right arises early, even where police are considering the use of extrajudicial measures instead of prosecution. In order to encourage young persons to retain counsel, the right to counsel is specifically referred to in a notice given to the youth's parents (discussed below). If the young suspect cannot afford to hire a lawyer, he will generally be referred to legal aid. In some cases, the court can order the attorney general to appoint counsel for the youth, or can order that the youth be represented by his own counsel, separate from counsel retained by his parents.

Notice to Parents

Except where a youth is 20 or older at the time of the first court appearance (having been charged while under 18), the police are required to give notice of the charge (and the youth's right to counsel) to a parent, or if no parent is available, to an adult relative or guardian. The purpose of this provision is to inform the parents so that they can help the youth with specific matters such as hiring a lawyer, and so that they can provide support during the legal proceedings.

Pre-Trial Detention

Sometimes a young suspect is detained in custody before trial—that is, he is not released on bail. The *Criminal Code* permits pre-trial detention where the suspect is considered dangerous to society or likely to escape the jurisdiction rather than attend at the trial. The YCJA imposes additional, very strict limits on the situations in which a young person can be detained before sentencing. A youth cannot be detained before trial unless, if convicted, he would be subject to incarceration even after considering the restrictions on custody imposed by section 39(1) of the YCJA. These restrictions forbid a custody sentence unless

- the young person has committed a violent offence;

- the young person has failed to comply with previous non-custodial sentences; or

- the young person has committed a serious offence (one that would attract a sentence of two years or more for an adult) and the young person has a criminal record.

The combination of these restrictions means, in essence, that a young person will not be detained before trial in the absence of violence, breach of probation, or the combination of a serious offence and a criminal record.

Medical and Psychological Assessments

The judge in a youth trial can order that the young person undergo a medical or psychological assessment. The court can order an assessment for one of a number of purposes, including

- to determine the appropriateness of **pre-trial release** (bail);

- to determine whether the young person can be subject to an adult sentence;

- to support an appropriate choice of youth sentence; or to support the choice of appropriate conditions for conditional release (probation).

In rare cases, the court can order that the young person be detained for the purpose of a medical or psychological assessment.

Records

The YCJA protects the identity of young offenders by banning publication of their names, to discourage labelling of young persons as criminals. The avoidance of labelling is viewed, by most psychologists, as a way of reducing the likelihood that the young person will reoffend because he has a reputation for criminal behaviour to live up to. By not publishing identifying information about young offenders, the justice system seeks to protect their reputation in the community, recognizing that the young sometimes make mistakes because they lack maturity. By protecting the privacy of young people, the courts seek to prevent a criminal charge from limiting the future opportunities of the young offender.

The publication ban imposed by the YCJA is not absolute. Under section 110, the legislation prohibits the publication of information "that would identify the young person as a young person dealt with under this Act." However, some exceptions apply with respect to violent offences.

EXTRAJUDICIAL MEASURES (DIVERSION)

Extrajudicial measures are ways of dealing informally with youth involved in criminal activity, as an alternative to prosecution through traditional criminal procedure (charge, trial, and sentencing). The decision about whether to use extrajudicial measures in a particular case is made by the police, and the YCJA makes it compulsory for the officer(s) involved to consider this option.

The typical point at which police will consider the use of extrajudicial measures is when they have enough evidence to lay a charge. For example, police may be called when a schoolyard brawl escalates and is considered an assault by school administrators. Arriving upon this kind of scene, police normally have sufficient eyewitness evidence to lay an assault charge, and are therefore required to consider extrajudicial measures before they do so.

In deciding whether extrajudicial measures are appropriate, police will consider factors such as the following:

- the degree of violence used in committing the offence;

- the demeanour of the youth (whether he is apologetic and remorseful or belligerent);

- the youth's past criminal history; and

- the youth's age.

In general, diversion is most appropriate for first offences, younger offenders, offences that do not involve violence, and situations in which the offender has clearly taken moral responsibility for his actions. Some studies suggest that there is a link between the use of less punitive measures for first-time young offenders and reduced recidivism. More specifically, commencing a formal criminal process against first-time young offenders is a stronger predictor of subsequent criminal behaviour on the part of the offender, while responses such as a police warning or no specific police action are most consistent with non-recidivism.

The following extrajudicial measures may be used, where appropriate, by the police (or, in some circumstances, by Crown prosecutors) instead of prosecution:

- choosing to take no further action;

- administering a warning;

- administering a caution;

- referring the young person to a counselling program; or

- imposing an extrajudicial sanction, requiring the young person to participate in a sanctions program.

A warning is spoken—for example, "You are not being charged for this offence, but if you do it again, you *will* be charged"—and is usually not communicated to the youth's parents. A **caution** is formal, and the parents will be informed. There are two kinds of cautions: police cautions and Crown cautions. The procedure for police cautions depends on local police policies; however, it is generally expected that a police caution will take the form of a letter to the young offender and her parents, or, in some situations, a meeting between the young offender, the parents, and a senior police officer to discuss the incident. A Crown caution typically arises where a case has been referred to a Crown prosecutor. The youth may or may not have been charged, but the Crown has decided not to prosecute. A Crown caution typically takes the form of a letter to the youth and the parents.

A referral to a counselling program requires the consent of the young offender. From a practical perspective, however, it seems unlikely that a young person will withhold consent if he knows that the alternative is likely to be a criminal charge. Programs that may be appropriate for such referrals include recreation programs, counselling agencies, child welfare agencies, and mental health programs. Since social service workers are often involved in these programs, they may, as a result of diversion, find that their clients include young offenders engaged in rehabilitation.

The assistance provided by these programs is supposed to help young people not to reoffend. Because the circumstances of young offenders vary widely, assistive programs will have the best chance of succeeding if they provide an individualized approach. For example, if a 13-year-old is getting into fights at school, she might benefit from participating in an anti-bullying education program. If a 17-year-old homeless youth has been caught shoplifting winter gloves, he might benefit from job search support and referral to shelter housing. Justice Canada notes that the use, and presumably the success, of assistive programs "depends greatly on the extent to which police–community partnerships have been developed." (See chapter 12 for further discussion of police–community partnerships.)

Extrajudicial sanctions are a sort of hybrid between assistance and punishment. Sanctions are designed to address criminal behaviour more serious than the type that warrants a warning, caution, or referral. For example, the police or the Crown may refer a young offender to a sanctions program if the offence in question is not his first criminal offence, or if the offence involved a low to moderate degree of violence. Serious violence almost always results in a charge; however, a sanction may be appropriate where the circumstances of the offence include a mitigating factor—for example, where a 14-year-old first-time offender is involved in a serious assault resulting in injury to another person but where there is clear evidence of significant provocation of the offender prior to the assault.

The YCJA provides that extrajudicial sanctions can only be imposed where other extrajudicial measures would be inappropriate. This limitation is important in order to address, at least partially, the concern that the imposition of sanctions on a person who is suspected of committing an offence and has not had the opportunity to defend himself in a court of law violates a guaranteed right under section 11(d) of the Charter: "the right ... to be presumed innocent until proven guilty." However, there is no doubt that many young offenders prefer to comply with sanctions as a way to avoid criminal prosecution, and the resulting criminal record if the offender is convicted.

Before extrajudicial sanctions may be imposed, the following conditions must be met:

- There must be a sanctions program in the jurisdiction of the offence.
- The police (or Crown) must believe that the program is appropriate for the offender.
- The offender must give her informed consent.
- The offender must accept responsibility for the incident.
- The Crown must have enough evidence, if the incident were to form the basis of a charge, to prosecute that charge.

Sanctions involve the performance of activities similar to what is commonly known as community service. For example, offenders may be required to volunteer their time to a community cleanup project. If the sanction can be tied to the offence, it should be; for example, a young person who has committed an act of vandalism may be required to clean up graffiti that he or she has applied, as well as other graffiti at the same site or another site. Tying the sanction to the offence reinforces the principle of restorative justice—achieving justice by requiring the offender to make concrete amends to the victim or others in the victim's situation.

Social service workers who are involved in administering sanctions programs, may be called upon to use their creativity in recommending and supporting sanctions that incorporate the principle of restorative justice. However, an important consideration in designing any sanction will be the need to ensure that the youth's participation in the sanction does not pose a danger to anyone, or cause discomfort or embarrassment to a victim. Some victims may want nothing to do with a young person who has wronged them, and this wish must be respected.

SENTENCING

From a social services perspective, the most significant improvements made by the YCJA over the predecessor YOA are refinements to the provisions governing sentencing and the rights of youth in custody.

The purpose of sentencing is stated in section 38(1) of the YCJA:

> to hold a young person accountable for an offence through the imposition of just sanctions that have meaningful consequences for the young person and that promote his or her rehabilitation and reintegration into society, thereby contributing to the long-term protection of the public.

This goal is supported by a set of explicit principles, followed by highly detailed rules, to be applied by the courts in deciding on the sentence that is most appropriate in each particular case. Generally, these principles and rules reflect a strong preference for alternatives to detention in custody for convicted young offenders. Consistent with the goal reproduced above, the sentencing options emphasize rehabilitation and personal accountability. For those cases in which incarceration is deemed to be necessary to protect the public, the YCJA provides rules regarding custody, including facility choices and placement review, which are designed to support the principle of applying the least restrictive measures appropriate in the circumstances.

The principles to be applied in sentencing are set out in sections 38(2) and (3) of the YCJA. Section 38(2) requires a judge to choose a sentence that

- is consistent with other youth sentences for the same offence committed in similar circumstances;
- is "proportionate to the seriousness of the offence and the degree of responsibility of the young person for that offence";
- is the least restrictive sentence available that is capable of achieving the purpose of sentencing (in section 38(1));
- is most likely to rehabilitate and reintegrate the young person into society; and

- promotes a sense of responsibility in the young person, and acknowledgment of the harm done to victims and the community.

Section 38(3) also requires a judge to take into account "aggravating and mitigating circumstances," including the harm done to the victim (and whether it was intentional or foreseeable), any reparation made by the young person to the victim or the community, and any previous findings of guilt of the young person.

Also worthy of particular note, for social service workers, are sections 29(1) and 35 of the YCJA. These sections hint at the complicated interplay between the child protection system and the youth criminal justice system. Section 35 provides that a youth court may, in addition to any other order made at any stage in the criminal proceedings,

refer the young person to a child welfare agency for assessment to determine whether the young person is in need of child welfare services.

This section is probably designed to encourage courts to view the youth criminal justice system as separate from the child protection system, and to guide them in making dispositions for the right reasons.

Partly as a result of the modern youth criminal justice system's roots in the JDA/reform school system—but more importantly, for purely practical reasons—judges over the years have ordered custodial sentences (incarceration) for youth whose need for protection was at least as great as their need for correction. A very large proportion of cases of serious youth criminality are complicated by unmet needs for care, guidance, and protection. Experienced youth court judges commonly identify factors such as inadequate parenting, guidance, education, or housing as major contributors to a young person's problems with the law.

Where a young offender is in a very difficult life situation, judges have sometimes responded by imposing a custodial sentence in the hope that the conditions of custody—economic stability, for example, or access to education—will address some of the individual's unmet needs. Consider the case of a homeless youth arrested for prostitution or drug possession. Even if the charges are dubious, a judge may be inclined to sentence the youth simply to get him or her off the street and provide an opportunity for life change.

Though this response is based on an impulse to help, it has been condemned by policy makers, who recognize the dangers of using the criminal justice system as a means of achieving social welfare objectives. In their view, the two must be kept clearly separate: the criminal justice system should devote its resources to crime control and prevention, while the social welfare system should use its own resources to accomplish social welfare objectives.

Section 29(1) of the YCJA makes explicit reference to the inappropriateness of using the criminal justice system for social welfare purposes:

A youth justice court judge or a justice shall not detain a young person in custody prior to being sentenced as a substitute for appropriate child protection, mental health or other social measures.

Of course, whether sufficient "child protection, mental health or other social measures" will be in place to take up the slack depends on complicated issues of access, accountability, and funding. This is an issue that social workers and social service workers must grapple with throughout the course of their careers.

WEB LINK

For information on youth justice services available in Ontario, visit Operation Springboard at www .operationspringboard.on.ca.

Critical Perspectives

Gender Differences in Young Offenders?

Some criminologists maintain that there are important differences between young offenders based on gender. However, programs and services for young offenders may not take such differences sufficiently into account. In a paper prepared for the Youth Services Bureau of Ottawa, Mark Totten argues that because most young offenders are boys, programs for young offenders have a strong gender bias and girls are being underserved.

According to Totten, programs catering specifically to girls are needed. He suggests specific guidelines for the design of such programs, including the following:

- A theoretical perspective based upon young women's gendered trajectories into street life, the child welfare system, and the youth justice system. This perspective is founded upon the belief that most young women are *criminalized* for having been abused, for having mental health problems, and for committing *crimes of powerlessness*.

- Safe, supportive, and nurturing female-centred environment that encourages trust, bonding, and healthy relationships between staff and young women, between clients, and between co-workers.

- Risk-resiliency therapeutic models based on theories that address the physiological, psychological, and social needs of young women.

- A strengths-based approach which builds protective "pillows" against the unique risks faced by young women and develops resiliency.

- Diverse and competent *female* staff that reflect the client population in terms of gender identity, ethno-racial origin, and sexual orientation. It is not good enough to have "just any" female staff involved in this work. They must adhere to the feminist principles of a relational approach to young women's bio-psychosocial development. Male staff, no matter how competent, should *not* be introduced into the program until that point in time when young women have had time to heal from the various forms of traumatic abuse suffered at the hands of men. Failure to adhere to this basic principle of quality programs will result in young women being re-traumatized by male staff and continuing to relate to men in unhealthy ways.

- Utilization of gender-responsive assessment tools and individualized case plans that match appropriate therapy with the identified risk and protective factors of each young woman.

- Positive, gender-responsive work environment where manager–line staff relations and relations between line staff are modeled on the theoretical underpinnings of the therapeutic program. Staff should model non-traditional gender roles as much as possible.

- Therapeutic interventions and models (based upon feminist relational theories) that address healing from physical, sexual and emotional abuse; limited gender role socialization which results in the sexualization of feminity, the emotional caretaking of men, the deference to male authority and privilege, and the equation of love with sex; childhood disrupted attachments and traumatic losses; family relationships; substance abuse; self-mutilation; eating disorders; mental health problems which are rooted in childhood trauma (such as Post-traumatic Stress Disorder, Bipolar Disorder, Depression, Borderline Personality Disorder); assertiveness skills; and healthy relationships.

- Opportunities to develop skills in a range of gender-fair educational and vocational areas.

- Diverse female role models and mentors that reflect the Indigenous and ethno-racial backgrounds of clients.

- An emphasis on artistic, musical, linguistic, physical and other activities that focus on empowerment, self-respect, and self-efficacy. These activities should be based on a multiple intelligences approach and oriented towards supporting young women to identify and rely on their learning strengths.

- Education and counselling based on a harm reduction approach to reducing risks and increasing health (drug and alcohol abuse, smoking, prostitution, cutting and other forms of self-mutilation, abuse in dating relationships, Fetal Alcohol Spectrum Disorder, pregnancy, Hepatitus, HIV/AIDS, sexually transmitted infections).

- Emphasis on parenting education and training, including child development, infant care and stimulation, attachment issues, shaken baby syndrome, and non-coercive child rearing practices.

Source: Mark Totten, "Gender-Responsive Young Offender Services and the Need for Female Staff," paper prepared for the Youth Services Bureau of Ottawa, June 25, 2007. ◈

RIGHTS OF YOUTH IN CUSTODY

Part 5 of the YCJA is very detailed and covers a wide range of issues that can arise while a youth is in custody. These include

- the appropriateness of the level of custody (type of facility, level of security, etc.);

- reviews of, and changes to, the level of custody;

- the separation of young offenders from adults in custody;

- appeals by the young person of administrative decisions made about custody (level, etc.);

- "reintegration leave" either on compassionate grounds (for example, for medical treatment) or as preparation for discharge;

- "review" of the sentence (eligibility for parole);

- appropriate conditions for supervision (parole) orders; and

- consequences of breach of supervision (parole) conditions.

Part 5 of the YCJA should be read in conjunction with part V of the *Ministry of Correctional Services Act* (MCSA) and part V of the *Child and Family Services Act* (CFSA), which together guarantee the rights of, and provide protection for, youth in custody. The rights guaranteed under the CFSA apply to a "child in care," who may be a child in foster care, a child who is detained temporarily, or a child who is committed to custody under the YCJA.

The guaranteed rights of a young person in custody, under the provisions of the CFSA, can be summarized as follows:

- The right to receive regular visits from family members (except for Crown wards, who must make special application).

- The right to receive visits from a solicitor, an advocate, the Ombudsman, or a member of the provincial or federal Parliament.

- The right to send and receive mail that is not opened or read by others (except as limited by section 102(3) of the CFSA, which allows examination of mail, in the child's presence, for prohibited items such as weapons or drugs).

- The right to reasonable privacy and to his own possessions.

- The right to receive religious instruction and participate in religious activities of his choosing.

- The right to have a plan of care provided for him within 30 days of entering custody.

- The right to participate in the development of the plan of care.

- The right to food that is well balanced, appropriate, and of good quality.

- The right to clothing that is appropriate and of good quality.

- The right to medical and dental care.

Critical Perspectives

Youth Violent Crime: Media Messages Versus Realities

In April 2007, 33 people were killed when a student opened fire at Virginia Polytechnic Institute and State University in Blacksburg, Virginia. It was the most recent in a disturbing history of such attacks in the United States.

School shootings happen in Canada too. A recent example is the attack in 2006 at Dawson College in Montreal, which claimed the life of one student and left 19 other people wounded. The shooter was 25 years old, but younger gunmen have been implicated in similar incidents.

In 1999, at a high school in the rural community of Taber, Alberta, a 14-year-old student shot two 17-year-olds, leaving one dead. In 2007, in Toronto, a 15-year-old boy was shot and killed in his high school by two alleged teenage assailants (one of whom was under 18); they were charged with first-degree murder. There have been other violent crimes (some fatal) in Toronto and other Canadian cities involving youths in drive-by shootings and direct assaults on other youths with guns, knives, and beatings. Some of these attacks occur in the context of ongoing wars between rival gangs; others, such as the widely publicized case of Reena Virk, a BC high school student who was viciously beaten and drowned by two classmates, appear to be acts of bullying carried to the extreme. (The Virk case was notable, not only for the violence of the attack, but also for the fact that the teenager believed to be the principal aggressor was a girl.)

The brutality, and in some cases the randomness, of incidents like these grab the media's—and the nation's—attention. With rising public concern, many Canadians are demanding answers to the apparent "crisis" of youth violence.

However, statistics suggest that there is no such crisis. In Canada, the rate of crimes committed by young offenders (teenagers between the ages of 12 and 18) is relatively low; in fact, it declined by 33 percentage points between 1992 and 2002. Violent crime as a proportion of youth crime increased slightly in the same decade but decreased each year between 2002 and 2005, surpassing the decrease in adult violent crime during that period.

Timothy Hartnagel, a professor of sociology at the University of Alberta, has noted that media reports substantially distort our perceptions of youth crime. While Hartnagel attributes the current 25-year low in property crime by youths in part to good economic conditions and the aging of the population, he emphasizes that violent incidents like the Taber, Alberta shooting are usually committed by a tiny minority of seriously disturbed youth. Acknowledging the need for increased and stable funding to anti-criminogenic social programs in general, Hartnagel suggests that serious crime could be averted by targeting assistance at high-risk youth from a very young age. Among the factors he identifies as being associated with violent teenage criminality are impulsiveness, low intelligence, poor parenting, antisocial tendencies, and difficult socio-economic circumstances.

Source: Timothy F. Hartnagel, "The Rhetoric of Youth Justice in Canada" (2004), vol. 4, no. 4 *Criminal Justice* 355-74. ◇

- The right to an education that meets his aptitudes and needs, preferably in a community setting—that is, outside the facility. (Typically, however, youth in custody receive their schooling inside the facility.)

- The right to participate in recreational and athletic activities.

- The right to have his views heard on any issue that affects him to the extent that the young person is sufficiently mature.

- The right to be informed of his rights and how they can be enforced, the rules of the facility, and his responsibilities while in custody.

All social service workers who work in youth corrections should be aware of these rights, and should respect them when working with young offenders. The CFSA provides a complaints procedure under which a child in care can seek to enforce rights that he feels are being denied.

From a social services perspective, it is important to note that part 5 of the YCJA also provides for the designation of a **youth worker** (who could be a social service worker) for every young person sentenced to custody. The role of the youth worker is similar to that of a parole officer in the adult system. The youth worker, with the young person, prepares and implements a reintegration plan that sets out the most effective programs for the young person.

Part VI of the CFSA deals with the commitment to secure treatment to manage the behaviour of children and teenagers with serious mental disorders called **extra-ordinary measures** in the CFSA. This is not to be confused with extrajudicial measures under the YCJA.

Where a young offender is suffering from a mental disorder, the administration of a "secure treatment program" may be authorized to try certain measures to modify her behaviour. These measures can include locking up, the administration of psychotropic drugs (drugs that affect mental or emotional function), the use of mechanical restraints, the use of "aversive stimulation" techniques, or other techniques that may be prescribed to control behaviour.

Because these treatments are physically intrusive and can have side effects, their use is very closely controlled. Part VI of the CFSA establishes a procedure for deciding whether the use of the techniques is warranted, and a procedure by which the young person (or his representative) can challenge the decision to use them. Where social service workers are involved in the day-to-day care of youth in custody, and particularly where a social service worker is authorized to make decisions about the use of restraints, etc., the social service worker should undergo detailed training about the appropriate procedures that are to be followed every time extraordinary measures are used.

KEY TERMS

caution	extrajudicial sanctions	*parens patriae*
criminal responsibility	extraordinary measures	pre-trial release
disposition	juvenile delinquent	recidivism
diversion	labelling	young offender
extrajudicial measures	legal capacity	youth worker

REFERENCES

Canadian Charter of Rights and Freedoms, part I of the *Constitution Act, 1982*, being schedule B of the *Canada Act 1982* (UK), 1982, c. 11.

Child and Family Services Act, RSO 1990, c. C.11.

Criminal Code, RSC 1985, c. C-46.

Hartnagel, Timothy F., "The Rhetoric of Youth Justice in Canada" (2004), vol. 4, no. 4 *Criminal Justice* 355-74.

Juvenile Delinquents Act, RSC 1970, c. J-3.

Ministry of Correctional Services Act, RSO 1990, c. M.22, and General Regulation, RRO 1990, Reg. 778.

Totten, Mark, "Gender-Responsive Young Offender Services and the Need for Female Staff," paper prepared for the Youth Services Bureau of Ottawa, May 2004.

Young Offenders Act, RSC 1985, c. Y-1.

Youth Criminal Justice Act, SC 2002, c. 1.

REVIEW QUESTIONS

1. List at least three ways in which youth in conflict with the law differ from their adult counterparts.

2. What is criminal responsibility, and why is it considered not to apply to children under the age of 12?

3. List at least two criticisms of the *Young Offenders Act* (YOA) that led to the passage of the *Youth Criminal Justice Act* (YCJA).

4. What are "extrajudicial measures" for dealing with youth criminality?

5. List at least three rights or protections guaranteed to a young offender under the YCJA, and give at least one reason for each.

6. Because extrajudicial sanctions (as contrasted with extrajudicial measures in general) incorporate a punitive aspect, certain conditions must be met before these sanctions can be imposed. What are they?

7. The YCJA expresses a strong bias against the imposition of custodial sentences on youth except under narrow circumstances, and explicitly warns against the imposition of custodial sentences as a means of achieving "child protection, mental health, or other social measures". Why?

8. Part V of the YCJA provides for the protection of the rights of youth in custody. What other legislation addresses the right of young offenders held in a detention facility?

9. List at least three rights of a young person in criminal custody.

DISCUSSION QUESTIONS

Taking into consideration the principles of restorative justice, rehabilitation, and the need to be sensitive to victims, suggest an appropriate extrajudicial sanction for the young person accused of committing each of the following criminal acts:

1. A 17-year-old boy is visiting his girlfriend's home while her parents are at work. He "borrows" the keys to her father's Porsche (despite her protests) and takes the car for a joyride. He brings it back, undamaged, after an hour. He is accused of stealing the car. He is a licensed driver, and this is the first time he has committed an offence.

2. A 14-year-old girl is accused of hitting a classmate over the head with a heavy textbook, giving him a mild concussion. She did this, she says, because the boy had just grabbed her crotch, roughly and without her consent. The boy has a history of similar minor sexual assaults.

3. A 15-year-old girl is accused of stealing a neighbour's pet chinchilla and attempting to pass it off as her own pet, purchased with her own money. She repeatedly denies that she kidnapped the animal, though it clearly is the neighbour's dog and she can't produce a receipt showing that she purchased a chinchilla.

4. A 16-year-old boy is accused of pouring sugar into the gas tank of a school bus while on a class field trip, in an attempt to prevent the bus from running. The boy admits to having done the prank on a dare and is embarrassed and contrite.

CHAPTER 12

Community Policing

CHAPTER OBJECTIVES

After reading this chapter, you should be able to:

- Define "community policing" and describe the philosophy behind it.

- List the interest groups, stakeholders, and actors involved in community policing.

- Describe some of the programs used for the delivery of community policing.

- Explain the role that social service workers can play in the community policing system and the relationship between social services and law enforcement.

INTRODUCTION

Community policing caught the attention of the public in the last two decades of the 20th century. However, the concept isn't new; the cooperation of neighbours to ensure their mutual safety is as old as civilization itself. Loose associations of community members working together to provide security for each other pre-dated the introduction of formal government-sponsored police forces.

Today, the term "community policing" (sometimes referred to as **contemporary policing**) is typically used to describe a particular philosophy of police services delivery that is based on connections and partnerships with non-police members of the community. In the past several years, there has been renewed appreciation, in the justice system and in communities, for the benefits that can be derived from supporting police–community partnerships.

Community or contemporary policing is the delivery of police services by a partnership of community stakeholders and the police. One of the central aims of community policing is to be proactive—to create an environment that minimizes criminality, and to prevent crime. Traditionally, policing has been heavily reactive in nature: police are called after a crime has been committed, or after a conflict has gotten out of control.

For example, a traditional policing approach to a recurrent problem of after-hours vandalism outside a nightclub might be for police to attend at the scene after receiving calls from local residents who have heard windows breaking late at night. A community policing response might involve preventive strategies such as increasing street lighting in the area, encouraging club owners to have security personnel stand outside to ensure that patrons clear the area, and having police perform regular foot patrols of the neighbourhood in the hour after closing.

Community policing programs are extremely diverse. Many of them benefit from the pairing of local law enforcement services with social services. This chapter describes some of the community policing initiatives that have been adopted in Ontario communities. It will show that social service workers can play an important role in supporting local crime prevention strategies.

STRUCTURE OF COMMUNITY POLICING IN ONTARIO

WEB LINK

Information about community policing initiatives in Ontario is available at the OPP website: www.opp.ca.

Community policing decisions are typically made by community policing committees, established and maintained by communities to work as partners with the police. In 2006, the Ontario Provincial Police (OPP) reported working in "active problem-solving partnerships" with over 350 different community policing committees in Ontario.

There are three kinds of community policing committees:

- consultative committees, which act as a conduit of communication between the police and the community;

- multifunctional committees which identify issues and undertake to solve them; and

- interagency committees which are multifunctional but include the participation of local service agencies.

A community need not choose just one of these types of committees; if appropriate, all three (or a hybrid of two or more) can be present in the same community. The three types are not intended to be hierarchical in nature—that is, none is intended to be a subcommittee of another.

The functions typically performed by each of these committees are described in more detail below.

Consultative Community Policing Committees

Consultative community policing committees act primarily as a liaison between the police and the community. They solicit and gather information about community opinion, often through the use of focus groups, surveys, or other consultative methods.

For example, the police may invite community input on a particular issue. The consultative committee will consult groups and individuals in the community and report back to the police with suggestions on how the issue might be addressed. The committee may also investigate issues that have been brought to its attention by community members. The committee is not involved directly in either funding or delivering policing programs or initiatives in the community.

Multifunctional Community Policing Committees

Multifunctional community policing committees identify issues of importance to the community and use problem-solving strategies to address those issues, often with police involvement. Committee members from the local community will assume active problem-solving roles appropriate to civilians, such as participation in Block Parent or Neighbourhood Watch programs.

Multifunctional committees help to coordinate community resources to fund local programs, and often undertake fundraising campaigns to support their activities or to finance a specific project. Fundraising is discussed later in this chapter.

Police and the committee are accountable to each other for fulfilling their respective responsibilities as determined in the problem-solving process.

EXTRA CREDIT

Community Policing in Arnprior, Ontario

Arnprior, Ontario has a well-established community policing committee that runs the following programs:

- "Wear It to Win" bicycle helmet awareness contest

- "Crayon Crackdown"—children draw impaired-driving awareness pictures that are glued onto paper bags distributed by the Liquor Control Board during the Christmas season

- anti-bullying program—presented to schools by a community policing liaison officer

- "Vial of Life"—a program provided in partnership with Shoppers Drug Mart to help make medical and prescription information available to emergency medical service personnel when a patient is unable to communicate

- food bank food drive

- bursary program for high school students entering the police foundations college program

- participation in "Honeywell Safety Day," a safety initiative pioneered by local businesses

- School Drop-In Program—casual/occasional police officer presence in local schools

- "Pumpkin Patrol"—a special Hallowe'en evening safety patrol

- presence/assistance at various community activities (for example, Canada Day celebrations) to offer programs such as child fingerprinting or drug awareness

The committee has a well-organized website with a special area for members only. Volunteers are encouraged to visit the committee office in the local shopping centre to drop off an application. The website provides links to community partners, such as an organization that supports seniors in the community, the library, and child-care centres. The website also provides a useful resource for safety measures, such as "How to Prepare an Emergency Survival Kit."

The committee's major fundraising initiative is an annual "Jail or Bail" event. This is a mock court hearing at which high-profile community members (for example, the mayor, a hospital administrator, owners of major businesses, and service club representatives) are brought before a "judge" to face amusing made-up charges. To "get out of jail," the accused must make "bail." Bail money is deposited to the committee's account and used to fund community policing programs. ◈

Interagency Community Policing Committees

Interagency community policing committees are similar in their goals and activities to multifunctional community policing committees, but with the added element of multi-agency participation. This means that instead of or in addition to individuals, the committee's membership includes local service agencies or interest groups. For example, a community policing committee in an urban centre may include representatives of the local retailers association.

In Ontario, police services provide local detachments with an "outreach directory" of social service and other agencies in the community. This (along with the community "Blue Book" or a similar directory) is a good place to start in identifying potential member agencies.

EXTRA CREDIT

The Peel Committee on Sexual Assault: A Creative Interagency Approach to Crime Prevention

The Peel Committee on Sexual Assault (PCSA) does not define itself specifically as a community policing committee, but the functions that it performs are consistent with community policing principles. It is a fascinating example of a complex interagency project.

The PCSA is an interagency partnership of agencies from three sectors: law enforcement/justice, medical services, and social services. It consists of one main committee and at least eight subcommittees; other ad hoc committees are formed, as needed, to deal with individual issues. Its membership includes a dazzling array of agencies. For example, one of its subcommittees—the Sexual Assault Emergency Response Protocol Committee (SAERP)—engaged the participation of 16 different agencies (including 7 social service agencies and police agencies at both the provincial and regional levels) in the development of an interagency protocol for responding to sexual assault emergencies.

The PCSA's statement of purpose reflects the kind of proactive approach to criminality that is at the heart of community policing:

> The Peel Committee on Sexual Assault is a group of service providers working collaboratively to establish a comprehensive and effective community response to end sexual violence. We envision a community that will not tolerate sexual violence.

To achieve those aims, the PCSA recognizes the importance of a **multidisciplinary approach**. A multidisciplinary approach seeks to incorporate, in its pursuit of solutions, knowledge and methods from two or more areas of expertise. In the case of the PCSA, the disciplines involved are law enforcement, medicine, and social services.

By serving on interagency committees and participating in interagency projects, social service workers can make their expertise and skills accessible to law enforcement personnel and vice versa. The resulting exchange of information and ideas often produces creative solutions that these community agencies could not have arrived at by working alone.

More information about the PCSA is available at www.sexualassault-peel.com. ◇

COMMUNITY PROFILE: IDENTIFYING NEEDS

One of the first tasks of a community policing committee is the preparation of a community profile. Community profiling is intended to identify specific policing and crime prevention needs, the community's priorities, and the resources available to meet those needs. A useful community profile should include the following information:

- demographics: age, family status, cultural background, first language, etc., of local residents;

- crime rates, patterns, and trends;

- the issues and concerns that local residents identify as high priority; and

- the perceptions of local residents about the adequacy of policing and social services in the community.

Demographic information can be gathered directly (for example, by going door-to-door) or from government sources such as Statistics Canada. Demographic information can help identify potential community vulnerabilities for crime. For example, if there is a high proportion of seniors in a community, the community may want to develop programs that educate seniors about financial scams that tend to target the elderly. Or, if there are many families with young children in the community, issues such as traffic calming in residential neighbourhoods may be a high priority.

Crime rates, patterns, and trends can often be determined by reviewing historical "calls for service" (911 and other calls made to police). Reviewing calls for service can allow crimes to be plotted on a map to determine trouble zones; it can allow the committee to identify times of the day when police coverage might need to be increased; and it can assist in "distinguishing fact from fiction" when it comes to comparing the actual crime rate with public perceptions. (This last issue is discussed briefly in chapter 11 in the context of youth crime.)

To determine the resources available in a community, the OPP recommends the following checklist as a starting point:

- civic associations;
- Chamber of Commerce;
- business improvement associations;
- community development agencies;
- First Nations/Aboriginal band councils;
- Native friendship centres;
- public sector organizations (i.e. city hall, public housing etc.);
- educational institutions;
- community service agencies;
- community taskforce/coalition members;
- non-profit voluntary groups (e.g. United Way, Scouts Canada);
- service clubs (Lions, Rotary, Kiwanis, Kinsmen);
- public agencies (e.g. public transportation, social assistance);
- ethnic/racial/multicultural organizations;
- recreation service providers; and
- social work agencies.

Community profiles should be updated every few years, or sooner if necessary. Demographics and crime trends may vary over time, resulting in changed needs and priorities. Likewise, the resources available to support crime prevention initiatives may change.

The community profile provides the community policing committee with a basic framework for working with police partners to select or develop programs designed to address the identified needs. Community policing programs are discussed below.

PROGRAMS

After the committee has been constituted and the profiling process has been completed, the committee should develop an action plan. The action plan should identify the problem(s) and the goal(s) to be achieved. It should outline the police and community strategies that will be implemented to address the problem(s) and realize the goal(s). It should also detail the tasks to be performed by each participant, such as the police, the public, and social service agencies. Finally, the action plan should provide for a method of measuring success and failure, so that the strategies may be revised and improved if necessary.

The OPP has developed a model known as "PARE" (Problem, Analysis, Response, Evaluation), involving the following steps:

1. *Problem identification.* What are the problems or symptoms that need to be addressed?

2. *Analysis.* Consider victims, offenders, and the circumstances; determine the impact, seriousness, and complexity of the problem; and prioritize goals such as eliminating or reducing harm.

3. *Response.* Develop strategies, such as enforcement, prevention and visibility, policy and legislative initiatives, public education, and agency participation; assign tasks; document the plan; and execute the plan.

4. *Evaluation.* Analyze plan results; learn from mistakes.

An action plan paves the way for the development and delivery of community policing programs. The following examples illustrate the range of initiatives and programs that may be spearheaded by community policing committees.

Police strategies

- The use of new enforcement strategies: where local cottagers report that boaters regularly drink alcohol on their boats, police may monitor that lake for a few days in the hope of deterring regular offenders.

- Enhanced visibility: police may increase their visibility in a problem neighbourhood or at a problem time of day by patrolling the area (whether on foot or horseback, or by bicycle, motorcycle, etc.).

- Education campaigns: police may produce pamphlets or deliver seminars on an identified risk, to alert potential victims and discourage offenders. For example, police may hold a seminar to educate a targeted group about recently identified e-mail scams.

■ Extended use of existing strategies: police who operate a holiday RIDE program may set up a checkpoint at a new location in response to community concerns about impaired drivers.

Civilian strategies

■ Community cooperative security programs: common examples are Neighbourhood Watch and Block Parents.

■ Anti-**criminogenic** social programs: local residents may organize after-school recreational programs for unsupervised teens or work with health-care and social service agencies to provide needle exchange programs for drug addicts.

■ Social welfare programs: community residents may set up a soup kitchen in a neighbourhood church to help relieve poverty, and thus perhaps reduce shoplifting from local grocery stores.

■ Environmental improvement campaigns: committee members may lobby for municipal lighting to be improved on a wooded pathway to reduce nighttime assaults.

■ Recommendations to politicians for changes to provincial legislation or municipal bylaws.

Joint police–civilian strategies

■ Mediation or other alternative dispute resolution approaches to interpersonal conflicts: police may suggest mediation instead of the use of a restraining order to resolve a feud between neighbours, and a community agency may agree to deliver the mediation services.

■ Alternative sentencing or diversion approaches: where permitted by law, such as under the *Youth Criminal Justice Act*, police may divert offenders away from the normal justice process and into anti-criminogenic social programs delivered by community agencies.

Given the broad range of programs outlined above, it is clear that there are many opportunities for social service workers to contribute to community policing initiatives.

Assistance in identifying and developing community policing programs may be available through Public Safety Canada's National Crime Prevention Strategy. This federal government program seeks to prevent crime by addressing root causes such as family violence, school problems, and drug abuse. The program offers expertise and support in developing community partnerships. It also provides grants to help fund local initiatives that are consistent with program objectives. Those objectives are

■ to promote partnerships between governments, businesses, community groups, and individuals to reduce crime and victimization;

■ to assist communities in developing and implementing community-based solutions to local problems that contribute to crime and victimization;

■ to increase public awareness of, and support for, crime prevention; and

■ to conduct research on crime prevention and establish best practices.

WEB LINK

For more information on the National Crime Prevention Strategy and grant applications, visit the Public Safety Canada website at www.publicsafety.gc.ca.

FINANCING COMMITTEE ACTIVITIES AND DELIVERING PROGRAMS

To accomplish the committee's goals, committee members will usually become involved in raising money, recruiting volunteers, and/or contracting for services. These activities give rise to a number of legal issues—for example, the committee's obligation to report taxable income, and the legal liability of committee members. These issues in turn involve decisions about the formal structure of the committee (for example, whether it should operate as a non-profit corporation), which will determine its legal status. These are complex matters, and a detailed discussion is beyond the scope of this book (though some of these concerns are briefly addressed below and in part VI).

This section provides an overview of the financing and program delivery functions of a community policing committee. The last section provides a short discussion of liability issues.

Fundraising

The committee will obviously need a source of funds to pay for its activities. As suggested above, a committee may be eligible for a program grant under the National Crime Prevention Strategy. Committee members should also research whether they may be eligible for provincial or local government support. Most committees, however, will rely on funds raised in the community.

The resource list compiled in constructing the community profile will identify some potential sources of funds. For example, local service organizations may commit to make regular donations to help pay for ongoing activities of the committee. Member organizations may contribute in the form of in-kind donations—for example, shared office space or accounting services. Often the committee will also seek contributions from local residents through various fundraising events such as raffles, community barbecues, T-shirt sales, and direct donation campaigns.

Fundraising is subject to legal regulation. While a discussion of fundraising law is beyond the scope of this chapter, committee members in charge of fundraising should be aware that they have a duty to inquire about the legalities of any fundraising scheme they may be planning.

Volunteers

Volunteer recruitment and management is vital to any community-based organization. The use of volunteers saves money, gets the job done, and builds community support and enthusiasm for community policing goals. Like fundraising, the use of volunteers may have legal implications. Committee members charged with the recruitment and supervision of volunteers should inform themselves about the legislation and regulations that apply to volunteers. Some of these issues will be touched on in chapter 17. The OPP suggest that a community policing committee should form a subcommittee to handle the recruitment of volunteers.

Managing volunteers is an art. The manager of volunteers faces the challenges of recruiting, retaining, and motivating skilled and busy people without being able to rely on the usual employer's toolkit of rewards (payment and benefits) and sanctions (threats of demotion and/or job loss). Managing volunteers is very different from managing employees. For example, when working with volunteers, it is essential to find non-economic ways of expressing appreciation and gratitude for the individual's efforts. In addition, the management of performance problems will require advanced skills in negotiation, diplomacy, and sometimes conflict resolution.

Many useful books and other resources on volunteer management are available in libraries, on the Internet, and in retail outlets. A committee member who is charged with managing volunteers should take the time to learn from the wisdom of others who have succeeded at this task.

Contracts with Suppliers

A community policing committee may need to enter into contracts with suppliers of goods or services, either to carry out internal functions (such as accounting) or to deliver specific programs in the community. Consider, for example, an after-school sports program designed to provide a supervised activity for grade 9 students between the time that school is dismissed and their parents return home from work.

As suggested above, such contractual arrangements raise various legal issues. Some of the concerns related to liability are outlined below.

COMMITTEE LIABILITY

While no serious liability issues involving community policing committees appear to have arisen in Ontario to date, it is conceivable that a committee that takes improper actions could be liable under the common law of tort or contract, as discussed in chapters 2 and 13.

With respect to tort claims, it's important for committee members to know that the Ontario government's general insurance policy, covering torts committed by government employees, does not cover community policing committees or their members. This means that committee members could be liable to pay damages for torts that they commit in the performance of their committee duties.

The risk of a lawsuit depends in large part on the activities engaged in by the committee and how the activities are carried out—whether by the committee directly or by an agency under a contract for services. When services are performed under a contract with a service provider, and the services are performed in the normal course of the provider's business, the provider is generally liable for tort claims that arise from the use of those services. This protection from liability is part of what the committee pays for when it contracts for services instead of providing them directly. To ensure that this is how liability will be managed, a committee should have all of its important contracts reviewed by a lawyer—especially those that involve risky activities.

The concept of **vicarious liability** involves one party being liable for the actions of another. In general, this form of liability depends on a degree of control and supervision over the person or corporation who commits the tort by the person or corporation whom the victim claims is vicariously liable. For example, an employer may be held vicariously liable for torts committed by employees during the ordinary

WEB LINK

For links to information on volunteering and volunteer management, visit the Volunteer Resource Centre at www.volunteer.ca.

course of their employment. It is unlikely that a community policing committee would be found vicariously liable for services performed by competent service providers under contract, but it is worthwhile to have a lawyer review the committee's planned activities for problems from the perspective of vicarious liability.

Depending on the circumstances, it may be prudent for the community policing committee to purchase insurance coverage to protect against tort claims.

Consider, for example, a community policing committee that wants to create a skateboard park to keep teens from skateboarding in municipal parking lots. It decides to hold a trick-skateboarding competition as a fundraising event. A lawyer may advise the committee to carry insurance in case any of the skateboarders are hurt in the competition. The committee would have to factor in the cost of this insurance when calculating appropriate entry fees and ticket prices for the event.

With respect to contract problems, one of the main issues that can arise for committees is capacity to contract. For a committee to be able to enter into contracts with service providers, it will need to be a **legal person**. A legal person is either an individual person or a corporation. A committee that expects to enter into contracts on a regular basis may find that it needs to become a non-profit corporation in order to do this. A lawyer can discuss the pros and cons of incorporation with the members of the committee, and can apply for incorporation on their behalf. This option is discussed in chapter 21.

KEY TERMS

community policing

contemporary policing

criminogenic

legal person

multidisciplinary approach

vicarious liability

REFERENCES

Youth Criminal Justice Act, SC 2002, c. 1.

REVIEW QUESTIONS

1. Is community policing a new concept? Explain.

2. What are the key aims of modern community policing committees?

3. What are the three main types of community policing committees, and how do they differ?

4. Why is it important for a community policing committee to develop a community profile, and what should it include?

5. What kinds of community organizations may be of help in supporting community policing? Can you think of any that aren't specifically mentioned in this chapter?

6. What are the four key steps that make up the PARE model for a community policing action plan?

7. List at least two community policing initiatives that might be undertaken by police and two that might be undertaken by civilian members of a community policing committee.

8. What kinds of resources is a community policing committee likely to need before it can implement these programs, and how can it gather these resources?

9. Can members of a community policing committee be sued if someone comes to harm as a result of any decisions they make in that capacity? What steps can they take to limit their liability?

DISCUSSION QUESTIONS

Consider each of the following community security issues. After reading the issue, jot down all the solutions you can think of that might help to make the community more secure. Be prepared to discuss your suggestions, particularly in terms of the resources that would be needed to carry out the solution, such as police personnel, volunteers, social service agency support, and funding.

1. Parking has become a serious problem at your local shopping mall. The mall is large and always busy, and drivers are often forced to drive around the lot several times looking for a space. There are frequent fender-bender accidents, drivers are causing property damage by parking illegally on neighbouring lawns, and several "road rage" assaults have been reported to mall security and to the police.

2. Now that spring is here, residents on a street that borders a ravine have begun to report that teenagers are gathering nightly on the lawns at the edge of the ravine; they stay until the wee hours of the morning, talking loudly, and playing music on car radios. Sometimes the neighbours smell marijuana smoke, and there have been two large multiparty brawls, which appear to have occurred between students from the two rival high schools in the area.

3. Your neighbourhood contains a small urban park that borders a commercial area with several restaurants. Nearby residents have recently complained that most mornings the municipal garbage bins in the park are full, crammed with loose refuse and large plastic bags. Often bags have been left leaning up against bins, and some have been torn apart by animals, leaving garbage scattered over walkways and the lawn. The smell is terrible, and the garbage is attracting wasps; some residents are concerned about rats. Parents with small children are avoiding the park, as are joggers, dog owners, and other regular users. The residents suspect that garbage is being dumped by local businesses, as a way of avoiding the city's commercial collection fee.

PART V

The Courts

CHAPTER 13

The Trial Process

CHAPTER OBJECTIVES

After reading this chapter, you should be able to:

- Describe the structure of the Ontario court system.

- Demonstrate a general understanding of pre-trial issues.

- Describe the stages of a criminal trial and list the trial participants.

- Describe the stages of a civil trial and list the trial participants.

- Explain the role of evidence in the civil and criminal legal systems, and list the types of evidence.

- Describe the role of witnesses and the types of questions witnesses may be asked.

- Explain how a witness prepares for giving testimony in court.

INTRODUCTION

As demonstrated in many chapters of this book, social service workers will often have clients who are dealing with legal issues as well as social and psychological issues. They may be charged with or victims of a crime; they may be involved in family law or child protection disputes; or they may have to use the court system to establish or defend their legal rights, such as under the residential tenancy legislation.

Sometimes clients are required to attend court, and social service workers can provide an important support during this process. The legal system, and court in particular, can be intimidating for many clients, and they may find the experience extremely stressful. Because of the significant repercussions of their conduct in court, it is important that they be able to overcome their fears and other emotions, so that they can put their best face forward.

Social service workers may also be called upon to testify in a professional capacity at a trial involving a client. Whether you are directly involved or assisting a client in a court proceeding, you will need to understand court procedure and what is expected of a witness. This chapter describes the Ontario court system, court procedure in criminal trials and civil actions, and the role of a witness in a court proceeding.

STRUCTURE OF THE ONTARIO COURT SYSTEM

Criminal offences and some civil disputes are tried in either the Superior Court of Justice (formerly the Ontario Court, General Division) or the Ontario Court of Justice (formerly the Ontario Court, Provincial Division). The jurisdiction of each of these courts in criminal and civil matters is described in more detail below. Ontario also has several specialty courts, such as Family Court to deal with family law cases and Small Claims Court to deal with minor civil disputes.

EXTRA CREDIT

Ontario's Gladue Court

In 1999, the Supreme Court of Canada released an important decision in a case called *R. v. Gladue*. One of the key findings in *Gladue* was that Canada's justice system at the time relied too heavily on incarceration as a response to criminality, especially in cases involving Aboriginal offenders.

One of the responses to the *Gladue* decision was the creation of a special branch of the Ontario Court of Justice, called the Gladue Court. The Gladue Court has three Toronto locations and handles only cases involving Aboriginal offenders. Aboriginal offenders include status and non-status Indians, Métis, and Inuit who identify themselves as such.

The intention in creating a separate court for Aboriginal people charged with criminal offences is to provide a venue in which the unique circumstances of these individuals are taken properly into account in the pursuit of justice. Judges and others who work in this court are specially trained in Aboriginal issues.

For a report of the *Gladue* decision, see *R. v. Gladue*, [1999] 1 SCR 688. More information about the Gladue court is available from the Aboriginal Legal Services of Toronto at www.aboriginallegal.ca. ◈

The Superior Court of Justice operates as both a trial-level court and an appeal court for some matters. It also hears judicial reviews of administrative decisions, discussed in chapter 2.

Decisions of the Ontario Court of Justice in respect of certain minor criminal offences and provincial offences may be appealed to the Superior Court of Justice. Decisions of the Superior Court of Justice may be appealed to the Ontario Court of Appeal.

As the name suggests, the Ontario Court of Appeal only hears appeals; it does not conduct trials. Moreover, it hears only those cases in which there is a legal issue to be clarified or an issue of importance to the public interest. For this reason, a party who wishes to appeal a civil matter must apply to the court for "leave" (permission) to appeal. In criminal cases, the accused may appeal the Superior Court's decision "as of right"—that is, the Court of Appeal cannot refuse to hear the appeal.

Most Court of Appeal hearings are before a three-judge panel, although a larger panel may hear certain very significant cases. There are no juries at the Court of Appeal, because the issues being examined involve questions of law, rather than determinations of fact.

A party who wishes to appeal a decision of the Ontario Court of Appeal may apply for leave to appeal to the Supreme Court of Canada. The court will review the decision and decide whether to grant or deny leave, depending on whether there are sufficient legal grounds. A decision of the Supreme Court is final.

CRIMINAL PROCEDURE

Criminal Trials

"Criminal procedure" refers to the rules and legal traditions that govern the conduct of trials of persons accused of criminal offences.

In a criminal trial, the **prosecutor** of the charge is the government, represented by the Crown attorney (the Crown); the person accused of the charge is the **defendant** or **accused**, and is usually represented by a lawyer who specializes in criminal defence law. For the police and the Crown, charging and prosecuting a suspect involves a certain degree of discretion. In general, if there is sufficient evidence to support the offence, the police will lay a charge. For the Crown, a decision to prosecute or not prosecute turns on an assessment of whether the evidence available is sufficient to support a conviction.

Once the police have laid charges and the Crown has decided to prosecute, the accused must go to court and present a defence if she hopes to escape a criminal conviction. The alternative is to plead guilty and thus avoid a lengthy trial. Sometimes the defendant can negotiate with the prosecution to plead guilty to a lesser charge. This is called a **plea bargain**. A plea bargain saves considerable time and money and removes the risk inherent in a trial, where the outcome is never certain. Many defendants are willing to accept a plea bargain in order to avoid the risk of conviction on a more serious charge and a heavier sentence.

Critical Perspectives

Plea Bargains and the Notion of Justice

When Paul Bernardo was accused of murdering two school girls, the testimony of his former wife, Karla Homolka, was key evidence in securing a conviction. To obtain her cooperation, the Crown negotiated a plea bargain: 12 years for manslaughter in return for her testimony against him. When videotapes were subsequently disclosed, which showed that Homolka was not a submissive and reluctant participant in the crime under the control of a dominating husband, but rather a willing and enthusiastic accomplice, there was public outrage over Homolka's sentence. Questions were raised as to why Homolka was not tried for first-degree murder. The Crown's position was that Bernardo's conviction was not a sure thing, even with the videotapes. The Crown did not want to risk going to trial without Homolka's testimony.

Plea bargains are a matter of course in criminal courts across the country, and rarely do they attract such controversy. However, the procedure does raise ethical issues. Do innocent people sometimes plead guilty to a lesser charge so as to avoid possible conviction for a more serious offence? Do plea bargains offend important sentencing principles, including deterrence, the protection of the public, and consistent treatment of offenders who have committed similar crimes? Do plea bargains give priority to expediency and cost savings at the expense of justice? ◇

Criminal Courts

Criminal trials are conducted in either the Superior Court of Justice or the Ontario Court of Justice. The court that will hear a particular case depends on the nature of the offence as determined by the *Criminal Code* (discussed in chapter 9). Summary conviction offences are tried in the Ontario Court of Justice. Indictable offences are tried in the Superior Court of Justice. Where hybrid offences will be tried depends on the election to proceed by summary conviction or indictment.

The *Criminal Code* prescribes that an indictable offence will be tried by judge and jury. If the offence is a hybrid offence and the prosecution has elected to proceed by way of indictment, the accused is typically allowed to choose either trial by a judge and jury or trial by a judge alone.

As discussed earlier, appeals of decisions in criminal trials may be made to the Superior Court of Justice, in the case of Ontario Court of Justice decisions, or to the Ontario Court of Appeal, in the case of Superior Court decisions.

Rules of Criminal Procedure

The primary source of criminal trial procedures is the *Criminal Code*. While individual courts also have their own procedural rules, the *Criminal Code* prescribes most of the steps in the prosecution of a criminal offence, from charging to sentencing.

PRE-TRIAL PROCEDURES

Before a criminal trial begins, there are many preliminary steps, some of which have been discussed in earlier chapters of this book. When a person is suspected of committing an offence, the alleged offence must be investigated and evidence must be collected. The investigation stage often includes an interview of the suspect and all witnesses. When the evidence is sufficient to support a reasonable belief that the suspect committed the offence, a charge is laid. All of these procedures must be conducted according to strict rules imposed by the common law, the *Criminal Code*, and the *Canadian Charter of Rights and Freedoms*.

Depending on the circumstances in the particular case, various **hearings** and **motions** may be held or brought in court, either before or at the start of a trial. Three examples are described below: a bail hearing, a hearing to determine whether the accused is mentally fit to stand trial, and a preliminary inquiry.

Bail Hearing

Part XVI of the *Criminal Code* sets out detailed procedural rules governing the detention of an accused in custody pending trial. Generally, except in the case of the most serious offences and unless the accused pleads guilty to the charge, a person who has been charged with an offence and detained in custody following his arrest is entitled to a bail hearing before a judge or a justice of the peace, "without unreasonable delay" (usually within 24 hours or three days). The *Criminal Code* refers to this hearing as a **judicial interim release** hearing (section 515).

Generally, the court will order the release of the accused unless the prosecution can show cause (give reasons) as to why he should be kept in custody or released subject to certain conditions, such as requiring him to stay away from victims or requiring that a bond be posted on his behalf. In determining whether or not to release an accused while awaiting trial, the court may consider whether the accused poses a danger to society or may flee the jurisdiction to avoid trial.

Hearing to Determine Fitness to Stand Trial

For a trial to be fair, the accused must be capable of understanding what is going on; of understanding the consequences he faces as a result of the trial; and of understanding, instructing, and receiving advice from his lawyer. If the accused is mentally incapable of any of these things, the trial cannot proceed. Where there is a question regarding the fitness of the accused, a hearing may be held before the trial (or at any time in the subsequent proceedings).

Section 2 of the *Criminal Code* states that a person is "unfit to stand trial" if he is unable, because of a mental disorder, to conduct a defence or to instruct counsel to do so, and, specifically, if he is unable to

    (a) understand the nature or object of the proceedings,
    (b) understand the possible consequences of the proceedings, or
    (c) communicate with counsel.

The trial judge may order an assessment of the accused to assist in determining his mental fitness (section 672.11 of the *Criminal Code*). If the accused is found to be unfit to stand trial, he may be committed to a mental institution until such time as he is fit to stand trial. In other words, a finding that the accused is unfit to stand trial will not remove the charges against him or save him from possible conviction; it will simply postpone the trial.

Preliminary Inquiry

A preliminary inquiry may be held where the accused is being tried in the Ontario Superior Court of Justice (that is, for an indictable offence or a hybrid offence prosecuted by indictment). It is not automatic but may be requested by either the accused or the prosecution. The purpose of the preliminary inquiry is to provide an opportunity for the Crown and the accused to present evidence and make submissions before a judge sufficient to establish that the accused either should or should not stand trial for the offence charged. Generally, on hearing the evidence, the judge will either order the accused to stand trial ("commit" him to trial) or discharge him.

The procedural rules governing a preliminary inquiry are contained in part XVIII of the *Criminal Code*. Essentially, the issue before the court is whether or not there is sufficient evidence against the accused to support prosecution of the charge leading to possible conviction. The test must be met with respect to each offence charged. Where an accused is charged with more than one offence, the judge may find that there is sufficient evidence to support a trial on some of the charges but not others. In this case, the judge will commit the accused to stand trial only on those supported charges. Where the evidence at the preliminary inquiry warrants, the judge can also commit the accused to trial for new offences that were not part of the original set of charges.

STAGES OF A CRIMINAL TRIAL

If the accused is committed to trial on at least one charge, the trial goes ahead. The following is a simplified outline of the stages of a typical criminal trial:

1. The jury is selected.

2. Any pre-trial motions are heard.

3. The charges are read and the plea is entered into the trial record.

4. The prosecution makes an opening statement.

5. The defence makes an opening statement.

6. The prosecution presents its evidence (calling witnesses and/or introducing physical evidence).

7. The defence presents its evidence.

8. The prosecution presents its closing arguments.

9. The defence presents its closing arguments.

10. The judge instructs the jury on how to apply the law.

11. The jury deliberates and delivers its **verdict**.

12. If the accused is found guilty, the judge hears submissions from the prosecution and the defence and imposes a sentence.

A criminal case is decided by a **trier of fact** and a **trier of law**. If the trial is by judge alone, the judge will act as both trier of fact and of law. If the trial is by judge and jury, the trier of fact will be the jury and the trier of law will be the judge.

The trier of fact examines the evidence to decide what is true and what is not true, and whether there is sufficient evidence to prove, beyond a reasonable doubt, that the accused is guilty of the charge. For example, if the accused is charged in a shooting, the trier of fact will decide whether or not there is sufficient evidence to prove, beyond a reasonable doubt, that he was the person who pulled the trigger.

The trier of law is always the judge. It is the judge's job in every trial to interpret the law and apply it to the proven facts of the case. The judge, for example, decides the legal question of whether a specific piece of evidence should be admitted (included and given consideration). In a trial by judge and jury, the judge must interpret the applicable law for the jury and, once all the evidence has been presented, must instruct the jury about how to apply the law to the evidence.

CIVIL PROCEDURE

Civil Actions

"Civil procedure" refers to the rules and legal traditions that govern the conduct of civil (non-criminal) trials. Civil actions arise when one party begins legal proceedings against another party in pursuit of a remedy for a harm or expected harm—for example, a wrongful act or omission, or a violation or breach of legal rights. The most common civil remedy is damages—monetary compensation for a loss or injury. However, there are other remedies available under civil procedure, such as judicial orders in custody disputes and judicial reviews of decisions of administrative tribunals.

Most civil actions never reach court. It is very common for conflicts that have escalated into lawsuits to be solved or settled through negotiation or mediation at some stage prior to trial. "Settling out of court" is a worthy objective, since trials are often very expensive for all parties (and for taxpayers as well). Litigation also tends to polarize the parties, creating additional animosity. For a business deal gone wrong, this may not be a serious concern; however, in other cases, such as family law disputes, the effect on children can be devastating.

A party to a civil action may be an individual, a corporation, or a public authority such as a municipal agency or a provincial ministry. In civil court, each party, including government parties, appears on its own behalf; that is, there is no Crown prosecutor as in a criminal trial.

Depending on the type of proceeding, the person who has begun the lawsuit is called either the **plaintiff** or the **applicant**, and the person who is opposing it is called either the defendant or the **respondent**. The defendant in a civil lawsuit may, in addition to defending against the plaintiff's claim, file her own **counterclaim** against the plaintiff.

Most Ontario civil trials are presided over by a judge. A party may request a jury to decide questions of fact and/or to assess the amount of damages in some cases. A jury trial is not available in all cases, such as those heard in Small Claims Court or with respect to family law issues. Jury trials tend to be longer and more costly than trials by judge alone.

The jury in a civil trial is made up of six people, who serve alongside the judge. As in criminal proceedings, the jury is the trier of fact and the judge is the trier of law. The judge applies the law to the facts, as they are determined by the jury. In this way, the judge and jury work together to come to a decision in the case.

Civil Courts

Most civil disputes are tried in the Superior Court of Justice, Family Court, or Small Claims Court.

The Superior Court hears civil trials where the damages being claimed are over $10,000. It has two sets of procedures: the regular procedure, which applies to cases where the damages claimed are over $50,000; and the simplified procedure, where damages up to $50,000 are at stake.

Small Claims Court hears civil matters where the amount of damages claimed is $10,000 or less. It offers a much simpler court procedure than the Superior Court of Justice, and parties appearing in Small Claims Court often choose not to be represented by a lawyer.

Rules of Civil Procedure

Ontario has issued *Rules of Civil Procedure* in a regulation under the Ontario *Courts of Justice Act*. The rules are very long and comprehensive, and a detailed discussion is beyond the scope of this chapter. The following outline provides an overview of the stages in a civil lawsuit in the Superior Court of Justice.

BEFORE TRIAL

1. Informal attempts at resolution are often made by the parties.

2. If these efforts are unsuccessful, the plaintiff serves the defendant with a statement of claim and files one with the court.

3. The defence serves and files a statement of defence, and sometimes a counterclaim.

4. The parties attend a mandatory mediation session to see if they can resolve some or all of the issues without going to court.

5. If the parties have not resolved the case, they begin preparing for trial by

   a. preparing an affidavit of documents (a sworn document containing all relevant documents in the party's possession);

   b. attending at discoveries (meetings to share evidence with the other side); and

   c. answering undertakings (promises, usually to provide information) that have been made in the discovery stage.

6. The parties attend a settlement conference with a judge, who tries to facilitate a settlement.

7. If the matter does not settle, a trial date is set. (The trial must be before a new judge.)

8. The court hears any **pre-trial motions or applications** (hearings on issues collateral to the subject of the dispute, such as the admissibility of a particular document into evidence).

STAGES OF A CIVIL TRIAL

1. The plaintiff makes an opening statement. (Sometimes the defence, usually with leave of the court, makes an opening statement immediately after the plaintiff's.)

2. The plaintiff presents evidence (calling witnesses and/or introducing physical evidence). This is usually the longest part of the trial.

3. The defendant makes an opening statement (unless it followed the plaintiff's opening statement).

4. The defendant presents evidence.

5. The plaintiff has an opportunity to present response evidence (restricted to addressing new issues raised by the defence).

6. The plaintiff makes closing arguments.

7. The defendant makes closing arguments.

8. The judge and/or jury considers the evidence and arguments, and renders a decision.

Interruptions to the Trial Process

Often, unfortunately, the process is not quite so seamless. It is very common in litigation for parties to ask for **adjournment**—a judicially approved delay by which the trial, or a stage of the trial, is postponed. This may occur in both criminal and civil proceedings. A party may ask for an adjournment because he or she cannot be available on a scheduled court date, or to replace a lawyer, accommodate a witness, or comply with an order of the court (for example, an order to obtain missing information or to provide such information to the other party).

Trials can also be interrupted by motions and applications to resolve side issues, or by "voir dire" hearings, where the judge decides issues of admissibility of evidence. These kinds of interruptions mean that witnesses may not always get a chance to appear to give testimony on the day that they expect to do so. Instead, they may have to come back on a later day, or come to court for more than just one day.

EVIDENCE

There are three primary justice functions of our legal system:

1. to determine the facts underlying the civil dispute or the crime;

2. to apply the law and arrive at a finding of fault or guilt; and

3. to impose a penalty (either a common-law judgment or a criminal law sentence) against the party at fault or the offender.

The first phase—fact determination—is driven by the presentation and testing of **evidence**. As explained above, in both the civil and the criminal courts, each party is given the opportunity to "present its case." For the plaintiff or the prosecution, this means the introduction of all the evidence it has at its disposal to prove the required elements of the common-law claim or the criminal law offence, respectively. For the defence, presenting its case means introducing evidence that tends to *disprove* those elements, pointing out that there are elements left unproven, and/or introducing evidence that supports a different set of facts.

The rules governing the use of evidence at Canadian trials were developed through common-law decisions. This means that the roots of many of these rules can be found in case law. Some rules of evidence have been codified in statutes like the *Criminal Code* or the *Canada Evidence Act*. However, evidence law has a strong common-law tradition and continues to evolve through case law.

Types of Evidence

The evidence that a party may present to prove or disprove a fact or an element can take a number of forms, but these fall into two broad categories: physical evidence and oral evidence or testimony.

PHYSICAL EVIDENCE

Physical evidence is an actual physical object. In a criminal case, for example, it could include a murder weapon, a DNA sample, or a bloodstained article of clothing. In a civil case, physical evidence might include photographs of damage to a plaintiff's property or a consumer item, such as a defective appliance. A subcategory of physical evidence is documentary evidence, such as a written contract or a medical report.

Physical evidence generally forms part of the trial record. It is introduced when a witness makes reference to it, and it is produced by the lawyer and identified by the witness, and then given to the court. There is therefore a direct link between physical evidence and oral evidence.

ORAL EVIDENCE (TESTIMONY)

Oral evidence, or **testimony**, is provided by **witnesses**. Witnesses are asked to appear at the trial to give the court information that is relevant to the issue before it (the claim, in a civil case, or the offence, in a criminal case). Witnesses may be brought to court by the plaintiff, the prosecution, or the defendant and are required to swear or affirm that their testimony will be truthful.

There are two main types of witnesses: regular witnesses and expert witnesses. Regular witnesses are asked to testify about their general and direct knowledge of the case. They are expected to stick to observations that are specifically relevant to the case and to avoid expressing opinions on those observations. Expert witnesses, on the other hand, may have no direct knowledge of the case but are called to provide an informed opinion on a particular question. For example, an expert medical witness may be called to provide an expert opinion about whether a baby with a broken arm could have broken the arm on his own, or whether the physical evidence points to injury by some other person. While expert witnesses generally are entitled to express opinions, those opinions must be defensible on the basis of the expert's credentials and generally accepted science. The opposing party is entitled to call its own expert witness to provide a contrary opinion.

Evidentiary Standards

In both civil and criminal cases, the party who is required to prove the claim or the charge is said to have the **burden of proof**, or the "onus." The **standard of proof** is the degree of proof that the party must produce to be successful. In other words, the standard of proof refers to how convincing the proof must be.

In civil trials, the standard of proof is a **balance of probabilities.** This means that the party making a claim (or counterclaim) against the other must prove that the basis for the claim is more likely than not to be valid. This standard applies to the key elements of a civil claim and to the claim as a whole. Before a judgment can be awarded, the trier of fact, taking into account all of the individual facts, must be convinced, on a balance of probabilities, that the legal elements of the claim (or counterclaim) have been established.

In criminal trials, the standard of proof is **beyond a reasonable doubt**. This means that the sum of all the facts pointing to guilt must be so convincing that no reasonable person would question that conclusion. This standard is based on the principle that a person is "innocent until proven guilty." The standard of proof for a criminal charge is high because a criminal conviction carries a heavy stigma in our society, with serious long-term consequences for the offender, including, in some cases, imprisonment.

The burden of proof in criminal trials falls on the prosecution. The defence is not required to present any evidence, although it usually does so. There is no obligation on the accused to prove his or her innocence or even to question the arguments presented by the prosecution.

BEING A WITNESS

Sometimes a social service worker has a client who is required to attend court in a family law, criminal, or other matter, or a social service worker may herself be asked to testify in a criminal or civil proceeding in a professional capacity—that is, as an expert witness. Giving verbal testimony can be nerve-wracking for anybody. Some degree of anxiety is to be anticipated, but knowing what to expect and good preparation can assist a witness in being more comfortable on the witness stand. This section provides some tips and guidelines to keep in mind when you are preparing yourself or a client for a court appearance.

The Questioning of Witnesses

Witnesses are generally summoned to appear in court by means of a **subpoena**—a legal document that compels a witness's appearance by force of law. When a witness is called to the stand by the party who requested his appearance, it is generally because it's hoped that the witness's evidence will be favourable to that party's case. In a criminal case, a witness to the crime would likely be called as a witness for the prosecution. For example, if a driver was shot and killed during a carjacking and a passenger survived, that passenger would be a witness.

The party who has called a witness in support of its case calls that witness to the stand and conducts an **examination-in-chief**. This examination will attempt to draw as much information out of the witness as possible by asking open-ended questions. Questions that contain crucial information and suggest an answer are leading questions and are not permitted in an examination-in-chief. For example, the prosecutor cannot ask her own witness, "Did the accused approach the car and bang on the window with the barrel of a gun to get the driver to lower it?" Instead, the prosecutor must elicit a description of the events from the witness. An open-ended question that would be permissible in the examination-in-chief would be, "What happened next?" When a witness is asked an open-ended factual question, she is expected to give a simple and straightforward answer —not adding other information or offering a personal opinion.

Often, if a lawyer asks a question that is not permitted under the law of evidence, the other party's lawyer will object. If this happens, the witness should remain quiet and not answer the question until the judge has made a ruling on the objection.

When the lawyer who called the witness has completed the examination-in-chief, the other lawyer gets a chance to examine the witness. This examination of the other party's witness is called **cross-examination**. In general, a lawyer who is conducting a cross-examination will try to control the content of the witness's answers. This is done by asking leading questions and questions that have very short answers (preferably "yes" or "no"). For example, the defence lawyer in the carjacking case might ask, "When the driver slowed for the red light, was his window open or shut?" This question limits the answer to one of two possibilities—either "open" or "shut."

For the witness, the key to handling questions in a cross-examination is to listen carefully to each question and reply to exactly what is asked, no less and no more. Lawyers conducting a cross-examination will sometimes try to shake a witness's confidence in his own observations or create opportunities for the witness to contradict either his own testimony or that of another witness of the examining lawyer. If this happens, the witness may pause before answering in order to give the examining lawyer an opportunity to object to the question.

Preparing for Court

In a January 2006 lecture at Loyalist College in Belleville, Ontario, Justice Stephen Hunter explained what is expected of a social service worker who testifies in a professional capacity regarding client matters. He emphasized that

> you are not a lay witness. You are a professional witness, and as such, you are there to give an opinion that has some expertise behind it. As a professional, you are subject to special rules, and those rules govern you.

For example, when you are called to the witness stand to give expert evidence, you will be asked questions that are designed to establish your professional qualifications. The credibility of your evidence will be enhanced if you have

- kept your qualifications up to date by pursuing continuing education about issues relevant to your particular area(s) of practice;

- kept records of your participation in these educational activities;

- taken advantage of opportunities to gain additional practical experience in the areas of practice about which you will be testifying; and

- documented this experience (for example, in your curriculum vitae).

You should ensure that your curriculum vitae is up to date, proofread it carefully to make sure there are no errors, and bring at least one copy (or preferably four) to court with you on the day of your appearance.

There are a number of other things you should do to prepare for giving evidence in court:

1. Review written information relevant to the case, including

   a. any notes you have made about the incidents about which you will be questioned;

   b. if the case relates to a client, the client's file;

   c. your copy of any statement that you have made to lawyers or police; and

   d. any other documents that may be useful in refreshing your memory of the events.

2. Don't make any changes to your notes, but highlight key points for easy reference.

3. Bring your notes to court (along with your curriculum vitae).

4. Confirm the time and exact location of the hearing the day before your scheduled appearance. Be sure you know how to find the hearing room.

5. If you are giving testimony in your professional capacity, speak with a supervisor who has attended this kind of hearing before. What was the experience like? What kinds of questions were asked? Does your supervisor have any suggestions or advice for you?

EXTRA CREDIT

Preparing Child Witnesses

Social service workers may sometimes have children as clients, and child clients may occasionally be required to appear in court to give testimony. This typically happens in one of two situations:

- a child may appear in family court to give evidence about his preferences with respect to custody or access; or

- a child may appear in court in the course of a child protection proceeding or a criminal prosecution to give evidence about child abuse.

In the first situation, the child is typically an older child who has asked to be included in the proceedings. It is rare for a family court to compel the appearance of a child who does not want to testify. When working with a child who is going to court willingly, you may need to describe the stages of a trial to the child, focusing on what happens during examination-in-chief and cross-examination. You may want to have a conversation with the child about what it means to tell the truth, and you may want to explain to the child that it is not her job to attempt to influence the court in favour of one party or another; her testimony, if given honestly, will assist in that process. If you think that the child has an unrealistic view of what court will be like, you may wish to accompany her to sit in on a trial. Many trials are public (less so in family court); allowing the child to observe the questioning of a witness, even if the case is quite different from her own situation, may help to prepare her for her court appearance and show her that a cross-examination is a normal part of the trial process.

A child who is a victim of child abuse may be quite young and reluctant to testify in court. Intimidation is very common in child abuse cases. The child may be afraid of testifying against the person who tried to intimidate and frighten him, particularly, for example, if the person threatened to hurt or kill the child (or a member of the child's family) if he ever tells anyone about the abuse. Clearly, giving testimony in an abuse case will be a very stressful event for any child.

While a social service worker with general skills may talk to the child witness about court procedures, it is preferable to arrange for a specialist trained in child psychology, and, ideally, a specialist in preparing children to testify in court, to work with the child.

Some regions have special programs set up to deliver child witness preparation services. Social service workers should investigate the availability of these services in their community so that they can make appropriate referrals of their child clients.

More information about preparing child witnesses is available from the Peel Region Child Witness Preparation Program at www.peelcc.org and The Centre for Children and Families in the Justice System (at the London Family Court Clinic) at www.lfcc .on.ca. ◇

6. Speak with the lawyer representing the party who has called you as a witness. Ask any questions that you have about the trial process and your role in it. Try to find out what kind of questions you are likely to be asked in examination and cross-examination.

7. If you have some idea of the questions that you may be asked, think about how you will answer.

8. If you are not comfortable speaking in a formal setting, and you expect to be asked to testify on future occasions, consider obtaining training in public speaking.

Giving Testimony

The following are some tips to keep in mind when you are on the witness stand:

- Dress neatly and professionally and arrive on time.

- Find out the correct form of address for speaking to the justice or judge, such as "Your Honour," and make sure you use it.

- Keep your notes at hand, but ask the judge's permission first before you consult them.

- Speak slowly, clearly, and audibly.

- Be aware of your body language: don't fidget.

- Be courteous and respectful toward the court and all participants in the proceeding.

- Don't volunteer information; wait until you are asked a question.

- Answer questions truthfully to the best of your knowledge.

- If you don't know the answer to a question, say so: don't guess.

- If you make a mistake, say so.

- In general, it is best to keep your answers brief. If the lawyer wants more information, he will ask a followup question.

- Don't exaggerate or speculate.

- Avoid slang.

- Avoid using professional jargon unless it is relevant to the matter on which you are testifying or necessary for accuracy.

- If you would like to emphasize a particular answer, it can help to turn toward the judge and address him or her directly.

- Don't express your personal views of the other parties in the case, especially the defendant in a criminal trial or the opposing party in a civil lawsuit. Objectivity makes you more credible; bias makes you less so. Credible testimony is the most helpful contribution you can make to the trial process.

- If the cross-examining lawyer is aggressive, stay calm and try to avoid reacting to upsetting questions.

- Be clear about the difference between your client's interests, your own interests, and the interests of your employer (if applicable).

- Remember that you have a duty at all times to tell the truth. If you are giving testimony about a client, you must act in the best interests of the client as far as is consistent with telling the truth.

KEY TERMS

accused

adjournment

applicant

balance of probabilities

beyond a reasonable doubt

burden of proof

counterclaim

cross-examination

defendant

evidence

examination-in-chief

hearing

judicial interim release

motion

oral evidence

physical evidence

plaintiff

plea bargain

pre-trial motion/application

prosecutor

respondent

Small Claims Court

standard of proof

subpoena

testimony

trier of fact

trier of law

verdict

witness

REFERENCES

Canada Evidence Act, RSC 1985, c. C-5.

Canadian Charter of Rights and Freedoms, part I of the *Constitution Act, 1982*, being schedule B of the *Canada Act 1982* (UK), 1982, c. 11.

Courts of Justice Act, RSO 1990, c. C.43.

Criminal Code, RSC 1985, c. C-46.

Gladue, R. v., [1999] 1 SCR 688.

Rules of Civil Procedure, RRO 1990, Reg. 194.

REVIEW QUESTIONS

1. In what roles might a social service worker be required to appear in court?

2. What is a plea bargain, and why might a person accused of a crime negotiate one?

3. Does a finding that an accused is unfit to stand trial result in withdrawal of the charge or acquittal?

4. Is a preliminary inquiry held in every criminal case?

5. In a criminal case, who decides whether the necessary elements of the offence have been proven beyond a reasonable doubt?

6. What kinds of remedies may be awarded at the end of a civil trial?

7. Why is it necessary, in a civil case, to seek leave to appeal a trial decision to the Ontario Court of Appeal?

8. List at least three steps in the litigation process that take place before a civil trial begins.

9. What are the civil and criminal standards of proof? Why is the standard of proof higher in a criminal case than it is in a civil case?

10. What is a leading question, and when is it permitted?

11. List at least five things you can do to prepare for a court appearance.

12. What should you bring to court?

CHAPTER 14

Notes and Reports

CHAPTER OBJECTIVES

After reading this chapter, you should be able to:

- Understand the importance of note taking in social service practice.

- Describe ways of improving the clarity and understandability of notes.

- Explain the use of good judgment in making decisions about content.

- Demonstrate an awareness of confidentiality concerns in making notes and writing reports about clients.

- Explain how the preparation of reports differs from note taking.

- Describe how your notes might be used in court.

INTRODUCTION

Accurate and timely note taking is a crucial skill for social service workers. It is important for workplace efficiency, and it is critical to protect against liability.

Documenting work in progress is a necessary component of keeping organized and prioritizing when dealing with heavy client caseloads. Information that is undocumented may be quickly forgotten or inaccurately recalled. By taking a few extra minutes to jot down notes summarizing all phone calls and meetings with clients, and internal discussions about clients, you will be able to pick up a file several weeks later and, at a glance, update your knowledge of the case. If co-workers are involved with the same client, "notes to file" are a valuable communication tool, keeping everyone informed. "To do" lists and action points are also helpful to keep you focused on what needs to be done.

In the event that you are asked to justify your decisions or actions with respect to a client, reliable and detailed notes will back you up. Your notes are evidence that you considered the issue carefully and fully, and responded in a competent and responsible manner. Without this documentary trail, you put yourself at risk of allegations of negligence.

Besides generating notes for personal or internal agency use, social service workers may also need to produce reports designed to be read by others, such as social workers, judges and lawyers, or government administrators. While internal notes are primarily designed as memory aids for the social worker or to provide information to colleagues, reports have different and often quite specific purposes. A social

> ## POLICY EXCERPT
> ### Standards of Practice for Record Keeping
>
> The Ontario College of Social Workers and Social Service Workers, in its *Standards of Practice Handbook*, sets out the following requirements for record keeping:
>
> > The creation and maintenance of records by social workers and by social service workers is an essential component of professional practice. The process of preparation and organization of material for the record provides a means to understanding the client and planning the social work and social service work intervention. The purpose of the social work and social service work record is to document services in a recognizable form in order to ensure the continuity and quality of service, to establish accountability for and evidence of the services rendered, to enable the evaluation of service quality, and to provide information to be used for research and education. College members ensure that records are current, accurate, contain relevant information about clients, and are managed in a manner that protects client privacy.
>
> Source: Ontario College of Social Workers and Social Service Workers, *Standards of Practice Handbook*, available online at www.ocswssw.org. ◇

service worker's duty both to respect client privacy rights and to communicate honestly with agencies entitled to receive reports means that considerable judgment is required in preparing external reports.

This chapter provides guidelines on note taking and report writing, with a focus on the use of notes and reports in court or other legal proceedings. Each office or agency has its own policies with respect to records management, which should be reviewed carefully to ensure that the records you produce and maintain serve the functions for which they were designed.

NOTE TAKING

General Considerations

In taking notes, you are creating a written record of certain events. Before you begin, you should ask yourself the following questions:

- Who will read these notes?
- What will the reader be hoping to learn from them?
- Is the reader familiar with the context, or must I provide background information?
- What are the privacy implications of making these notes?
- What is my own purpose for making these notes?

In the simplest scenario, you will be keeping notes for your own future use. In that case, you should make notes in the format that you find most useful, without worrying about providing background information. However, it is important to keep in mind that in some circumstances, notes recorded for personal use may need to be made available to others, such as colleagues, or perhaps the client. Your notes may even be used in a legal proceeding; for example, you may be required, in your professional capacity, to give testimony based on your notes in a court of law. For this reason, any notes relating to the practice of your profession should be accurate, and free from offensive or inappropriate content that would reflect badly on you or on the agency where you work. (Justice Stephen Hunter has offered this advice to social service students: when making notes, assume that the next person who will read them is your worst enemy!)

If you are keeping notes that are intended to be read by others—for example, in a setting where clients are served by multiple professionals—there will be additional considerations. For example, you will need to consider whether what you write is understandable to the intended reader, and whether the notes provide sufficient information.

In the course of your practice, you may encounter situations in which legal issues may arise. In such situations, it is advisable to take notes in case you need to rely on them to protect yourself or your employer organization. The following are just a few examples:

- A resident in a group home tells a social service worker that she has been harassed by another resident. The social service worker documents the allegation and any steps she has taken to address it.

- A social service worker who manages staff takes disciplinary action against a staff member. She records the action taken in the employee's file (in case the agency needs to terminate the employee at some future time).

- A social service worker uses an extraordinary method (for example, restraints or forced isolation) to manage the behaviour of a mentally ill client in an institutional setting, or participates in such an intervention. He records the circumstances of the decision and the method of intervention used.

- A social service worker witnesses an incident of child abuse involving a client. She takes notes recording what was observed and documenting the report to the children's aid society, as required by the CFSA.

- A social service worker working in a long-term care facility reports an instance of abuse of a patient by a co-worker and documents it.

In these situations, it is prudent to take notes so that you can substantiate your actions and your reasons for taking them, in case the incident forms part of a subsequent investigation or legal claim. This type of note taking is especially challenging, and the keys to getting it right are to be thorough, honest, accurate, and neutral. Sometimes notes taken in these contexts need to be used at a later time to generate a report.

Usefulness and Understandability

Your notes will be useful only to the extent that they can be understood by the reader, and that they provide all the information that is required. In reviewing your notes for understandability, you may find the following checklist helpful.

1. Did you make the notes as soon as possible after receiving the information? Timeliness in making notes promotes accuracy.

2. Do your notes follow a well-organized structure—for example, chronological order?

3. Are your notes dated? If you make notes in a shared notebook or file, are they marked as yours?

4. Did you write out, in full, any pertinent details and check the accuracy of the information recorded (including the spelling of names, addresses, and phone numbers)?

5. If you used abbreviations, did you work from a list of accepted or recognized abbreviations, or provide explanations of what they refer to?

6. Did you make it clear which portions of your notes are direct quotations of another person's words by using quotation marks?

7. Did you provide enough information to answer the following questions about the matter described and the individuals, agencies, etc. involved?

- Who?

- What?

- When?

- Where?

- How?

CASE IN POINT

A Duty to Evaluate?

Social service workers are usually expected to take a neutral position in writing notes and reports; unlike social workers, they do not perform diagnostic functions. However, sometimes a social service worker may be called upon to act in a decision-making or evaluative capacity, requiring him to record his assessment of a particular situation. Consider the following scenario.

You are supervising the first session of a recreational program for cognitively impaired adults. Your supervisor has asked you to carefully observe the participants who have enrolled to ensure that there is no one in the group who might pose a threat to the other participants. As the session unfolds, one man seems increasingly angry. For no apparent reason, he yells at two other participants. Though he does nothing more than this, his presence makes you nervous, and some of the other participants seem to be avoiding him.

In your notes, you provide a neutral description of the session, mentioning only that "Jamie Parsons raised his voice on two occasions."

In this situation, limiting your notes to that neutral statement amounts to not living up to your responsibilities.

Your obligations to your supervisor and to the safety of your clients, in this situation, require that you form and express an opinion about whether Jamie Parsons might pose a threat to the group. In some circumstances, failing to evaluate a situation and include an assessment in the written record may have detrimental consequences.

For example, in the judicial inquiry into the death of Kim Anne Popen (a 1982 child abuse case), Judge H. Ward Allen was critical of a social worker for omitting "an evaluative component" from her notes. In particular, the social worker neglected to express, in her notes, any opinion about the fitness of the parents to care for their child. While making such fundamental judgments about clients is generally beyond the role of a social service worker, the recreational program scenario above is a realistic example of a situation in which your notes should go beyond the neutral facts of a situation.

Judicial Inquiry into the Case of Kim Anne Popen (Toronto: Queen's Printer, 1982). ◇

Generally, it is not appropriate to attempt to answer the question "Why?" Often, you will be reporting on the actions of others, and you cannot be sure that you understand the motivations for someone's actions, or the underlying causes of an event. Attempting to do so can make you appear less than impartial, if the matter is ever reviewed, or can inappropriately narrow the scope of an investigation.

Making useful, understandable notes requires careful consideration of what information should and should not be reported, and how it should be reported. Some guidelines are suggested below.

Choices About Information

Notes should be focused and concise. Including unnessary or excessively detailed information will only reduce the readability and impact of important content. For the purpose of building a rapport with your client, you may sometimes listen to his ideas about quite irrelevant matters, but those conversations need not be recorded. Personal comments should also be avoided; if you must note something negative about a client, you should do so in language that is professional and as neutral as possible.

To illustrate the choice of appropriate information, consider a situation where you are making notes of a client interview to determine employability. Information obviously worth recording would be details about education and work experience, and about the kind of work sought. It would also be useful to note factors that could restrict the client's availability for certain kinds of employment; for example, "She has school-age children and might have difficulty working afternoon and night shifts" or "He was fired from a job that involved sales, which he says he hates." Anecdotes about friendships in previous workplaces are probably not important. You should avoid value judgments, such as "He claimed to have excellent customer service skills, but I think he was just being arrogant." Instead, keep it factual. If the client claims to be fluent in English but you have trouble understanding her when she speaks, you might write, "Offered to refer client to language training program; she declined" (presuming you did make such an offer).

Finally, it can sometimes be useful to note gaps in information, or to note that you have not observed something that you expected to observe. This can serve as a reminder, to yourself or to colleagues, of matters that should perhaps be investigated further. In the context of the employability interview described above, you might discover that there is a gap of a few years in the client's employment history and that the client is reluctant to provide information about what he was doing during that time. Since the reason could affect his eligibility for a particular job (for example, if he was serving time in prison), further attempts should be made to obtain an explanation from the client.

Revising Notes

Sometimes it is necessary to make changes in your notes—for example, if you discover an error, or if you want to include additional information. When and how you make such revisions will depend on the kind of work you do and the format you use for recording information. However, in all circumstances, you should follow certain procedures in altering your notes.

The first rule is that, unlike personal notes, notes made for professional purposes should never be destroyed.

The second rule is that, since your notes may be used by others, you should make your changes clear. For example, in handwritten notes or a typewritten copy, use a single line to strike out, and write the correction above or after this line. It is good practice to date and initial any changes of substance (as opposed to trivial changes such as corrections in spelling), particularly if your notes are part of a file to which several people contribute.

Some professionals use notebooks with numbered pages, both for easy reference and for security of the record, since it is immediately evident if an entry has been torn out. If you use this type of note-taking system, never tear out a page; it may appear that you are trying to hide something. Instead, strike through the page with a diagonal line. You should not be reluctant to correct inaccuracies, but you should do so by crossing out in a way that doesn't obliterate the entry, or by adding new, more accurate information on another page.

If you make notes in an electronic format (on a computer), the safest way to make a change is to save the previous entry as a draft, and work from a new version of the document, saving any previous versions for your records. Alternatively, you can use a word processing program that "tracks" changes. These programs often note changes using strike-throughs or different colours, and can save the date and time of the change. Many of these programs are designed to manage documents that are accessed by more than one user, tracking the deletions and additions of each.

Privacy Considerations

The introduction of the federal *Personal Information Protection and Electronic Documents Act* and the Ontario *Personal Health Information Protection Act, 2004* added a new layer to the issue of protecting clients' privacy. The topic of privacy is discussed in detail in chapter 22. It is difficult to give specific recommendations about privacy protection here, because social service workers work in a wide range of settings. However, some general guidelines can be suggested.

- Be aware of concerns about privacy and the confidentiality of client information.

- Be familiar with your employer's policy with respect to client privacy.

- If you need to request, share, or use personal information about a client, ensure that the appropriate releases have been obtained.

- Never share your notes unless you have been given permission to disclose them from every person mentioned in them. (Your office may have obtained releases to permit certain kinds of disclosure; inquire whether this is the case.)

- If you are authorized to disclose your notes, make sure you understand the scope of that authorization: to which client(s) and to what information it applies, and to whom the information can be disclosed.

- If in doubt about your right to disclose certain information, withhold the information until you have checked with a supervisor or obtained a new release from the client.

Typically, in a setting where you are expected to take notes to facilitate the provision of client services, there is a certain expectation of privacy associated with the content of those notes. In many cases, people who have interests that are opposed to your client's interests (for example, the other party in a lawsuit) will not be able to gain access to your notes. There are, however, exceptions. As discussed in chapter 1, unlike the communications between a lawyer and a client, what is said between a social service worker and her client is not considered privileged (protected from disclosure in court). Also, some statutes or court orders can force you to disclose the content of communications with a client. You might also, under certain circumstances, feel a moral obligation to disclose information to a third party, such as if you believe your client is suicidal.

As a result, you should never promise a client confidentiality unless you are certain that you can guarantee it. You should also not allow the client to be lulled into a false sense of security about talking with you. In some cases, it is necessary to warn a client ahead of time that there are certain kinds of information that you cannot keep to yourself. This gives the client the opportunity to decide whether or not to censor what she chooses to tell you.

If you know that a party who is opposed to your client could gain access to your notes, you should use extra care when deciding what information to include in them. This means that you can use discretion in recording unfavourable or unflattering details, but it doesn't allow you to omit information that you ought to record.

Using a notebook with numbered pages is helpful in protecting sensitive information: you can record such information on a separate page, resuming the text of your notes on a new page. This can make it easier to limit access to this information by others. (See, for example, the discussion below under the heading "Using Your Notes in Court.")

REPORT WRITING

Report writing differs from note taking in two key ways:

- Reports are prepared specifically for use by persons other than the writer.
- Reports are usually written for a specific purpose other than just the creation of a written record.

Reports may also differ in other ways, including the following:

- A report may be prepared in collaboration with other colleagues, professionals, etc.
- The organization or content of a report may be formally prescribed, instead of being left to the preference of the writer.
- The writer may be required to express opinions and/or make recommendations.

While the range of reports that social service workers may encounter in their work is almost limitless, the general function of those reports is universal: they provide a formal framework by which a person who has direct knowledge of or experience with a client, event, or set of circumstances can communicate that knowledge or experience to a third party (a supervisor, an administrator of an agency, a commit-tee, etc.).

The following examples indicate the kinds of reports that social service workers may be required to contribute to or write:

■ *Human resources reports*: A social service worker who supervises other employees may be required to report to a senior manager on the performance of those subordinates.

■ *Reports in family relations contexts*: A social service worker who works in a supervised access program may be asked to prepare a report for a court on how well this approach is working for a particular family and whether there are any problems.

■ *Reports for use by care workers or health-care professionals*: A social service worker may be asked to observe a candidate for long-term care and report on the extent of the candidate's need for assistance with daily living.

■ *Reports in the corrections context*: A social service worker who counsels offenders serving custodial sentences may be asked to prepare a report about some aspect of an inmate's progress or behaviour for use in an early release assessment.

■ *Reports in the context of making social benefits decisions*: A social service worker who is an intake officer for a social benefits program, such as Ontario Works, may be required to prepare regular reports for program administrators on whether or not individual clients are complying with participation requirements.

You can probably think of many more examples.

When preparing a report, you will benefit from having thorough and clear notes from which to work. If there is a prescribed format, you should be careful to follow it. This may mean converting content that is organized in one way in your notes into a different format for the report. You may also have to supplement the information in your notes with additional background information, if the intended readers of the report do not have your knowledge of the context—the client, the issue or event, and the circumstances. In effect, you must put yourself in the reader's shoes and ask yourself what he needs to know.

Often, you will be required to strike an appropriate balance between your duty to the client, or to your employer, and your obligations as the author of the report. For example, if you are an intake officer with Ontario Works, and you are preparing a report about an applicant for benefits who you feel is not prepared to comply with participation requirements, you may have a duty to express that opinion even though it would disappoint the applicant. Your duty to your employer and the goals of the program supersede your obligations to the applicant.

Similarly, if you are working as a parole officer, or in a program for inmates of a correctional facility, you may be required to report on a client's suitability for early release. If you have concerns about the client, you must report them, even if doing so appears to be against the client's interest. In such situations, where you are required to draw unfavourable conclusions about a client, explain your reasons truthfully and briefly; avoid unnecessary elaboration. Ideally, well in adance of making your report, you will have laid the groundwork with the client, advising him

1. that you are required to make reports about him in the course of your work;

2. that your reports must be truthful and accurate; and

3. that there are important limits on the confidentiality of communications between you and him.

The general guidelines for writing reports are similar to those for note taking, and can be summarized as follows:

1. In making reports, you should always be scrupulously honest.

2. You should be neutral in your comments unless an opinion is specifically required.

3. You should use appropriate and professional language:

    a. avoid labels or comments that could be construed as racist, sexist, elitist, or otherwise discriminatory;

    b. no matter how strong your private opinions, refrain from making judgmental or damaging remarks about anyone, even a person whose behaviour toward your client is extremely offensive and upsetting;

    c. avoid comments that could reflect poorly on you as a professional, or on your employer; and

    d. avoid any comments that might suggest bias or a desire to cast blame on another party.

Finally, you should remember that your reports, or your notes, may be viewed by the client at some later time. Therefore, you should take care always to communicate with the sensitivity that is expected of you as a helping professional.

DOCUMENTARY EVIDENCE IN LEGAL PROCEEDINGS

Evidence, in the context of civil litigation or criminal proceedings, is anything that tends to support or disprove a conclusion. In many legal proceedings, a significant portion of the evidence presented takes the form of written documents, collectively referred to as "documentary evidence."

Generally, a document filed with the court is not by itself considered sufficient proof of its contents. In most cases, the court requires a witness to attend in court to give oral testimony about the document—who made it, when it was made, and whether its contents reflect the truth. For example, in a case involving child abuse, a court presented with allegations of child abuse written in a private letter from one person to another will not automatically accept the letter as evidence. In order to establish the reliability of the evidence, the party seeking to have it admitted by the court must call the writer of the letter to testify about the letter and its contents.

It is important for social service workers to understand the role of documentary evidence in legal proceedings, and court or tribunal procedures for testing the reliability of such evidence. From time to time, cases arise where notes and other written records created by social service workers are brought forward as evidence for or

---

EXTRA CREDIT

Business Records as Documentary Evidence

Section 30 of the *Canada Evidence Act* provides a special rule for the use of business records as evidence. Basically, this rule provides that

1. if a record is kept in the normal course of business, and

2. if it is kept consistently according to the organization's policy or protocol,

that record is admissible in court as proof of its contents.

This means that even if the employee who made the record cannot be found (has long since left the employer, moved away, etc.), the person seeking to rely on the record will likely be able to have it admitted into evidence without supporting testimony.

The rationale behind this rule is that business records are kept for a business purpose, and therefore are not likely to be self-serving (made for the benefit or advantage of the person creating the record), or to be made in an attempt to influence litigation.

For social service agencies, this rule should be an important motivator for the development and maintenance of standard business records and of policies to guide their use. An example of a record that might be kept by a social service agency would be an Occurrence Report kept by staff at a halfway house. If all of the staff fill out these reports in standard form whenever there is an occurrence (and the agency has a policy that defines "occurrence"), the agency would have a strong argument for being able to admit these records as proof of their contents whether or not the staff who made them are available to testify.

It is also useful to remember that the business records rule applies in reverse, to some extent. Where an organization keeps certain records in the usual course of business, but the records, when produced, do not contain references to events that a party alleges have happened, if those events are of a type that the organization's policies require staff to document, the court can consider the absence of these references as support for the fact that the events alleged to have occurred did not in fact occur. ◈

---

against a party in the case. In these circumstances, the social service worker who prepared the document may be called to testify in court or at the hearing.

A social service worker may also be called to give oral testimony in a case involving a client or the social service worker's employer, and she may rely on her notes and reports to refresh her memory. This section provides some suggestions that you may find useful if your professional work places you in either of these situations.

Using Your Notes in Court

If you are required to give testimony in court, you will be permitted to bring your notes with you and to consult them as a memory aid. To avoid fumbling with your notes on the witness stand, carefully review them on the day before your court appearance, so that you can quickly locate the information you need. (Refer to the checklist in chapter 13 for other suggestions on preparing to testify in court.)

When you testify, you must ask the judge's permission before you refer to your notes, and you will not be permitted to simply read from your notes. The lawyers who question you will want you to describe your current recollection of the events in question; your notes are intended to remind you of important details you may have forgotten.

If you choose to rely on your notes in court, the judge will likely allow the other party's lawyer to examine them, and perhaps make photocopies. If your notes relate to more than one client, you have a duty to protect the information about the clients who are not the subject of the court case. You can do this by providing the other party's lawyer with only those pages that apply to the relevant client. If you use a notebook from which it is not possible or acceptable to remove pages, you can use elastic bands to separate the notes that you are required to disclose from the notes that you need to keep confidential.

If you are asked a question and your truthful answer differs from what you have written in your notes, you must give that truthful answer and be prepared to explain to the court why your notes, in your opinion, are not accurate.

Being Cross-Examined on Your Notes

If your notes have been provided to the opposing party's counsel as part of the disclosure process, they may have been entered as an exhibit in the case and may form part of the public record. If this has happened, it is likely that you will be cross-examined on the content of your notes by the other party's lawyer. Make sure you have a copy of the notes in front of you before this cross-examination begins. If you don't have them, tell the judge, so that you can be provided with a copy.

Your credibility as a witness—the degree to which the judge and jury believe you—can directly affect the weight that will be given to your evidence. For this reason, you will be most helpful to your client if you deliver your testimony in a straightforward way, without excessive elaboration or attempts to hold back information.

If you are asked about a passage in your notes that you cannot immediately recall, do not rush your answer, even if the cross-examining lawyer is pressuring you. Take a moment to think, and, if necessary, ask permission to consult your notes; then, once you're sure, answer the question. It is in the interests of justice for you to answer accurately, not instantly, and you need to avoid making a mistake that the opposing lawyer can use to cast doubt on your credibility.

Since the objective of cross-examination is to undermine the other party's case, the cross-examining lawyer may attempt to find inconsistencies in your testimony, or between your testimony and your notes, so that it appears that you are lying or fabricating information. Rather than react defensively, stay calm, and remember that your duty is to be truthful. If you have made a mistake in an earlier statement, if you have made a mistake in your notes, or if you simply don't remember something, you must say so. But also keep in mind that it is never appropriate for counsel to badger or harass a witness, nor are you obliged to answer the same question twice. If this happens, pause to allow the lawyer for your side to object; or state that you are feeling bullied, or that you have already answered the particular question. Your statement will form part of the court record.

REFERENCES

Canada Evidence Act, RSC 1985, c. C-5.

Ontario College of Social Workers and Social Service Workers, Code of Ethics and *Standards of Practice Handbook*, online at www.ocswssw.org.

Personal Health Information Protection Act, 2004, SO 2004, c. 3, Sch. A.

Personal Information Protection and Electronic Documents Act, SC 2000, c. 5.

Samuels, Marilyn, and Elayne Tanner, *Managing a Legal and Ethical Social Work Practice* (Toronto: Irwin Law, 2003).

REVIEW QUESTIONS

1. How can good note taking help a social service worker or social service agency to manage a heavy caseload?

2. What kinds of questions can you ask yourself before you prepare your notes to improve their usefulness?

3. How can note taking help to protect a social service worker or his agency from liability or other challenges (for example, allegations of professional incompetence)?

4. Why might a social service worker's notes be admissible in court long after he has left the social service agency?

5. When making notes, it is useful to answer the following questions: who, what, when, where, and how? However, it is generally not appropriate to ask, "Why?" Why not?

6. Should a social service worker ever include an opinion in her notes?

7. Are communications between a client and a social service worker protected by privilege?

8. If a social service worker has recorded confidential personal information about a client in her notes, and a third party (for example, a potential landlord) requests access to those notes, what should the social service worker do?

9. When writing a report, a social service worker should be aware of certain differences between report writing and note taking. Describe at least four of these differences.

CHAPTER 15

Accessing Legal Services

CHAPTER OBJECTIVES

After reading this chapter, you should be able to:

- Understand when legal advice and representation should be obtained.

- Explain how the legal profession is regulated.

- Describe in general terms how paralegals differ from lawyers.

- Understand how a person with limited financial resources may obtain the services of a lawyer.

- Explain the criteria used to establish a person's eligibility for legal aid.

- Describe how the legal aid system works, from the point of view of the lawyer and of the client.

INTRODUCTION

The clients of social service workers often require lawyers to advise them on a variety of legal issues (relating, for example, to employment law, immigration law, landlord–tenant law, family law, and criminal law) and to represent them in court or before administrative tribunals. It is important that social service workers be able to identify legal issues that require the attention of lawyers, so that they can help their clients to find a lawyer when appropriate. It bears repeating that while social service workers may provide clients with basic legal information, such as that included in this text, they must be very careful not to advise clients about what to do.

There may also be occasions when a social service worker needs to consult a lawyer on her own behalf. This chapter is a practical guide to obtaining the services of a lawyer or a paralegal in Ontario, including subsidized services (legal aid). It also discusses, briefly, advocacy resources outside the legal profession that may be able to assist individuals who, because of their circumstances, are not adequately served by the existing social support network.

LAWYERS AND PARALEGALS

Qualifications and Professional Regulation

While the law is publicly accessible—anyone can look up cases and statutes in a library, or online—a person with legal training is often needed to decipher it. The amount of legal training needed depends on the complexity of the issue. For example, some legal transactions, such as entering into a lease with a landlord, may be simple enough for non-lawyers to accomplish on their own. In fact, the legislature and the courts have made efforts to make the handling of some of the simpler and more common issues, such as defending against a parking ticket or even taking a case to Small Claims Court, accessible to people who cannot afford, or choose not to engage, a legal representative.

Whether or not a person seeks legal representation generally depends on the complexity of the matter and on how much is at stake. For example, it may be sensible to defend a $30 parking ticket on your own, but it is unwise to defend a charge of impaired driving without a lawyer, because the consequences of losing at trial include possible loss of your driver's licence and even imprisonment. A lawyer who has experience in criminal law will be better able to protect your rights and present a persuasive case in court.

Lawyers qualified to practise in Ontario have a three-year law degree from a Canadian university, or the foreign equivalent, and have undergone an apprenticeship period, known as "articling." They have also passed examinations for admission to the Law Society of Upper Canada, the regulatory body of the legal profession in Ontario. Members of the Law Society are expected to conform to a code of conduct, and they are required to carry professional liability insurance. Anyone who questions the credentials of a person who claims to be a qualified lawyer, or who wants to know whether a particular lawyer has ever been disciplined for professional misconduct, can ask the Law Society to provide this information. The Law Society also offers a referral service to assist people seeking legal advice (discussed below).

In Ontario, **paralegals** are permitted to represent clients on relatively simple matters, such as civil claims tried in Small Claims Court, minor traffic offences, and issues adjudicated by administrative tribunals. Paralegals have some training in matters of law and legal procedure but have not passed the exams for qualification as a lawyer. Regulation of paralegals, establishing minimum standards of professional practice, was introduced in 2006 and is in the process of implementation. Paralegals will be required to meet specific educational standards, pass a licensing examination, and carry professional liability insurance. A separate governing body will be created to regulate paralegal practice, including the investigation of complaints and the imposition of disciplinary sanctions if necessary.

The primary advantage of using a paralegal rather than a lawyer is the cost: paralegals are much less expensive. Many paralegals are knowledgeable, competent, and honest, and provide good service at a reasonable price in their area of practice.

As noted above, all practising lawyers must be insured, and, once regulated, paralegals will be required to do so as well. (In the meantime, before hiring a paralegal, it is prudent to obtain confirmation that he or she has insurance coverage.) Insurance is very important because it protects clients against **fraud** and negligence.

WEB LINK

For more information about individual lawyers, about obtaining a referral, or about the regulation of paralegals in Ontario, visit the website of the Law Society of Upper Canada at www.lsuc.on.ca.

Keep in mind that you cannot sue a lawyer or a paralegal for losing your case. A successful malpractice suit is possible only where you have been harmed because your legal adviser has done something that is fraudulent, otherwise malicious, or clearly negligent. After all, even the most conscientious professionals may occasionally make minor administrative or tactical mistakes or errors of judgment. Professional liability insurance is designed to cover those circumstances in which a lawyer (or paralegal) has done something that falls below the accepted standard of competence and professional care.

Suppose, for example, that you are injured in a bus crash and the legislation requires that you file a claim for damages against the transit company within two years. If you instruct your lawyer to file a claim and she fails to do so by the specified deadline, you almost certainly have grounds for a negligence claim against your lawyer. If the court agrees that the claim is valid, you will be awarded compensation based on the loss you suffered as a result of your lawyer's mistake. In other words, the amount of compensation you are awarded will depend on the amount of money you would have won in your trial against the transit company, adjusted for the likelihood that you would have won that case and the expense of pursuing it.

Finding Legal Representation

There are many ways to choose a lawyer in Ontario. You might ask a friend or colleague to recommend a lawyer; you might choose a lawyer whose office you pass every day on your way to work; or you might look in the local telephone directory. You can also make use of lawyer referral services provided by the Law Society of Upper Canada and the Canadian Bar Association. The Law Society charges a very small fee to use the service, and all lawyers who accept referrals under the system offer a free 30-minute consultation to potential clients. The service is neutral: it simply lists lawyers by name, not according to any kind of rating system, so that all participating lawyers have an equal chance of being referred.

People who have limited financial resources to pay for a lawyer's services, and who are eligible for subsidized legal assistance, may find a lawyer by applying to a legal aid office or a community legal clinic. These options are discussed in a later section of this chapter.

Some lawyers are generalists, practising in a variety of areas. Others, especially at large firms, specialize in particular areas, such as insolvency law or family law. Specialists often cost more, and their expertise is usually not required for routine legal matters. If a complex issue arises, any lawyer should be able to either research it or seek the advice of a specialist. When a potential client begins looking for a lawyer, she will typically be asked about the nature of her legal issue. If the lawyer does not practise in that area, the client should feel free to ask for the name of a lawyer who does. Good lawyers are usually happy to provide referrals to their colleagues.

Paralegals are listed in the local telephone directory, but many people may prefer to seek a referral from a friend or colleague who can vouch for the competence and credentials of a particular person. It doesn't hurt to ask for references from other satisfied clients. Finally, in choosing either a paralegal or a lawyer, it's important that the client feel comfortable with the legal adviser on a personal level, so that they can work well together.

Legal Fees and Other Costs

Lawyers calculate their charges for legal services in three main ways:

- *Hourly rate.* The most common type of billing is by the hour. Most lawyers charge an hourly rate that reflects the lawyer's level of experience. Often, in more complex cases, a senior lawyer will work on the more difficult aspects of the case and others in the firm—junior lawyers or articling students—will handle the more routine details. In such cases, the senior lawyer's time is charged at a higher hourly rate and the work done by other staff is charged at a lower rate. Some lawyers charge different rates for different kinds of work, such as a higher hourly fee for court time.

- *Transaction-based flat fee.* Some lawyers charge a flat fee for routine transactions—for example, handling the sale of a residential property or an **uncontested divorce**. These fees generally apply only to transactions that follow the usual pattern. Flat fees can also apply to stages in a proceeding; for example, a lawyer could charge a flat fee to file a statement of claim or defence, a separate flat fee to conduct discoveries and attempt settlement out of court, and an hourly rate thereafter if the matter goes to trial.

- *Contingency fees.* In a case involving a claim for monetary compensation, the lawyer and the client may agree to a **contingency fee** arrangement, whereby the lawyer's fee is calculated as a percentage of any amount recovered in the action. If the client loses the case, the lawyer loses too. The advantage of this arrangement is that clients with a strong case but little money are able to afford representation. There are strict rules governing contingency fee arrangements, including maximum contingency payment rates, and a contingency fee may not be appropriate in some cases. Understandably, lawyers prefer to accept contingency fees only in cases with a reasonable likelihood of success. For example, if a client has a strong case in a damages claim for, say, $200,000, she may agree to pay the lawyer 18 percent of the money recovered from the defendant. If the client is awarded $200,000, she will pay the lawyer $36,000. If she is awarded $180,000, the lawyer will get $32,400. However, if the claim fails, the lawyer will get nothing.

In addition to legal fees, clients must pay for the lawyer's disbursements. **Disbursements** are out-of-pocket expenses incurred in the course of representing the client; they include photocopying costs, courier costs, court filing fees, and fees to obtain experts' reports.

Some lawyers occasionally take on a worthwhile legal cause on a ***pro bono*** basis. The full term, *pro bono publico*, means "for the public good"; the short form, *pro bono*, is widely used to refer to legal work undertaken without charge. In general, a lawyer will accept a *pro bono* case where legal aid funding is not available but the litigant's claim is worthy of support for ethical or moral reasons. One example would be a case where a person has been convicted of a criminal offence and has gone to jail, but maintains his innocence in circumstances that strongly suggest wrongful conviction. A criminal defence lawyer might take on an appeal on a *pro bono* basis in the interests of justice, and for his or her own personal or professional reasons. Anyone who has a case that is unusually significant to the broader community,

CASE IN POINT

Profile of a Pro Bono Case

In 1999, the Supreme Court of Canada made an important ruling on the disclosure of evidence to the defence in criminal cases involving sexual assault.

The case of *L.C. v. Mills* (cited as *R. v. Mills*) involved the Crown's appeal of a successful Charter challenge by a sexual assault defendant of recent amendments to the *Criminal Code*. Sections 278.1 to 278.91 of the Code created a scheme that requires the defendant in a sexual assault case to prove the relevance of the complainant's (the alleged victim's) psychiatric or other counselling records to the defence before a court may order disclosure of these records to the defendant. These provisions are controversial because they require an accused to establish the importance to his defence of records that he has not yet seen before he can get access to them.

The *Mills* case, in a nutshell, required the court to weigh the accused's right to make full answer and defence in a criminal matter against the complainant's privacy rights.

The courts routinely grant a defendant access to a victim's medical records that relate to an assault. In *Mills*, however, the requested records were counselling records. The court received submissions from 15 different parties (10 provincial attorneys general and 5 public interest groups) who presented arguments against allowing a defendant direct access to a complainant's counselling records. They maintained that disclosing such records to a defendant would open the door to potential misuse, because the trauma of sexual assault often leads to feelings of guilt and self-blame on the part of the victim.

This argument helped to influence the court in deciding that the *Criminal Code* provisions, which were designed to balance the accused's disclosure interests against the complainant's privacy interests, amounted to a reasonable and justifiable limit on the accused's Charter rights. Thus, the court overturned the lower court's decision and upheld the *Criminal Code* provisions as constitutional.

Aleck Trawick, a lawyer with Blake Cassels & Graydon, represented the Canadian Mental Health Association, one of the 15 **intervenors**, on a *pro bono* basis. Mr. Trawick took the case because he believed that the protection of the privacy rights of sexual assault complainants is an issue of general public importance.

Details of this case and the Supreme Court's decision can be found in *R. v. Mills*, [1999] 3 SCR 668. ◇

and/or likely to attract the interest of the media, and who lacks the resources to pay legal fees, should consider consulting a lawyer who is known for doing *pro bono* work.

SUBSIDIZED LEGAL SERVICES

Sources of Legal Assistance

LEGAL AID ONTARIO

In Ontario, the principal source of subsidized legal assistance is a publicly funded but independent agency called Legal Aid Ontario (LAO). LAO delivers legal assistance in accordance with the *Legal Aid Services Act*. The mandate of LAO is to

> promote access to justice throughout Ontario for low-income individuals by means of providing consistently high quality legal aid services in a cost-effective and efficient manner.

To qualify for **legal aid**, a candidate must meet specified criteria, discussed in more detail below. In general, the candidate must have a low income, and the legal assistance requested must meet a basic need—for example, the need to defend oneself against a serious criminal charge. Individuals seeking legal aid must submit an application to LAO. If successful, the candidate is granted a legal aid certificate that he can use to obtain legal assistance, either from a lawyer in private practice or from an LAO staff lawyer.

Lawyers who agree to provide services pursuant to a legal aid certificate are reimbursed by LAO for their services, but the amount they can charge must be within a specified range (referred to as "the legal aid tariff"). The amount that may be charged depends on the lawyer's experience and the legal matter involved. At the time of writing, the legal aid tariff ranged from $70 to $88 an hour, a rate that is a fraction of the "going rate" for privately paid legal services. For this reason, many lawyers either refuse to take legal aid cases or limit the number of legal aid clients that they will accept.

COMMUNITY LEGAL CLINICS

Legal assistance is also available from community legal clinics. These clinics are funded by LAO, and their availability and the diversity of their legal practice varies from region to region. Community legal clinics often have a small complement of staff lawyers who supervise students, paralegals, and/or other lawyers, some of whom may serve on a volunteer basis. According to LAO, community legal clinics can do other work besides simply assisting clients directly and individually: "clinics also can engage in test cases, public legal education, community organizing, and other law reform initiatives."

DUTY COUNSEL

If a person is required to appear in court and she has not yet secured legal assistance or representation, she may request the services of duty counsel. **Duty counsel** are lawyers who are available in the criminal and family courts to provide "emergency" legal representation to unrepresented individuals. Duty counsel can also attend at mental health facilities to assist patients in exercising their rights under mental health law.

The role of duty counsel used to be restricted to the client's first appearance in court, but it has expanded somewhat, in recognition of the fact that duty counsel not only assist the client but also help to make the court system as a whole function more efficiently.

Qualifying for Legal Aid

Legal aid is available to low-income individuals who need help with any of the following legal matters:

1. Family law disputes that involve

    a.   seeking custody of a child;

    b.   seeking access to a child;

    c.   child protection proceedings;

  d. gaining access to spousal or child support;

  e. preventing a spouse from selling or destroying family property; and

  f. negotiating rights to assets that could provide the client with income, such as registered retirement savings plans or pensions.

 2. Immigration and refugee matters that involve

  a. refugee hearings (attempts to gain refugee status);

  b. sponsorship and deportation appeals; and

  c. detention reviews.

 3. Mental health hearings and appeals.

 4. Litigation to gain access to

  a. workplace safety and insurance benefits (sometimes referred to as workers' compensation);

  b. social benefits (for example, Ontario Works benefits or disability benefits); and

  c. employment insurance appeals.

 5. Criminal law matters in which there is a probability of incarceration if the client is convicted.

Legal aid is not available to assist a client with

- wrongful dismissal;
- change of name;
- personal bankruptcy;
- power of attorney;
- money lent to others or money owed to others;
- sponsorship of relatives for immigration;
- commercial litigation;
- libel, defamation, and slander; or
- real estate matters.

To determine eligibility for legal aid, LAO scrutinizes the financial position of the applicant, his spouse and/or partner, and any dependent children. The first step of the legal aid financial test is a review of assets. The assets scrutinized most closely are cash and investments, such as RRSPs. LAO does not typically require a person to sell her house to pay for legal fees, but she may be required to seek a loan by way of a mortgage against the house before she can be eligible for legal aid.

The next step is an assessment of income. LAO sets a series of income thresholds below which applicants (other than those who have assets) are generally considered eligible for legal aid. These thresholds (shown in figure 15.1) are related to family size and correspond, more or less, to the income brackets for social assistance (Ontario Works, discussed in chapter 8).

Figure 15.1   Income Thresholds for Legal Aid in Ontario, 2007

Family size	Monthly maximum	Yearly maximum
1 person...............................	$601	$7,212
2 people..............................	$1,075	12,900
3 people..............................	$1,137	$13,644
4 or more people	$1,281	$15,372

Source: Data obtained from Legal Aid Ontario at www.legalaid.on.ca/en/getting/Financial.asp.

If an applicant's income is above the threshold, LAO will conduct a detailed financial assessment. This assessment compares an applicant's income against his expenses to determine financial means. The assessment applies ceilings for housing expenses; for example, if a person has a low income but very high mortgage costs, only a portion of these costs will be counted as an expense in calculating the applicant's financial means. However, necessary expenses, such as medical expenses for a chronic condition, are taken into account in determining eligibility.

In some cases, an applicant will be required to pay a share of the legal costs while LAO pays the remainder, or he may be asked to agree to repay the legal costs in the future. A promise to repay may be secured—for example, by a lien placed on the applicant's house. When a person recovers money in the course of litigation paid for by legal aid, legal aid costs must be at least partially repaid from the amount awarded.

OTHER AVENUES FOR ADVOCACY

Lawyers advocate for their clients on particular legal matters, such as the defence of a drug trafficking charge, a claim for child support, or the appeal of a Social Benefits Tribunal decision. Social service workers are often involved in social **advocacy** on a broader scale. They represent their client's needs and interests on a personal level, but also work to effect political and social change. This may involve lobbying for funding, petitioning for changes to laws, and attempting to change attitudes and behaviours in society. Clients also may play an active role in social advocacy.

Example

You have a client, Marisa, with a 10-year-old daughter, Jenna, who suffers from attention deficit hyperactivity disorder (ADHD). The school that Jenna attends has implemented a behaviour modification program and is tolerating the child's disruptions in the classroom, but Marisa is concerned that her daughter is not reaching her full potential. She believes that smaller class sizes and individual attention would enable a more student-focused approach to teaching. She would like to see a completely different learning model implemented for ADHD children, which would change the classroom to fit the child, rather than change the child to conform to the typical classroom.

Marisa wants to draw attention to what she perceives as a gap in the education system. She asks you how she can influence the government to change the law, requiring school boards to support special needs, and also providing the necessary funds. How can you help your client to make her voice heard?

A wide range of organizations, including many charitable organizations, regard advocacy as an important part of their mandate. Often, they represent a particular interest group or focus on a particular set of issues. The following list provides just a few examples:

- the Canadian Mental Health Association;

- the War Amps;

- Jewish Students Canada (a division of B'nai Brith Canada);

- the Sex Workers' Advocacy Network (SWAN); and

- the Hamilton Homeschool Association.

The organizations that perform advocacy for their members number in the thousands. Advocacy activities can range from basic attempts to raise awareness about an issue (such as creating a website) to fully funded, well-organized campaigns designed to put pressure on politicians to introduce legislation that recognizes important legal and human rights for the organization's members and other people who are similarly situated.

Social service workers can assist their clients in getting in touch with the appropriate advocacy organizations. In this way, clients can work toward improving their own situation and that of others like them.

WEB LINK

For Internet sources on various topics related to social advocacy in Ontario, see the websites and links listed at www.canadiansocialresearch.net.

KEY TERMS

advocacy	fraud	*pro bono*
contingency fee	intervenor	uncontested divorce
disbursements	legal aid	
duty counsel	paralegal	

REFERENCES

Legal Aid Services Act, 1998, SO 1998, c. 26.

Mills, R. v., [1999] 3 SCR 668.

REVIEW QUESTIONS

1. Why should a social service worker be able to identify common legal issues on behalf of her client?

2. Under what circumstances might a person reasonably choose to represent himself in a legal matter?

3. What are the differences between a lawyer and a paralegal?

4. What is a contingency fee?

5. What are disbursements?

6. What are the differences between having a legal aid lawyer and being represented by a community legal clinic?

7. What are the two main factors that are considered in deciding whether a client is eligible for legal aid?

8. List at least three kinds of legal matters for which legal aid certificates are not available.

CHAPTER 16

Alternatives to the Court System: Alternative Dispute Resolution

CHAPTER OBJECTIVES

After reading this chapter, you should be able to:

- Define alternative dispute resolution and explain the benefits of this avenue to justice.

- Describe four different alternative dispute resolution mechanisms.

- Understand when disputes are well suited to alternative dispute resolution and when they are not.

- Explain the concept of restorative justice and distinguish it from the traditional justice system.

INTRODUCTION

Chapter 13 provided an overview of the court system in Ontario, including a discussion of criminal and civil trial procedures. It's important, however, to recognize that the majority of disputes between parties—whether they be individuals, corporations, or government bodies—are not resolved in a courtroom. According to the Ministry of the Attorney General, over 90 percent of civil cases in Ontario settle before trial.

Litigation is a highly formalized, adversarial process. It is notoriously expensive, and, in most cases, it can only produce a win/lose result: one party's victory is the other party's defeat. Litigation has the potential to alienate the parties: it can turn relatives or friends into enemies, and permanently sever business or commercial relationships.

In some high-conflict cases, where one party has acted unscrupulously, litigation is the appropriate avenue to resolution. Most conflicts, however, are not so sharply drawn, and the parties could benefit from a more creative, collaborative approach—a solution that benefits both sides.

Alternatives to litigation begin at the very informal, interpersonal level. When conflicts arise, there is almost always an opportunity for the parties in conflict to negotiate a solution. For example, where the child of divorced parents is resisting the continual movement from one home to another prescribed by a custody agreement, the parents do not need to take their problem to court. They can, perhaps with the child's input, negotiate a new agreement to govern the child's residence. If appropriate, they can request a consent order (discussed in chapter 3) formalizing the new agreement, but there is usually no obligation to do even this. Another example is a landlord-tenant dispute, where a tenant has complained to a landlord that there is no running water. To resolve the issue, the parties might negotiate a schedule for repair and possibly a partial rent rebate.

Where parties have not been able to solve their problems on their own, sometimes all that is needed is a more structured process. **Alternative dispute resolution (ADR)** is a term used to describe a range of recognized strategies—for example, assisted negotiation, mediation, and arbitration—that are designed to help resolve disputes without recourse to the traditional court system. The common element in structured ADR strategies is the involvement of a neutral third party.

Social service workers may be able to assist clients in accessing ADR services. Social service workers may also be engaged directly in ADR in the course of advocating for their clients. Consider, for example, a women's shelter client whose Ontario Works benefits have been suspended because she has failed to live up to the terms of her agreement to participate in job search activities. The client may ask the social service worker to speak to Ontario Works on her behalf, to explain that an intensive trauma counselling program that the client has been participating in has taken up more time than anticipated in the previous month. If the social service worker persuades Ontario Works to revisit its suspension decision, she has engaged—successfully—in a form of ADR.

GOALS OF ADR

ADR comes in many forms, ranging from negotiation at one end of the spectrum to binding arbitration at the other. The principal ADR mechanisms, and the differences between them, are described in the next section. The goals of ADR vary somewhat, depending upon the particular mechanism that is used. In general, however, ADR is designed to support parties in conflict in their efforts to fashion their own solutions and avoid the expense of litigation. Even binding arbitration, which is similar to court in that the decision maker imposes a decision on the parties, is less expensive than going to court, and it gives the parties much more control over the process.

Fact finding—the collection of evidence, and proving one party right and the other wrong—is less important in ADR than in traditional litigation. While the courts strive to deliver answers to legal questions, ADR strives to deliver solutions, and, where possible, to preserve or restore relationships.

FIGURE 16.1   Alternative Ways of Resolving Disputes

	Negotiation	Mediation	Arbitration	Litigation
Participation in process	Voluntary.	Voluntary, unless the parties agree otherwise beforehand.	Voluntary, unless the parties agree otherwise beforehand.	Involuntary.
Formality	Usually informal and unstructured although the parties can agree to structure if they wish.	The degree of formality and structure will depend on the mediator and the extent to which the parties accept the mediator's proposals to formalize and structure the process.	Less formal than litigation, but much more formal and structured than negotiation or mediation.	Highly formal, following a process prescribed by the rules of civil practice.
Control of process	Parties control the process and may proceed with or without negotiation "rules."	Mediator and the parties control the process, normally with the mediator proposing rules for the process and the parties agreeing.	Arbitrator controls the process.	Judge controls the process.
Outcome	Private agreement, enforceable as a contract.	Private agreement, enforceable as a contract.	Private decision by arbitrator that is usually binding, unless the parties agree beforehand to non-binding arbitration. Decision may be subject to court review and enforceable by legal action.	Public decision by judge, supported by reasoned analysis and enforceable by the court.

From a more practical perspective, ADR saves money and time by allowing parties to avoid expensive and time-consuming litigation. In disputes where money is on the line, an early settlement leaves more money in the pockets of both parties.

From an interpersonal perspective, ADR may be a healthier way to settle problems than recourse to litigation. The reason is that in ADR, there are no rules of evidence that prohibit the parties from talking about issues that are not legally relevant, but of importance to them. Many conflicts have their roots in hurt feelings. By providing a context of open discussion in which these subjective issues can be raised, ADR presents the opportunity for the healing of damaged relationships and reconciliation of the parties.

Example

Thomas's elderly father, Albert, recently suffered a serious stroke, and was declared incapable of making health-care decisions or managing his financial affairs. While Albert is recovering in a nursing home, Thomas obtains a court order making him his father's legal representative. After being advised that Albert will need nursing care for life, Thomas sold his father's house and made arrangements for a permanent placement in long-term care. Albert's health gradually improved and he is now seeking to challenge the court order that gave his son the power to make these decisions.

If this matter went to court, evidence would be called to establish whether or not Albert was in fact incapable at the time of the order, whether Thomas's application for the order was proper, and whether the decision to sell the house was within the terms of the order. Little or no court time would be devoted to more subjective issues—for example, Albert's perception that his son's decision was hasty, or Thomas's perception that he had to act quickly to secure a top-quality care placement that was not expected to be available for long.

If, instead, the dispute is resolved through an ADR process, such as mediation, these non-legal issues can be raised and discussed. Albert will have the opportunity to express his resentment over being "parented" by his child, and Thomas will have the opportunity to express his anxiety about his father's welfare. These considerations will become part of the solution that is ultimately proposed. Albert may even withdraw his challenge to Thomas's appointment. Not only will the legal conflict be resolved but the father–son relationship may be preserved.

ADR MECHANISMS

Negotiation and Assisted Negotiation

Negotiation is the formal word for "working things out." People negotiate with each other on a daily basis. Consider, for example, a driver who lives on a main commuter route into the city and is trying to enter a flow of steady rush-hour traffic from her driveway. If she had to wait for a break in the traffic, she might be there for a very long time. However, most drivers in this situation will negotiate entry into the line of traffic by making eye contact with oncoming drivers. If an approaching driver returns the eye contact, nods, and slows to let the waiting driver in, then the parties have successfully negotiated an exception to the traditional right-of-way rules.

Not all negotiations are this simple. When parties have been thrown into conflict by some kind of negative event, their natural motivation to be generous and reasonable diminishes. Reaching a solution may require the passage of some cooling-off time, a number of failed attempts, and possibly even an apology. Sometimes this process can be facilitated by the parties' delegation of their role in the negotiation to someone who was not part of the dispute, and who therefore lacks the emotional baggage that can slow the process. This is **assisted negotiation**.

In theory, a negotiator can be anyone with the expertise to understand and resolve the issue in dispute. Sometimes it is appropriate to appoint a lawyer as the negotiator; negotiating on the part of clients is sometimes the most important aspect of a lawyer's work. However, if legal expertise isn't required, someone else may be an equally effective negotiator. A social service worker can provide this kind of assistance as long as it is within the limits of her role and training. The extent to which a social service worker is permitted to negotiate with others on behalf of a client should be explicitly addressed in her contract of employment and/or in the employer's policies. Social service workers may not give legal advice and should not negotiate directly with a lawyer who is representing someone in conflict with her client.

In addition to these considerations, there are three keys to successful negotiation:

- The client must trust the negotiator.

- The client must give the negotiator specific instructions about the results she wants, any concessions or admissions she is willing to make, and any limits on the negotiator's freedom to work toward an agreement.

- The negotiator must work within the client's instructions, request clarification of those instructions if any uncertainty develops, and act in the best interests of the client at all times.

Neutral Evaluation and Conciliation

Neutral evaluation and conciliation describes a process in which parties in conflict jointly consult an independent party for an impartial assessment of the dispute. As in the case of negotiation, this happens informally in many everyday situations. For example, a man is shopping for a suit, accompanied by his wife. He tries one on but thinks it makes him look fat. His wife says no, it makes him look distinguished. They see a salesperson nearby and ask him what he thinks: does this style suit the shopper, or would another style suit him better?

A more formal and more serious example of neutral evaluation is a pre-trial conference in a criminal case. The evaluation is made by a judge, but not the one who will preside over the trial itself. At the pre-trial conference, the prosecutor and defence counsel meet with the judge to discuss the issues in the case and, where appropriate, to attempt to narrow the issues for trial. For example, an accused involved in a massive brawl between opposing fans after a hockey game may be charged with both assault causing bodily harm and attempted murder. After listening to both sides, the judge may conclude that the evidence relating to the attempted murder charge is weak and conviction on that charge is unlikely. The judge may advise the parties that, in the interests of fairness and efficiency, the prosecutor should drop the attempted murder charge and proceed with the assault charge alone. The judge at a pre-trial conference may not make a binding decision, but only may make recommendations.

As in the case of negotiation, neutral evaluation and conciliation can be performed by a professional (such as a judge) or by an ordinary person, like the salesperson in the first example. The one factor that qualifies a person as an evaluator of disputes is experience or expertise. The salesperson presumably knows something about suit styles that flatter the customer; the judge has expertise in criminal law and experience with criminal trials. In view of the evaluator's expertise, while the parties are not obligated to act on his opinion, they may well be influenced by it when deciding about next steps.

Social service workers may sometimes be called upon to evaluate situations within their knowledge or experience. Consider, for example, a social service worker who supervises the meetings of a residents' council in a long-term care facility. The residents are brainstorming about ideas for their autumn social. One group of residents would like to have a Hallowe'en party. Another group would like to have a "fantasy draft" hockey pool party complete with betting. When asked which proposal is more likely to win the approval of management, the social service worker may point out, with reasonable confidence, that the long-term care facility will be unlikely to lend its support to any kind of gambling-related activity.

While this kind of advice is clearly within the scope of the social service worker's role, advice-giving situations need to be handled with extreme care. For example, you have a client who wants to apply for subsidized housing, but you think he isn't eligible because he has some assets. Even if you have some experience with housing assistance, it would be inappropriate to talk the client out of making an application, since you cannot be sure how the eligibility criteria will be applied in a particular case. Whenever a client requests an evaluation and the underlying question is whether he should take further steps to pursue a right or entitlement, the correct answer, for a social service worker, should always be either "yes" or a recommendation to consult a lawyer or some other qualified person (such as an administrator at the agency that provides the assistance or entitlements).

Mediation

Mediation involves having the parties meet to discuss their conflict in the presence of an independent third party—also called a **neutral**. The mediator facilitates the discussion, helping to encourage appropriate disclosure and to keep the talks productive. The mediator does not make a decision; instead, he supports the parties in coming to their own voluntary settlement, which is eventually converted into a written settlement agreement that binds the parties.

If the talks are unproductive, the parties can terminate the mediation process. In general, anything that has been said during mediation is **without prejudice** to any future legal proceedings; that is, it cannot be used against the parties in court. This encourages the parties to be open and candid in expressing their concerns.

There are many different styles of mediation, often depending on the personality and approach of the mediator. Facilitative mediation is a more "hands-off" style, whereas in evaluative mediation, the mediator is more actively involved, providing opinions about the arguments and proposals advanced by the parties.

Where parties attending mediation have filed court documents and intend to go to court if mediation fails, they are sometimes said to be negotiating "in the shadow of the law." Especially in a situation in which the legal precedents are clear, the mediator may have a general idea of how the court would likely decide the dispute. If one of the parties is unrealistic in his demands, advising the parties of the likely outcome of a trial may help to reframe the negotiations.

In some circumstances, parties are permitted to bring a support person to a mediation session. This support person is not generally a lawyer but rather a friend, a relative, or a counsellor such as a social service worker. Having a support person at a mediation session can help if the party is intimidated by the process, or by the other party; it is sometimes difficult to sit face-to-face with a person with whom you have an unresolved conflict.

As a social service worker, if you are asked to attend a mediation session as a support person, you should understand that your role is to be there as a resource to your client if needed. It is generally not appropriate for support people to take a significant part in the discussions, or to be very active in providing advice. It is usually better to wait for questions to be addressed to you before you speak. Your client

---

EXTRA CREDIT

ADR Chambers

ADR Chambers is a unique example of an ADR service provider. "Chambers" is the word generally used to refer to an office in a court building in which a judge has private discussions with counsel and sometimes witnesses. These discussions are often held in an attempt to resolve issues that are affecting the progress of litigation.

ADR Chambers is so named because its membership began with a group of retired judges. Membership has since grown to include lawyers, but the organization still puts an emphasis on conducting alternative dispute resolution against a backdrop of experience with the traditional legal system. Services offered by ADR Chambers include mediation, arbitration (including provision of a specialized panel to deal with Aboriginal issues), neutral evaluation, international dispute resolution, and "private appeals."

A private appeal is a hearing before an ADR panel following a decision by a trial court, where the parties agree to pursue an appeal of the decision through ADR Chambers rather than through a provincial appeal court. When the parties decide to proceed by private appeal, they sign a document stating that they are relinquishing their rights to a regular appeal and that they agree to be bound by the decision of an ADR Chambers appeal panel (usually a panel of three arbitrators). For the parties, one advantage of a private appeal is speed in resolving the dispute: the appeal can be conducted shortly after the trial decision is handed down. Another advantage is a degree of control in deciding who will hear the appeal: often, each party chooses one panel member, and the two chosen will appoint the third.

More information about ADR Chambers is available online at www.adrchambers.com.

◇

---

may be helped by your presence alone—by simply having someone else in the room who understands the story from his perspective.

MANDATORY MEDIATION

Mediation is an alternative to litigation in any civil dispute. Generally, it is chosen at the option of the parties; however, in certain circumstances, the parties are required to attempt mediation before seeking resolution in a civil court. Mandatory mediation became law in Ontario in 1999 when new rules were added to the *Rules of Civil Procedure*. One of these rules requires parties in all case-managed, defended, non-family civil matters scheduled for trial in Toronto, Ottawa, or Windsor to attempt mediation before going to trial. Another rule imposes mandatory mediation in wills and estates cases in the same cities.

"Case management" refers to procedures that have been established in cities with busy courts, with the objective of alleviating bottlenecks in the justice system. Under case management, the parties are required to meet specific deadlines in completing certain stages of the trial process, in an effort to speed up the disposition of cases before the courts.

Where a case is under case management, the parties must choose a mediator within 30 days of the filing of the first statement of defence. If the parties cannot agree on a mediator, the Local Mediation Co-ordinator chooses one for them. The parties then schedule the date on which mediation will commence. Each party is required to file a statement of issues with the mediator, summarizing the party's case as he sees it. The statement of issues must be filed no later than 7 days before the scheduled mediation date.

The parties are required to attempt mediation within 90 days of the filing of the first statement of defence. While they are not required to agree to a settlement, they must attend and make an attempt to mediate for at least three hours. Most mediations, whether successful or not, take no more than 2 days.

The parties share the cost of the mediation. There is a set maximum fee for the first three hours, which varies according to the number of parties involved (figure 16.2). After the first three hours, if the parties want to continue, they can negotiate an hourly rate for the mediator's time.

A mediation session is not necessarily held at the court; it can be held wherever it is convenient for the parties. A neutral location—for example, the mediator's office—is usually best. The parties must attend in person, with lawyers if they are represented. Mediation sessions are private; the only people allowed to attend are the mediator, the parties, and their lawyers, unless everyone agrees to the inclusion of another person. The purpose of this rule is to encourage full disclosure of all issues. For many parties, the privacy provided by mediation—not having "dirty laundry" aired in public or being required to reveal sensitive business or financial information—makes it an attractive alternative to litigation.

If the parties manage to achieve resolution of the dispute at the mediation session, the terms of resolution are drafted as a settlement agreement, which is filed with the court. The court can then enforce the agreement against a party who fails to honour it, in the same way that a court can enforce a trial judgment. If the parties do not settle, the mediator must prepare a report that states this and file it with the court.

MEDIATION IN FAMILY LAW CASES

As noted above, mediation is not mandatory in family law cases. The reason is that in family disputes there is often an imbalance of power between the parties, which makes mediation inappropriate. (This situation is discussed further in a later section.) However, where this obstacle does not exist, family disputes can benefit greatly from mediation. Where there are children involved, ongoing contact between the parties is necessary and important; and a process that diminishes conflict rather than polarizing the parties in adversarial positions has significant long-term advantages.

Achieving a settlement through mediation can give family members a sense of having cooperated in the outcome, which can motivate them to honour the terms of the agreement. Mediation can also help family members to resolve non-economic

Figure 16.2   Mandatory Mediation: Schedule of Fees for First Three Hours (Maximum for 2007)

No. of parties	Maximum fee
2	$600
3	$675
4	$750
5+	$825

EXTRA CREDIT

Ontario Statutes That Recognize ADR

ADR in some form such as arbitration or mediation is specifically allowed or provided for by law to resolve a wide range of disputes. Ontario statutes that express a role for ADR include:

- the *Workplace Safety and Insurance Act, 1997*;
- the *Residential Tenancies Act, 2006*;
- the *Professional Engineers Act*;
- the *Police Services Act*;
- the *Labour Relations Act, 1995*;
- the *International Commercial Arbitration Act*;
- the *Personal Health Information Protection Act, 2004*;
- the *Insurance Act*;
- the *Children's Law Reform Act*; and
- the *Condominium Act, 1998*. ◈

---

aspects of their conflict, thereby laying the foundation for reasonable relations in the future.

To encourage the mediation of family disputes in appropriate cases, the government provides and financially supports family mediation services through family mediation programs administered by the courts. These programs offer mediation services with costs charged on a geared-to-income scale. The mediators who work in these programs are certified in accordance with established standards, and they follow guidelines issued by the Ministry of the Attorney General in screening applicants for mediation services. (These guidelines are discussed further below in the context of imbalance-of-power concerns.)

WEB LINK

Information on family mediation programs is available from Ontario's Ministry of the Attorney General, online at www .attorneygeneral.jus.gov .on.ca.

Arbitration

Arbitration is the most formal of ADR processes, and the closest to litigation in style. The parties attend before a neutral person (or sometimes a panel of three neutrals) and deliver their arguments. The arbitrator or panel then renders a decision. Unless the parties have agreed otherwise, an arbitral decision is final and binding.

Arbitral decisions are often pursued as part of a larger negotiation. For example, before coming to arbitration, the parties may have already reached agreement about some aspects of the dispute, and the binding arbitration may be needed only to resolve a couple of outstanding issues on which there is an impasse. Thus, like other forms of ADR, arbitration supports party-based decisions even though a final decision may be imposed by the arbitrator.

Evidence given at arbitration hearings is subject to certain rules, but usually these are less formal than the rules of evidence that apply in court. Unless the parties and their arbitrator are working according to an agreed-upon set of arbitration rules, the procedures that will apply in the arbitration are those prescribed by the applicable provincial arbitration legislation. Ontario's *Arbitration Act* governs such issues as jurisdiction, reviewability of arbitral decisions by courts (like judicial review of the decisions of administrative boards), and the timing of various parts of the process such as the delivery of the arbitrator's order. The *Arbitration Act* applies to all arbitration prescribed or permitted by statute in Ontario unless the legislation expressly states otherwise.

Arbitration is prescribed by a statute governing the parties or by an agreement between them, or entered into voluntarily as a means of avoiding litigation after the dispute has already arisen.

An example of arbitration prescribed by statute is found in section 7 of Ontario's *Insurance Act*. Section 7 applies in circumstances where a claim arises that could potentially be covered by more than one insurer and a dispute arises as to which insurer is liable to satisfy the claim. In such cases, section 7 requires that the dispute be settled by arbitration instead of litigation. The arbitration process is governed by the rules created by the *Arbitration Act*.

In the context of the *Insurance Act*, arbitration limits expensive litigation between insurance companies to the benefit of consumers because this cost is inevitably passed on in the form of higher insurance premiums.

Where there is no applicable statute, parties may negotiate an agreement or contract that sets out terms governing the relations between them. A common example is a collective agreement between unionized workers and company management. The contract may include an **arbitration clause** requiring that disputes arising in respect of the terms of the contract be resolved through arbitration. An arbitration clause may be included in many kinds of contracts, such as marriage contracts, employment contracts, and commercial contracts.

RECOGNIZING WHEN ADR MAY NOT BE APPROPRIATE

While ADR offers clear advantages over litigation in many cases, it is not appropriate to every situation. There are two primary reasons why ADR may not be appropriate in a particular case:

- At least one of the parties is motivated to pursue litigation rather than settle out of court.

- The parties are in unequal bargaining positions, by reason of the historical pattern of their relationship or because of other circumstances, making it unlikely that ADR would produce a fair outcome.

Motivation to Pursue Litigation

In general, parties in conflict are motivated to settle the dispute by ADR: it provides a relatively speedy and inexpensive route to resolution of the issue, and it achieves a reasonable compromise between competing interests. However, in some situations, at least one of the parties is influenced by other considerations that outweigh the potential benefits of settlement.

An analogy is found in the way the justice system deals with crimes. When a crime is committed, a conflict arises between the victim and the perpetrator, and also between the perpetrator and society. However, there is no mechanism in traditional criminal law for "settling" criminal cases. Dropping charges and plea bargaining are close approximations; but generally, our justice system and social values don't readily accommodate the notion of negotiated compromise as an adequate response to an act of criminal wrongdoing. (Indeed, as discussed earlier, some people question whether the kind of negotiation involved in plea bargaining is consistent with the principles of justice.) While there is some limited provision in our system for amends to be made between an offender and his victim (see the discussion on restorative justice below), the trial of criminal offenders in public courts and the sentences imposed on conviction include an important social penalty—namely, public denunciation of the offender for his actions. This need for formal recognition of a person's wrongdoing can make ADR inappropriate in certain non-criminal cases as well. Consider the following example.

Example

Bonita has a job that is interesting and pays well, but she is suffering constant harassment and threats from a co-worker. The co-worker, jealous about being passed over for a promotion, has destroyed Bonita's personal property, calls her at home to harass her after hours, and threatens to spread damaging and untrue gossip about her in the office. Bonita asks the management to address the problem, but the company takes no action and the harassment continues. Bonita's mental health suffers, eventually forcing her to resign. Later, she learns from someone in HR that this is the third time that harassment by the same co-worker has driven another employee out of the company.

Given the circumstances, Bonita decides to sue the employer, claiming damages for **constructive dismissal**. The employer offers to settle the claim out of court by paying Bonita 75 percent of what she might expect to receive through successful litigation (an attractive offer, considering the legal costs of taking the employer to court). However, Bonita feels that in accepting the settlement, she would, in effect, be condoning the employer's tolerance of harassment in the workplace, and also perpetuating such behaviour, insofar as the co-worker's actions would escape public exposure. For this reason, Bonita is unwilling to settle and instead prefers to pursue the claim in court.

ADR is most attractive to parties who can put a dollar value on the resolution they want, and who are not strongly motivated by the desire to set a legal precedent, to make an example of the other party, or to pursue their rights as a matter of principle. As a social service worker, you will encounter many clients who simply want what they are entitled to—access to their children, for example. In the absence of imbalance of power issues (discussed below), it is often appropriate to support the efforts of these clients to find and use ADR services.

You may also encounter the occasional client who is willing to pursue a **test case**, enduring the rigours of litigation in an effort to benefit others in his situation. Depending upon the public importance of your client's case, it may not be appropriate to encourage the client to mediate. Instead, you may choose to help the client find an advocacy group or a lawyer who is willing to take on the case on a *pro bono* basis (discussed in chapter 15).

Imbalance of Power

ADR may not be appropriate where there is an **imbalance of power** in the relations between the parties, or where one party is intimidated by the other. This is very common in families with a history of domestic abuse. Where one party has been subjected to violence or abuse by the other party, the abused party is unlikely to be capable of negotiating with the abuser as an equal. There may be undercurrents of influence between the parties that even a mediator would miss, and this subtle intimidation may cause the abused party to settle for much less than a court would award.

The Ministry of the Attorney General recognizes the limitations of ADR in such circumstances:

> Mediation is not appropriate for everyone, particularly in cases where there has been violence or abuse. Where one party is afraid of, or intimidated by, their spouse/partner, mediation may not be a good idea.

This concern is reflected in the ministry's guidelines for screening applicants under the government's family mediation program. The criteria to be met include the following:

- abuse has not occurred that has rendered either party incapable of mediating
- no harm will come to either party or the children as a result of mediating
- the parties' desire to mediate is voluntary
- any inequality in bargaining power can be managed so as to ensure that negotiations are balanced and procedurally fair
- parties are psychologically ready to mediate and have the capacity to do so
- the complexity of the case does not exceed the mediator's education, training and competence.

(These criteria can be found on the ministry's website referred to earlier in this chapter.)

Imbalance of power does not occur only in the divorce context; it can be a factor in any situation involving parties who have a history of conflict. The following are examples of other situations where intimidation or unequal bargaining power may make ADR unsuitable:

- disputes over wills or estates;
- disputes between parents and children—for example, where a child is seeking a power of attorney over a parent or authority to make medical decisions on the parent's behalf;
- landlord and tenant disputes where the tenant is hard to house because of a criminal record or serious financial problems; and
- employment matters where there have been allegations of harassment.

This is not an exhaustive list; capacity to mediate depends on the facts of the situation and the particular parties involved. In general, however, individuals who are vulnerable because of age, mental health or mental capacity problems, extreme poverty, lack of education, or a history of abuse may not be effective advocates for their own rights in the context of ADR.

RESTORATIVE JUSTICE

"Putting things right" is a central goal of ADR, and also the core of the concept of restorative justice. Restorative justice is an approach that applies some of the principles of ADR to criminal disputes. It is a philosophy that has broad application within the justice system, and not just in the context of ADR. Because one of the goals of restorative justice is to repair relationships and restore harmony in the community, this chapter is a fitting place to provide an overview of the concept.

The Royal Canadian Mounted Police (RCMP) provide the following extended definition of restorative justice:

> Restorative Justice is a philosophy which holds community healing as its cornerstone. Like community policing, it's a way of doing business differently. Unlike the current adversarial system which is based on punishment, restorative justice encourages dialogue and responsibility for past behaviour, while focusing on future problem-solving and offender accountability. Ideally, the victim, the offender and the community should be involved in "making things right" to enable all parties to be returned to their pre-crime states. Restorative justice views crime as a violation of one person by another not simply as a breaking of the "law".

WEB LINK

The RCMP provides additional information about restorative justice on its website at www.rcmp-grc.gc.ca.

Supporters of restorative justice note that there are certain pitfalls inherent in the traditional justice system's approach to crime, including the following:

1. *Fact-finding focus.* The traditional system has a very strong fact-finding focus (gathering of evidence, proof of facts to establish a conviction, etc.) and may overlook important subjective aspects of justice—for example, the impact of emotions, the human drive to resolve interpersonal conflicts, and the capacity for problem solving through communication.

2. *Offender focus.* The traditional system tends to focus on the offender—his behaviour, his guilt, his rights in the investigative process, etc. This focus may neglect the importance of the victim's perspective and the context of the community as a whole.

3. *Punishment focus.* The traditional system tends to focus on punishment, following complicated sentencing guidelines and precedents to determine whether the punishment fits the crime. This focus draws attention away from other values, such as compensation of the victim and resolution of interpersonal conflicts on an emotional level.

4. *Win/lose focus.* The traditional system turns on a clearcut decision about conviction or acquittal; one party wins and the other loses. This focus all but eliminates the possibility for compromise and creative problem solving.

5. *Alienation.* The traditional system tends to alienate parties from each other and from the system. In training materials for Community Justice Forum participants, the RCMP describes this effect as follows:

This traditional system often provokes a sense of alienation for both victim and offender. The stigma of charges can alienate the offender from his community. Additionally, if found guilty s/he may be removed from the community to serve a sentence in a correctional facility or halfway house. Similarly, the victim is often isolated and alienated by this process. Victims often complain that they have no voice in the system. They may emerge from the court process, disillusioned and angry.

In contrast, restorative justice initiatives seek to shift the focus to aspects of justice that are often neglected in the traditional system: subjective perceptions of the "crime"; victim and community perspectives; compensation and reparations; conflict resolution and creative problem solving; and the healing of relationships in a way that maintains a sense of community among justice system participants. An example of this approach is the use of sentencing circles in Aboriginal communities (discussed in chapter 9).

KEY TERMS

alternative dispute resolution (ADR)

arbitration

arbitration clause

assisted negotiation

constructive dismissal

imbalance of power

mediation

negotiation

neutral

test case

without prejudice

REFERENCES

Arbitration Act, 1991, SO 1991, c. 17.

Children's Law Reform Act, RSO 1990, c. C.12.

Condominium Act, 1998, SO 1998, c. 19.

Insurance Act, RSO 1990, c. I.8.

International Commercial Arbitration Act, RSO 1990, c. I.9.

Labour Relations Act, 1995, SO 1995, c. 1, Sch. A.

Personal Health Information Protection Act, 2004, SO 2004, c. 3, Sch. A.

Police Services Act, RSO 1990, c. P.15.

Professional Engineers Act, RSO 1990, c. P.28.

Residential Tenancies Act, 2006, SO 2006, c. 17.

Rules of Civil Procedure, RRO 1990, Reg. 194.

Workplace Safety and Insurance Act, 1997, SO 1997, c. 16, Sch. A.

REVIEW QUESTIONS

1. Why can it be an advantage to settle a legal dispute out of court?

2. List four ADR mechanisms.

3. What are the keys to successful negotiation?

4. What happens if mandatory mediation (or, often, voluntary mediation) fails to produce a solution to the parties' dispute?

5. What happens if parties who have filed court documents succeed in reaching a settlement through mediation?

6. When is a dispute resolved through arbitration?

7. What factors should be taken into account by the parties in a family dispute before embarking on mediation?

8. Are there situations other than family matters in which there can be an imbalance of power?

9. Why is motivation important in deciding whether it is appropriate to resolve a dispute through ADR?

10. List a few of the principles or values of restorative justice.

DISCUSSION QUESTIONS

People frequently enlist the assistance of others to negotiate resolutions to disputes. The following are a few examples of assisted negotiation in action. Read them, and think about scenarios in which a social service worker might be called upon to negotiate on behalf of a client. With your class, discuss at least three situations where ADR may apply in the social services context.

1. Nivedita approaches Leesa in the sandbox with the message that Susie is sorry she smashed Leesa's castle and would like to help build a new one if Leesa wants.

2. Mr. Leporati leans over the fence to tell Mr. Blevins that Mrs. Leporati didn't mean to hurt Mrs. Blevins's feelings by not inviting her to the lunch party she gave last week. He explains that the lunch party was for the members of Mrs. Leporati's book club. Perhaps Mr. and Mrs. Blevins would like to come over for a barbecue after work on Friday?

3. Animated movie production companies Dizzy Inc. and Flixar Ltd. are in constant competition. Dizzy has an outstanding multimillion-dollar lawsuit against Flixar for breach of contract that arose out of a failed collaboration 10 years ago; however, Flixar has made an offer to purchase a majority of the shares in Dizzy and Dizzy is considering the offer. Bad publicity about either the lawsuit or the potential takeover would benefit neither party. Each company hires a specialist in strategic negotiation to assist in communicating with the other party in a way that will protect the company's interests in the coming talks.

PART VI

Employment, Immigration, and Housing

CHAPTER 17

Employment Law

CHAPTER OBJECTIVES

After reading this chapter, you should be able to:

- Identify at least one federal statute and three provincial statutes that create rights for employees.

- Understand the difference between reliance on employment standards legislation and recourse to the common law when employment issues arise.

- Suggest the steps that a person might take to assert his rights on termination of employment.

- Describe the resources, including legislative schemes, available to employees who suffer a work-related injury or illness.

- Describe the legislation that has been put in place to provide for safe workplaces in Ontario.

INTRODUCTION

In Canada today, most of the working population earn a livelihood by working for an employer. To facilitate access to employment, and provide for safe and reasonable working conditions, the federal and provincial governments have enacted a number of statutes that require employers to respect certain employee rights and comply with certain employment standards. These statutes have been passed against a backdrop of common-law principles that have evolved over time.

Employment legislation is designed, in part, to address the imbalance of power that often exists between employers and employees. Employees need to work in order to support themselves, and especially in times of high unemployment, employers may exploit this need by dictating terms of employment that favour their own interests over those of their employees. Before employment laws were passed, employees were reluctant to complain about poor working conditions or inadequate pay, because the employer could simply fire them and find others to fill their jobs.

The union movement arose to address this inequity in bargaining power. Labour unions can win higher wages and better working conditions for employees by threatening collective action such as a strike. Since replacing an entire workforce is much more problematic than firing a single employee, employers tend to be more responsive to the demands of unions than to the demands of individual employees. In fact, the pendulum has swung so far that sometimes unions are criticized for abusing their power over employers.

In some workplaces, unionization has contributed in part to the recognition of rights for non-union employees. Today employers are aware that they must treat employees fairly, if they hope to compete with unionized workplaces and preserve their good image in the business community. In times of low employment, employees may also find that they are in an advantageous bargaining position, as employers compete for human resources.

Social service workers are often called upon to work with clients who have lost their job, are having trouble finding employment, or are prevented from working for reasons of poor health or disability. Other clients may be employed but facing difficulties in the workplace. There are many federal and provincial statutes that may apply in such circumstances, including employment insurance, employment standards, human rights, and workplace health and safety legislation. It is important that social service workers acquire a broad understanding of employment law and the applicable statutes, so that they can recognize issues and pursue remedies and resources for their clients. This chapter is a starting point for the development of that understanding. As in other chapters, the discussion focuses on the law that applies in Ontario.

EMPLOYMENT AS A CONTRACT

In essence, employment law is based on the concept of **contract**. All employment relationships, whether they're described as "permanent" or "contract," are based on a contract between the employer and the employee. Where employees belong to a union, the individual employment contract is replaced in whole or in part by a **collective agreement**—a contract between the union, which represents its members, and the employer.

Employment contracts can be in writing, but they do not have to be. Written contracts are easier to prove, but an oral agreement or understanding may also be legally binding. If the employer tells the employee that work hours are between 8 a.m. and 4 p.m., and the wage is $12.00 per hour, and the employee starts work on that basis, those terms are binding.

Contracts set out terms that govern the employment relationship. These typically include a job description, the expected hours of employment, the rate of pay, the method and timing of payment, employment benefits, and other details, depending on the nature of the work. Generally, the employer and the employee are free to arrange their relationship as they wish. However, employee rights that are established or protected by statute cannot be relinquished by contract. These include statutory obligations imposed on employers with respect to such matters as minimum wages, vacation time, notice of termination of employment, and provision of a safe working environment.

A comprehensive review of the statutes that contain provisions regarding employee rights is beyond the scope of this chapter. The discussion that follows focuses on the application of the law—and particularly employment legislation—in several areas where issues arise relating to employee rights. While this discussion includes reference to human rights legislation, the scope and application of these statutes are described in more detail in chapter 20.

DISCRIMINATION AND HARASSMENT

The federal and provincial governments have enacted human rights legislation that prohibits discrimination and harassment in an employment setting, on specified prohibited grounds. Each jurisdiction has a slightly different list of prohibited grounds, but these typically include race, nationality, religion, sex, disability, family status, criminal record, and age (over 18).

Both direct and indirect discrimination are prohibited. For example, an employer who advertised a job opportunity restricted to "white Canadian" applicants would be discriminating directly on the prohibited grounds of race and nationality. An employer who required "excellent skills in writing and speaking English" for the job of gardener could be considered to be discriminating indirectly on the prohibited grounds of national or ethnic origin and/or race.

Human rights legislation makes an exception for **bona fide job qualifications**— specific skills or training that a prospective employee needs in order to perform the job. For example, while it would usually not be reasonable to require a gardener to have "excellent skills in writing and speaking English," this would be a reasonable requirement for a high school English teacher. Likewise, a bona fide job qualification for a truck driver would be a valid driver's licence, even though this requirement would exclude an applicant who is legally blind, and thus would violate the prohibition against discrimination based on disability. Human rights legislation recognizes that in some circumstances, discrimination is legitimate. However, the onus is on the employer to prove the reasonableness of the job requirements and performance standards.

Social service workers commonly work with "hard to employ" clients who may face discrimination on prohibited grounds, such as disability, single parent status, or ethnic origin. Discrimination is often difficult to prove, especially at the interview stage, when most applicants are rejected without explanation. Clients with poor English skills or a lack of job experience face many barriers to employment, not all of which are attributable to prohibited discrimination.

Social service workers need to be able to recognize employer conduct that is contrary to human rights legislation, so that they can provide information and support to clients, and a referral to a lawyer if necessary. The Ontario Human Rights Commission is a good source of information, and individuals who believe that their rights have been violated may make a formal complaint to the commission. The scope and application of Canada's human rights laws and the procedures in the event of violation are discussed in more detail in chapter 20.

Some specific types of discrimination, such as offering different employee benefits based on age, sex, or marital status, are prohibited by Ontario's *Employment Standards Act, 2000* (ESA). In these cases, an employee may choose to seek a remedy under that Act, using the procedure described in the next section.

Critical Perspectives

Mandatory Retirement

Until recently, employers in Ontario had the option of instituting a policy of mandatory retirement for their employees at age 65. Many employers adopted such a policy in the belief that by 65, most workers have become less productive. Mandatory retirement allowed employers to, in effect, terminate older employees without having to make costly termination settlements. The policy also had the advantage of flexibility, since employers could enter into a contract with the employee to continue working after retirement if he chose to do so. Mandatory retirement was an *option* for employers, not required.

With an aging population that, overall, enjoys better health than in previous decades, there has been a growing recognition that many people in their 60s are fit and willing to work past 65. This has resulted in political pressure to recognize the value of older workers and to preserve their right to work. In Ontario, the *Human Rights Code* was amended to provide that, effective December 12, 2006, discrimination in employment on the basis of age is prohibited with respect to any person over 18 years of age. While employers may still deny employment to persons aged 18 and under, they may no longer discriminate against people aged 65 or older by forcing them to retire or by refusing to hire them.

While this change has many supporters, there are others who point to its negative effects for both employers and employees. For example, without the option of mandatory retirement, employers who wish to terminate older workers must either show cause for dismissal (at some cost to the employee's reputation and self-esteem) or pay out very large termination packages for long-term employees. In the case of employees who are in fact becoming less productive as they approach 65, the employer may decide to terminate the employee sooner than it would if a policy of mandatory retirement were in place. In addition, employers may perceive that there is greater risk in hiring employees over 65 because it is uncertain how long they will be able and willing to go on working productively. Maintaining an older workforce may also be more costly to employers since they may have to accommodate more employees with age-related disabilities. ◇

TERMS OF EMPLOYMENT

Every province in Canada has legislation to regulate the quality of the work environment. Some statutes, including Ontario's ESA, impose minimum standards governing the terms of employment—for example, pay and time off. The ESA also provides for an administrative review procedure to allow an employee to seek a remedy where an employer fails to comply with a legislated standard. These provisions are discussed below.

Wages

Minimum wages are legislated in all provinces. Ontario's minimum wage is prescribed by a regulation under the ESA. The minimum wage varies across the country, and there may be a separate and lower minimum wage for certain occupations (typically in the service sector where it is usual for employees to receive tips) or for employees under the age of 18.

Ontario Human Rights Code

RSO 1990, c. H.19

Objective: To prevent discrimination and harassment in employment, housing, and the delivery of goods and services, on grounds including race, sex, religion, handicap, and age.

Target Population: Provincially regulated employers, landlords, and goods and services providers.

Program Administration: The Ontario Human Rights Commission investigates complaints, attempts to settle complaints, carries out public education, formulates public policy, and does research.

Administrative Tribunal: The Human Rights Tribunal is independent and "quasi-judicial." It hears complaints and makes decisions.

Summary: The Ontario *Human Rights Code* prohibits discrimination and harassment in employment, housing, and the delivery of goods and services by both the private and public sector and it provides a complaint mechanism for those who believe their rights were violated. If, after an investigation, the Ontario Human Rights Commission determines that the Code was infringed, it may impose fines and other remedies such as compensation. ◇

Hours of Work and Time Off

The ESA legislates the maximum hours of work per week and the minimum periods of rest during shifts for most occupations. An employee who works longer than a standard workweek may be entitled to overtime pay.

The ESA prescribes a list of public holidays, sometimes called statutory holidays, which employees are generally entitled to take off with pay when the holiday falls on a regularly scheduled workday. There are exceptions for certain occupations, such as essential services, and employees who are required to be at work on a public holiday are typically entitled to overtime pay (generally time-and-a-half).

Once employees have completed a minimum qualification period of typically one year, they are entitled to take paid vacation. The details of vacation entitlements and the amount of vacation pay may vary in different jurisdictions, but in general, employers are not allowed to substitute pay for earned vacation time except in limited and specified circumstances.

Leave periods are also available in some circumstances. Generally, a leave period, such as for illness, family emergency, or pregnancy, is unpaid, but the employee's job is secure; that is, he is entitled to resume his duties on his return.

Perhaps the most important leave is pregnancy and parental leave, available to employees who have worked for the employer for a minimum number of weeks before the leave begins. In Ontario, parental leave is available for an employee who has recently become the mother or father of a child, whether by birth or adoption. The employer is not required to pay wages or salary during pregnancy or parental leave, though some employers do. The employer is required to continue its contributions to employee benefit plans, such as medical insurance; and during the period of leave, the employee may be entitled to claim benefits under the federal *Employment Insurance Act.*

Enforcing Employment Standards

WEB LINK

For information about employers' obligations under the *Employment Standards Act, 2000* and the procedure for seeking a remedy in a case of non-compliance, visit the Ministry of Labour's website at www.labour.gov.on.ca.

WEB LINK

To find a Service Ontario centre near you, visit the government's website at www.gov.on.ca.

As a social service worker in Ontario, you may encounter a client who has been denied a legislated employment right under the ESA. In such a situation, the employee should first seek a remedy from the employer by bringing the matter to the employer's attention and requesting compliance with the ESA. The request should be made in writing. Ontario's Ministry of Labour has created a "Self-Help Kit" (which is available online at the ministry's website) to assist employees in drafting such a letter.

If a written request to the employer does not result in resolution of the problem, the employee may choose to file a complaint with the Ministry of Labour. However, before doing so, he should seek advice from a lawyer. Generally, filing a complaint under the ESA precludes filing a lawsuit on the same issue. In some cases, such as wrongful dismissal (discussed below), the remedy available from a court is substantially greater than that offered by the ESA, so the pros and cons of the two ways of proceeding should be carefully weighed. Also, if the workplace is unionized, the provisions of the collective agreement govern, and the process for dealing with a dispute is grievance arbitration pursuant to the collective agreement.

If the employee decides to proceed with a formal complaint, he should fill out the ministry's claim form, either online at the ministry website or in person at a ServiceOntario Information Centre. (These information centres are found in more than 60 communities across Ontario.) Once the claim is filed, the ministry first tries to negotiate a resolution. If this fails and the ministry believes that the complaint has validity, an investigation may be launched.

Investigations are conducted by employment standards officers. After investigating, the employment standards officer may order an appropriate remedy against the employer, such as requiring payment of unpaid wages, or requiring payment of

LEGISLATIVE SHORTCUT

Employment Standards Act, 2000

SO 2000, c. 41

Objective: To set minimum standards for working conditions.

Target Population: Non-unionized employees governed by the laws of Ontario, and their employers.

Program Administration: Complaints are investigated by an employment standards officer, who may order payment of unpaid wages, compensation, or fines.

Administrative Tribunal: Challenges to the decisions of employment standards officers are heard by the Ontario Labour Relations Board.

Summary: The *Employment Standards Act, 2000* imposes minimum standards for the treatment of employees, with respect to such matters as wages, overtime, vacations, parental leave, and notice of termination (or pay in lieu of). ◇

compensation for violation of the ESA. Fines, payable to the ministry, may also be imposed. Generally, an employer is not ordered to reinstate an employee whose employment was terminated, but there are two exceptions: where the employee was fired for pursuing his or her rights; and where an employee was fired for taking a leave of absence to which he was legally entitled.

Where either the employer or the employee wishes to challenge the results of an investigation, a review process is available. Reviews involve a hearing before the Ontario Labour Relations Board (OLRB), an administrative tribunal. Parties usually have lawyers to represent them at these proceedings. As a social service worker, you may be called upon to assist a client in obtaining a lawyer, legal aid, or the services of a community legal clinic for this purpose. Helping clients to access legal services is discussed in detail in chapter 15.

WORKPLACE HEALTH AND SAFETY

According to the Association of Workers' Compensation Boards of Canada, 928 workers were killed and over 340,000 suffered injury or illness in Canadian workplaces in 2004. The youngest and least experienced members of the workforce are at the highest risk.

To help minimize workplace accidents and illnesses, each province has passed legislation designed to regulate physical conditions in the workplace, such as the exposure of employees to health and safety hazards, and to prescribe the duties of employers to protect employees from such hazards. In Ontario, the main workplace safety statute is the *Occupational Health and Safety Act* (OHSA).

Provincial governments have also enacted workers' compensation legislation to provide for the payment of compensation where an employee suffers a loss of income as a result of a work-related injury or illness. In Ontario, the governing statute is the *Workplace Safety and Insurance Act, 1997* (WSIA). Generally, the WSIA provides that an employee with a valid claim against an insured employer is entitled to compensation, and the employer is protected from legal action and potential liability for damages. The WSIA and the OHSA are discussed in more detail below.

Health and Safety Standards

The OHSA is a fairly general statute that establishes health and safety standards for particular workplaces and hazards via 35 separate regulations. This legislative scheme mandates a cooperative approach to safety by prescribing the respective role of employers, supervisors, and workers themselves. For example, if hazards present at a worksite call for the use of protective eyewear, the employer is responsible for providing the eyewear and establishing a usage policy, including, for example, posted reminders. Supervisors are responsible for enforcing the policy, and individual workers are responsible for protecting themselves by using the eyewear in accordance with the employer's rules.

The legislation also provides for the appointment of health and safety representatives in smaller workplaces and joint health and safety committees (JHSCs) in larger workplaces. Health and safety representatives are appointed by workers, while JHSCs include both worker and management representatives. The health and safety

WEB LINK

Information about workplace injuries and illness is available from the Association of Workers' Compensation Boards of Canada online at www.awcbc.org. For information on workplace safety specifically targeted to young workers, visit www.prevent-it.ca.

representative or JHSC is responsible for identifying and monitoring health and safety hazards in the workplace, developing strategies for minimizing the risks from those hazards, reporting to the Ministry of Labour about health and safety issues, and investigating workplace accidents and incidents of work-related illness.

Health and safety representatives and members of a JHSC are responsible for knowing the health and safety standards and rules that apply to their particular workplace, and for communicating those standards and rules to supervisors and workers. For example, many chemicals used in workplaces are subject to the Workplace Hazardous Materials Information System (WHMIS), which requires special labelling of the prescribed chemicals and record keeping through the use of material safety data sheets (MSDS). In such workplaces, it is the responsibility of the JHSC to establish and maintain this system.

If an employee perceives that he is at risk on the job, or becomes injured or ill through his work, the first step, after addressing his immediate medical needs, is to

---

LEGISLATIVE SHORTCUT

Occupational Health and Safety Act

RSO 1990, c. O.1

Objective: To minimize workplace accidents and illnesses.

Target Population: All workers and employers in Ontario.

Program Administration: Ministry of Labour.

Administrative Tribunal: Disputes are heard by the Ontario Labour Relations Board.

Summary: The *Occupational Health and Safety Act* is a fairly general statute that is given specific operation to particular workplaces and hazards via 35 different regulations. The Act prescribes a cooperative approach to safety by prescribing roles for employers, supervisors, and workers themselves. It requires the creation of "joint health and safety committees," made up of worker representatives and management representatives, who report to the Ministry of Labour. ◇

Workplace Safety and Insurance Act, 1997

SO 1997, c. 16, Sch. A

Objective: To provide compensation for workers who incur injuries or illness due to their jobs, and to protect employers from lawsuits.

Target Population: Workers and their employers.

Program Administration: The Workplace Safety and Insurance Board administers the Act.

Administrative Tribunal: The Workplace Safety and Insurance Appeals Tribunal hears disputes.

Summary: The *Workplace Safety and Insurance Act, 1997* creates a no-fault insurance system designed to eliminate the need for lawsuits by injured workers against their employers. Employers pay premiums into the insurance fund and eligible workers are compensated. ◇

contact either the health and safety representative or the JHSC. The representative or JHSC will encourage the worker to get treatment and will begin to investigate the hazard or incident.

Workplace accidents and illnesses resulting in lost worktime must be reported to the Ministry of Labour. Workplaces should also keep a record of *all* work-related accidents and illnesses. This information will be useful in identifying risks and preventing other occurrences. In the case of serious accidents where the employer has been negligent in protecting an employee, the Ministry of Labour has the power to impose fines and even imprisonment to deter future incidents. Employees who lose worktime and income because of a work-related injury or illness may seek compensation under the WSIA, as described below.

Workers' Compensation

THE WSIA REGIME

To compensate employees for work-related injuries and illnesses, and to minimize recourse to expensive lawsuits in such cases, Ontario instituted an insurance scheme, established and governed by the WSIA and mandatory for most workplaces where a risk to worker health or safety exists. The insurance fund is created and maintained by employer-paid premiums, which are calculated as a percentage of total payroll. The percentage varies depending upon the industry class and the safety record of the individual employer. This means that higher-risk industries—for example, construction or mining—bear a greater share of the burden for workers' compensation than lower-risk industries such as food services or retail sales. In addition, employers that are lax in applying health and safety standards pay a penalty in the form of increased premiums.

Employees are entitled to be compensated for work-related injuries or illnesses if their employer is insured. Certain employers, particularly in low-risk industries such as banking, are exempt from the application of the WSIA, but, generally, they may obtain coverage if they wish. Some of these employers may choose coverage because it protects them against potential lawsuits in the event of employee injury or illness. Business owners and contract workers are not covered by the WSIA because they are not employees.

The WSIA provides for the creation of two agencies to administer workers' compensation claims: the Workplace Safety and Insurance Board (WSIB) and the Workplace Safety and Insurance Appeals Tribunal (WSIAT). The WSIB functions as both a regulatory agency and an administrative tribunal. It receives and decides workers' claims for income support and rehabilitation services following a work-related injury or illness. It also decides employers' challenges of workers' claims. The WSIAT hears appeals of WSIB decisions. It is largely independent of the WSIB, but it is required to follow WSIB policies where applicable.

The procedure for making claims is described briefly below.

QUALIFICATION FOR COMPENSATION

To qualify for compensation under the WSIA, the employee must sustain the injury or illness in the course of his work. For example, an employee who is injured in a car accident on the way to work will generally not qualify; but an employee who drives a company delivery truck and is injured in a crash while making deliveries may be entitled to compensation under the WSIA. The circumstances in which the injury or illness occurred may also be relevant. For example, if an injury resulted from a wilful act of wrongdoing by the employee (say, the delivery truck driver was driving while impaired), the employee may not be eligible for benefits.

An employee will also not be entitled to compensation for chronic pain that is not clearly related to employment-related repetitive strain or a workplace injury, or for mental stress or anguish, unless it is attributable to a sudden and unexpected traumatic event in the workplace.

PROCEDURE FOR MAKING A CLAIM

When an employee is injured on the job, the employer is required to take steps to ensure that the employee gets appropriate first aid and, if necessary, is seen by a doctor. If the employee loses worktime or requires medical treatment other than first aid at the workplace, the employer is required to file a report of the incident within three days of its occurrence.

The filing of an Employer's Report (form 7) with the WSIB begins the process for making a workers' compensation claim. The employee must either sign the form 7, which serves as her authorization for the WSIB to access certain medical records, or file her own Worker's Report, a form 6. An employee should generally file her own report if she disagrees with the employer's version of the incident. An employee who sees a health-care practitioner should advise the practitioner of her plans to make a workers' compensation claim, because the practitioner is then required to file a Health Professionals Report, a form 8.

On receipt of a worker's claim, WSIB staff investigate the validity of the claim and decide whether to allow or deny it. If the employee has submitted a report challenging the employer's report, the WSIB will assess the merits of both reports in reaching its decision. If the employee or the employer disagrees with the decision, either party may request an internal review. If the ultimate decision of the WSIB is still not accepted, the dissatisfied party may appeal to the WSIAT.

In many workplaces, a health and safety representative or JHSC member will help the employee with filing a claim. However, in certain cases, a social service worker may be called upon to provide assistance—for example, if a client is injured while working in a program sponsored by Ontario Works.

BENEFITS

Depending on the circumstances, and subject to approval of the employee's claim by the WSIB or the WSIAT, a worker may be entitled to a range of income support and other benefits to compensate for injury or illness suffered on the job. These include the following:

- *Wages for the day of the injury.*
- *Health-care benefits* (such as payment for drugs to treat the condition).
- *Loss-of-earnings (LOE) benefits* (to replace lost income up to a statutory maximum that is adjusted annually for inflation).
- *Employment benefits* (the employer's share of premiums for 12 months after the accident).

WEB LINK

For more information on the procedures for filing claims and challenging decisions of the WSIB, visit www.wsib.on.ca. For information on appeals to the SIAT, visit www.wsiat.on.ca.

- *Retirement benefits* (payable at age 65 to some claimants).

- *Non-economic loss (NEL) benefit* (to compensate for residual pain and suffering, based on the degree of impairment).

- *Assistance in returning to work* (programs to support a worker's "early and safe return to work").

- *Survivor benefits for dependants* (including burial or cremation expenses for a worker who was killed on the job and grief counselling, income replacement or support, and return-to-work support for survivors).

A knowledgeable social service worker can assess whether a client is receiving all of the benefits to which he is entitled, and whether the client should be referred to a lawyer for assistance in pursuing his claim.

JOB LOSS

Because most people need to work in order to support themselves and their families, loss of employment is usually a significant life crisis. In some cases, unemployment brings a client into contact with a social service worker for the first time in his life. In other cases, the client may already be dealing with social service workers, and job loss may be symptomatic of other unresolved personal issues. Your role as a social service worker may be to help the client to secure income assistance, be it employment insurance or Ontario Works benefits, or to find a new job.

It is useful to understand the circumstances of the client's dismissal, and to be able to assess whether there may be grounds for a claim against the employer. While you must not advise the client on this or other legal matters, you should be able to identify issues that should be brought to the attention of a lawyer, so that you will know when it is appropriate to refer the client.

Generally, an employer is free to fire an employee, and is not required to specify a reason or justify the decision. However, there are some situations where an employee may challenge her employer's decision to fire her—for example, if she has reason to believe that her dismissal constitutes discrimination, or perhaps retaliation for asserting her statutory rights; or if the employee's job is protected by a collective agreement. In these limited cases, the employee may be entitled to get her job back.

Notice of Termination and Pay in Lieu of Notice

Generally, dismissed employees are entitled to either **notice of termination** or **pay in lieu of notice**. However, if the employee has engaged in conduct that justifies dismissal, he usually loses both of these entitlements and may be ordered to leave the workplace immediately.

When an employee receives notice of termination, the employer tells him in advance of the date on which his employment will end. If the employer chooses to provide "working notice," the employee will be expected to remain in his job for the duration of the notice period. If the employer prefers that the employee leave immediately (as is often the case), the employer must provide pay in lieu of notice—

compensation equal to the amount of salary or wages that he would have earned had he been given notice.

The length of the notice period and the circumstances in which an employer is excused from providing notice vary, depending on whether one relies on the provisions of the applicable employment standards legislation (in Ontario, the ESA) or on the common law. The differences are explained below.

Statutory Termination Provisions and Common-Law Rules and Concepts

If an employee is dismissed from her job without cause, and without being given proper notice or pay in lieu of notice, she may have a claim for termination pay under the ESA, or for damages for **wrongful dismissal** under the common law.

The ESA mandates minimum notice periods, which vary according to the period of employment. The current notice periods are shown in figure 17.1.

Compared to the minimum entitlement under the ESA, the notice obligations under common-law rules are much more generous to the employee, and more onerous for the employer. In some cases, the notice period can exceed one month per year of service. Also, while the ESA notice periods are based solely on length of service, common-law notice periods take into account additional factors related to the time it will likely take the employee to find a replacement job, such as the age of the employee and the type of work.

Both the ESA and the common law provide for specific exceptions to the notice obligations of the employer, based on the conduct of the employee. The ESA exceptions apply in circumstances of:

- wilful misconduct;

- disobedience; or

- wilful neglect of duty that is not trivial.

These exceptions are narrower in scope than the **just cause** exception under the common law. In general, circumstances that can form the basis of termination for just cause include:

- dishonesty that is prejudicial to the employer's economic interests or reputation;

Figure 17.1   Statutory Notice of Termination

Period of employment	Minimum notice of termination
3 months or less	No notice required
3 month to 1 year	1 week
1 to 3 years	2 weeks
3 to 4 years	3 weeks
4 to 5 years	4 weeks
5 to 6 years	5 weeks
6 to 7 years	6 weeks
7 to 8 years	7 weeks
More than 8 years	8 weeks

- serious insubordination or disobedience (including harassment of other employees);

- chronic lateness or unexcused absenteeism; and

- very serious incompetence.

In view of the differences between the statutory and common-law exceptions and notice obligations, a terminated employee who has not been given proper notice, or pay in lieu of notice, should consult a lawyer before asserting a claim.

An employee who is terminated without just cause after several years of service may consider suing the employer for wrongful dismissal. However, this will be a long and expensive process. An alternative route in satisfying a claim is to seek a negotiated settlement. Often, having a lawyer draft a demand letter is enough to trigger a process of negotiation between the employee and the employer that will lead to resolution of the claim.

A negotiated settlement may not match the amount that could be obtained by taking the employer to court. For example, an employee who is terminated after 12 years of service might accept an employer's termination pay offer that is more than the statutory minimum (8 weeks) but less than, say, the 12 months' pay that the employee might have been awarded at the end of a lawsuit. The reason for choosing the lesser amount is that it will typically be available immediately, whereas the lawsuit could take two or three years, and cost thousands of dollars in legal fees, with no assurance that the amount awarded will actually be paid.

If the employee is not seeking reinstatement, she should engage in a serious job search while she is waiting for settlement of her claim. As a social service worker, you will know that it is usually in a person's best interests to find a new job quickly, in order to minimize the financial and emotional toll of unemployment. If interim financial assistance is needed, a terminated employee may be eligible for employment insurance benefits (discussed below) or Ontario Works benefits (discussed in chapter 8).

Downsizing, Bankruptcy, and Layoff

Sometimes, a person loses his job because the employer can no longer afford to employ him. The employer may simply go out of business, or may **downsize** the workforce to cope with seasonal demands for a product or downturns in the company's fortunes or the economy. It's important to understand that even when financial pressures force a business to downsize, the employer's notice obligations still apply.

If an employer goes out of business and declares bankruptcy, there may be unpaid wages owing to employees. The *Bankruptcy and Insolvency Act* places wages near the top of the priority list for payment from the proceeds of the liquidation of the business. Employees of a bankrupt employer who are owed back pay should obtain legal advice on how to make a claim.

The ESA and related regulations provide special rules to govern situations where an employer terminates 50 or more employees within a four-week period. In general, these rules require the employer to file information about the reasons for the termination with the director of employment standards and to make provision to pay reasonable **severance**; however, in some circumstances, the employer is allowed to give less notice than is normally necessary.

If a company is experiencing financial difficulties or a loss of business that is expected to be temporary, it may lay off some employees in order to cut costs. With a **layoff**, there is an expectation that the employees will be asked to return to work when conditions improve. The ESA provides that if an employee who has been laid off is not called back to work after about three months, the employment relationship is considered to be terminated and the employee is entitled to payment in lieu of notice. The termination date is deemed to be the first day of the layoff.

Employment Insurance Benefits

If an employee is fired from his job for cause or because of misconduct, he may be denied benefits to which he would otherwise be entitled under the *Employment Insurance Act*. However, he may still be entitled to claim damages for wrongful dismissal. This is because the test for exclusion from employment insurance benefits is broader than the common-law concept of just cause. The following are some examples of conduct that could result in a refusal of benefits:

- absence without permission
- tardiness
- insubordination
- refusal to carry out an order or instruction
- refusal to work overtime
- hostile behaviour
- disrespectful conduct
- breach of rules
- inappropriate dress and appearance
- consumption of alcoholic beverages or drugs

WEB LINK

For more information about employment insurance benefits, visit the website of Human Resources and Social Development Canada at www.hrsdc.gc.ca.

When a fired employee applies for employment insurance benefits, he is generally asked about the reason for the termination. If the benefits officer suspects that he may have been fired for cause or misconduct, an administrator will contact the employer for details. If the employer suggests that the employee was terminated for cause, the employee will be invited to submit his own statement of the facts, and an administrative decision will be made about whether to grant or deny benefits. If benefits are denied on the basis of a finding of misconduct and the employee disagrees with this finding, he can appeal the decision.

If a person is found not to be eligible for employment insurance benefits, either because he was fired for misconduct or because he is otherwise ineligible (for example, he did not work enough qualifying hours), he may be able to apply for Ontario Works benefits.

Being fired for cause can make it more difficult for a person to find new employment. Social service workers who work with unemployed clients may need to provide extra support to help a client overcome a for-cause firing in her employment history. For example, the client may need to be coached about how to address the subject of the firing objectively, honestly, and professionally when asked about it in job interviews. She may also need help in negotiating with her former employer to provide the most constructive reference possible that is consistent with honesty.

KEY TERMS

bona fide job qualifications

collective agreement

contract

downsize

just cause

layoff

notice of termination

pay in lieu of notice

severance pay

wrongful dismissal

REFERENCES

Bankruptcy and Insolvency Act, RSC 1985, c. B-3.

Canada Labour Code, RSC 1985, c. L-2.

Canadian Charter of Rights and Freedoms, part I of the *Constitution Act, 1982*, being schedule B of the *Canada Act 1982* (UK), 1982, c. 11.

Canadian Human Rights Act, RSC 1985, c. H-6.

Employment Insurance Act, SC 1996, c. 23.

Employment Standards Act, 2000, SO 2000, c. 41.

Human Rights Code, RSO 1990, c. H.19.

Labour Relations Act, 1995, SO 1995, c. 1, Sch. A.

Mining Act, RSO 1990, c. M.14.

Occupational Health and Safety Act, RSO 1990, c. O.1.

Technical Standards and Safety Act, 2000, SO 2000, c. 16.

Workplace Safety and Insurance Act, 1997, SO 1997, c. 16, Sch. A.

REVIEW QUESTIONS

1. Define a bona fide job qualification. Give an example of a job qualification that could be considered a bona fide requirement for a particular job, but could be discriminatory and a violation of human rights if required for a different job.

2. List three rights provided to employees under the *Employment Standards Act, 2000*.

3. What is a joint health and safety committee, and what is its role?

4. What is the purpose of the *Workplace Safety and Insurance Act, 1997*?

5. Can an employer fire an employee without giving him a reason? What are the employee's rights in this situation?

6. What is the difference between statutory notice and common-law notice of termination?

7. Is a fired employee always eligible for employment insurance under the *Employment Insurance Act*?

CHAPTER 18

Immigration and Refugees

CHAPTER OBJECTIVES

After reading this chapter, you should be able to:

- Describe the central goals of Canada's immigration policy.
- List the classes under which prospective immigrants can apply for permanent resident status.
- Explain what is meant by sponsorship.
- List some of the factors supporting refugee protection.
- Understand the general admissibility rules that apply to applicants in all classes.
- Describe how social service workers can support newcomers who are seeking permanent resident status or who want to sponsor family members.

INTRODUCTION

Canada is a wealthy country with a highly developed social support system, a diverse population, and vast natural resources, making it an attractive destination for newcomers from around the world.

According to government records, more than 15 million people have immigrated to Canada since Confederation in 1867. In the last 10 years, approximately 220,000 immigrants and refugees have been admitted to Canada annually. The current immigration target is 1 percent of the total population or about 330,000 new immigrants per year.

The Canadian government's policy on **immigration** is guided by three main goals:

- to encourage the influx of skilled workers and entrepreneurs;
- to offer protection to people fleeing violence in their own country; and
- to reunite families by allowing immigrants to bring family members to Canada.

The implementation of Canada's immigration policy is governed by the *Immigration and Refugee Protection Act* (IRPA), which was passed into law in 2001, replacing the previous *Immigration Act*. The government department that administers this statute and its regulations is Citizenship and Immigration Canada (CIC). CIC is responsible for the following general functions:

- admitting immigrants, foreign students, visitors, and temporary workers who have the potential to enhance Canada's social and economic growth;

- resettling, protecting, and providing a safe haven for **refugees**;

- helping newcomers to adapt to Canadian society and become Canadian **citizens**; and

- managing access to Canada to protect the security and health of Canadians and the integrity of Canadian laws.

Because there are more applicants wanting to move to Canada than our immigration policy allows, CIC applies formal criteria to determine which applicants will be accepted. In general, Canada is most supportive of the entry of applicants who:

- have valuable skills needed by Canadian employers;

- have the means, ability, and ambition to become entrepreneurs in Canada, or to extend the operation of existing, successful business enterprises to Canada;

- have come to Canada for protection when fleeing persecution in their own countries, particularly under conditions of war; or

- are family members or dependants of immigrants in the first three groups.

LEGISLATIVE SHORTCUT

Immigration and Refugee Protection Act

SC 2001, c. 27

Objective: To govern immigration to Canada and the granting of refugee protection to persons who are displaced, persecuted, or in danger.

Target Population: Non-Canadians who wish to be here on a temporary or permanent basis to live, work, and/or go to school, either because they are fleeing persecution in their country of origin, or because they have decided for other reasons that they would like to be in Canada.

Program Administration: Immigration is administered by the federal government.

Administrative Tribunals: Disputes are heard by the Immigration and Refugee Board, the Immigration Appeals Division, and, potentially, the Refugee Appeals Division.

Summary: The *Immigration and Refugee Protection Act* provides criteria and procedures for admission of non-Canadians. Immigrants admitted on a temporary basis include visitors, students, temporary workers, caregivers, and others on humanitarian and compassionate grounds. Immigrants admitted permanently are skilled workers (marketable skills and language skills are measured on point system); entrepreneurs (assets, management experience and viability of business plan are examined); and sponsored relatives. To be admitted as a refugee, a claimant must have a "well-founded fear of persecution" based on race, religion, nationality, political opinion, or membership in a particular social group. ◇

In general, Canada does not support the entry of foreign nationals who:

- may pose a threat to national security;

- have a history of criminality or close connections to organized crime; or

- will likely impose a heavy burden on Canada's social support systems (for example, the medical system) without contributing to the Canadian economy.

The details of Canada's immigration and refugee policies are discussed in the sections that follow.

Social service workers may work with new immigrants and refugees in many different capacities. Newcomers to Canada often need help with finding housing, arranging for financial assistance, obtaining appropriate education and training, and securing employment. In addition, newcomers who are seeking formal **permanent resident status** or Canadian citizenship may need help with completing forms, making applications, upgrading language skills, obtaining police or medical clearances, or appealing immigration or refugee decisions. Social service workers can provide support in these and other ways, as discussed below.

IMMIGRATION CLASSES

An immigrant is any person who has come to Canada from another country with the intention of living here permanently. Many aspects of participation in Canadian life, including working and benefiting from Canada's social services, are restricted to Canadian citizens and **permanent residents**. To become a permanent resident, an immigrant must comply with Canada's immigration policy. Permanent residents may obtain citizenship if they meet additional criteria.

In order to successfully apply for and be granted permanent resident status in Canada, a foreign national must generally obtain an entry visa before leaving her country of origin. Visas are available to successful permanent residency applicants who fall into one of the following three categories:

- *Family class.* A person may be a family class applicant if he or she is the spouse, common-law partner, parent, child, or "other prescribed family member" (generally a grandparent) of a Canadian citizen or permanent resident (section 12(1) of the IRPA and related regulations). Family class entrants must be sponsored by the citizen or resident; **sponsorship** is discussed in greater detail below.

- *Economic class.* A person is an economic class applicant if he or she has good potential to become economically established in Canada (section 12(2) of the IRPA). This typically means one of two things: either the person has money to bring into Canada that will be used to begin a business enterprise, or the person has skills that are in demand by Canadian employers (especially if the immigrant can show proof of an offer of employment from within Canada).

- *Refugee class.* A person is a refugee class applicant if he or she meets the definition of a Convention refugee (discussed in the section on refugees

WEB LINK

For information about criteria for citizenship, visit the CIC's website at www.cic.gc.ca.

below) or is "in a similar circumstance"—that is, the person does not meet the definition of a Convention refugee, but the Canadian government deems that there are valid reasons to admit the person, "taking into account Canada's humanitarian tradition with respect to the displaced and the persecuted" (section 12(3) of the IRPA).

These general classes are defined and limited by detailed selection criteria set out in the regulations to the IRPA. For example, the regulations provide, for the purpose of defining family class applicants, a definition of spouse that includes anyone who has been in a conjugal relationship with the sponsor for at least a year. They also provide that a person is not eligible as a member of the family class if the applicant and the sponsor are claiming to be spouses only for the purpose of immigration. The declaration of a spousal relationship must be bona fide—meaning genuine.

Each of the three immigration classes is discussed separately below.

Family Class Immigrants and Sponsorship

Family members of Canadian citizens and permanent residents can be sponsored for immigration into Canada as part of the government's policy to reunite families. The following family members are eligible for sponsorship:

- spouses and common-law partners;

- children, including dependent biological children, dependent adopted children, and children under 18 to be adopted in Canada;

- parents;

- grandparents; and

- other orphaned dependants who are brothers, sisters, nieces, nephews, or grandchildren of the sponsor.

If the person who is seeking to immigrate is the sponsor's spouse or partner or dependent child, the sponsor and the applicant prepare a joint application package. The sponsor obtains the package from CIC, fills out the relevant portions of the application, and asks the applicant to provide the necessary documents. The sponsor then forwards the completed package to CIC.

If the applicant is living in Canada, CIC will interview the applicant and conduct the necessary medical, security, and criminal record checks. If the applicant is living in a foreign country, the sponsor will need to mail the application to the Canadian visa office in that country, and that visa office will review the application and conduct the medical, security, and criminal record checks.

If the applicant is not a spouse or partner or dependent child, the sponsor completes only his portion of the application and submits it to CIC. The applicant, after receiving an application guide from the sponsor (who will receive it from the appropriate visa office), must fill out a separate application form and submit it to the visa office, where it will be assessed.

If the application is being made on behalf of an adopted child, or a child whom the sponsor plans to adopt upon the child's arrival in Canada, the rules are somewhat more complicated and vary according to which of these circumstances applies.

Critical Perspectives

Sponsors on the Hook

What happens when a man sponsors his fiancée, who comes to Canada, breaks off the engagement, and goes on social assistance? He gets a bill for the repayment of thousands of dollars of welfare collected by the ex-fiancée. At least, that is what happened to Nedzad Dzihic, when the Yugoslavian woman he sponsored, Edina Zurko, used him to get to Canada and promptly left him. He claims he informed CIC immediately, but the department did nothing about it. Ms. Zurko successfully applied for social assistance, and some time later, Mr. Dzihic was sent a bill.

Mr. Dzihic is fighting his case in court, along with other deceived sponsors, arguing that his ex-fiancée breached the sponsorship agreement by failing to marry him. This raises many questions about the allocation of risk. For example, should the sponsor or the government be responsible when something goes wrong? Are sponsors taking on more responsibility than they realize? ◇

CIC will not accept a child for entry into Canada if there is reason to believe that the adoption will not create a true parent–child relationship, or that it has been done for the primary purpose of securing Canadian residency for a child. For example, if a permanent resident living in Canada does not have the financial means to sponsor her child, and so asks her neighbour to adopt and sponsor the child with the expectation that the child will actually live with the biological parent, CIC will decline the sponsorship application.

Also, before bringing a child into Canada after foreign adoption or for the purposes of adoption here, certain extra requirements must be met. For example, the sponsor will have to prove that the child was legally available for adoption in his home country, that a home study of the adoptive parents was performed (as is also required for domestic adoptions), that the adoption was made with the consent of the person who was originally the legal parent of the child, and that the original parental relationship was terminated by the adoption. Finally, CIC will need to be satisfied that the adoption was not made for gain—that is, that it was not a case of child trafficking.

In order to qualify as a sponsor, a citizen or permanent resident must prove that she is able to financially support the sponsored family member for a period of 3 to 10 years, depending on the age of the applicant and the familial relationship. The sponsor makes this promise in the form of an **undertaking** to CIC. She also signs a sponsorship agreement with the applicant, promising to support him, in return for the applicant's promise to make efforts to become self-supporting in Canada. The sponsor must provide financial information (for example, proof of salary) as evidence of her ability to support the applicant, which CIC will assess on the basis of established guidelines.

Economic Class

BUSINESS IMMIGRANTS

To promote economic growth, Canada welcomes the arrival of foreign businesspeople and skilled workers. There are three classes of business immigrants: investors, entrepreneurs, and self-employed people.

Investors

A person applying to immigrate as an investor must come prepared to make a minimum $400,000 "investment" to the Receiver General for Canada, who in turn disburses the funds to the provinces for use in job creation and economic development programs. This money is paid back, without interest, to the investor after five years.

Investor immigrants must also have a net worth of at least Cdn $800,000, and they must meet requirements specified in the regulations that indicate business acumen and managerial experience. These rules are intended to weed out those who might have the funds to "buy their way in" to Canada but lack the ability to run a successful business and contribute to the economy in the long term.

Entrepreneurs

The rules for people applying to immigrate as entrepreneurs are technically complex. In essence, an entrepreneur is a person who

- has gained business experience abroad;

- has a net worth of at least $300,000; and

- is demonstrably able, within 3 years of arriving in Canada, to acquire control and management of a minimum 33 $\frac{1}{3}$ percent interest in a qualifying Canadian business, and to create a full-time job for one additional person here.

The regulations define in quite complicated terms what is meant by a qualifying Canadian business. In essence, however, a business must be a real business that earns profits and employs people, not simply a tax shelter or another business operated chiefly to generate interest, dividends, or capital gains.

Self-Employed People

A person applying to immigrate as a self-employed person must work in one of three areas: athletics, cultural activities, or farming.

People who work in farming must have at least two years of farm management experience in the five years preceding their immigration, and must have plans to purchase and manage a farm here in Canada.

Athletes and people who participate in cultural activities (for example, musicians) must have either competed or participated at the international level, for two out of the five years preceding their arrival, or be self-employed (and self-supporting) in athletics or cultural pursuits.

Additional Requirements for Business Immigrants

A business applicant who meets all of the requirements for his class (investor, entrepreneur, or self-employed person) must also receive a passing score when assessed under five additional selection categories:

- education,

- employment experience,

- age,

- proficiency in English or French, and

- adaptability.

This selection grid is designed to predict the likely success of each applicant becoming economically established in Canada. It is similar to but less stringent than the self-assessment test used for applicants in the skilled worker class.

SKILLED WORKERS

A prospective immigrant who hopes to qualify in the skilled worker class must meet three criteria:

- She must receive a "passing" point score when assessed against CIC's skilled worker assessment grid (discussed further below).

- She must have at least one year's qualifying work experience (also discussed below).

- She must have sufficient savings to be able to support herself while she becomes settled in Canada.

The assessment grid allows CIC staff to score applicants in six categories, which include the same five categories as for business immigrants with the addition of "pre-arranged employment in Canada":

- education,

- employment experience,

- age,

- proficiency in English or French,

- pre-arranged employment in Canada, and

- adaptability.

In addition to getting a passing score, the applicant must show that she has at least one year's qualifying work experience. Qualifying work is either management work or work that requires university, college, or technical training. This work is defined under the National Occupational Classification as Skill Type O or Skill Level A or B:

- Skill Type O refers to legislators or senior and middle management workers in all types of industries.

- Skill Level A occupations are those for which a person normally requires a university education (whether or not he works as a manager).

- Skill Level B occupations typically require a college education or apprenticeship training.

MEETING LANGUAGE REQUIREMENTS

As indicated above, both the business and skilled worker categories of economic class immigrants require applicants to have some proficiency in at least one of Canada's two official languages (English or French). The CIC scoring grids rate four

WEB LINK
Prospective immigrants who would like to apply as skilled workers can get an idea of their likelihood of success by scoring themselves on CIC's online self-assessment test, available at www.cic.gc.ca.

WEB LINK

For more information about LINC programs in Canada, visit www.eslincanada.com or the CIC website at www.cic.gc.ca.

kinds of proficiency—speaking, listening, reading, and writing—on four proficiency levels: high, moderate, basic, and none.

Social service workers can help prospective immigrants to meet language requirements, either by working in language training centres or by referring clients to language schools or other sources of language training. Often, the best way for a newcomer to build speaking and listening skills is by practising with people who are fluent in the language and with other learners. Social service workers can help to develop, or can work in, recreational programs designed to provide opportunities for people to converse in English or French. Examples include book clubs, games nights, and other social clubs where conversation is encouraged.

New immigrants can also seek help in upgrading their language skills from LINC, the federal government's Language Instruction for Newcomers to Canada program. LINC offers free language training in English or French to adult newcomers. Social service workers should research the availability of LINC classes in their local area so that they have this information available to share with newcomer clients.

REFUGEE CLASS

According to CIC, in the last 10 years, 20,000 to 45,000 people a year have sought refugee status in Canada. People who wish to settle in Canada as refugees (as opposed to applying as immigrants in the family or economic classes) are assessed, not on the basis of how they can contribute to our economy or whether they can support themselves here, but rather on the basis of their need for protection.

Applying for Refugee Status

Applicants may be considered for refugee status under the IRPA as **Convention refugees** (section 96) or as **persons in need of protection** (section 97). A Convention refugee is a person who has a well-founded fear of persecution for reasons of race, religion, nationality, membership in a particular social group, or political opinion, and who is unable or afraid to seek protection from his country of nationality or residence. For example, a person who is subjected to threats and beatings because he belongs to an ethnic minority may be a refugee if his country does not offer protection by enacting and enforcing laws against such behaviour. This definition comes from the Geneva Convention, an international **treaty** or **convention**.

A person in need of protection is of broader scope and expands the definition of refugee beyond that of the Geneva Convention. A person in need of protection is a person in Canada whose removal to his country of nationality or former residence might subject him to torture, death, or cruel and unusual treatment or punishment.

Applicants may claim refugee status from either inside or outside Canada. If a person seeks status as a refugee while in his own country, he must apply to the United Nations High Commissioner for Refugees for a referral to a Canadian visa office, or be sponsored by a private sponsor who has been pre-approved by the CIC.

If a person seeks refugee status after arriving in Canada, she must first report to an immigration officer. The officer then has three days to decide whether her case is suitable for hearing by the Immigration and Refugee Board (IRB) for a determination. A case may not be suitable for an IRB hearing if the person is clearly ineligible

WEB LINK

For information about the proceedings of the Refugee Protection Division of the IRB, the Refugee Protection Division Rules, and a plain-language overview of IRB procedures, visit the IRB website at www.irb-cisr.gc .ca. A more detailed publication for applicants is also available on the website.

because of the country from which she has arrived, or because of serious criminal behaviour. Section 101 of the IRPA sets out detailed rules for determining eligibility for a hearing.

If the case is referred to the IRB for a determination, the IRB will hear the facts of the case and will decide whether the applicant meets the definition of a Convention refugee or a person in need of protection.

A person appearing before the IRB for a determination of his refugee status claim is not required, by law, to have legal representation; however, considering the importance of this hearing in the context of a person's life, social service workers who work with clients appearing before the IRB should do their best to assist those clients in finding legal advice. Refugee claimants can apply for legal aid, seek the help of a community legal clinic, or hire an immigration consultant. Besides having a legal adviser present, a refugee claimant may also want to be accompanied by the social service worker for moral support.

Because many refugees speak a language other than English or French, the IRB has an obligation to provide an interpreter who can speak the applicant's language to assist in the proceedings.

WEB LINK

For more on immigration consultants—a self-regulated profession—visit the website of the Canadian Society of Immigration Consultants at www.csic-scci.ca.

SPONSORSHIP OF REFUGEES

Refugees applying from abroad for permanent residence must be sponsored; that is, someone must undertake to provide financial support and assistance to enable the refugee to relocate in Canada. Any one of the following agencies or groups may sponsor a refugee:

- The Canadian government.

- A group of five Canadian citizens or permanent residents, all over the age of 17 and living in the area in which the refugee will be resettled.

- An agency that has a sponsorship agreement with the Canadian government, such as the Afghan Women's Organization. The government makes such agreements with qualifying agencies that regularly sponsor refugees in order to expedite the sponsor approval process.

- An organization, association, or corporation that is not party to a sponsorship agreement, and that operates in the area in which a refugee will be resettled and has the funds available to support a refugee—for example, a community church whose congregation has heard of the plight of an individual or a family.

Like all other immigrants, applicants for refugee status are subject to medical, criminal, and security clearance, as discussed below.

GENERAL ENTRY REQUIREMENTS FOR ALL PROSPECTIVE IMMIGRANTS

As well as meeting the criteria specified for each immigration class—family class, economic class, and refugee class—all prospective immigrants are subject to a medical examination and criminal record and security checks. These assessments are done to protect the Canadian public from individuals who might pose a risk from a public health or safety perspective.

Medical Examinations

All applicants for permanent residence in Canada must submit to a medical examination. Medical examinations may also be required for shorter-term visitors—for example, those who hold temporary work visas and work in a field in which protection of public health is essential (such as hospital care), those who expect to stay for six months or longer, and those arriving from a country with a high rate of communicable disease.

Medical examinations are conducted for two reasons: first, to determine whether the applicant has a communicable disease that could pose a risk to Canadians; and second, to determine whether the person suffers from a medical condition that would place an excessive demand on Canada's health-care system. Medical examinations are conducted by a "designated medical practitioner"—a physician from a list maintained by CIC. Examinations can include a physical examination, a mental health assessment, a review of past medical history, and "routine diagnostic tests." These tests can include urinalysis, a chest X-ray, and blood tests for syphilis and human immunodeficiency virsus (HIV).

Section 38(1) of the IRPA provides that a person is ineligible for permanent resident status if his or her medical condition(s) would impose an excessive burden on the health-care system. However, this does not apply to sponsored members of the family class, or to refugees or protected persons.

Critical Perspectives
Excessive Demand Exclusions

IRPA section 38(1), which permits the exclusion of applicants based on their potential to place an excessive demand on health or social services, is a fairly controversial provision, for several reasons:

- Canada's health-care system currently supports thousands of Canadian-born individuals who are suffering from medical conditions.

- The exclusion discriminates on the basis of timing of the onset of a medical condition. However, there is no certainty that, for example, a healthy entrant will not become sick soon after being granted status.

- It can be difficult to estimate accurately the burden that an individual will place on the social or health-care system; some critics suggest that the burden is overestimated in some cases and underestimated in others. Consider, for example, the burden of a symptom-free person with HIV compared with that of an apparently healthy two-pack-a-day smoker.

- The benefits to Canada of an immigrant's entry, from an economic perspective or otherwise, can sometimes far outweigh the burden the individual places on the social support network. Consider, for example, the achievements of many well-known people in Canada and around the world who have suffered illness or disability—Terry Fox, Stephen Hawking, Lance Armstrong, Stevie Wonder, and Manitoba MP Steven Fletcher. ◇

Criminal Background and Security Checks

All applicants must establish that they are not ineligible for permanent resident status on the basis of criminality. "Criminality" means that the accused

- was convicted in Canada of an indictable or hybrid offence, or of two or more offences of any kind (not arising out of the same occurrence), or

- was convicted of, or committed, an equivalent offence or offences in another country.

Where the applicant can show that he was pardoned, successfully appealed a conviction, or has since been rehabilitated, he may be found admissible.

The simplest means of establishing the lack of a criminal record is for the applicant to obtain a police certificate and provide it to CIC. A police certificate is an official document, signed by a police authority or government official, that indicates whether or not a person has a criminal record and, if so, the details of the offence(s). An applicant for permanent residence status must obtain a police certificate from every country in which he lived for six consecutive months or longer after reaching the age of 18. The police certificate(s) must have been issued no more than three months earlier than the date of the application for permanent resident status, and must be accompanied by a translation if written in a language other than English or French.

In some cases, a person may be inadmissible to Canada as a security risk even if he or she has no criminal record, if CIC is satisfied that the person has links to terrorism, organized crime, or groups (including governments) with a history of attempts to overthrow elected governments, to commit genocide, or to engage in serious human rights abuses. The IRPA sets out the details of these grounds of inadmissibility, but each individual case is decided on its own facts by the IRB.

APPEALS AND OPPOSING REMOVAL

Appeals by Family Class and Economic Class Immigrants

Where a person has applied to sponsor a foreign national as part of the family class, and CIC has declined to issue a visa for the foreign national, the sponsor may be able to bring an appeal of the decision before the Immigration Appeal Division of the IRB. Grounds for appeal include an error of law or fact, a procedural error, and other issues where the best interests of a child are at stake.

There is no right of appeal where an applicant has been found inadmissible for reasons of

- security,

- violation of human rights,

- serious criminal behaviour, or

- involvement in organized crime.

Appeals by Refugee Status Claimants

When the IRPA was first drafted, some commentators were highly critical of the legislation's lack of provision for appeals from refugee status decisions. In response, the drafters of the IRPA laid the groundwork, in the legislation for the introduction of a Refugee Appeal Division (RAD) of the IRB; however, implementation was delayed. At the time this book was written, the appeal division was still not in operation, and there appear to be no plans at present to move toward the implementation of the RAD.

If implemented, the RAD would consider appeals of Refugee Protection Division decisions "on the merits" of the particular appeal. This means that the RAD would review decisions based on alleged errors of fact and/or law. The process would not involve an in-person hearing; rather, the RAD would conduct a paper-based review of the decision. The RAD would not accept new information about the case, even if circumstances had changed, and would not consider reversing a decision of the Refugee Protection Division on humanitarian grounds.

Meanwhile, a refugee claimant whose claims is dismissed has the following options:

- seek judicial review (by the Federal Court of Canada) of the IRB decision that went against him;

- argue for permission to stay in Canada while a pre-removal risk assessment is conducted; or

- request to remain in Canada on compassionate and humanitarian grounds.

Pre-Removal Risk Assessment

Canada is committed to the international law principle of **non-refoulement**. This means that Canada has agreed not to send people who have arrived in Canada back to a country where they will be at risk.

When a person is denied permanent resident status, he must ordinarily leave Canada when his visitor's visa, study permit, or work permit, if any, runs out. (If he is a refugee, he may have none of these.) To ensure that this happens, the Immigration Division of the IRB may make a removal order directing that the person must leave. However, if the person believes that he would be at risk if he had to return to his country of origin, he can apply for a pre-removal risk assessment (PRRA).

Some people are not eligible to have a PRRA performed on their behalf. Ineligible applicants include:

- a person who has already been recognized as Convention refugee in another country to which he can return;

- a person who is subject to extradition (usually, removal by agreement between Canada's government and the government of another country for the purpose of facing criminal charges in the other country);

- a person who was not given a hearing by the Refugee Protection Division because he had arrived from a designated "safe" third country; and

- a repeat claimant who was removed from Canada within the preceding six months.

The assessment is usually a paper-based process, not an in-person hearing. PRRAs are conducted by CIC risk assessment officers. The CIC officer considers available information about conditions in the country to which the person is supposed to return, and then makes a determination as to whether the person, if returned, would be at risk of the following:

- persecution, as defined in the Geneva Convention;

- torture, as defined in the Convention Against Torture;

- execution; or

- cruel and unusual treatment or punishment.

After an application for a PRRA has been filed and while it is being considered, the person may stay in Canada. If the assessor determines that the person is not at risk, he must leave Canada.

If the assessment suggests that the person is at risk, he is generally permitted to apply for permanent resident status *unless* he is ineligible for reasons of security, serious criminality/organized crime, or human/international rights violations. If he is ineligible on these grounds, he will usually be permitted to stay only until conditions improve in the destination country.

Requests to Remain on Compassionate and Humanitarian Grounds

Section 25(1) of the IRPA provides that, where an applicant is found to be ineligible for permanent resident status and requests to remain in Canada on "compassionate and humanitarian grounds," the Minister of Citizenship and Immigration may grant permanent residence status on that basis.

The procedures for making a request on compassionate and humanitarian grounds are described in sections 66 to 69 of the IRP regulations. Requests can be made from either within or outside Canada, and must be submitted in writing along with an application for permanent residence status.

A person might make and be granted an application to stay on compassionate and humanitarian grounds where, for example, the person is a close relative of a Canadian citizen, but not a member of the family class, and depends on the Canadian citizen for financial support and assistance. The applicant may be the widowed sister of a Canadian citizen, with a young child whom she cannot support because she is disabled. Or perhaps the person has fled family violence in a "safe" country to come and live with a relative in Canada, and therefore does not qualify for refugee protection.

WEB LINK

For more information on human trafficking and migrant smuggling, visit the website of the federal Department of Foreign Affairs and International Trade at www.dfait-maeci.gc.ca and the website of The Future Group, a non-governmental organization dedicated to combatting human trafficking and the child sex trade, at www.thefuturegroup.org.

HUMAN TRAFFICKING AND MIGRANT SMUGGLING

Human trafficking, in the Canadian context, involves a person or a group that brings people into Canada from another country for financial gain or exploitation. These newcomers are generally from impoverished areas or families, do not meet immigration class criteria, and do not have sponsors in Canada. The traffickers use deception to convince the migrants to come to Canada, giving them inaccurate information about employment opportunities and their chances for resettlement here. In these respects, human trafficking is not unlike **human smuggling**.

The main differences between trafficking and smuggling are that in the latter case, the migrants pay the smugglers to get them into the country secretly and illegally, and the connection with the smugglers usually ends when the human "cargo" is delivered at the border, or, in some cases, abandoned. In the case of human trafficking, which often involves organized criminals, the victims may initially consent to move to Canada; however, on arrival, they are forced into unpleasant, difficult, or dangerous work, and they are required to pay the trafficker a percentage of the money they earn. They are prevented from either reporting their "employer" to the police, or simply leaving the situation, under threat of prosecution and deportation by Canadian authorities.

Social service workers should be alert to the issue of human trafficking, and should not be afraid to ask questions when they encounter people in circumstances that suggest they might be victims of this crime. Among the possible indicators are

- recent arrivals without permanent resident or refugee status and without family ties in Canada;

- sex trade workers from "exotic" cultures;

- children or minors from foreign countries whose immediate family is not in Canada; and/or

- newcomers who are fearful, or unwilling to talk about their immigration status or employment arrangements.

Victims of human trafficking who are under the control of criminals may resist offers of help. When there are grounds for possible concern about a client, a logical first step for a social service worker might be to ensure that the client understands Canada's immigration laws. The person may be under the influence of threats about

Critical Perspectives

New Law to Address Trafficking of Strippers

Under the *Immigration and Refugee Protection Act*, immigration officers have been unable to deny a work permit to someone who meets all the requirements to enter Canada, even if they believe there is a strong possibility of exploitation or abuse. For years "exotic dancers" have been brought into Canada by traffickers who enslave them once they are here. Many are forced into prostitution.

On May 16, 2007, Minister of Citizenship and Immigration Diane Finley introduced amendments to the Act intended to address this issue by giving the Minister of Citizenship and Immigration the authority to instruct immigration officers to deny work permits to foreigners, including exotic dancers, who could be subjected to humiliating and degrading treatment, including sexual exploitation, in Canada.

"It will also ensure that Canada's immigration system is not used by criminals to victimize people. For those people applying to enter our country, Canada represents hope, safety and a new start. This is one more measure that helps ensure that this hope is not shattered through exploitation, and that the expectation of safety within Canada is preserved," added Minister Finley. ◇

what will happen to her if she discloses her situation, and these threats may be based on misinformation. Arranging a confidential consultation with legal clinic staff or an immigration consultant may help to reassure the client and encourage her to take appropriate steps toward either obtaining permanent resident status or returning home.

KEY TERMS

citizen	immigration	refugee
convention	non-refoulement	sponsorship
Convention refugee	permanent resident	treaty
human smuggling	permanent resident status	undertaking
human trafficking	person in need of protection	

REFERENCES

Convention Against Torture and Other Cruel, Inhuman, or Degrading Treatment or Punishment (1984) 1465 UNTS 85; Can. TS 1987 No. 36.

Geneva Convention, 1951 Convention relating to the Status of Refugees and 1967 Protocol.

Immigration and Refugee Protection Act, SC 2001, c. 27.

REVIEW QUESTIONS

1. Why does Citizenship and Immigration Canada (CIC) impose qualifying criteria on immigration candidates?

2. What are the four general categories of immigrants favoured by Canada's immigration policy?

3. Which characteristics, in immigrants, are most strictly screened out by Canada's immigration policy?

4. What is permanent resident status, and why do immigrants to Canada need it?

5. Why are the family class immigration rules especially complex when it comes to children adopted abroad?

6. What support must a family class sponsor pledge to an applicant for immigration, and what must the applicant pledge in return?

7. What are the basic requirements for eligibility to enter Canada as a skilled worker?

8. How is a person's claim for refugee status assessed when he applies for that status while outside Canada? What about after arrival in Canada?

9. On what basis can a person be admitted as a refugee?

10. Which classes of prospective immigrants cannot, under the current law, appeal the decision to exclude them?

11. If an immigrant is afraid that she will be in danger if, after being denied refugee status, she is returned to her country of origin, what should she do?

12. What are some of the warning signs that might alert a social service worker to the possibility that a client or contact may be a victim of human trafficking?

DISCUSSION QUESTIONS

The following scenarios are based on actual cases heard by the IRB's Refugee Protection Division. Which applicants, do you think, would be eligible for refugee status, and which would not?

1. Jim Harris is a US soldier who, while deployed on a mission in Afghanistan, sought conscientious non-combatant status. His application was refused by the US military. When Mr. Harris received news that his unit would be deployed to Iraq, he left the unit without leave and came to Canada. He sought protection as a refugee on the basis that the court martial he would face in the United States for dereliction of duty would amount to cruel and unusual punishment.

2. Sean Kubrick, his wife, Mona, and their young children, Buttercup and Crystal—all US citizens—appear before the IRB seeking refugee status. Sean claims that, because he suffers from cancer and uses marijuana to relieve his symptoms, he cannot return to the United States. As a marijuana user, he fears persecution (which, he alleges, includes prosecution) and a possible jail term. Mona seeks refugee status on the basis that she may be prosecuted for helping to acquire marijuana for Sean, and that the children's aid society in her state has threatened to take Buttercup and Crystal into custody because of their father's use of an illegal substance.

3. Julio Mendes is a citizen of Colombia who attended university in the United States in the 1990s but returned to Colombia to provide for his family. In 2004, he began receiving telephone calls from a person who identified himself as a member of the Colombian FARC-EP guerilla organization. The caller demanded a payment of US $4,000 and made threats against Mr. Mendes and his family. Mr. Mendes sought protection from the Colombian government, but none was offered. Feeling that he had no alternative, Mr. Mendes fled to Canada and, upon arrival, immediately claimed refugee status. In the course of hearing his case, the IRB reviews evidence that the FARC-EP guerilla group has a history of violence, "disappearances," and other crimes against citizens throughout Colombia, and that the government has been unable to effectively prevent the group's criminal activities.

CHAPTER 19

Housing

CHAPTER OBJECTIVES

After reading this chapter, you should be able to:

- Identify the statute that governs relations between landlords and tenants in Ontario.

- Describe some of the legal rights and obligations of landlords and tenants.

- Describe the non-profit housing system in Ontario and explain how it is administered.

- List some of the rules that govern access to and retention of non-profit housing.

- Explain the concept of cooperative housing.

- Describe how human rights legislation protects access to housing.

INTRODUCTION

Social service workers can help clients with many aspects of housing. For example, they can

- find emergency shelter for abused women, runaways, and people living on the street;

- support clients in navigating the rental housing system and asserting their rights as tenants;

- assist clients in accessing non-profit subsidized housing or co-op housing; and

- help clients in financial difficulty to keep their home—for example, by assisting them in applying for income support and referring them to credit counselling, if necessary.

Adequate housing is fundamental to a person's health, security, and well-being. For most people, it is their largest single household expense. Those who can afford to purchase a home are generally less likely to seek assistance from a social service agency in meeting their housing needs than those who rent. Accordingly, this chapter will focus on issues related to rental housing—both unsubsidized rentals and government-subsidized housing for low-income families. Since these issues often involve tenants' rights, it is useful for social service workers to have a general knowledge of the legislation governing landlord–tenant relations. However, because the law in this area changes frequently, to be certain that a particular rule still applies, you will need to refer to the current legislation and any pending amendments.

RENTAL HOUSING

In an unregulated rental market, tenants are generally at a disadvantage in negotiating with landlords over rent, repairs, and other issues. To protect them, governments have enacted legislation regulating many aspects of the rental housing system. It has been a challenge for policy makers to arrive at a regime that achieves a fair balance between the rights of tenants and those of landlords, and landlord–tenant legislation has a history of frequent amendment. Ontario is no exception. It recently introduced a substantially revised statute, the *Residential Tenancies Act, 2006* (RTA), replacing the *Tenant Protection Act, 1997*.

A number of other statutes contain provisions governing the regulation of rental housing and the protection of tenants. This section describes how Ontario's legislative framework addresses the following concerns:

- *Safety*: compliance with legislated standards.

- *Rent*: provincial rent control and the procedure for increasing rent.

- *Contractual terms*: tenants' and landlords' rights and obligations.

Safety Standards

Several Ontario statutes prescribe standards for the construction of residential buildings, and the installation and maintenance of mechanical equipment in those buildings. These standards are designed to ensure the safety of occupants. Two examples of Ontario statutes prescribing these standards are the *Building Code Act* and the *Fire Protection and Prevention Act* (specifically, the fire code in regulation 388/97 under the Act).

Commercial multi-unit apartment buildings must pass building code, fire code, and electrical inspections before they can be used to house tenants. Buildings with elevators must also comply with the *Technical Standards and Safety Act*.

Home renovations to create rental units must also meet building code, fire code, and electrical standards. Rental units in private homes, such as duplexes and basement apartments, are required to be registered with the local property authority. Before renting the unit, the homeowner must

- ensure that local bylaws permit the rental of such units in private homes;

- have the apartment inspected by officials from the fire department and receive a notice of compliance; and

- have the apartment inspected by the Ontario Electrical Safety Authority.

A tenant cannot be prosecuted for renting a non-legal apartment; however, the tenant runs the risk of being forced to move out if the arrangement comes to the attention of local authorities. In addition, if the owner has not obtained legal registered status, this may be an indication that the apartment lacks important safety features.

Residential Tenancies Act, 2006

SO 2006, c. 17

Objective: To protect residential tenants from unlawful rent increases and unlawful evictions, to balance the rights and responsibilities of residential landlords and tenants, and to provide for the adjudication of disputes.

Target Population: Residential tenants and landlords in Ontario.

Program Administration: Ministry of Municipal Affairs and Housing.

Administrative Tribunal: Disputes between landlords and tenants are heard by the Landlord and Tenant Board.

Summary: The *Residential Tenancies Act, 2006* provides that a landlord may increase the rent only once per year where there is no change in tenant. The Act also provides for minimum rights for all tenants including the right to quiet enjoyment of the property and the right to have it maintained, and procedures for eviction. ◇

Before agreeing to rent an apartment, whether in a private home or a multi-unit building, a tenant should check for the following fire protection features:

- working smoke detectors;
- working carbon monoxide detectors (if applicable);
- separation from other living quarters by fire-resistant construction materials;
- modern electrical wiring with no signs of trouble (for example, lights that flicker);
- separate exit; and
- alternate exit, such as a large and accessible window.

Tenants must consider their own individual needs when assessing the safety features of an apartment. For example, an apartment on an upper level in a house, or above the main or second floor in a multi-unit building, would not be a good choice for a person who has difficulty climbing stairs.

Rent Control

Rent control refers to the government's regulation of maximum annual rent increases for rental properties. When there is high demand for rental properties and a low vacancy rate, landlords are often motivated to increase rents to maximize their income. Before the introduction of legislated caps on rent increases, tenants were vulnerable to being forced out of their homes because of rents they could no longer afford.

The first rent control legislation in Ontario was introduced during the Second World War. Today, rent control is governed by the new residential tenancies statute, the RTA, and regulations under that Act. The law provides that a landlord can increase the rent for a residential unit only once in a 12-month period, unless there is

WEB LINK

The current maximum rate of increase in residential rents is available from the Ministry of Municipal Affairs and Housing at www.mah.gov.on.ca.

a change in tenant. The government also announces, each year, the recommended maximum amount by which the rent may be increased, expressed as a percentage. The permitted rate of increase (often referred to as "the guideline") has declined since the 1970s, reflecting the decline in the inflation rate over this period. In 1975, the guideline was 8.0 percent; in 2006, it was 1.5 percent, the lowest rate since rent control began.

A landlord can apply to increase the rent above the permitted rate where the increase can be justified on the basis of additional costs, such as renovation of the unit or an unusual increase in fuel or electricity costs. The landlord must submit the application to the Landlord and Tenant Board (LTB) and inform the tenant of the requested increase. The tenant is entitled to contest the increase at a hearing of the tribunal. A landlord is also required to give a tenant notice of any increase in rent at least 90 days before the proposed increase will take effect.

If a landlord does not comply with the increase and notice requirements, and attempts to raise a tenant's rent above the guideline, the tenant can file an application with the LTB to have the rent reduced, or to have the increase limited to the maximum permitted by the guideline. Before taking this step, it is usually a good idea to discuss the proposed increase with the landlord directly, since it may be possible to resolve the issue informally.

Applications to the LTB are discussed briefly below.

Tenancy Agreements

All Canadian provinces have passed legislation that imposes limits on conditions that landlords and tenants may include in the contracts (tenancy agreements, or leases) that they make with each other. In Ontario, the RTA provides tenants with minimum rights that may not be contracted away; in other words, tenants may enforce these rights against landlords, even if the tenancy agreement they signed says otherwise. Rights of tenants include the right to quiet enjoyment of the premises, the right to have the premises maintained, and the right to occupy the premises until given proper notice of termination of the tenancy. Tenants also have the right of recourse to the LTB in the event of a dispute.

QUIET ENJOYMENT

Quiet enjoyment refers to the right to occupy and use the rented premises free from unexpected intrusions by the landlord. In general, a landlord cannot enter the rented premises except at the tenant's request (for example, to make a repair) unless the landlord gives the tenant notice of entry, usually at least 24 hours in advance. This restriction may be suspended or altered in case of emergency, or where the tenant is planning to move out and is required to provide access for the purpose of showing the premises to prospective new tenants.

MAINTAINING THE PROPERTY

The RTA governs maintenance of the property and the landlord's duty to keep the premises in good repair. Tenants are expected to facilitate maintenance by advising the landlord of problems and by giving the landlord reasonable access to the premises so that repairs may be made.

Where a problem relates to a vital service, such as plumbing or heating, the landlord is expected to fix the problem without delay. If the tenant is left without heat or water for more than a day or two because of the landlord's neglect, the tenant may apply to the LTB for a remedy. The LTB may make an order requiring the landlord to make the necessary repairs, or to compensate the tenant for having paid for the repairs herself. The LTB may also order a rent reduction. However, the tenant may not refuse to pay the rent, or pay only part of the rent, without an order from the LTB.

Tenants are responsible for day-to-day upkeep such as cleaning, and may be held liable to compensate the landlord for unusual damage to the property. "Normal wear and tear" will not give rise to liability.

NOTICE OF TERMINATION OF THE TENANCY

Because shelter is an essential need, the RTA limits the ability of landlords to evict tenants. Tenants are generally entitled to at least one month's notice of eviction, even if the tenant is not paying the rent or is otherwise in breach of the tenancy agreement. A tenant who comes home to find that the locks have been changed is almost always entitled to re-entry. If the landlord refuses, the tenant should call the police.

In certain circumstances, the RTA permits a landlord to evict a tenant with less than one month's notice. Examples of tenant behaviour that may justify a shorter notice period include the following:

- conducting an illegal "trade, business or occupation" on the premises, such as selling drugs;

- wilfully or negligently causing damage to the premises, such as kicking holes in the wall;

- interfering with the "reasonable enjoyment" of other tenants, such as hosting loud, late-night parties;

- seriously impairing the safety of another person on the premises, such as allowing a vicious dog to roam the building; and

- allowing occupation of the unit by more people than are permitted by local bylaws.

If the offending behaviour stops, the tenant may be allowed to stay.

Tenants are also required to provide notice of termination; the notice period varies according to the terms of the tenancy agreement. Generally, where a tenant has a 12-month lease, he must give notice at least 60 days in advance. If the tenant wants to move out before the expiry of the term, he still owes payment of rent for the remaining months of the lease. In this situation, the tenant may consider finding a new tenant to move in and **sublet**. Provided that the rent continues to be paid, the landlord may not unreasonably refuse to allow a **subtenant** to occupy the unit.

LANDLORD AND TENANT BOARD

The LTB was created to resolve problems that arise between landlords and tenants. Both landlords and tenants have the right to apply to the LTB for relief, depending upon the circumstances. The most common relief sought by landlords is an eviction order. Tenants typically come before the board requesting an order that the landlord make repairs. Either party can apply to the LTB for an order with respect to rent (raising or lowering it).

Proceedings at the LTB are relatively brief, and are designed to be simple enough to allow parties to represent themselves, without the presence of a lawyer. In order to assist clients who expect to appear before the LTB, a social service worker should become familiar with the board's procedures. These are available from the LTB website or from the local board office. The client will need to obtain a copy if she intends to represent herself.

In some cases, a client who wishes to apply to the LTB may benefit from the advice and assistance of a lawyer or paralegal. The role of a social service worker in helping a client to find affordable legal services is discussed in chapter 15.

NON-PROFIT HOUSING

Finding affordable housing is often difficult for low-income people, particularly in cities, where the demand for modestly priced rental accommodation typically exceeds the supply. To address this problem, government subsidies are available to non-profit housing providers.

All three levels of government—federal, provincial, and municipal—contribute funds for non-profit housing, as do many community organizations and charitable donors. Non-profit housing providers encourage the building of affordable housing units and offer these units to people who cannot afford to pay market rents. In non-profit housing, sometimes called social housing or supportive housing, rent is typically paid by tenants on a geared-to-income scale. Most housing advocates agree that to be considered "affordable," housing costs should not exceed 30 percent of family or household income.

The administration of non-profit housing in Ontario is currently governed by the *Social Housing Reform Act, 2000* (SHRA) and regulations. Relations between the tenants and the non-profit housing provider (the landlord) are governed by the RTA, except with respect to the amount of rent paid.

The Non-Profit Housing System

The non-profit housing system in Ontario is regulated by the Ministry of Municipal Affairs and Housing. Currently, non-profit housing is available from a complex patchwork of almost 1,500 public and private providers. A non-profit housing provider is any not-for-profit corporation that receives government subsidies to offset rents. A list of non-profit housing providers is included in regulation 298/01 (table 2) under the SHRA.

Until 2001, the Ontario government directly owned and managed non-profit "public housing" providers. However, with the introduction of a new policy known as "devolution," responsibility for the administration of most non-profit housing was shifted to the municipal level. The provincial and federal governments continue to provide funding for non-profit housing, but the "public housing" label has been dropped.

Under the present system, non-profit housing providers fall into three general categories:

WEB LINK

Information about the Landlord and Tenant Board, including application and hearing procedures, is available at www.ltb.gov.on.ca.

WEB LINK

The *Social Housing Reform Act, 2000* and regulations can be found at two websites: www.e-laws.gov .on.ca and www.canlii.org.

Social Housing Reform Act, 2000

SO 2000, c. 27

Objective: To provide for the administration of social housing programs by service managers.

Target Population: People in Ontario who are unable to pay market rent for housing.

Program Administration: The provincial and federal governments provide funding, but the administration of most non-profit housing is carried out by service managers at the municipal level.

Administrative Tribunal: Not applicable—review is available before an eligibility review officer.

Summary: The *Social Housing Reform Act, 2000* and regulations govern eligibility for public housing and provide that local service managers may make rules that apply to the projects and providers under their control. The Act requires a coordinated access system to fairly manage applications for non-profit housing. Potential tenants may also apply for a subsidy that allows them to pay rent-geared-to-income rent. ◇

- *Private non-profits.* These providers have no direct link to government. They can be community agencies, or housing organizations or projects created by service clubs, religious organizations, or ethnic groups. An example of such a provider is the Ja'Fari Islamic Housing Corporation in the region of York.

- *Municipal non-profits.* These providers are 100 percent owned and operated by local service managers (municipalities). More than 100 Ontario municipalities operate non-profit housing projects.

- *Local housing corporations.* These providers were formerly owned by the province and are now owned by local service managers. Unlike municipal non-profits, they are managed by their own separate and distinct boards.

Currently, the supply of non-profit housing in Ontario falls far short of the demand: in the summer of 2006, there were approximately 224,000 non-profit housing units and 158,000 additional applicants on waiting lists. While new units are under construction or in the planning stages, these will not come close to meeting existing and projected needs. It is hard to argue with critics who describe the present state of affordable housing in Ontario as a crisis.

The non-profit housing system serves several client groups. While many occupants are low-income earners or recipients of social assistance, a substantial number are people who require assistance with daily living. According to the ONPHA, non-profit housing units are allocated as follows:

- Seniors: 32 percent

- People with special needs (including mental illness, developmental disability, chronic homelessness): 11percent

- Other families and single individuals: 57 percent

Critical Perspectives

Does Ontario Deserve a Failing Grade for Housing?

The Ontario Non-Profit Housing Association (ONPHA) reports that 42 percent of Ontario households are spending more than 30 percent of their income on housing, and 20 percent are spending more than 50 percent. According to the ONPHA, Canada is "the only industrialized nation without a national housing strategy."

In the late 1980s and early 1990s, Ontario added an average of 7,500 non-profit housing units each year. Between 1996 and 2000, however, no new units were added, and fewer than 500 units were added between 2000 and 2005. The availability of for-profit rental housing is declining as well: the number of rental apartments that have been demolished or converted to condominiums in the last 10 years surpasses the number of new units created for the rental market.

The Centre for Equality Rights in Accommodation (CERA—a non-profit advocacy group) suggests that the supply of rental housing is only part of the problem. In many areas of the province, there is sufficient rental housing available; the problem is that the working poor and people on social assistance cannot afford it. CERA calls for a needs-based shelter supplement to assist those in the most desperate circumstances.

More information on advocacy for affordable accommodation is available from the Centre for Equality Rights in Accommodation at www.equalityrights.org/cera. ◊

Applying for Housing

To ensure fairness and maximize efficiency, the SHRA mandates the creation of a coordinated access system to manage applications for non-profit housing. Coordination is important since it would be inefficient and unwieldy if individuals submitted multiple applications to a number of housing providers. Under the coordinated access system, applicants across the province fill out a standardized application form to be placed on the list for non-profit housing in the applicant's area. An applicant can apply to be considered for particular buildings only, or for any non-profit housing unit in the community that is appropriate to her needs. Applying for the first available space usually shortens the waiting time on the list (which, in some areas, can be as much as 10 years).

Applications must be made in person at a **coordinated access centre** in the applicant's area. Many of these centres are operated by community organizations that have taken on the task of helping people find housing. A list of coordinated access centres in communities across the province is available from the ONPHA.

Some non-profit housing providers are excluded from the coordinated access system, including federally managed projects (which fall outside the jurisdiction of the SHRA), housing for the homeless or hard to house, and residential facilities managed by the Ministry of Health and Long-Term Care and the Ministry of Community and Social Services. People who are looking for housing that falls into one of these categories generally have to apply to the non-profit provider directly.

The rules that govern eligibility for housing are prescribed, in part, by the SHRA and related regulations. However, section 75(5) of the SHRA provides that a service

WEB LINK

For the location of coordinated access centres and information about non-profit housing providers, visit the website of the Ontario Non-Profit Housing Association at www.onpha.on.ca.

manager (municipality) can make local rules that apply to the projects and providers under its control. For this reason, the specific rules relating to applications and eligibility can vary from community to community. The following discussion summarizes the more important rules in the legislation and regulations that generally apply to all applicants.

To qualify to be placed on the waiting list for housing, applicants must

- be Canadian citizens, permanent residents, or persons who have applied for refugee status;

- have no unpaid arrears of rent from a prior non-profit housing placement;

- have no convictions for misrepresentation of income or for fraud in the last two years;

- be able to live independently without special care or support (unless such assistance is offered by the non-profit housing provider); and

- commit to selling any permanent residence that the applicant or family owns within six months of moving into non-profit housing.

Regulation 368/01 under the SHRA defines high-need households and sets maximum household income limits for non-profit housing applicants in each region. Regulation 298/01 provides rules governing many aspects of the application process, including the following:

- the procedure for requesting consideration as a member of a special priority group;

- the consequences of becoming ineligible for subsidy while living in non-profit housing, or of becoming ineligible to occupy a unit of the size the tenant is living in;

- the calculation of subsidized rents; and

- the procedure for requesting a review of a housing decision.

An applicant for non-profit housing can apply for a subsidy that will allow her to pay **rent geared to income** (RGI)—that is, below market rent. About 80 percent of non-profit housing residents pay RGI. Residents who pay market rent include former RGI tenants who no longer qualify for the subsidy because their financial situation has improved, and residents who occupy non-profit housing for non-economic reasons, such as disability. Market rent for non-profit housing is generally more affordable than market rent in the for-profit sector.

While non-profit housing units are generally awarded on the basis of financial need and seniority on the waiting list, some non-profits are permitted to give priority to applicants in special circumstances—for example, victims of family violence. When an applicant reaches the top of the list for one of the buildings she has applied for, she will be offered a unit. She has the right to refuse the unit, but after three refusals, her name will be removed from the list.

An applicant can also be removed from the list for failing to notify the coordinated access centre, within 10 days, of a change in information such as address, phone number, income, or citizenship/residence status.

Continued Eligibility

Once an applicant has been accepted for non-profit housing, and has qualified for an RGI subsidy, he must continue to qualify in order to retain the unit and the subsidy. While stability in housing is an important goal, it is more important to match the service to the need. When affordable housing is so scarce, it isn't fair for people to remain in non-profit housing if their income increases substantially, or to remain in the assigned unit if members of the family move out and the remaining members become **overhoused**—that is, occupying a unit that is larger than they need.

Section 67(2) of the SHRA allows the service manager in charge of a non-profit housing provider to review a tenant's eligibility status on a periodic basis. While an applicant remains on the waiting list, a review is conducted every 24 months. Once a tenant is living in a non-profit housing unit, a review is conducted every 12 months. As part of the review, the applicant or tenant is required to provide any documentation requested by the review officer that is relevant to the review process.

Section 12 of regulation 298/01 lists facts and circumstances that may lead to a finding of ineligibility. They include the following:

- At the time of application, the applicant failed to meet one of the basic eligibility criteria for being put on the waiting list.

- The applicant or tenant has ceased to meet one of the basic eligibility criteria (for example, because his application for refugee status has been rejected).

- The applicant does not meet a local eligibility criterion (imposed by the local service manager).

- The applicant has not notified the service manager of changes in information provided on the application form.

- The tenant, or family, has occupied the unit for more than six months and has not yet sold a permanent residence that he, or a family member, owns.

- The applicant has declined to accept any of three offers of non-profit housing, or the tenant has declined to move to a smaller unit despite a request to do so by the service manager and being offered three different units.

- The tenant has failed to comply with a rent increase based on a review of RGI.

As well as complying with requests for information and eligibility reviews, an applicant or tenant has an ongoing obligation to make reasonable efforts to obtain financial assistance from all available sources. These sources may relate to more than one member of the household and can include the following:

- spousal support or child support,

- employment insurance benefits,

- Ontario Works benefits,

- disability benefits,

- pension benefits, and

- money promised under an immigration sponsorship agreement.

A **family support worker**, designated under section 159(3) of the SHRA, may assist anyone eligible for an RGI subsidy in pursuing financial support from persons with a legal obligation to provide it. Family support workers (who may be trained as social service workers) perform a role similar to that described in chapter 8, in the context of income assistance. However, family support workers designated under the SHRA are also granted the authority to collect and disclose personal information from clients for the purpose of bringing legal proceedings to enforce general rights to financial assistance, or to enforce legal judgments (for example, from a personal injury lawsuit), on behalf of housing clients.

Generally, there is an expectation that a person who is owed money, such as unpaid child support or other debt, should collect that money before asking for public assistance. However, if to do so would pose a risk to the person's safety—for example, if it might disclose her whereabouts to a violent ex-spouse—she may be exempt from the obligation to pursue her right to support.

Challenging Non-Profit Housing Decisions

The SHRA provides that a service manager must give notice to applicants and tenants of any decisions regarding, for example, their eligibility for housing, continued eligibility, an increase to geared-to-income rent, or the type of unit for which they qualify. Where the service manager is required to make a decision that could have adverse consequences (for example, the applicant is found to be ineligible for non-profit housing, or the tenant will have to move because he no longer qualifies or has become overhoused), the applicant or tenant has a "right to comment" under section 80 of the SHRA. The particulars of how to exercise this right are described in section 55 of regulation 298/01. Comments must be in writing and must be submitted within a specified time after notice of the decision.

If a decision is unfavourable, the applicant or tenant (referred to as a "household member") may be entitled to request an internal review under section 82 of the SHRA. The following are the kinds of decisions that can form the subject of an internal review:

- eligibility for RGI assistance,
- eligibility for special-needs housing,
- type of accommodation,
- waiting list category into which the household has been placed,
- amount of RGI payable by the household, and
- deferral of RGI payable by the household.

The process for internal review is described in section 58 of regulation 298/01. Social service workers should note that the tenant or person affected must request the review in writing and deliver the request to the service manager, supportive housing provider, or lead agency that made the decision in question, within 10 business days of receiving notice of the decision.

The person who conducts the review cannot be the same person who made the original decision. In most cases, the reviewer has 10 business days to complete the review and a further 5 business days to give the tenant or affected person notice of the decision. Certain kinds of reviews must be completed within a shorter time frame, and in some cases, the local rules governing service managers allow them to take longer than 15 days to report. An applicant or tenant who requests a review should try to find out when a decision can be expected.

> ### WEB LINK
>
> An innovative form of non-profit housing has been developed by Habitat for Humanity, an international non-profit organization, which builds low-cost houses with the help of volunteers and sells them to recipients on a non-profit basis. The Toronto office has completed more than 100 homes in the area since 1988. For more information, visit www.habitat.org or www.torontohabitat.on.ca.

CO-OPERATIVE HOUSING

About a quarter of a million Canadians live in housing co-operatives. The majority of housing co-operatives are non-profit; the co-op is owned by a not-for-profit corporation, which operates the co-op for the benefit of the members and has no other commercial purpose.

Although sometimes included in the definition of social housing, **co-operative housing** differs from non-profit tenant housing in that the members of a housing co-operative are not tenants in the true sense. Each member has a quasi-ownership interest in the co-op and a share of the responsibility for its management and day-to-day operations. Members delegate decision-making authority to a board of directors, elected by themselves. In addition, members organize and work on committees with responsibility for specific functions, such as indoor and outdoor maintenance.

Co-op members pay a monthly housing fee (and often, on admission to the co-op, fees for the first and last months), plus a membership charge and a damage deposit. These fees are similar to rent. A member of a co-op cannot sell her unit or her ownership interest in the unit.

Housing co-ops and their members are not subject to provincial residential tenancies legislation (in Ontario, the RTA). Instead, they are regulated by legislation governing cooperative organizations (which include co-ops formed for purposes other than housing, such as product marketing, retail sales, and financial services). Under Ontario's *Co-operative Corporations Act* (CCA), co-ops retain the authority to create and pass bylaws governing their management and operation. The CCA deals mainly with corporate governance issues (for example, how members of the co-op vote on administrative matters). Co-op bylaws usually deal with specific issues; for example, in a housing co-op, who is responsible for making repairs and what happens if a member is in arrears in paying his housing fees. Every member of a housing co-op is expected to comply with its bylaws and rules. It is therefore important for a new member to obtain a copy of those bylaws and rules, and to make sure that she understands her rights and responsibilities as a member.

One of those rights is the entitlement to propose and vote on changes to the bylaws and rules. The decision of the majority must be accepted, even if a member disagrees with it. If a serious conflict arises, and a member has exhausted all means of resolving it within the democratic structure of the co-op, the member may need to hire a lawyer to determine whether the co-op is acting within the scope of the law and its own bylaws. For example, in a case of eviction, the co-op must comply with the relevant provisions of the CCA, as well as the Ontario *Human Rights Code* (discussed below).

The government (federal and/or provincial/territorial) may provide some financial support for the development of cooperative housing and assistance with monthly housing charges for some co-op members, similar to the subsidy available through RGI for tenants in non-profit housing.

As a social service worker, if you have a client who is interested in moving into cooperative housing, you should make sure that he understands the kinds of responsibilities associated with living in a co-op. You can assist the client in finding out what options are available by directing him to a local co-operative housing association.

WEB LINK
More information on co-operative housing is available from the Canada Mortgage and Housing Corporation at www.cmhc-schl.gc.ca and the Co-operative Housing Federation of Canada at www.chfcanada.coop.

ACCESS TO HOUSING: HUMAN RIGHTS ISSUES

Since everyone needs shelter, human rights abuses in the context of access to housing have a particularly serious impact. As discussed earlier (and in more detail in chapter 20), federal and provincial human rights legislation prohibits discrimination on specified grounds. In Ontario, the prohibited grounds include sex, age, race, family status, and disability. Receipt of public assistance is an additional prohibited ground of discrimination specific to housing: landlords may not discriminate against tenants and prospective tenants because they are receiving public assistance.

Examples of discrimination that may be prohibited by Ontario's *Human Rights Code* include the following:

- refusing to rent to an unmarried couple;

- asking for a higher amount of rent from a gay or lesbian couple;

- refusing to rent to a disabled person because she was unable to fill out the application form;

- refusing to rent to families with young children; and

- asking for a deposit greater than the last month's rent because the prospective tenant is receiving public assistance.

An exception is made permitting restricted access to a housing program aimed specifically at helping people of a particular disadvantaged group, such as mentally ill single men or teenaged parents. This kind of "reverse discrimination" is permitted because such programs are designed to relieve hardship for people who may otherwise face obstacles in finding the housing they need.

Key Issues

While many human rights abuses can arise in the housing context, three issues are of particular interest, being the subject of important court decisions. These involve refusal of housing on the basis of rent-to-income ratios, on the basis of youth, and on the basis of an "adults only" rental policy. Each of these forms of discrimination is discussed below.

RENT-TO-INCOME RATIOS

In the past, it was not uncommon for private landlords in Ontario to require prospective tenants to provide information about their income, so that the landlord could assess the risk that a particular applicant might be unable to pay the rent. The landlord applied what is known as a rent-to-income ratio to decide whether the applicant could afford the apartment. Typically, the rule was that rent could not exceed 30 percent of income.

In the 1990s, this practice was challenged before an Ontario human rights board of inquiry. In *Kearney v. Bramalea Ltd.*, a landlord refused to rent apartments to three low-income applicants on the basis that the rent amounted to more than 30 percent of their income. The complainants were represented by a lawyer who took the case on a *pro bono* basis. The issue in the case was of wider public interest because the use of rent-to-income ratios can leave people homeless and forced to live in shelters even though they are able and willing to pay rent. Often the people who are put in this position are those with modest incomes and heavy financial responsibilities, such as young single parents and recent immigrants.

The board of inquiry found that the use of rent-to-income ratios is a discriminatory practice, and that the evidence (including a 1999 research report prepared for the Ontario Human Rights Commission) showed that low-income tenants are no less likely to default on the rent than other tenants.

The board of inquiry also found that while it is acceptable for a landlord to request references from previous landlords and to conduct a credit check, it is not acceptable to refuse to rent to an applicant who has no references and no credit history (as opposed to bad references and/or a bad credit history). Again, young people, newly separated single parents, and new immigrants often cannot provide such information, and denying them access to housing on this basis constitutes indirect discrimination.

YOUNG PEOPLE

Landlords are often hesitant to rent apartments to young people in their teens and early 20s, because of a common perception that they will likely default on the rent or be otherwise irresponsible. However, the law is clear that anybody aged 18 and over may rent an apartment; and teens aged 16 and 17 who have withdrawn from parental care and control can rent and can sign the lease in their own right. A landlord is not entitled to require that a parent sign the lease or accept responsibility under the lease on behalf of a young person.

"ADULTS ONLY" BUILDINGS

A landlord may legally designate a building exclusively for people aged 65 and over. However, apart from this "seniors exception," it is discriminatory and illegal to designate a rental apartment as "adults only," or to refuse to rent to someone on the basis that he has children. It is also discriminatory to refuse to rent a unit on the basis of the number of intended occupants unless to do otherwise would violate a local overcrowding bylaw. Most overcrowding bylaws require that the home have a minimum of approximately 100 square feet of space per occupant. This figure generally allows for households where children share bedrooms.

Acting on an Abuse of Rights

If a social service worker encounters a client who is having trouble finding housing, and it appears that he is encountering barriers to access, the social service worker should ask specific questions about his experiences in searching for accommodation. What kinds of questions have landlords been asking? Have landlords given any reasons for either refusing to provide an application for housing or turning down the client's application? If so, what were those reasons?

If the social service worker uncovers evidence of discrimination, as a first step it may be appropriate for the client to go back to the landlord and try to resolve the problem informally. If the client is able to arrange a personal interview with the landlord, the social service worker might offer to accompany him. Sometimes it is enough to make the landlord aware of the client's legal rights.

If informal attempts to resolve the problem don't help, the social service worker can refer the client to an advocacy agency for tenants. There are dozens of these. Some examples are:

- the Federation of Metro Tenants' Associations;

- the International Union of Tenants;

- the Tenant Advocacy Group (affiliated with the Ontario Coalition Against Poverty); and

- the Advocacy Centre for Tenants Ontario.

Advocacy groups have experience with a wide range of tenant issues, and may be able to bring direct or political pressure to bear on landlords.

WEB LINK

Visit a website created by Toronto's Parkdale Tenants Association to award a "Lord of the Slums" title to a "deserving" landlord and post photos of apartments with unacceptable living conditions at www.torontoslumtourism.com.

Critical Perspectives

Assisting Clients Who Are Hard to House

The Ontario *Human Rights Code* prohibits discrimination in the "occupancy of accommodation" and specifies an additional prohibited ground, receipt of public assistance. In other words, a landlord may not refuse to rent on the basis that a person is dependent on public income support. In addition, a landlord may not refuse to rent to a person who is 16 or 17 years old provided that she is no longer under parental care and control.

Despite the protections provided by human rights law, social service workers have many clients who encounter persistent obstacles in their search for accommodation. Helping these **"hard-to-house" clients** often involves advocacy, as well as practical assistance such as providing information about housing options and referrals to appropriate agencies.

While difficulty in finding housing can be explained, in part, by a chronic shortage of affordable rental accommodation, landlords are sometimes reluctant to rent to individuals and families in certain circumstances. These include

- unemployment;

- reliance on social assistance;

- family status (for example, single parent, common-law relationship, same-sex relationship);

- family size (number of dependants relative to income);

- mental illness (difficulty in adapting to independent living or communal housing);

- physical or mental disability;

- a criminal record or recent release from prison;

- lack of financial references (a problem for young renters); and

- lack of rental references (a problem for first-time renters such as new immigrants and young people).

Clients who have no success in applying to commercial landlords may consider renting an apartment or a room in a house. However, they should be aware that rental units in private homes do not always comply with safety standards and bylaws. Moreover, the Ontario Code permits landlords to discriminate in accepting a tenant where the tenant shares the kitchen or bathroom with the owner.

Sometimes attempts to solve these housing problems lead to the creation of ghettos, where low-income families or minority groups are concentrated in housing projects in a particular neighbourhood. This may offer some advantages, such as having many neighbours with a shared language and culture; however, it tends to further marginalize groups that may already be disadvantaged. In recognition of this issue, many social housing projects strive for a mix of rent-geared-to-income and market-rent residents.

When seeking housing for clients, social service workers must strike a balance between the ideal and the practical. While it is not possible to take every difficult landlord to court, discrimination in housing will continue to flourish unless somebody speaks up. Clients who are motivated to stand up for their rights should be directed to legal aid and provided with appropriate support by social service workers. ◇

Ultimately, a tenant who has grounds for a formal complaint may bring his case to the attention of the Ontario Human Rights Commission. The procedure is discussed in chapter 20. A social service worker may provide assistance with a referral to a lawyer, if required, and may also provide support during the hearing process.

WEB LINK

For more information about tenants' rights, visit the website for the Advocacy Centre for Tenants Ontario at www.acto.ca. This organization works with legal clinics, tenant associations, and other groups and individuals concerned about housing issues, through test case litigation, lobbying and law reform, and public legal education.

KEY TERMS

coordinated access centre

co-operative housing

family support worker

hard-to-house client

overhoused

quiet enjoyment

rent control

rent geared to income

sublet

subtenant

REFERENCES

Building Code Act, 1992, SO 1992, c. 23.

Co-operative Corporations Act, RSO 1990, c. C.35.

Fire Protection and Prevention Act, 1997, SO 1997, c. 4.

Human Rights Code, RSO 1990, c. H.19.

Kearney v. Bramalea Ltd., [2001] OJ No. 297 (Div. Ct.).

Residential Tenancies Act, 2006, SO 2006, c. 17.

Social Housing Reform Act, 2000, SO 2000, c. 27.

Technical Standards and Safety Act, 2000, SO 2000, c. 16.

Tenant Protection Act, 1997, SO 1997, c. 24.

REVIEW QUESTIONS

1. List three fire safety features that tenants should look for in choosing rental housing.

2. What is rent control, and why is it important?

3. Under what circumstances may a landlord enter the tenant's unit?

4. What should a tenant do if there is a problem with a vital service such as plumbing or heating?

5. Name the three general categories of non-profit housing providers and briefly explain the differences between them.

6. How does one apply for non-profit housing?

7. What is rent geared to income (RGI)?

8. People who apply for or live in non-profit housing are expected to make reasonable efforts to obtain financial assistance from all available sources. Name three possible sources.

9. What are rent-to-income ratios, and what is their significance?

10. How can a social service worker assist a client who says she is having trouble finding housing because the landlords she has approached are discriminating against her?

DISCUSSION QUESTIONS

List a variety of approaches that a community may explore in solving the housing problems of people with low income and others who are vulnerable or hard to house. Consider temporary and long-term solutions. What are the advantages and disadvantages of each approach?

Other Aspects of the Legal Context

CHAPTER 20

Human Rights Legislation

CHAPTER OBJECTIVES

After reading this chapter, you should be able to:

- Identify the federal and Ontario statutes that define and protect human rights.

- List the human rights that are protected under Canadian law, and some that are not.

- Describe the scope of application of the federal and Ontario human rights statutes.

- List the grounds on which it is illegal to discriminate under these statutes.

- Explain how a person can seek redress for a violation of human rights.

INTRODUCTION

Canada, like most other countries, recognizes that every individual has certain rights that are essential to personal dignity and the preservation of society. The range of recognized rights varies greatly and includes, for example, the right to life and liberty, the right to safety from violence, the right to basic health care, the right to food and shelter, the right to equality before and under the law, the right to free speech, and the right to religious belief and practice. Individual countries may not formally recognize all of these rights; however, many have agreed to endorse certain rights set out in international treaties. Treaties to which Canada is a **signatory** include the following:

- the Convention on the Prevention and Punishment of the Crime of Genocide,

- the International Convention on the Elimination of All Forms of Racial Discrimination,

- the International Covenant on Economic, Social and Cultural Rights,

- the International Covenant on Civil and Political Rights,

- the Convention on the Non-Applicability of Statutory Limitations to War Crimes and Crimes Against Humanity,

- the International Convention on the Suppression and Punishment of the Crime of Apartheid,

- the Convention on the Elimination of All Forms of Discrimination Against Women,

- the Convention Against Torture and Other Cruel, Inhuman or Degrading Treatment or Punishment,

- the Convention on the Rights of the Child, and

- the International Convention on the Protection of the Rights of All Migrant Workers and Members of their Families.

Often, the content of international human rights law can influence the development of human rights legislation within individual countries, and this is true of Canada. As a signatory to international human rights treaties, Canada is expected to reflect principles of international human rights law in its domestic laws.

In Canada, the rights of individuals are protected primarily by the *Canadian Charter of Rights and Freedoms*, and by human rights statutes. The Charter, as part of Canada's constitution, is paramount over other legislation. This means that where legislation conflicts with the terms of the Charter, that legislation is void. For example, in 2004, the Supreme Court ruled that the definition of "spouse" in many statutes violated the right to equality because it was restricted to heterosexual relationships. As a result, the law was changed to conform to the Charter right to equality.

Critical Perspectives

Universal Human Rights, Cultural Diversity, and National Autonomy

Are **human rights** universal, superseding culture and religion, or are they relative, merely expressing the culture and beliefs predominant in western democracies? This boils down to a basic question that has troubled philosophers for centuries: How does one know what is morally right?

Having tolerance and respect for cultures and religions different from one's own is itself a cultural value, reflected in the concept of multiculturalism. We are all familiar with this in Canada. It finds expression in our human rights laws that protect, for example, the right of Sikh students to wear a kirpan (a ceremonial dagger) in public schools. However, there are limits to the freedoms that Canadians will tolerate. For example, the custom of female genital mutilation is a criminal offence in Canada. We draw the line when a cultural value transgresses a prohibition under Canadian law, such as inflicting personal injury or harm.

There are many cultural and religious practices that are incompatible with the human rights expressed in international treaties, and this incompatibility can cause conflict and resentment. Should human rights laws formulated by one group of countries be extended to all, at the expense of longstanding traditions and values? And what happens when it is Canada that is found to be in violation of human rights? Consider the case of *Waldman v. Canada*, ccpr/c/67/D/694/1996, in which the Human Rights Committee (established under the International Covenant on Civil and Political Rights) ruled that Canada's funding of Roman Catholic schools, and not schools of other religions, violates international human rights law. ◈

The Charter is an important safeguard of individual rights in a democratic society, where the prevailing values reflect the will of the majority. The Charter places limits on what the government may do—in the laws it enacts, in the services it provides, in the policies it espouses, and in the conduct of its employees. However, the Charter does not govern the conduct of the private sector. Human rights legislation fills this gap.

These statutes are of interest to social service workers, because of their commitment to helping people in our society who are vulnerable or disadvantaged. An important part of the social service worker's role is to speak on behalf of and provide support to **marginalized** clients—those who are consigned to the fringes of community life, and often overlooked or ignored. People who are poor or belong to a minority group, or who are incapable of defending their own interests because of mental illness, addiction, or disability, are often at risk of being denied their statutory rights.

THE CANADIAN CHARTER OF RIGHTS AND FREEDOMS

Chapter 2 provided a general introduction to the Charter and listed some of the key rights and freedoms guaranteed under its provisions. When you read the Charter, you will quickly see how relevant it is to professionals working in the social service sector. Many of its provisions could apply in the course of everyday practice.

In chapter 2, attention was drawn to the importance of section 1, which limits the scope of application of the Charter where such limits are reasonable, are prescribed by law, and can be "demonstrably justified in a free and democratic society." This section describes how Charter rights can be asserted where a violation is believed to have occurred.

Enforcing Charter Rights

If a law or government action adversely affects a party in apparent violation of a Charter right, that party may seek a remedy by formal application to a court (section 24(1)). Legal arguments made in the course of litigation that assert the violation of Charter rights are known as Charter challenges.

Charter challenges involve a two-step process:

- *Step 1*: The person claiming that a Charter right has been violated must prove that the violation occurred, and that it arose by operation of the law or by government action.

- *Step 2*: The burden then falls to the government to prove that the right in question can be limited in accordance with the law, and why.

If the government succeeds in proving that the limit on the right is reasonable, the challenge fails and the law remains unchanged. If the court finds that the limit is not reasonable and demonstrably justified, the party raising the challenge is entitled to a remedy. Charter remedies to address violations are numerous and include:

- excluding evidence in a criminal trial that was obtained in a manner that infringed the Charter limits on search and seizure;

- court-ordered amendment of legislation to remove an offending section of a statute; and

- declaration that a statute contrary to the Charter is of no force and effect.

Unless a Charter challenge arises in a criminal matter, where the accused is entitled to legal aid if he cannot afford a lawyer, access to legal aid is not guaranteed. Plaintiffs who wish to make a Charter challenge in a civil matter may need to look elsewhere for financial assistance. If you are searching for legal representation for a client's Charter case, it may be helpful to identify:

- advocacy groups that specialize in helping people in the client's situation; and

- other potential plaintiffs who are in the same position as the client (to help bolster the case).

A lawyer may be persuaded to take on the case *pro bono*. As discussed in chapter 15, this will depend on the issues and facts of the case; but it never hurts to ask.

CASES IN POINT

Charter Challenges: Sections 7 and 15(1)

Several cases of interest to social service workers have formed the subject of Charter challenges under sections 7 and 15(1). The issues and decisions in these cases are described briefly below.

Cases Decided Under Section 7

Section 7 provides:

Everyone has the right to life, liberty and security of the person and the right not to be deprived thereof except in accordance with the principles of fundamental justice.

- *Buhlers v. British Columbia (Superintendent of Motor Vehicles)* (1999). Suspending a person's driver's licence (and thus preventing him from using his car) without a trial, under the administrative suspension rules of BC traffic law, does not violate "liberty" as expressed in section 7.

- *Rodriguez v. British Columbia (Attorney General)* (1993). Section 241 of the Criminal Code, which prohibits assisted suicide, does not violate the right to "liberty" (that is, liberty to choose the timing and manner of one's death) as expressed in section 7 of the Charter.

- *Singh v. Minister of Employment and Immigration* (1985). The rules governing the determination of refugee status that were in place at the time of the determination that the Singh family were not Convention refugees were found to be inconsistent with the principles of section 7 the Charter. The Supreme Court confirmed that all people on Canadian soil (including refugee claimants) were entitled not to be deprived of security of the person except in accordance with the principles of fundamental justice. The court ordered that the refugee determination process be changed to incorporate some of those principles, including a right, on the part of refugee claimants, to be heard in the decision-making process.

For a more detailed account of these decisions, see *Buhlers v. British Columbia (Superintendent of Motor Vehicles)* (1999), 132 CCC (3d) 478 (BCCA), leave to appeal to the Supreme Court of Canada refused; *Rodriguez v. British Columbia (Attorney General)*, [1993] 3 SCR 519; and *Singh v. Minister of Employment and Immigration*, [1985] 1 SCR 177.

Cases Decided Under Section 15(1)

Section 15(1) provides:

> Every individual is equal before and under the law and has the right to the equal protection and equal benefit of the law without discrimination and, in particular, without discrimination based on race, national or ethnic origin, colour, religion, sex, age or mental or physical disability.

- *Schachter v. Canada* (1992). Schachter, a new father, challenged a provision of the former *Unemployment Insurance Act* (replaced by the *Employment Insurance Act*) that granted 15 weeks of benefits to adoptive fathers, on the basis that it discriminated against natural fathers. Schachter was successful, and the government's response to his challenge paved the way to paternity leave for all fathers. *Schachter* is considered to be an especially important case because, as a result of the remedy ordered by the court, the government was required to extend the payment of employment insurance benefits in order to ensure equal treatment.

- *Vriend v. Alberta* (1998). Vriend, a gay man, was dismissed from his job because of his homosexuality. He brought a complaint under BC's human rights statute, but his claim failed because sexual orientation was not listed as a prohibited ground for discrimination. Vriend then raised a Charter challenge under section 15 and succeeded. The Supreme Court ordered that sexual orientation should be "read in" as a prohibited ground in all provincial human rights legislation. Discrimination on the basis of sexual orientation is now illegal across Canada.

- *Eldridge v. British Columbia (Attorney General)* (1997). Eldridge, who was born deaf, argued that the failure of the BC medicare system to fund sign language interpreters to facilitate deaf patient–doctor communications constituted discrimination on the basis of disability. The Supreme Court agreed and ordered that the medicare system in BC take steps to accommodate the needs of disabled patients so that they would have equal access to health care.

For a more detailed account of these decisions, see *Schachter v. Canada*, [1992] 2 SCR 679, available online at www.canlii.org/en/ca/scc/doc/1992/1992canlii74/1992canlii74.html; *Vriend v. Alberta*, [1998] 1 SCR 493, available online at www.canlii.org/en/ca/scc/doc/1998/1998canlii816/1998canlii816.html; and *Eldridge v. British Columbia (Attorney General)*, [1997] 3 SCR 624, available online at www.canlii.org/en/ca/scc/doc/1997/1997canlii327/1997canlii327.html. ◇

HUMAN RIGHTS LEGISLATION

While the Charter guarantees certain rights by prohibiting governments from making laws or authorizing actions that infringe those rights, human rights legislation provides protection against infringement of other specified rights through the actions of other persons, including individuals, corporations, and administrators of government offices and agencies. In particular, human rights statutes codify the right to be free from discrimination or harassment on specified grounds, such as race, sex, or disability, with respect to access to, or receipt of, goods and services, employment, and housing. For example, refusing to serve a customer in a restaurant because of his race, deciding not to hire someone because of her sex, or refusing to rent an apartment to someone because of his disability, would be in violation of human rights law.

Service providers should be aware of their obligation not to discriminate against clients on the basis of any of the prohibited grounds. Social service workers may also be called upon to assist clients who have experienced discrimination or harassment in employment, housing, or the provision of goods and services, contrary to human rights legislation.

The federal human rights statute is the *Canadian Human Rights Act*. At the provincial level, each province and territory has its own human rights statute, which is applicable to matters under provincial or territorial jurisdiction. Ontario's statute is called the *Human Rights Code* (referred to here as "the Ontario Code"). The scope of application of each statute is described below.

Jurisdiction

THE FEDERAL STATUTE

The *Canadian Human Rights Act* prohibits discrimination and harassment in matters that fall under the jurisdiction of the federal government, as prescribed by the division of powers set out in the *Constitution Act, 1867*. As you have learned, many aspects of the day-to-day lives of social service clients—housing, employment, education, family services, and health care—are governed primarily by the provinces. Matters that fall into the federal regulatory sphere, and are subject to the protection provided by the *Canadian Human Rights Act*, include the following:

- immigration,
- employment in the federal public service,
- telecommunications,
- federal taxation,
- the federal pension system,
- the design and administration of federal aid programs (excluding programs targeted to specific disadvantaged groups), and
- the approval of plans, in federal spheres of activity, that are designed to assist people with disabilities.

WEB LINK

For information on the the *Canadian Human Rights Act*, and the procedure for seeking a remedy in the event of a violation, visit the website of the Canadian Human Rights Commission at www.chrc-ccdp.ca.

ONTARIO'S STATUTE

The Ontario Code applies to the following matters under the jurisdiction of the province (including those delegated to municipalities):

- property, including housing, real estate, and the regulation of residential tenancies;
- civil rights, including contract and tort rights, most aspects of the family law, and a wide range of commercial and economic rights;
- the incorporation of provincial companies;
- the regulation of employment;
- public hospitals and health care; and
- education.

WEB LINK

For information on the application of Ontario's *Human Rights Code*, and the procedure for seeking a remedy in the event of a violation, visit the website of the Ontario Human Rights Commission at www.ohrc.on.ca.

Prohibited Grounds

Both statutes list prohibited grounds of discrimination. Although there are some differences, generally they include the following:

- race,

- national or ethnic origin,

- colour,

- religion,

- age,

- sex,

- sexual orientation,

- marital status,

- family status (including pregnancy and childbearing),

- physical or mental disability (including dependence on alcohol or drugs), and

- pardoned criminal convictions.

Attributes or characteristics that are not on the list include educational background, political opinion, and personal appearance (such as style of dress, hairstyle, piercings, and tattoos). Discrimination on these grounds is not prohibited by the federal Act or the Ontario Code. It is important to familiarize yourself with the prohibited grounds in both jurisdictions.

CASE IN POINT

Is the Non-Medical Use of Marijuana a "Disability"?

Addictions such as alcoholism or drug use may qualify as disabilities. The scope of human rights law with respect to drug use was recently thrown into question by a ruling of the Alberta Court of Queen's Bench in *Alberta (Human Rights and Citizenship Commission) v. Kellogg Brown & Root (Canada) Company*. The court held that casual marijuana use is a "disability" and should be treated no differently than other disabilities in the hiring process.

The complainant in the case was a recreational marijuana user who had applied for a job working in an oilsands operation. The company's screening process included a pre-employment drug test. When the complainant tested positive for marijuana, he was denied employment.

A panel of the Alberta Human Rights and Citizenship Commission had ruled against the worker. In overturning the decision, the Alberta Court of Queen's Bench criticized the employer's zero tolerance drug policy as an unacceptable limitation on the man's right to work, considering that he never used marijuana while on the job.

For a report of the decision, see *Alberta (Human Rights and Citizenship Commission) v. Kellogg Brown & Root (Canada) Company*, 2006 ABQB 302, available online at www.albertacourts.ab.ca/jdb/2003-/qb/civil/2006/2006abqb0302.cor2.pdf. ◇

Discrimination

The federal and Ontario statutes prohibit both **direct discrimination** and **indirect discrimination** (also called **adverse impact discrimination**). An example of direct discrimination is refusing to hire people of a particular faith. Indirect discrimination is more subtle. For example, an applicant for a job whose manual dexterity is

---

CASE IN POINT

Is a Coroner's Inquest a "Service"?

In a May 2006 decision, the Ontario Human Rights Tribunal ruled that coroner's inquests are a "service" within the meaning of Ontario's *Human Rights Code*, in that they provide information to the family of a deceased person. As a provider of a service to which the Code applies, the Coroner's Office must comply with the "prohibited grounds" requirement in deciding which cases will or will not be investigated.

The decision involved two cases where a complaint was brought by the family of a psychiatric patient who had died while being detained in a psychiatric facility. In the first case, Thomas Illingworth died while under chemical and physical restraints. In the second case, Melba Braithwaite died in the shower while under treatment with drugs that her daughter had requested not be used on her. In each case, the family asked the Coroner's Office to conduct an inquest, but the request was denied.

The tribunal ruled that it is discriminatory for inquests to be mandatory for a person who dies in prison but discretionary for a person who dies while he or she is an involuntary patient in a psychiatric facility.

The issue of discrimination in the application of the *Coroner's Act* to mentally ill patients has been receiving attention since 2002. At the time this book was written, the government had not yet amended the law to make inquests mandatory when deaths occur in psychiatric facilities; but in light of this ruling, it is expected that this change will be made.

A report of the tribunal's decision can be found at *Braithwaite v. Ontario (Attorney General)*, 2006 HRTO 15, currently under appeal to the Divisional Court, available online at www.canlii.org/en/on/onhrt/doc/2006/2006hrto15/2006hrto15.html. ◇

---

limited by arthritis would be disqualified by a company policy requiring all job applicants to meet a minimum typing-speed standard, even though the particular job for which he was applying would involve very little typing. Indirect discrimination is often unintentional: the owner of an apartment building without a wheelchair ramp may not intend to discriminate against people in wheelchairs, but this will be the result. Human rights legislation places an obligation on service providers to ensure that they are not discriminating unintentionally.

Both statutes prohibit discrimination in employment, housing, and the provision of goods and services. Goods and services include those provided commercially in the private sector and those provided by government in the public sector. This definition includes the services of social service workers.

DUTY TO ACCOMMODATE

In many cases, human rights legislation imposes a duty on employers, landlords, and goods and services providers to accommodate the special needs of employees, tenants, and customers and clients. This is particularly important in employment. For example, if an employee is unable to work on particular days for religious reasons, or requires a special chair because of a back injury, it is the responsibility of the employer to accommodate these needs.

The **duty to accommodate** is quite demanding and requires employers to go to considerable expense if necessary—though not to the point of **undue hardship**. The effort required of the employer will vary, depending on the employer's resources and the employee's particular needs. Employers may even be required to adjust the job description to accommodate an employee or job applicant. However, an employer is not required to accommodate an applicant who lacks a bona fide job qualification (discussed in chapter 17).

Social service workers who work with disabled job seekers can help them to assess their job skills, identify jobs that make the best use of those skills, and approach employers with confidence. If a candidate meets resistance, the social service worker should be prepared to assist the client in drawing the employer's attention to his obligations under human rights legislation. In some cases, the client may need assistance and support in bringing a discrimination-based complaint. The procedure is described later in this chapter.

Harassment

Both the federal and the Ontario statutes prohibit **harassment**. Harassment differs from discrimination in that the harasser need not be in a position of power—that is, in a position to subject the victim to "unequal treatment." Generally, harassment means behaving in such a manner as to trouble or annoy the victim, or to make him uncomfortable. If such behaviour causes the victim to fear for his safety, it may constitute **criminal harassment** under section 264 of the *Criminal Code.*

Harassment is defined in the Ontario Code, much more broadly than in the *Criminal Code*, as "engaging in a course of vexatious comment or conduct that is known or ought reasonably to be known to be unwelcome." This definition suggests repeated behaviour rather than a single event.

Both human rights statutes prohibit harassment in the context of employment and housing, but only the federal Act prohibits harassment in the provision of goods and services. Harassment is prohibited on the same grounds as discrimination (as enumerated in the particular statute). In the employment setting, an employer may be held responsible for the harassment of an employee if the employer is aware of it and fails to take reasonable steps to make it stop.

Figure 20.1 provides some examples of conduct that may be considered harassment.

SEXUAL HARASSMENT

Sexual harassment is singled out in both the federal and Ontario human rights statutes because it is such a prevalent and serious issue. While the majority of sexual harassment complaints involve women complaining about harassment by men, men may also be sexually harassed by women; and both men and women may be harassed by others of the same sex.

Sexual harassment is defined broadly by the courts to include a wide range of behaviour. Obvious examples are threats, stalking, sexual touching, and assault (any of which could be considered a criminal offence). However, the following conduct may also constitute sexual harassment:

- sexual jokes, comments, or insults within earshot of a person;
- sexually explicit images displayed in the workplace (calendars, posters, figurines, computer screen savers, etc.);

Figure 20.1   Examples of Harassment in the Context of Employment, Housing, and Provision of Services

	Basis for harassment			
Context	Sex	Race/ethnic origin	Family status	Disability
Employment	Pictures of women in bikinis are posted on the lunchroom bulletin board by some of the male staff.	Some employees make ethnic and racial jokes targeting minorities in the presence of fellow-workers who belong to those groups.	Members of a work group openly express their resentment that their workload will be much heavier when their pregnant co-worker goes on leave.	Whenever a difference of opinion arises between a manager and an employee who has a history of alcoholism, the manager asks, "Are you drunk?"
Housing	An apartment superintendent slips sexually suggestive notes under the door of a tenant who lives alone, making her anxious and uneasy.	An apartment superintendent makes derogatory remarks about the cooking smells from an apartment occupied by an immigrant family.	A landlord regularly makes rude remarks to a single-parent tenant about her five young children.	An apartment superintendent grumbles to a tenant in a wheelchair about the effort required to keep the access ramp free of snow and ice in the winter.
Provision of services	Male workers at a post office wink and exchange whispers when attractive young women come in to buy stamps and pick up mail.	A passenger on an airplane makes racial slurs in the presence of a passenger belonging to the impugned race, and flight attendants who overhear him do not react or intervene.	On an interprovincial train trip, an attendant repeatedly asks a passenger with a crying baby to keep the child quiet.	Employees at a restaurant laugh at an obese customer, mimic her awkward gait, and ask her several times if she is sure she doesn't want to order a dessert.

■ staring or inappropriate compliments;

■ unwanted hugging or similar touching;

■ requiring an employee to wear a revealing uniform.

If a client tells you that she has been sexually harassed, you should encourage her to record the details of the incident(s) in writing, including the date and time, the precise conduct or remarks that she found offensive, and the names of any witnesses. If the client decides to proceed with a formal complaint of sexual harassment, you may be called upon to provide emotional support. It is fairly common in sexual harassment cases for the complainant to be questioned about the incident, including, for example, her reaction to the harasser's actions. Those who are asked to investigate the claim will want to determine whether the complainant said or did anything to encourage the alleged harasser, and she may find it upsetting to face suggestions that she may have welcomed the advances. Victims often feel shame and blame themselves. Your role may include helping the person to sort through these feelings.

Enforcing Human Rights

People who believe that their human rights have been denied or violated can make a complaint to either the Canadian Human Rights Commission (CHRC), in the event of a violation of the federal Act, or to the Ontario Human Rights Commission (OHRC), in the event of a violation of the Ontario Code. For violations of the Ontario Code, possible remedies include an order requiring payment of monetary losses suffered by the complainant, compensation for mental anguish of up to $10,000, and additional fines of up to $25,000.

A complaint should be made as soon as possible after the event. The procedure is outlined below.

1. The complainant contacts the appropriate commission and obtains a complaint form.

2. The complainant files the complaint with the commission, which then informs the person or party against whom the complaint is made.

3. The person or party who is the subject of the complaint must prepare and file a written response.

4. Various means of resolution are explored, such as mediation (described in chapter 16).

5. If the issue remains unresolved, the commission may choose to investigate the complaint.

6. If there is an investigation, it typically involves reviewing the complaint and the response, and, if necessary, interviewing the parties or other individuals.

7. The investigator prepares a report and communicates the commission's findings to the parties, who may respond.

8. The case may be resolved at this point by arriving at a settlement, through negotiation or mediation, based on the investigator's report.

9. If the case is not resolved, it is reviewed by the commission, which then decides what action to take. For example, the commission may

    a. refer the parties to a conciliator, and/or approve a settlement arrived at by the parties;

    b. refer the parties to the Canadian Human Rights Tribunal or the Ontario Human Rights Tribunal for adjudication; or

    c. dismiss the complaint.

10. If the case goes before a tribunal, the tribunal will schedule and conduct a hearing and issue a decision.

11. The tribunal may declare that the complaint was without merit, or it may offer a remedy in favour of the complainant. Remedies can include

    a. an order that the discriminatory practice stop, including a change to policy;

b. compensation to the victim for lost wages and/or other losses that resulted from the discriminatory practice;

c. compensation to the victim for additional costs of obtaining alternative goods, services, facilities, or accommodation, and for any expenses incurred by the victim as a result of the discriminatory practice; and

d. compensation for pain or suffering that the victim suffered as a result of the discriminatory practice.

12. In certain cases, decisions of the Ontario tribunal can be appealed to the Divisional Court.

Hearings before a human rights tribunal are quite formal, and parties are generally represented by a lawyer. A support person, such as a social service worker, may also attend. Parties may be called to give oral testimony, and there may be other witnesses, including expert witnesses, called by either side.

If a party makes a complaint to the CHRC or the OHRC, regardless of the outcome—whether it is settled at mediation, dismissed by commission staff, settled after conciliation, dimissed by the tribunal, or decided in favour of the complainant—the person who is the subject of the complaint may not make reprisals against the complainant. **Reprisals** include any action or statement that is intended to punish, threaten, intimidate, or discriminate against the complainant.

KEY TERMS

adverse impact discrimination	indirect discrimination
criminal harassment	marginalized
direct discrimination	reprisal
duty to accommodate	sexual harassment
harassment	signatory
human rights	undue hardship

REFERENCES

Alberta (Human Rights and Citizenship Commission) v. Kellogg Brown & Root (Canada) Company, 2006 ABQB 302, available online at www.albertacourts .ab.ca/jdb/2003-/qb/civil/2006/2006abqb0302.cor2.pdf.

Buhlers v. British Columbia (Superintendent of Motor Vehicles) (1999), 132 CCC (3d) 478 (BCCA).

Canadian Charter of Rights and Freedoms, part I of the *Constitution Act, 1982*, being schedule B of the *Canada Act 1982* (UK), 1982, c. 11.

Canadian Human Rights Act, RSC 1985, c. H-6.

Constitution Act, 1867, 30 & 31 Vict., c. 3 (UK).

Coroner's Act, RSO 1990, c. C.37.

Criminal Code, RSC 1985, c. C-46.

Eldridge v. British Columbia (Attorney General), [1997] 3 SCR 624.

Human Rights Code, RSO 1990, c. H.19.

Rodriguez v. British Columbia (Attorney General), [1993] 3 SCR 519.

Schachter v. Canada, [1992] 2 SCR 679.

Singh v. Minister of Employment and Immigration, [1985] 1 SCR 177.

Vriend v. Alberta, [1998] 1 SCR 493.

REVIEW QUESTIONS

1. Why are the laws governing human rights of interest to social service workers?

2. Name six prohibited grounds of discrimination under Canada's and Ontario's human rights statutes.

3. Explain what is meant by indirect or adverse impact discrimination.

4. What is the duty to accommodate, and how does it apply in the employment context?

5. What is harassment, and how is it different from discrimination?

6. List five examples of sexual harassment.

7. Can an employer be held responsible for the harassment of an employee?

DISCUSSION QUESTIONS

Your client describes incidents in her workplace that sound to you like sexual harassment. She says that several women in her office are receiving similar treatment. None of them have complained because they are afraid that if they do, they will be fired. What should you tell your client? What is your appropriate role in helping the client to seek a remedy?

CHAPTER 21

Not-for-Profit Organizations

CHAPTER OBJECTIVES

After reading this chapter, you should be able to:

- Explain the differences between a sole proprietorship, a partnership, and a corporation as a legal structure for carrying on a business.

- List advantages and disadvantages of incorporation.

- Explain what is meant by a not-for-profit corporation.

- Describe the differences between a for-profit and a not-for-profit corporation.

- Understand the advantages and disadvantages of charitable status, and the requirements for becoming a registered charity.

INTRODUCTION

Not-for-profit (or **non-profit**) **organizations** are created and operated for a purpose other than making a profit. Examples in the social services sector include children's aid societies, homeless shelters, victims' services agencies, addictions treatment facilities, and subsidized housing corporations. Many not-for-profit organizations do earn revenues (for example, from fees or fundraising activities) and these revenues may exceed the operating expenses of the organization; but net earnings are not returned as profits to the owners or investors, but are transferred to beneficiaries in the form of services or social benefits. Not-for-profit organizations may qualify for preferential tax treatment or government subsidies, provided that they meet specific eligibility criteria and operate within strict rules.

Many social service workers work for or perform administrative functions within not-for-profit organizations. This chapter is designed to help you to understand the legal environment within which these organizations operate.

LEGAL STRUCTURE OF A BUSINESS

Businesses are carried on through a variety of organizational structures. The three most common forms are sole proprietorships, partnerships, and corporations. The laws and regulations that apply to a business vary depending on the structure of the business organization. The choice of structure affects many aspects of management of the business, including liability (responsibility for debts and other obligations of the business), financial reporting, and taxation.

Generally, any of the above structures may be used for a business, whether it is operated for profit or not for profit. Before considering the reasons for operating as a non-profit entity in the social services sector, it is useful to explain the fundamental differences between sole proprietorships, partnerships, and corporations.

Sole Proprietorship

The simplest kind of business organization is a **sole proprietorship**. It is a business owned entirely by one individual (the proprietor). There is no legal distinction between the business and the proprietor: the proprietor is liable for the debts of the business and for any claims related to the conduct of the business. Contracts made with the business are actually made with the proprietor directly, not with a separate business entity. This is the case even if the proprietor operates the business under a name other than his own.

There is no reason why sole proprietors cannot work on a non-profit basis, and many do. In addition, professionals who work for profit in social services, such as psychologists, psychiatrists, social workers, and lawyers, often operate as sole proprietors, and many provide *pro bono* services as a small part of their total practice.

It is relatively simple, from a legal perspective, to operate as a sole proprietorship. A sole proprietorship comes into existence, without being formally "created," at the moment the proprietor begins doing business. Ontario requires a business operated under a name other than the proprietor's name to be registered with the Ministry of Government and Consumer Services. Otherwise, apart from the proprietor's obligation to report business income and expenses on his personal income tax return, and to register for and remit payroll and sales taxes (if applicable), there are no onerous reporting requirements associated with operating in this way.

The major disadvantage of operating as a sole proprietorship is that the owner is not protected from liability. Creditors and plaintiffs may seek payment of debts owed by the business, or damages awarded by a court, from the owner's personal assets, such as his home and savings. The owner's personal liability extends beyond his own actions to those of any employees as well.

Partnerships

A **partnership** is much like a sole proprietorship, except that it allows for the equal participation of two or more owners (who often are, but need not be, individuals). Like a sole proprietorship, a partnership has no separate legal existence apart from its owners.

Partnerships may be formed for a variety of business purposes, including investment and the provision of certain professional services. Many professionals (such as lawyers, accountants, or doctors) form partnerships in order to share overhead and other business costs, and to better serve clients. Partners often enter into partnership agreements that formalize the terms of their association, such as what happens when a partner wants to withdraw from the partnership.

As with a sole proprietorship, the major disadvantage of a partnership is the exposure to liability. In traditional partnership structures, each partner is jointly and severally liable for all debts and liabilities of the business. Joint and several liability means that each partner is legally responsible for any debts and obligations of the partnership. Thus, for example, if a partner is unable to pay his share of a judgment against the partnership, or make good on a contract, the other partners will be liable for the full amount of the claim. Unlimited liability is problematic in some business contexts. Therefore, Ontario and some other jurisdictions have enacted legislation to permit limited liability for certain types of partnerships, including professional partnerships.

While it is relatively uncommon for a social service worker to be a partner in a partnership, social service workers are sometimes employed by professional partnerships, and they often have dealings with such partnerships in the course of their

EXTRA CREDIT

General Partnerships, Limited Partnerships, and Limited Liability Partnerships

Ontario law recognizes three basic types of partnerships: general partnership, limited partnerships, and limited liability partnerships. General partnerships and limited liability partnerships are governed by the *Partnerships Act*; limited partnerships are governed by the *Limited Partnerships Act*.

In a general partnership (the traditional structure), all partners share equally in the decision making (which, in large partnerships, may involve voting for or appointing representatives), the profits, and the liability. Shared (joint and several) liability is a concern because any partner can be held liable not only for his own actions but also for the actions of other partners. For example, if a lawyer in a law firm causes harm to a client by the negligent delivery of legal services, all partners in the firm may be responsible to pay the damages award.

A limited partnership is a special structure comprising one or more general partners, with unlimited liability, and one or more limited partners, with limited liability. A general partner carries on the business of the partnership on behalf of the limited partners (subject to certain restrictions) and has all the rights and obligations of a partner in a general partnership. A limited partner contributes money or property to the partnership but does not actively engage in the business of the partnership; essentially, a limited partner is a passive investor. A limited partner is entitled to share in the profits of the partnership in proportion to his financial contribution, and his liability is limited to the amount of the contribution.

A limited liability partnership is a type of partnership available only to certain professions, including lawyers, accountants, and some health services professionals. A limited liability partnership is similar to a general partnership except with respect to liability. Each partner is jointly and severally liable with respect to the debts and obligations of the partnership *other than* liabilities arising from the negligence of any other partner, or any employee, agent, or representative of the partnership. In the event of negligence, the client's pursuit of a remedy is limited to the responsible partner alone, and does not extend to any other partners. ◇

practice. For example, a social service worker may work with a law firm on matters of concern to her employer, in referring clients who need legal advice, or on her own account when legal issues arise relating to her practice.

In dealing with a partnership, it is useful to remember that in most cases, any one partner can bind the others via a contract. However, recourse in the event of negligence may be limited in some partnership arrangements.

If you are considering working in partnership with other individuals, it's important to choose partners whom you trust on both a personal and a professional level. Even if you do trust your partners, it's prudent to arrange insurance coverage that takes into account the fact that you may be liable not only for your own actions, but also for the actions of your partners.

Corporations

Unlike a sole proprietorship or a partnership, a **corporation** has a separate legal identity independent of its owners. A corporation comes into existence by incorporation under a governing corporate statute, such as Ontario's *Business Corporations Act* or the *Canada Business Corporations Act*, or by a special act of the federal Parliament or a provincial legislation. Under corporate law, a corporation is created by filing articles of incorporation with the appropriate government office, followed by the issuance of a certificate of incorporation.

There are many different kinds of corporations, including

- share capital corporations,

- professional corporations,

- not-for-profit corporations,

- not-for-profit charitable corporations,

- co-operative corporations,

- condominium corporations, and

- corporations governed by special statutes (such as municipal corporations, certain hospitals, religious organizations and other charities, and federal and provincial Crown corporations).

As separate legal entities, corporations can own property; enter into contracts, including borrowing money; and sue and be sued. Almost all corporations provide limited liability for the owners in respect of the debts and obligations of the corporation. This means that, generally, an owner (such as a **shareholder**) or a member (of a not-for-profit corporation) is not personally liable for the debts of the corporation, and his liability in respect of a claim against the corporation is limited to the amount of his investment or interest in the corporation.

Limited liability is one of the main advantages of a corporation over other business structures. There are two others that should be noted:

- *Perpetual existence*: Generally, a corporation continues to exist even if there are changes in ownership, unless a majority of the owners vote to dissolve the corporation.

- *Tax advantages*: Federal and Ontario tax statutes provide a complex set of tax measures from which owners of corporations can benefit.

Disadvantages include complexity and compliance with a vast array of rules under corporate, taxation, and other regulatory statutes.

Generally, corporations are operated with the expectation that the business will generate a profit. Funds required to establish and conduct the business are raised through the issuance and sale of shares. Share ownership entitles each investor to a proportionate share of the profits of the business, which may be received through periodic payments of dividends out of corporate earnings or in the form of proceeds from the eventual sale of the shares. Shareholders also bear a share of any losses, since a reduction in profits will generally reduce the value of the shares.

Social service workers, among those in other professions referenced in section 3.1(2) of the *Business Corporations Act*, may practise by way of a professional corporation.

Corporations may also be created for non-profit purposes, and some of these not-for-profit corporations may qualify to register as charities. The distinctive features of not-for-profit corporations, the procedure for incorporation, and the advantages of charitable status are described in the next section.

NOT-FOR-PROFIT CORPORATIONS

Not-for-profit organizations are generally exempt from paying income tax. They are required to file a special income reporting form, called a Non-Profit Organization Information Return. Not-for-profit organizations may also be eligible for rebates of goods and services tax (in some provinces, harmonized sales tax) paid on taxable supplies.

Many social service agencies operate as not-for-profit corporations—for example, children's aid societies. Each children's aid society is a separate corporation with a voluntary board of **directors**. Not-for-profit corporations differ from for-profit corporations in several respects:

- A not-for-profit corporation does not issue shares and has members instead of shareholders. Members do not "own" the corporation and are not permitted to benefit personally from any profits earned by the corporation.

- Any earnings of the corporation must be "incidental to" its principal objects and "in furtherance of" those objects. A corporation's objects are simply the goals it wishes to achieve. For example, as discussed in chapter 19, a not-for-profit corporation may be dedicated to providing affordable housing for people with limited financial means. The corporation will receive plenty of money in the form of rents paid by tenants. However, since the corporation's principal object is to provide affordable housing, rents will be set at an amount that matches, rather than exceeds, the cost of providing the housing (including administration and maintenance expenses).

- Any profits earned by the corporation must be retained for the benefit of the clients that the corporation was created to serve. In the case of an affordable housing corporation, profit could be retained in a reserve for future repairs. No money in excess of salaries may be passed on to the directors (the people who manage and control the corporation) or, as noted above, to the members.

Incorporation is not essential for individuals and agencies with altruistic objectives; in fact, hundreds of unincorporated organizations successfully carry on non-profit activities in Ontario. Incorporation imposes reporting responsibilities; however, the main advantages of incorporation—limited liability and perpetual existence—make it attractive to some service providers.

Procedure for Incorporation

The procedure for incorporating a not-for-profit organization depends on the jurisdiction in which it intends to operate. A corporation that aims to provide services in several provinces may find it advantageous to incorporate under the federal statute (that is, the *Canada Corporations Act*), whereas a corporation whose operations will be limited to a particular municipality, or to communities in Ontario, will prefer to incorporate under the provincial *Corporations Act*. In the case of a not-for-profit corporation seeking charitable status, there are advantages to federal incorporation. For simplicity, the discussion that follows will focus mainly on the procedure for incorporation under the Ontario statute.

In Ontario, not-for-profit status may be conferred, at the discretion of the attorney general, on corporations whose primary objective is service to the community. The Ministry of the Attorney General identifies five main types of not-for-profit corporations:

- general type, including ratepayers' associations, business or trade associations, and community organizations;

- sporting and athletic organizations;

- social clubs;

- service clubs such as Rotary, Lions, Kiwanis, and Optimist; and

- charities, including religious organizations and other organizations that undertake activities for the benefit of society.

Social service workers may be involved in setting up a not-for-profit corporation "from scratch" or in obtaining corporate status for an existing non-profit service agency. The Ministry of the Attorney General publishes a *Not for Profit Incorporators' Handbook*, in which it notes that it is possible to incorporate a not-for-profit company without the assistance of a lawyer. However, hiring a lawyer to guide prospective directors through this process is a good investment, even for small corporations. Where controlling costs is paramount, at the very least a lawyer should be consulted to identify the steps that the directors can do themselves, such as preparing a first draft of the corporate objects and, later, a draft of the bylaws.

Not-for-profit corporations are registered by applying for the issuance of "letters patent." To obtain registration as a not-for-profit corporation, a group of prospective directors will need to take the following steps:

1. *Choose a corporate name.* There are rules restricting the choice of a corporate name. For example, in order to successfully register a name in Ontario (or any other jurisdiction), the name must be unique and not

easily confused with corporate names already registered in that jurisdiction. The name must also not be too general, such as "The Used Clothing Exchange." Once a potential name is chosen, the applicants must do an official database search, called NUANS (newly upgraded automated name search), to ensure that the name is not already taken.

WEB LINK
For more information about the NUANS computerized search system, visit www.nuans.com.

2. *Prepare and file an application for incorporation.* Before doing this, some prospective incorporators may need to check with a government agency first, if the proposed corporation's objects fall within the supervision of a particular government ministry. For example, if the corporation is being set up as an affordable housing provider, the incorporators should contact the Ministry of Municipal Affairs and Housing before proceeding with the incorporation.

   The Ontario application form is available from the Ministry of Government and Consumer Services, Companies and Personal Property Security Branch. As part of the application, the prospective incorporators will need to establish a head office address; name at least three directors; and prepare a statement of the corporation's primary (and secondary, if any) objects.

3. *Organize the corporation.* When the corporation receives the letters patent, the new directors will need to take certain steps to ensure that the corporation is ready to operate. The Ministry of the Attorney General provides the following list:

WEB LINK
For more information about incorporation, visit Ontario's Ministry of Government and Consumer Services at www.mgs.gov.on.ca.

   a. establishing a directors' quorum,

   b. adoption of bylaws,

   c. banking and financial arrangements,

   d. adoption of a corporate seal,

   e. appointment of auditors, and

   f. appointment of officers.

Once created and operating, the new corporation will need to keep up to date with reporting, accounting/auditing, and tax obligations. Most corporations hire a lawyer and an accountant to help with these responsibilities.

When a for-profit corporation is dissolved, its assets are sold and the profits are distributed to the shareholders in proportion to their shareholdings. When a not-for-profit corporation is dissolved, the distribution of the assets depends on how this eventuality has been addressed in the corporate bylaws. In most cases, the proceeds from the sale of the assets can be distributed among the directors/incorporators. This changes, however, if the corporation has status as a charity, as discussed below.

Charitable Status

A not-for-profit corporation may qualify for registration as a charitable corporation. The advantage of registration as a **charity** is that the corporation can then issue official receipts for donations. A receipt allows a donor to deduct a portion of the donation from his income in calculating income tax; this tax treatment supports the organization's charitable activities by encouraging gifts and donations.

A disadvantage of charitable status is that charities are subject to strict regulation by the Canada Revenue Agency (CRA). Regulation includes restrictions on the kinds of business activities a charity may engage in. For example, corporations with charitable status are currently permitted to spend no more than 10 percent of their annual budget on advocacy activities. For this reason, agencies that intend to rely heavily on advocacy as a means to help their clients typically forgo charitable status.

A registered charity must also comply with annual reporting requirements. In the public interest, the CRA maintains a registry of charities, which publishes information about each charity, including the names of directors and past directors, the charity's address, details of the charity's application for registration (which includes a statement of the charity's objects), and, in the event of deregistration, the reasons for the revocation of charitable status. To verify compliance, and to keep this database up to date, the CRA requires charities to file an annual information return. The return includes details of the charity's financial circumstances and tax obligations, and this information may be disclosed to the public. Failure to file an annual return can result in deregistration of the charity.

To obtain registration as a charity, the directors of a not-for-profit corporation must apply to the CRA; the application form is available online, via mail, or at a CRA district taxation office. The review and registration process may be slow; Charity Village, an online community resource for charities, reports that it can take from 6 to 18 months.

In deciding whether a not-for-profit organization is eligible for charitable status, the CRA applies the following criteria:

- The organization's activities and purposes must provide a tangible benefit to the public.

- Either the public as a whole or a significant segment of the public must be eligible for the benefits provided by the organization. That is, the beneficiaries may not be a restricted group, or one whose members share a private connection, such as a social club or a professional association with a specific membership.

- The charity's activities must be legal and must not be contrary to public policy.

A key difference between registered charities and other not-for-profit corporations is that when a charity is dissolved (ceases to exist), it is required to distribute any assets that it owns at the time of dissolution (or the proceeds of those assets) to other charities. This money may not be paid out to the founders, directors, or members of the organization.

WEB LINK

For more information about how to set up a charity, visit the website of Charity Village at www.charityvillage.com.

WEB LINK

For more information about the criteria for charitable status, and to download the application form for registration, visit the Canada Revenue Agency's website at www.cra-arc.gc.ca.

KEY TERMS

charity

corporation

director

not-for-profit (or non-profit) organization

partnership

shareholder

sole proprietorship

REFERENCES

Business Corporations Act, RSO 1990, c. B.16.

Canada Business Corporations Act, RSC 1985, c. C-44.

Canada Corporations Act, RSC 1970, c. C-32.

Child and Family Services Act, RSO 1990, c. C.11.

Corporations Act, RSO 1990, c. C.38.

Limited Partnerships Act, RSO 1990, c. P.16.

Partnerships Act, RSO 1990, c. P.5.

REVIEW QUESTIONS

1. What are the requirements in Ontario for starting a business as a sole proprietorship?

2. What is joint and several liability, and why is it a disadvantage of partnerships?

3. What kind of business structure can be used to provide services on a not-for-profit basis? Is one particular structure more attractive than any other, and if so, why?

4. What are the principal disadvantages of incorporation for a not-for-profit organization?

5. What must prospective incorporators do before they decide on the name of the new corporation?

6. What is a not-for-profit organization? What is a registered charity?

7. What are the criteria that a not-for-profit corporation must meet in order to qualify for charitable status?

CHAPTER 22

Privacy and Access to Information

CHAPTER OBJECTIVES

After reading this chapter, you should be able to:

- Describe the client confidentiality principles prescribed for social service workers by the Ontario College of Social Workers and Social Service Workers.

- Describe at least three scenarios that pose a challenge to social service workers from a client confidentiality perspective.

- Identify several federal and Ontario statutes that regulate the disclosure and use of personal information.

- Understand the steps that a private sector organization should take to ensure compliance with the federal *Personal Information Protection and Electronic Documents Act*.

- Describe the procedures under the federal and Ontario statutes for requesting access to information and making a complaint in the event of non-compliance with privacy law.

INTRODUCTION

The nature of social service work requires social service workers to speak with clients about matters that most people consider highly personal and private: family relationships, finances, employment issues, and mental and physical health, among others. Sometimes personal information is revealed during counselling; in many cases, it is required for the purpose of determining a client's eligibility for assistance under a range of programs and services provided by government and private agencies.

Social service workers have a legal, professional, and moral responsibility to handle clients' personal information with care and discretion. Failure to live up to that responsibility can result in legal and professional sanctions, as well as the loss of clients' confidence and trust. The *Standards of Practice Handbook* of the Ontario College of Social Workers and Social Service Workers provides detailed guidelines for the protection of confidential information, in support of the following general principle:

> College members respect the privacy of clients by holding in strict confidence all information about clients. College members disclose such information only when required or allowed by law to do so or when clients have consented to disclosure.

Protecting client privacy is also a legal requirement under a number of federal and provincial statutes. Here we will focus on four statutes:

- the *Privacy Act* (federal);

- the *Personal Information Protection and Electronic Documents Act* (federal);

- the *Freedom of Information and Protection of Privacy Act* (Ontario); and

- the *Personal Health Information Protection Act, 2004* (Ontario).

The discussion that follows provides a general overview of the professional standards and statutory rules governing the collection and protection of information, and access to information from public sources.

PROFESSIONAL STANDARDS

The obligation to protect client confidentiality imposed by the Ontario College of Social Workers and Social Service Workers is a strict one. According to the *Standards of Practice Handbook*, the only circumstances under which information may be divulged are

- when disclosure is required by law; or

- when the client has consented to the disclosure.

Disclosure Required by Law

Disclosure required by law means required by statute or court order. For example, the duty to report the suspicion of child abuse is mandated by the *Child and Family Services Act* (CFSA). In other cases, a court may order the disclosure of information for use as evidence in a legal proceeding. This can pose a moral dilemma for social service workers, as well as create practical concerns.

For example, if a client raises the subject of sexual feelings toward a child and wants to talk about his struggle to control such feelings, the social service worker should immediately warn him of the duty to report suspicion that a child may be at risk of harm. Even though encouraging the client to speak freely could better enable protection of the child, until information is actually disclosed the social service worker's duty is to the client. The social service worker must warn the client of the possible consequences of disclosure, even if doing so may put a child at risk. However, if the client nevertheless discloses information, the social service worker's duty to report supersedes the duty of confidentiality.

A court may order disclosure to be used as evidence—for example, discussion of criminal acts committed by the client. Again, the social service worker has an obligation to warn the client that such information could be used against him in a court of law.

More controversial is the subject of the use of the therapeutic records of victims of crime as evidence called by the accused perpetrator in his or her defence. With respect to domestic violence and sexual offences, victims often wrongly blame themselves. Courts are sensitive to this issue, and don't wish for victims to shy away from seeking needed counselling for fear that their most private feelings will be exposed and even used against them. Nevertheless, clients should be warned that, in some cases, a court may order the disclosure of such information. When deciding how information is conveyed in their clinical notes, social service workers may wish to keep in mind how these notes might be used in court. (See chapter 14.)

Disclosure by Consent

Disclosure by consent is disclosure made in conformity with privacy legislation—that is, it is allowed, rather than required, by law. Generally, privacy legislation permits the disclosure of "personal" information only with the written consent of the person. The consent limits disclosure to the purposes specifically described; it does not give blanket permission to reveal the information.

Client information of any kind may be disclosed with the consent of the client. It is important to document all client consents in writing, so that there is no misunderstanding. In documenting consents, the following points should be kept in mind:

- Each new proposed disclosure requires a new consent, or a carefully drafted consent to ongoing disclosure. For example, where a social service worker is helping a client who is looking for work and the client has consented to disclose details of a disability to a particular potential employer, the social service worker should not automatically treat this consent as applying to *all* potential employers.

- Before the client signs a consent to disclosure, the applicable privacy laws should be explained to her. For example, the client should be assured that any person to whom the information is provided is under an obligation to protect it from further disclosure.

- The terms of any consent should be as specific as possible. The information subject to disclosure should be precisely described, and all persons to whom the information will be disclosed should be clearly identified.

- All consents are revocable; that is, the client can suspend consent at any time. The client must be advised of his right to revoke a consent.

Consulting Colleagues

Social service workers often share clients or work in agencies in which a client's file is shared with other co-workers. It should be made clear to the client which people within the agency are entitled to access her information.

In environments where colleagues may discuss their clients' cases, they should take care to ensure that these conversations are not overheard by other clients or by anyone else who is not entitled to receive confidential client information. This means being discreet about conversations in lunchrooms and staff rooms, ensuring privacy when on the telephone, and avoiding discussing clients in settings where other clients may be present, such as group therapy rooms, gymnasiums and recreational facilities, public areas of community centres, and waiting rooms.

Group Therapy

Group therapy, and certain other group programs, can pose a challenge to confidentiality, because information is shared not just with the counsellor but also with other participants. Group therapy specifically involves discussion of personal information, often of a highly sensitive nature.

Most people who are interested in group therapy are prepared to share in this way; however, all participants in this kind of program should be asked to sign consents ahead of time. It's also important that clients understand that they have been entrusted with each other's private information, and that they have an obligation of confidentiality toward each other. This means that information revealed in the group setting should not be discussed outside that context.

Meeting in the Community

Particularly in small communities, or in tight-knit ethnic communities, a social service worker may have non-professional contact with clients and former clients. This may include running into each other at the grocery store, being neighbours, being the customer of a client who works in a local business, or having friends or even relatives in common.

The parameters of the relationship should be discussed with each client. For example, the social service worker should explain that if she sees the client on the street with someone she doesn't know, she will not greet the client until he acknowledges her. This is to protect the client from being asked, "How do you know her?" Caution is also necessary when using a client's case as an anonymous case study. In a small community, people are more easily identified.

If a social service worker inadvertently breaches a client's confidentiality, she has a moral responsibility to report the breach to the client immediately.

Suicidal Clients

What if a social service worker has reason to believe that a client may harm himself? Should the social service worker disclose her suspicions to someone who can help? Arguably, there is an implied consent to do whatever is necessary to stop a client from committing suicide. However, a disclosure, if unexpected, can erode the client's trust.

Where a social service worker believes that a client may be suicidal, the best course of action is probably to report the suspicions to a supervisor at the first available opportunity, and to encourage the client to see a helping professional (such as, a psychiatrist) who is better able to treat the client. This referral should be made without delay, and the social service worker should follow up to ensure that the client has in fact sought the help suggested.

FEDERAL LEGISLATION

The two key federal privacy statutes that protect personal information are the *Privacy Act* and the *Personal Information Protection and Electronic Documents Act* (PIPEDA). Both statutes are administered by the Privacy Commissioner of Canada.

Privacy Act

The *Privacy Act* was introduced in 1983. It governs the handling of personal information by a list of over 150 federal government offices and agencies, including

- the Department of Health,
- the Department of Finance,
- the Canada Mortgage and Housing Corporation,
- the Canada Post Corporation,
- the Canada Revenue Agency,
- the Canadian Human Rights Commission, and
- the Correctional Service of Canada.

The *Privacy Act* regulates the collection, retention and safe storage, disclosure, and disposal of individuals' personal information by the federal government. Personal information generally includes information relating to race, religion, age, and marital status; health records, criminal records, employment records, financial records, addresses, social insurance numbers, and even personal opinions.

The *Privacy Act* also mandates access by individuals to their own personal information held by the regulated agencies, and allows individuals to request that corrections be made to this information. Social service workers who work in listed federally regulated agencies need to understand their obligations under this law. The discussion that follows summarizes some of the more important points to keep in mind.

LEGISLATIVE SHORTCUT

Privacy Act
RSC 1985, c. P-21

Objective: To protect the privacy of individuals with respect to their personal information held by a federal government institution, and to provide individuals with a right of access to that information.

Target Population: Anyone whose personal information is held by any of the more than 150 offices and agencies of the federal government and anyone interested in such information.

Program Administration: The Office of the Privacy Commissioner of Canada investigates complaints and reports on findings and recommendations.

Administrative Tribunal: The Office of the Privacy Commissioner reports on the findings of its investigations and makes recommendations, but does not make binding rulings. If the matter is not settled based on the report, the complainant must seek review by the court.

Summary: The *Privacy Act* regulates the collection, retention and safe storage, disclosure, and disposal of individuals' personal information by the federal government. Personal information generally includes information relating to race, religion, age or marital status, health records, criminal records, employment records, financial records, addresses, social insurance numbers, and even personal opinions. ◇

MANAGING PERSONAL INFORMATION

If, as a social service worker working in a federal agency, you are unsure of your employer's privacy policies, you should speak up and request appropriate support or training with respect to how personal information is collected and managed in your office.

As a general rule, no personal information collected by a federal agency can be used for a purpose other than the purpose for which it was collected, and that purpose must be defined in specific terms and communicated to the information provider at the time the information is sought. While in the possession of the agency, the information must be securely protected to prevent unauthorized access.

PERMITTED DISCLOSURE

Personal information must not be disclosed except for specified reasons or in specified circumstances, including the following:

- for the purpose for which it was collected and with the consent of the provider;

- as specifically permitted by another statute;

- for certain narrowly defined research purposes;

- as ordered by a court; or

- where the public interest in disclosing the personal information clearly outweighs the invasion of privacy that would result from disclosure. (See Extra Credit, below.)

Before disclosing personal information, it is important to ensure that the disclosure falls within one of these categories. In some cases, you may be permitted to disclose part of the information that you have about a client but required to keep the rest confidential.

ACCESSING PERSONAL INFORMATION

Social service workers serving clients whose information was collected by a federal agency may need to assist clients in accessing their own information, and requesting corrections to it. Section 13 of the *Privacy Act* describes the process for obtaining access to one's own personal information.

The government maintains a directory (actually, a collection of four separate publications) called Info Source, which can help individuals find out which federally regulated institutions are holding their personal information. The request must be made in writing to the agency holding the information. Upon receiving the request, the agency or institution is usually required to respond within 15 days.

For example, an individual who successfully obtained a pardon of a criminal offence might want to confirm that his criminal record, held by the National Parole Board, reflects his pardoned status. The National Parole Board is on the list of agencies governed by the *Privacy Act*, and a social service worker may be asked to assist in this process.

WEB LINK

To find out which federally regulated institutions are holding a client's personal information, access Info Source at the public library or online at www.infosource.gc.ca.

EXTRA CREDIT

Public Interest Disclosures

Section 8(2)(m) of the *Privacy Act* permits the disclosure of personal information in situations where the public interest in the disclosure clearly outweighs the invasion of privacy caused by the disclosure. The provision is intended for use in exceptional circumstances only; and disclosures may be made under this provision only after the head of the information-collecting institution has performed an evaluation to determine that the public interest outweighs the invasion of privacy.

According to the Privacy Commissioner of Canada,

> the [information-collecting] institution has a duty to notify the Privacy Commissioner that it will be disclosing personal information in the public interest. The Privacy Commissioner may express concerns, if any, with the proposed disclosure and may, if appropriate, notify the individual whose information will be disclosed. It is, however, ultimately the institution's decision as to whether it will or will not release the information, and how much it will release. The Privacy Commissioner has no authority to prevent the disclosure.

The Privacy Commissioner of Canada acknowledges that the media and government departments may differ in their views of what is meant by public interest. While the commissioner maintains that section 8(2)(m) should be used sparingly, there are clearly instances in which disclosure will be in the public interest; the commissioner provides, as an example, the situation where an individual who may pose a threat to the community is released from a correctional institution.

Nevertheless, the commissioner emphasizes that the provision does not justify generalized disclosures:

> Section 8(2)(m) is not a "loophole" in the *Privacy Act* which simply allows government departments and agencies to make information public when it should remain private. The provision is applied in unique, fact-specific situations. It is not designed to deal with the disclosure of personal information on a systematic or routine basis. Rather, it is an important section in the Act, which provides institutions with a tool they may need to effectively balance an individual's right to privacy with the public's need to know.

Source: Privacy Commissioner of Canada, information obtained online at www.privcom.gc.ca. ◇

COMPLAINTS

A client who is dissatisfied with the handling of her personal information or her request for access may seek the help of a social service worker in making a complaint under section 29 of the *Privacy Act*. Briefly, the complaint procedure is as follows:

1. The individual makes a complaint in writing to the Privacy Commissioner of Canada.

2. The commissioner notifies the head of the institution that a complaint has been made and specifies the nature of the complaint.

3. The commissioner may choose to investigate the complaint if it is satisfied that there are reasonable grounds to do so.

WEB LINK

More detailed information about the application and administration of the *Privacy Act*, including access and complaint procedures, is available from the Privacy Commissioner of Canada at www.privcom.gc.ca.

4. The commissioner conducts the investigation in private, calling witnesses and subpoenaing information as appropriate; however, both parties are given the chance to make representations.

5. The commissioner communicates the findings to the parties. Depending on the nature of the complaint, the commissioner determines whether or not the individual should be given access to the information requested, or makes another kind of recommendation (for example, that the institution change its procedures to avoid inappropriate disclosures in the future).

Personal Information Protection and Electronic Documents Act

When PIPEDA came into force on January 1, 2004, it brought sweeping changes to Canadian privacy law, extending the regulation of the collection, handling, disclosure, and disposal of personal information to organizations in the private sector. The purpose of PIPEDA is set out in section 3:

> to establish, in an era in which technology increasingly facilitates the circulation and exchange of information, rules to govern the collection, use and disclosure of personal information in a manner that recognizes the right of privacy of individuals with respect to their personal information and the need of organizations to collect, use or disclose personal information for purposes that a reasonable person would consider appropriate in the circumstances.

PIPEDA is designed primarily to govern the collection, use, and disclosure of personal information for commercial activities, or for the management of federal employees. Organizations subject to the *Privacy Act* are exempt from the operation of PIPEDA, because the scheme of both acts is substantially similar. Since Ontario's *Personal Health Information Protection Act, 2004* (PHIPA) is also substantially similar to PIPEDA, the PHIPA governs privacy in the health sector in Ontario, to the extent of its application (as discussed below).

MANAGING PERSONAL INFORMATION AND PERMITTED DISCLOSURE

The Privacy Commissioner of Canada provides the following plain-language summary of PIPEDA:

- If your business wants to collect, use or disclose personal information about people, you need their consent, except in a few specific and limited circumstances.

- You can use or disclose people's personal information only for the purpose for which they gave consent.

- Even with consent, you have to limit collection, use and disclosure to purposes that a reasonable person would consider appropriate under the circumstances.

- Individuals have a right to see the personal information that your business holds about them, and to correct any inaccuracies.

- There's oversight, through the Privacy Commissioner of Canada, to ensure that the law is respected, and redress if people's rights are violated.

LEGISLATIVE SHORTCUT

Personal Information Protection and Electronic Documents Act

SC 2000, c.5

Objective: To establish rules to govern the collection, use, and disclosure of personal information in a manner that recognizes the right of privacy of individuals and the need of organizations to collect, use, or disclose personal information.

Target Population: Customers or employees whose personal information is collected, used, or disclosed in the course of commercial activities by federally regulated businesses (such as banks, airlines, and telecommunications companies) and customers (but not employees) of provincially regulated businesses in provinces that do not have substantially similar legislation governing provincially regulated businesses. In provinces that have legislation that is substantially similar to PIPEDA (such as British Columbia, Alberta, and Quebec), PIPEDA does not apply to provincially regulated businesses.

Program Administration: The Office of the Privacy Commissioner of Canada investigates complaints, reports on findings, and makes recommendations.

Administrative Tribunal: The Office of the Privacy Commissioner reports on the findings of its investigations, but does not make binding rulings. If the matter is not settled based on the report, the complainant must seek review by the court.

Summary: PIPEDA governs the collection, use, and disclosure of personal information for commercial activities, or for the management of federal employees. Organizations subject to the *Privacy Act* are exempt, because the statutes are substantially similar. Also, with respect to personal health information, Ontario's *Personal Health Information Protection Act, 2004* governs privacy in the health sector in Ontario. ◇

The website of the privacy commissioner provides a wide range of resources to assist private sector organizations in complying with PIPEDA. Establishing policies and procedures to manage the handling of personal information in accordance with the law is an essential step in setting up any kind of service business; and for existing businesses, auditing procedures for compliance with PIPEDA are a must.

Organizations should take the following steps to comply with PIPEDA:

1. identify the purposes for which the business needs to collect personal information, and narrow the scope of such collection to fit those purposes;

2. develop a procedure for obtaining and renewing consents to use or disclose information, and develop a privacy policy that is available for review by customers;

3. develop internal policies for the use of information;

4. establish procedures and physical facilities for the secure storage of information files and electronic data;

5. establish guidelines for the retention and eventual secure destruction of personal information; and

6. appoint a privacy officer or committee to monitor compliance with privacy laws.

CASE IN POINT

Does PIPEDA Apply to Not-for-Profit Organizations?

A parent filed a complaint with the privacy commissioner under PIPEDA alleging that the scholarship committee of a private school divulged his financial information to people who were not on the committee, without his consent. The school argued that PIPEDA did not apply and that the Privacy Commissioner of Canada had no jurisdiction to rule on the matter, because the school's core activity was education and it was a not-for-profit corporation designated as a charitable organization by the Canada Revenue Agency.

The Privacy Commissioner of Canada ruled that it had no jurisdiction under PIPEDA with regard to information disclosed by a private school where the school was not engaged in any commercial activities.

Importance

Not-for-profit organizations and charities are not governed by PIPEDA. However, other privacy legislation may apply.

Source: Privacy Commissioner of Canada, PIPEDA Case Summary no. 345, decided 2006 July 5, obtained online at www.privcom.gc.ca. ◇

COMPLAINTS

Social service workers may encounter clients who have complaints about the invasion of their privacy in violation of PIPEDA. Requests for access or corrections to information and complaints about inappropriate disclosures are handled by the Privacy Commissioner of Canada. The complaint procedure is very similar to that for complaints under the *Privacy Act*, and it commences with the submission by the complainant of a written complaint to the privacy commissioner.

To minimize the submission of complaints on issues that have been addressed previously, and to assist organizations in avoiding compliance pitfalls, the Privacy Commissioner of Canada publishes summaries of its decisions on complaints that have been resolved. These are available online at the commissioner's website, cited above.

ONTARIO LEGISLATION

Ontario has two key privacy statutes, the *Freedom of Information and Protection of Privacy Act* (FIPPA) and the *Personal Health Information Protection Act, 2004* (PHIPA). FIPPA applies to provincial government organizations. A similar statute, the *Municipal Freedom of Information and Protection of Privacy Act*, applies to municipal governments and agencies in Ontario. It is not discussed separately here.

All three statutes are administered by the Information and Privacy Commissioner of Ontario. The commissioner is appointed by the legislature, but is independent of the ruling government. The commissioner investigates complaints about the mishandling of individuals' personal information by public sector information gatherers, and manages requests for access to information. Complaints about mishandling of personal information by private sector information gatherers fall under the federal PIPEDA, discussed above.

Freedom of Information and Protection of Privacy Act

The *Freedom of Information and Protection of Privacy Act* is intended to provide a right of access to information, based on the principle that information should be available to the public. The statute provides for an independent body to make decisions about the disclosure of government information, and it also offers privacy protection to individuals who may be affected by the disclosure.

Examples of kinds of information that a social service worker or her client might wish to access include the following:

- the government's reasons for denying a benefit that the client has applied for;

- the government's criteria for making a decision with respect to social benefits;

- the government's reasons for declining to provide requested funding or grants to a not-for-profit corporation or other charitable project; and

- a list of corporations or projects that have received government funding.

Like the federal *Privacy Act*, the Ontario FIPPA provides a mechanism for individuals to inquire about the information that government holds about them, and to request corrections to that information. If an individual believes that the information is incorrect, and the government disagrees and refuses to make the requested

LEGISLATIVE SHORTCUT

Freedom of Information and Protection of Privacy Act

RSO 1990, c. F.31

Objective: To provide a right of access to Ontario government information based on the principle that information should be available to the public, and to protect the privacy of individuals with respect to information about them held by Ontario government ministries and agencies.

Target Population: Anyone whose personal information is held by an Ontario ministry, agency, board, commission, community college, university, or district health council.

Program Administration: The Information and Privacy Commissioner of Ontario investigates complaints about the mishandling of individuals' personal information by public sector information gatherers, and manages requests for access to information.

Administrative Tribunal: Information and Privacy Commissioner of Ontario.

Summary: FIPPA provides for an independent body to make decisions about the disclosure of government information, and it also provides rules for the government's handling of people's personal information. The legislation and the regulations made under it regulate the collection, use, disclosure, storage, and disposal of personal information. ◇

Municipal Freedom of Information and Protection of Privacy Act

RSO 1990, c. M.56

Objective: To provide a right of access to municipal government information, based on the principle that information should be available to the public, and to protect the privacy of individuals with respect to information about them held by municipal councils and their boards and agencies.

Target Population: Anyone whose personal information is held by municipal councils and their boards and agencies in Ontario.

Program Administration: The Information and Privacy Commissioner of Ontario investigates complaints about the mishandling of individuals' personal information by public sector information gatherers, and manages requests for access to information.

Administrative Tribunal: Information and Privacy Commissioner.

Summary: The *Municipal Freedom of Information and Protection of Privacy Act* provides for an independent body to make decisions about the disclosure of government information, and it also provides rules for the government's handling of people's personal information. The legislation and the regulations made under it regulate the collection, use, disclosure, storage, and disposal of personal information. ◇

correction, the individual has a right to request that a "statement of disagreement" be attached to the information, and that this statement be provided to all government holders and users of the information to which FIPPA applies. These include all Ontario government ministries, agencies, and boards; most provincial commissions; community colleges; and district health councils.

Like the *Privacy Act*, FIPPA provides rules for the government's handling of personal information. The legislation and the regulations made under it govern the collection, use, disclosure, storage, and disposal of personal information.

ACCESSING INFORMATION

The first step for an individual seeking access to information is to direct the request to the agency that holds the information. Only if the agency refuses the request, or fails to provide access, should an individual seek recourse from the IP commissioner.

Besides creating a mechanism for allowing individuals access to their own information, FIPPA allows individuals to request access to "general" government information. This is information that is not about the individual himself or other third parties, but rather about the government and its dealings.

The government is not required to disclose all information. It shall not disclose information that would infringe on the privacy interests of a third party (another individual, for example), and it is also not allowed to disclose Cabinet records. Other kinds of information are subject to government discretion, that is, the government can decide whether or not to disclose it. These categories of information are

- information about intergovernmental relations, if the information was received in confidence;

- advice or recommendations within the organization;

- law enforcement;

- defence;

- information that could prejudice the financial or other specified interests of the organization;

- solicitor–client privilege;

- information that could endanger the health or safety of an individual;

- information already available to the public or soon to be published.

COMPLAINTS

FIPPA sets out the procedure for pursuing disclosure where the agency that holds information denies a request for access. Requests are to be made in writing and generally must be responded to by the agency within 30 days. Efforts are made to resolve complaints informally. If informal negotiations are unsuccessful, the Information and Privacy Commissioner may conduct a formal review, which may result in an order to disclose the information. In most cases, the agency is required to change its procedures to ensure that similar violations of individual privacy will not occur in the future. Applicants whose requests are denied by the agency and are not made subject to disclosure by the commissioner have a right of appeal to the courts.

Like the federal privacy commissioner, the Information and Privacy Commissioner publishes reports of some of the cases that it has resolved as a reference for individuals and information gatherers.

CASE IN POINT

Security of Private Records

A couple was left alone to wait in an Ontario legal aid office. The wife looked through a stack of stapled papers that had been left on the desk (scratch pads using the blank reverse of old documents), and noticed that the printed side contained personal names, telephone numbers, social insurance numbers, and notations indicating whether the person had applied for legal aid before. The wife removed some sheets from the office and delivered them to her provincial member of Parliament, who filed a complaint under FIPPA with the Information and Privacy Commissioner.

The Information and Privacy Commissioner investigated the complaint and found that the information disclosed was personal information, and that it was not "disclosed" in compliance with FIPPA. The legal aid office took measures designed to ensure that confidential documents would no longer be used to create scratch pads, but the Information and Privacy Commissioner recommended additional steps. These included circulating memorandums about privacy issues to all staff (not just senior staff), posting privacy protection information on bulletin boards across the province (not just in the affected office), and establishing a training program on privacy issues for new employees.

Importance

Special care should be taken to ensure that, in any part of an office to which clients or visitors have access, all personal information—including out-of-date, "recycled" client records—is kept in secure storage and cannot be viewed by unauthorized persons. Offices that wish to use old documents as scratch paper should exercise extreme care in doing so.

Note, also, that Legal Aid Ontario is a not-for-profit organization. As discussed in a case summary cited earlier in this chapter, the federal PIPEDA does not apply to not-for-profit organizations. Ontario's FIPPA evidently covers privacy violations in this sector.

Source: Information and Privacy Commissioner of Ontario, Information and Privacy Commissioner's Investigation no. PC-000025-1, reported December 13, 2000, obtained online at www.ipc.on.ca. ◈

Personal Health Information Protection Act, 2004

The PHIPA has already been discussed in the context of hospitals and long-term care facilities (chapter 7). That chapter also covers the PHIPA's purposes, the health-care providers to which it applies, the definition of personal health information, and other important issues.

In Ontario, the PHIPA applies in lieu of the health information provisions of PIPEDA, because the PHIPA has been declared "substantially similar" to PIPEDA in respect of those provisions. In health-care settings regulated by the provincial government, either the PHIPA or FIPPA (but generally not both) applies: FIPPA applies to district health councils; the PHIPA applies to all other "custodians" of personal health information. As noted above, the PHIPA is administered by the Information and Privacy Commissioner.

OTHER LEGISLATION

There are other federal and provincial statutes that contain provisions governing the management of personal information in specific contexts, such as the financial sector. For example, the federal *Bank Act* regulates the use and disclosure of personal financial information by federally regulated financial institutions. Similarly, provincial legislation regulates the use and disclosure of personal information by credit reporting agencies.

KEY TERMS

disclosure by consent

disclosure required by law

REFERENCES

Child and Family Services Act, RSO 1990, c. C.11.

Freedom of Information and Protection of Privacy Act, RSO 1990, c. F.31.

Municipal Freedom of Information and Protection of Privacy Act, RSO 1990, c. M.56.

Ontario College of Social Workers and Social Service Workers, Code of Ethics and *Standards of Practice Handbook*, online at www.ocswssw.org.

Personal Health Information Protection Act, 2004, SO 2004, c. 3, Sch. A.

Personal Information Protection and Electronics Documents Act, SC 2000, c. 5.

Privacy Act, RSC 1985, c. P-21.

WEB LINK

More detailed information about the applications and administration of FIPPA and the PHIPA is available from the website of the Information and Privacy Commissioner of Ontario at www.ipc.on.ca.

REVIEW QUESTIONS

1. What are the potential consequences of violating a client's personal privacy?

2. In what circumstances is it acceptable to divulge client information, according to the Code of Ethics and *Standards of Practice Handbook* of the College of Social Workers and Social Service Workers?

3. If a social service worker thinks that a client may disclose information to her that she would be required by law to disclose, what should she do?

4. List at least two things that a client should be told at the time that she is asked to provide written consent to disclosure of her personal information.

5. What are two important things to remember when drafting a consent to disclosure?

6. If a social service worker believes that a client may be suicidal, what steps should he take?

7. Identify two privacy statutes that apply to social service agencies and employees within the federal government.

8. If you are a social service worker working in a federally regulated agency and you are uncertain about whether you can disclose certain information, what should you do?

9. If you have a client who is concerned that an Ontario government agency has information on file about her and that information is inaccurate (for example, she is a client applying for Ontario Works benefits and the government has on file that she is married, when she is not), what can she do? How can you help?

10. What should you or a client do if the information wanted is not personal information but rather general Ontario government information? (For example, in a client's case, it may be information about why her disability claim was denied; or in your case, it may be information about which agencies received government grants that your agency had applied for but not obtained.)

DISCUSSION QUESTIONS

The following scenarios raise the potential for a breach in client confidentiality. How might each situation be handled, either at the time it arises, or by prior preparation?

1. You are the leader of a local chapter of Alcoholics Anonymous. Nina is a regular attendee. Another participant, Mario, runs into Nina and her mother in the local grocery store and asks, "So, are you coming to the meeting tonight?" Nina's mother asks Nina, in front of Mario, how the two have met. Nina looks very uncomfortable.

2. André and Larry are fathers who participated in a court-ordered anger management program as a condition of gaining unsupervised access to their children. The two men did not get along during the course of the program. They run into each other at a swim meet in which their children are participating. Also at the meet is Belinda, a neighbour of André's. When André offers to drive Belinda's daughter home at the end of the swim meet, Larry overhears and cautions Belinda about letting her daughter ride with André.

3. You work as a counsellor in a program designed to build self-esteem and lifestyle skills for overweight teenagers. Nadjma is one of the program participants. You run into Nadjma and her grandmother at a symphony performance, and Nadjma introduces you as "my fat-group counsellor, Sophie." Her grandmother then launches into a friendly barrage of questions, asking you about the program and Nadjma's participation.

CHAPTER 23

Liability Issues

CHAPTER OBJECTIVES

After reading this chapter, you should be able to:

- Identify three categories of legal or professional consequences that can arise from poor performance of a social service worker's duties.

- Describe the complaint and discipline process of the Ontario College of Social Workers and Social Service Workers.

- Explain the possible consequences of a breach of professional standards.

- Identify two types of criminal charges that could be laid against a social service worker as a consequence of her actions on the job.

- Understand the concepts of criminal and civil negligence and their application to social service workers.

- Provide suggestions for how social service workers can limit their exposure to professional or legal sanctions or damages.

INTRODUCTION

Very few people choose a career in social services for purely economic reasons. Rather, they are motivated by a sincere desire to help disadvantaged people to overcome their problems and lead happier and more productive lives. For this reason, social service workers seldom harm others out of malice or recklessness. However, mistakes happen. Social service workers often carry large caseloads. Overwork, inexperience, lack of support, and other factors can contribute to situations in which a social service worker fails to take correct action on behalf of a client, or makes an error in judgment.

There are three main kinds of consequences that social service workers can experience in the event of serious errors:

- sanctions for professional misconduct;

- criminal charges; or

- lawsuits under the **civil law** of torts.

Reasonable everyday errors or missteps made in the course of performing assigned duties are unlikely to land a social service worker in legal trouble. Problems tend to arise, instead, where an error is unreasonable given the circumstances—for example, where a social service worker's efforts have fallen markedly below the recognized standards of the profession. Taking actions that are outside the acceptable scope of your professional duties, such as giving legal advice, can also cause problems. Finally, any action motivated by malice, personal gain, or other inappropriate objectives is automatically outside the scope of a social service worker's duties, and can lead to legal or professional consequences.

PROFESSIONAL MISCONDUCT AND INCOMPETENCE

WEB LINK

To review the Code of Ethics and *Standards of Practice Handbook* published by the Ontario College of Social Workers and Social Service Workers, for access to Discipline Committee decisions, and for more information about how to make a complaint, visit www.ocswssw.org.

As explained in chapter 1, the professions of social work and social service work are regulated by the Ontario College of Social Workers and Social Service Workers. One of the key goals of the college is to maintain standards of practice that promote high-quality service to clients, and thereby build public confidence in the work of social service. To this end, the college has authority to call its members to account for failure to meet the established standards of the profession. This section describes the college's procedure for reviewing complaints and the disciplinary sanctions that may be imposed in cases of incompetence or professional misconduct.

Complaints and Discipline

An instance of professional incompetence or misconduct typically comes to the attention of the college when someone—often a client, or a family member of a client—makes a written complaint about the social service professional to the college. A complaint is defined as

> an expression of concern about the conduct or actions of a member relating to professional misconduct, incompetence or incapacity on the part of a member of the College.

"**Professional misconduct**" is defined as

> conduct that violates the *Social Work and Social Service Work Act*, the regulations under that Act, or the by-laws of the College.

"Incompetence" generally means

> being unable to do one's job properly through lack of experience, skill, effort, or application.

"Incapacity" is different from incompetence and means

> not being able to do one's job because of a physical or mental condition or disorder.

When a complaint is made, the college provides the social service worker with a copy or written summary of the complaint. The social service worker has at least 35 days to prepare a written response. The response is delivered to the complainant, who is allowed to provide additional information for clarification. If necessary, the college makes additional inquiries (for example, speaks to other witnesses) to obtain any other information that may be needed.

COMPLAINTS COMMITTEE

Once the information has been gathered, the complaint is reviewed by a three-member panel of the Complaints Committee. The panel does not hear oral submissions; it only reviews documents. The panel is generally required to provide a decision and written reasons within 120 days, where possible, but sometimes the process takes longer.

The panel of the Complaints Committee can take a range of actions, which include the following:

- doing nothing;

- requiring the social service worker to appear before the committee to be "cautioned" (given a formal warning);

- taking "any action permitted by the legislation or by-laws" (such as referring the matter to a mediator for an attempt at resolution);

- referring the matter to the Discipline Committee to make a determination regarding professional misconduct or incompetence of the member; or

- referring the matter to the Fitness to Practice Committee to make a determination regarding incapacity of the member.

The panel of the Complaints Committee does not have authority to make an order of damages. Complainants who are seeking monetary compensation must pursue a civil lawsuit (discussed later under the heading "Tort Lawsuits").

DISCIPLINE COMMITTEE

When a complaint is referred to the Discipline Committee, the college can temporarily suspend the social service worker's membership, pending resolution of the complaint.

The Discipline Committee deals with complaints through a formal hearing process with oral submissions and witness testimony. The hearings are usually open to the public. Because an adverse discipline decision remains on the member's record and can have a significant impact on her future career, it is a good idea for anyone facing discipline to hire a lawyer. For example, if the college proposes to suspend the individual's membership pending the resolution of the complaint, she has 14 days in which to prepare written submissions about why the membership should not be suspended. A lawyer's advice would be very useful for the purpose of drafting these submissions.

If the Discipline Committee finds the member guilty of professional misconduct or incompetence, it may make any of the following orders (as provided in section 26 of the *Social Work and Social Service Work Act, 1998*):

1. Revocation of any certificate of registration held by the member under this Act.

2. Suspension of any certificate of registration held by the member under this Act for a specified period, not exceeding 24 months.

3. Imposition of specified terms, conditions or limitations on any certificate of registration held by the member under this Act.

4. Direction that the imposition of any of the above be postponed for a specified period and not be imposed if specified terms are met within that period.

CASE IN POINT

Professional Misconduct: Sexual Involvement with a Client

Two recent discipline cases published on the website of the Ontario College of Social Workers and Social Service Workers, turned on allegations of sexual involvement between a member of the college and a client or former client. The decision of the Discipline Committee and the sanctions imposed in each case reflect the particular circumstances and the member's willingness to take responsibility for his or her actions.

Disgraceful, Dishonourable, and Unprofessional Conduct

The client was a counselling client with a history of being sexually abused and of engaging in self-harming behaviour. He was actively suicidal.

The member (a social worker) realized that she was sexually attracted to the client and decided that she needed to transfer the case to a colleague at the same agency. However, despite the client's vulnerability, of which she was aware, she initiated and engaged in a sexual relationship with him. She eventually terminated this relationship, and the client filed the complaint.

The Discipline Committee found that as a result of the member's impropriety, the client suffered substance abuse problems, health problems, and social isolation issues.

The member showed a lack of remorse about her conduct, accusing the former client of having "ruined her life" by bringing the complaint. This lack of appreciation of the impropriety of her conduct seems to have influenced the committee's decision with respect to penalties. Although the member had resigned after the complaint was filed, the committee, having deemed her conduct to have been "disgraceful, dishonourable" and professional misconduct, imposed the following penalties:

- a reprimand was noted on the member's file;

- the college's decision and reasons were published on the college's website, in the college's newsletter, and on the newswire with the member's name included; and

- the decision and findings were to be "made known to social work regulators in other provinces and to the American Association of Marriage and Family Therapists."

Dishonourable and Unprofessional Conduct

The member (also a social worker) cooperated closely with the college after the complaint was lodged. He and the college filed an agreed statement of fact explaining the conduct in issue. According to the statement, the member had encountered the client as a psychotherapy patient. The client, who began seeing the member for therapy when he was 17, suffered from a social functioning disorder.

The member developed a dual relationship with the client that involved seeing the client extensively on a social basis, providing the client with alcohol, viewing pornography with the client, discussing his sexual orientation with the client, and disclosing to the client that he felt sexually attracted to him. The summary of the facts notes that "the Member allowed a relationship of excessive emotional dependency by the client upon the member to develop, and used the therapeutic relationship to meet the Member's own personal needs."

The Discipline Committee took into account the fact that, once the complaint was filed, the member acknowledged his wrongdoing and cooperated with the college. As a penalty, the committee ordered that:

- the member be reprimanded and the reprimand be entered on the member's record;

- limitations/conditions be entered on the member's record, restricting his scope of practice for two years, so that he would not be in a position to engage in the same conduct again;

- a summary of the findings and order be published, with identifying information removed; and

- the member undergo "intensive insight-oriented psychotherapy" for two years, and the college be permitted to monitor the psychotherapy.

Case reports obtained from the Ontario College of Social Workers and Social Service Workers, published online at www.ocswssw.org. ◇

Additional orders are available if the member is found guilty of professional misconduct (but not incompetence), as follows:

1. Reprimand, admonishment or counselling, and if considered warranted, recording of such on member's record.

2. Fine to a maximum of $5,000.

3. Publication of the case, in detail or in summary, with or without the name of the member, in the official publication of the College and in any other manner or medium considered appropriate in the particular case.

4. Costs of the discipline hearing to be paid by the member.

The college maintains a register of members, with a record of any revocation or suspension of an individual's membership. In some cases, the college can order that the fact that a member was found guilty of disgraceful or dishonourable conduct, or professional misconduct, be entered on his permanent record.

CRIMINAL OFFENCES

The *Criminal Code* covers a wide range of criminal acts, and it's conceivable that a social service worker could commit a variety of crimes in the course of her work. This chapter, however, will focus on two of the more common criminal charges that may arise in the social services context: assault and criminal negligence.

Assault

There are many provisions of the *Criminal Code* that deal with assault. Assault ranges from unwanted and intentional physical contact (including touching) to violent physical aggression against another person. Where force is involved, or the use of a weapon, it is an offence not only to commit such an act but also to threaten to do so.

The penalties for assault offences vary according to the nature of the assault (sexual or non-sexual), the circumstances, whether a weapon was involved, and the degree of harm inflicted. For example, where the assault causes no lasting physical harm, the *Criminal Code* tends to impose higher penalties for sexual assault than for minor non-sexual assault. The reason for this is that sexual assault includes a component of humiliation or affront to the dignity that is not as common in the case of minor non-sexual assault.

Sexual assaults against children, disabled persons, or individuals in a relationship of trust or dependence with the assailant are punished more harshly because of the vulnerability of the victim and/or the breach of trust. The *Criminal Code* also recognizes, by imposing higher penalties, the greater severity of assaults that involve the use of a weapon or result in lasting physical harm.

The criminal law was discussed in some detail in chapter 9 (including the key concepts of *actus reus* and *mens rea*) and will not be reviewed here. A detailed discussion of the various assault provisions is also beyond the scope of this chapter. However, it is important to recognize that assaults do sometimes occur in the social services context, including circumstances where a service provider is charged with assault of a client.

There are three key situations in which the risk of assault or sexual assault is elevated:

- where a social service worker serves clients who tend to be violent or resistant to physical treatment or care;

- where a social service worker who is sexually attracted to children or teenagers is allowed unsupervised individual access to these clients; and

- where a social service worker allows a dual (personal and professional) relationship to develop with a client.

Each of these situations is discussed below.

VIOLENT CLIENTS

The risk of assault is present whenever a client is difficult to manage physically, or "hard to handle." This category includes a wide variety of clients and service contexts. Consider the following examples:

- a 2-year-old client who is prone to tantrums;

- a 9-year-old autistic client who becomes unresponsive and violent when he feels upset;

- a 20-year-old mentally ill client who becomes violent when she suffers delusions;

- a 40-year-old client who becomes violent while under the influence of alcohol;

- a 93-year-old client with Alzheimer's who physically resists necessary care (bathing, being moved for bedding changes, etc.).

Social service workers who work with physically hard-to-handle clients should receive thorough training in the use of restraints (physical restraints and/or submission holds) and other measures involving the application of force. The use of restraints is permitted in certain settings (for example, hospitals that treat mental illness) within very strict guidelines.

The use of force permitted by law is very limited. In general, no individual can use force against another unless it is explicitly provided for by a statute, or unless the statute provides that those who are empowered to carry out its objectives cannot be sued for so doing. Even then, a person who is carrying out a public or statutory duty must use the minimum force necessary under the circumstances. Using excessive force takes a person outside the protection of these laws, and the person's only defence, in those circumstances, may be self-defence under the criminal law.

Federal statutes that authorize the use of some level of force and/or limit the liability of those who carry out public duties include:

- the *Criminal Code*,

- the *Customs Act*, and

- the *Corrections and Conditional Release Act*.

Ontario statutes include:

- the *Public Authorities Protection Act*,

- the *Police Services Act* (specifically, regulation 926 made under that Act),

- the *Mental Health Act,*
- the *Child and Family Services Act,* and
- the *Ministry of Correctional Services Act.*

As a general rule, unless you have been made aware of a specific employment policy permitting the use of force in your work, and unless you have undergone appropriate training in support of that policy, as a social service worker, you should avoid the use of force completely. In fact, unless physical care is included in your job description (as it may be if you work in a daycare centre or a long-term care facility), you should try to avoid any physical contact with clients, particularly those who are known to be hard to handle.

SEXUAL ABUSE

Pedophiles and individuals who seek to exploit vulnerable adults and/or teens often apply for jobs that will bring them into contact with potential victims. While employers should perform criminal background checks and reference checks on *all* employees, this is essential in the case of those who will be allowed access to children and vulnerable clients. Even if these checks uncover no areas of concern, it is good policy for employers to ensure that new employees are closely supervised in the first few months of their employment. Only after the employer develops informed trust in an employee should he or she be permitted to work in an unsupervised setting with an individual child, teenager, or vulnerable adult. Finally, any complaints about an employee's behaviour must be thoroughly investigated, and the employee's access to vulnerable clients should be suspended pending resolution of the complaint.

To prevent unwarranted suspicion or accusations, social service workers should be diligent in avoiding any behaviour that might be deemed inappropriate, including suggestive or ambiguous comments and, particularly, physical contact with clients. Occasionally, a client might initiate touching, for example, a developmentally delayed or very young client with whom you interact in a recreation program might spontaneously hug you at the end of a session. In this situation, without rebuffing the client, you should keep the hug brief and, if possible, gently discourage such contact. For example, you might explain to the client that in your culture, hugging is for family and best friends. If the behaviour is repeated, or if you aren't sure how to handle the situation, you should report it to your supervisor and ask for guidance in dealing with this issue on future occasions.

MINIMIZING RISK

The best policy on the question of physical contact is to exercise extreme caution, particularly in high-risk situations. Unless it is part of the job, limit physical contact with clients to, at most, a brief and formal handshake, preferably initiated by the client.

At the same time, it is fair to say that, generally, a social service worker is unlikely to be charged with assault in an incident involving accidental contact. An assault charge arising out of a social service worker's performance of her duties is most likely to be laid when the conduct complained of is clearly intentional, is sexually motivated, involves the use of excessive force, or contravenes recognized professional standards.

Employers also should do their part to minimize the risk of assault charges against their employees. After all, if a charge is laid, the employer's reputation may be tarnished as well. The following are effective ways of minimizing risk:

- carefully screening job applicants;

- supervising new employees who work with children and/or other vulnerable clients;

- developing a detailed policy for the use of restraints and/or force, if applicable;

- developing a detailed policy with respect to dual relationships;

- providing training for employees on such matters as physical contact with clients, handling violent or aggressive clients, and sexual harassment; and

- promptly and thoroughly investigating all complaints.

Criminal Negligence

While assault generally implies some degree of action, the concept of negligence, which also exists in tort law, implies a lack of action in circumstances where action (or caution) is warranted.

Criminal negligence is more severe than civil negligence. The precise differences are beyond the scope of this book; it suffices to say that, generally, only particularly serious derelictions of duty attract criminal charges. Criminal negligence is also likely to be charged only where there is a widely accepted duty (for example, a statutory duty) on the accused to take the action that he or she is accused of not taking. Civil negligence is discussed later, under the heading "Tort Lawsuits."

Section 219 of the *Criminal Code* creates the basic offence of criminal negligence:

219. (1) Every one is criminally negligent who
    (a) in doing anything, or
    (b) in omitting to do anything that it is his duty to do,
shows wanton or reckless disregard for the lives or safety of other persons.
    (2) For the purposes of this section, "duty" means a duty imposed by law.

Unlike most criminal offences, criminal negligence does not require proof of intent. To support a charge, the prosecutor must prove that the accused had a legal duty to act, and failed to do so.

As this book has shown, there are many laws that impose specific duties on social service workers. Where neglect of those duties has serious consequences, a charge of criminal negligence could arise. For example, failing to follow up on child abuse or neglect has the potential to attract criminal (and civil) sanctions that go beyond the offence provisions of the *Child and Family Services Act*. In the case of *R. v. Heikamp and Martin*, discussed in chapter 3, where a baby died in his mother's care despite children's aid society involvement, the child protection worker assigned to the case was charged with criminal negligence.

Under section 218 of the *Criminal Code* it is also an offence to abandon or expose a child to harm where his or her life or health is permanently at risk. The definition of "abandon or expose" in section 214 specifically extends the scope of liability to include not just the child's parents but other persons as well:

"[A]bandon" or "expose" includes

>　　(a) a wilful omission to take charge of a child by a person who is under a legal duty to do so, and

>　　(b) dealing with a child in a manner that is likely to leave that child exposed to risk without protection.

Section 215 of the *Criminal Code* also has direct application to social service workers who work with children, in that it imposes "a legal duty ... to provide necessaries of life for a child" on a "parent, foster parent, guardian or head of a family." Child protection is only one possible area in which social service workers might be exposed to the risk of criminal negligence. Other areas include any work that involves caring for vulnerable persons, including those who are elderly, mentally ill, or physically ill, disabled, or developmentally delayed.

Many cases in which criminal negligence has been charged have involved the failure of parents to properly care for their children. In the Kim Anne Popen case, discussed in chapter 14, one of the baby's parents was convicted for failure to protect the baby from her other parent. However, it is easy to imagine other situations in which a charge of criminal negligence might be laid in the social services context. For example, a social service worker might fail to report to a supervisor that a child disclosed suicidal feelings, or to take other appropriate action. If the child later committed suicide without anyone having attempted to intervene, it is possible that the social service worker could be charged with criminal negligence.

To minimize the risk of being charged with criminal negligence, it is important that you understand the duties of your job, and perform them conscientiously. If you are unsure of what to do in a particular situation, it is imperative that you ask for help. If you feel overwhelmed by your workload to the point where you believe that individual clients may be neglected, it is your responsibility to report this to a supervisor, and to request extra help.

From the perspective of the employer, the following safeguards are important:

- providing adequate training and supervision to all staff;

- responding promptly to requests for guidance and/or assistance;

- managing the workload of staff to ensure that clients receive the services they need; and

- seeking background checks, including criminal records, before hiring.

CIVIL LAWSUITS

Tort Liability

Tort liability was discussed briefly in chapters 2 and 13. **Torts** fall into two basic categories: **intentional torts** and **unintentional torts**. An intentional tort, as the name suggests, is harm caused intentionally to one person by another. The events that form the basis for an intentional tort lawsuit are often similar to those that give rise to offences under criminal law—the key difference being that in the latter case, a criminal charge is laid and prosecuted by the Crown. There are other important differences as well, and these will be discussed below.

Unintentional torts are based on the civil concept of negligence. There are a number of elements that must be proved by the plaintiff in a negligence case—namely, duty of care, standard of care, causation, and remoteness. These also will be explained below.

INTENTIONAL TORTS

As indicated above, there are significant differences between an intentional tort lawsuit and a criminal charge, in particular:

- A intentional tort lawsuit is a civil action brought by the plaintiff (the person wronged) and tried in civil court, whereas a criminal charge is prosecuted by the Crown and tried in criminal court.

- The civil standard of proof is lower. The plaintiff need only prove the case on a balance of probabilities, rather than beyond a reasonable doubt as required in criminal cases. This means that torts are often easier to prove than crimes.

- If the tort is proven, the penalty is an award of monetary compensation (**damages**) that must be paid by the defendant (the tortfeasor) to the victim/plaintiff. A criminal charge, if proven, may result in a fine and/or imprisonment, depending on the seriousness of the offence.

- In recent years, there has been a proliferation of intentional tort lawsuits arising from sexual assault of children and vulnerable adults by caregivers and other service providers. As a result of these lawsuits, many of which have been successful, there is a new awareness in the community, and among social service professionals of the potential for sexual mistreatment of children.

- Employers should ensure that their employees are well supervised, especially when working with one child or small groups of children. Employers should also respond promptly to any complaints or concerns, by carrying out a thorough investigation and suspending the employee's access to children or vulnerable adults pending the results of the investigation.

UNINTENTIONAL TORTS: NEGLIGENCE

The tort of negligence is grounded in certain rights that flow from the relationships between individuals (parent to child, neighbour to neighbour, social service worker to client, etc.). These relationships may give rise to a duty of care. If there is no duty of care, there can be no tort of negligence. In Canada, the law of torts does not recognize a "good Samaritan" rule or principle compelling people to help each other. If a person is drowning in a river, a passerby may be morally obligated to throw a flotation device, or call for help, but he has no legal duty to do so.

Duty of Care and Standard of Care

Before there can be any liability for the tort of negligence, the plaintiff must prove that a legal **duty of care** was owed to him, and that the defendant failed to carry out that duty to the standard of what is "reasonable" in the circumstances. The duty of care and the standard of care are key elements in proving civil negligence, and it is important to understand how the courts apply these concepts. In the case of a social service worker–client relationship, in the great majority of cases, there will be a duty owed.

Once the duty of care is established, the court will have to decide whether the actions of the social service worker fell below the **standard of care** that is appropriate. Social service workers are held to the objective, but somewhat vague, standard of the "reasonable" social service worker. What would a "reasonable" and competent social service worker do in the circumstances?

To determine what you must do to meet the standard of care required of you, you will need to consult sources already discussed elsewhere in this book. These include

- the code of ethics and standards of practice established by the College of Social Workers and Social Service Workers;

- your job description;

- the policies of your employer;

- the terms of any licence under which your employer operates; and

- any statutes and/or regulations that govern the work that you do.

Causation and Remoteness

In addition to proving the existence of a duty of care and a breach of the standard of care owed, the plaintiff must also prove causation, and that the harm caused was not too "remote."

To prove causation, the plaintiff must show that the harm resulted from the negligence. For example, if a social service worker reveals the location of a safe house for abused women, and as a result a woman is attacked there by her husband, the social service worker may be found to have "caused" the harm to the woman, because "but for" the disclosure of this confidential information, the incident would not have occurred. The husband could, of course, also be found liable for the same incident.

CASE IN POINT

Suing the Government

A couple of interesting lawsuits have been filed in Alberta recently, claiming damages against the provincial Department of Child Welfare for administrative decisions made in the 1970s and 1980s.

In one case, *Mr. K v. E.K.*, the plaintiff (Mr. K), a young man, is suing Child Welfare for allegedly failing to take sufficient measures to protect him from abuse at the hands of his mother (another defendant in the lawsuit), despite a number of complaints made to Child Welfare on his behalf when he was a child.

In another case, a sexual assault victim is suing her young assailant in civil court (subsequent to a criminal trial). She has named Child Welfare as an additional defendant in the lawsuit. Her claim against Child Welfare alleges that, in failing to adequately protect her rapist when he was an abused child, Child Welfare contributed to an upbringing that made him more likely to be violent toward her.

Both cases were still pending when this book was written. ◇

The test for remoteness is foreseeability. Was the harm caused foreseeable by the defendant? In the example above, if the disclosure of the whereabouts of the shelter led to the client fleeing, and being hit by a car on the street outside, a court would likely find that the injuries sustained were too remote from the social service worker's wrongful disclosure. A reasonable social service worker could not be expected to foresee this event as a consequence.

Vicarious Liability

It is important to realize that unprofessional practice that results in harm to a client can have legal consequences not only for the social service worker but also for his employer.

Generally, under the doctrine of **agency**, an employer may be held responsible for mistakes of his employees made in the course of carrying out their duties. Agency applies to actions of an employee taken in the line of duty—that is, actions taken on the employer's time that are within the employee's job description. In addition, in limited circumstances, employers can be held accountable, under the doctrine of **vicarious liability**, for actions that fall outside the scope of the employee's work. For example, vicarious liability could arise where the employer ignores complaints from clients alleging inappropriate sexual advances or touching by a social service worker, and eventually a client sues the social service worker for sexual battery under the law of torts. Knowing about (and ignoring) the social service worker's inappropriate behaviour while promoting his access to vulnerable clients will likely make the employer liable to compensate the victims, even though the social service worker's actions fall outside the scope of his duties in his job description.

Where a social service worker's actions result in liability for the employer, the consequences may be worse than just costing the employer money. Many social service providers operate on a non-profit basis. The cost of a lawsuit may force the service provider to go out of business. Proven harm to a client may also cause the agency to lose a licence that it requires to do business (for example, a daycare licence under the *Day Nurseries Act*, or status as a non-profit housing provider for the purpose of government funding).

Social service workers must realize that failing to perform their job to expected professional standards, and within the requirements of the law, not only harms existing clients, but may also result in reduced access to services for others in the community. In addition, successful lawsuits erode the public trust in social service providers.

INSURANCE AND WAIVERS

While the most important strategy for staying out of legal trouble is for social service professionals to do their job to the best of their ability, there are additional ways in which an agency can manage the risk of a lawsuit, including insurance and waivers.

Liability insurance protects against negligence lawsuits by compensating victims. By paying an affordable and predictable premium, a social service agency can protect itself against damages awards. Insurance may also make it possible to settle claims at an earlier stage, resulting in lower legal fees and limiting harm to the agency's reputation in the community.

Besides purchasing insurance, a social service agency may want to consider using waivers. A **waiver**, sometimes called a release, is a contract that explains the risks involved in certain activities and provides that the client accepts the risk. For example, a waiver may set out the risks of participating in a sports program, or the risk of disclosure of confidential information through participation in group therapy. In signing the waiver, the participant acknowledges the risk and agrees not to sue if such harm occurs. A waiver typically

- advises the participant of the most well-known risks in detail, and sometimes explains that there may be other risks that cannot be foreseen;

- advises the participant that by signing the waiver and participating in the activity, he or she is voluntarily assuming known and unknown risks; and

- explains that as a result of signing the waiver, the participant is barred from making any future legal claims based on harm arising from his or her participation in the activity.

A waiver cannot provide protection against all lawsuits. For example, the obligations and responsibilities set out by statute may not be overridden by waiver. In some cases, courts have found that the person who signed a waiver did not understand either the nature of the risks or the effect of the waiver. In these circumstances, the waiver is typically not valid. In other cases, the courts have found that the particular harm that came to the participant was outside the scope of the waiver.

If a service provider wants to use a waiver, it should seek legal advice regarding wording and determine the extent to which it can be relied upon. Regardless of how carefully worded a waiver may be, it will not apply if the participants are unable to understand it. Staff who supervise the handing out and return of waiver forms will require training in how to present the waiver. Ideally, the staff member should cover the following points:

- Explain the effect of the waiver—that, by signing it, the participant is assuming risk.

- Explain the known risks of the activity, even if these are spelled out in the waiver.

- Ask the client if she understands the risks.

- Ask the client if she understands the effect of the waiver.

- If the client signs the waiver but says anything that suggests she does not agree to assume the risk or to release the agency from liability, write this down and report it to the supervisor before the client participates in the activity.

- Check the signed waiver to be sure that the client has printed and signed her name, and has included the date on which it was signed.

The use of waivers does not eliminate the obligation of social service workers to follow all safety rules and policies of their employer, and to serve their clients conscientiously and to the best of their ability.

KEY TERMS

agency	professional misconduct	vicarious liability
damages	standard of care	waiver
duty of care	tort	
intentional tort	unintentional tort	

REFERENCES

Child and Family Services Act, RSO 1990, c. C.11.

Corrections and Conditional Release Act, SC 1992, c. 20.

Criminal Code, RSC 1985, c. C-46.

Customs Act, RSC 1985, c. 1 (2d Supp.).

Day Nurseries Act, RSO 1990, c. D.2.

Mental Health Act, RSO 1990, c. M.7.

Ministry of Correctional Services Act, RSO 1990, c. M.22.

Mr. K v. E.K., 2004 ABQB 159 (CanLII).

Ontario College of Social Workers and Social Service Workers, Code of Ethics and *Standards of Practice Handbook*, online at www.ocswssw.org.

Police Services Act, RSO 1990, c. P.15.

Public Authorities Protection Act, RSO 1990, c. P.38.

Social Work and Social Service Work Act, 1998, SO 1998, c. 31.

REVIEW QUESTIONS

1. Name three kinds of consequences that can arise when social service workers commit serious professional errors.

2. Identify three kinds of behaviour that are most likely to land a social service worker in trouble.

3. Why would a person choose to become a member of the Ontario College of Social Workers and Social Service Workers if it means having to abide by standards of practice and a code of ethics?

4. If a complaint against a registered social service worker is referred to the Discipline Committee of the college and the committee finds the member guilty of incompetence or professional misconduct, what consequences can follow?

5. What additional penalties can be imposed if a registered member of the college is found guilty of professional misconduct?

6. Identify the three most common situations in which social service workers assault clients.

7. Under what kinds of circumstances may a social service worker use force against a client?

8. What must the prosecution prove in order to establish criminal negligence?

9. When might social service workers have a legal duty to act, within the meaning of the offence of criminal negligence?

10. If, instead of being charged with criminal negligence, a social service worker is sued for civil negligence, what is the likely penalty if the suit is successful?

11. What consequences can a social service worker's negligence have for her employer?

12. What is the difference between a duty of care and a standard of care?

Glossary of Terms

absolute discharge   A sentencing order that imposes no penalty on an accused; the accused is found guilty but is deemed not to have been convicted and receives no formal criminal record, although court files and police files are retained.

abuse of process   An improper action or series of actions on the part of the police or the prosecution that undermines the fairness of the criminal procedure.

access   In the family law context, a formal legal arrangement that establishes the terms upon which a non-custodial parent can spend time with his or her child.

accommodation   In the employment law context, any action on the part of an employer that is designed to assist an employee with special needs in doing a job—for example, the purchase of computer hardware that helps a visually impaired employee read electronic documents.

accreditation   The official recognition, by a professional association or government body, of an organization's successful achievement of standards or criteria.

accused   A person against whom a criminal charge has been laid and who has not yet been convicted; usually used with respect to indictable offences.

actus reus   The physical act or omission that, when combined with the required intent (if any), constitutes an offence.

adjournment   A delay in a trial for which a judge has given permission.

administrative discretion   The choices made every day by government administrators and employees when responding to particular circumstances.

administrative law   The body of law that governs how government administrators and employees exercise the decision-making powers granted to them under statute.

administrative segregation   A term used in corrections to refer to the practice of keeping an offender separate from the general offender population, either for his or her protection, for the protection of the offender population, or as a disciplinary measure.

administrative tribunal   A body or a panel that hears disputes and makes formal decisions with respect to the administration of a legislative scheme, program, or system—for example, the Social Benefits Tribunal.

adverse impact discrimination   Discrimination that is indirect, and often unintentional.

advocacy   The making of representations or arguments on behalf of another party or parties in an effort to help them.

advocate   (v.) To make representations or arguments on behalf of someone else; (n.) a person who undertakes advocacy.

agent   A person who acts on behalf of another (the principal) and who can bind the principal to contracts with third parties.

aggravating circumstances   In the criminal law context, a factor that tends to support the charging of a more serious offence or the imposition of a more serious penalty; for example, it's an aggravating factor for a crime to be motivated by racial hatred.

alternative dispute resolution (ADR)   The resolution of interpersonal conflicts that might otherwise form the basis of legal proceedings through alternative means, such as mediation or arbitration.

appeal   A hearing (including a paper-based decision-making process) for the purpose of formally reconsidering an earlier decision of a court, tribunal, or administrator on a point of law.

appeal court   A court that reconsiders a decision made by a trial court or administrative tribunal on a point of law.

applicant   A person who has initiated a legal process.

arbitration   A form of alternative dispute resolution in which parties submit their dispute to an individual arbitrator or an arbitral board, who makes a decision that the parties have agreed, in advance, will be binding.

arbitration clause   A term of a contract that provides that any disputes arising in respect of the terms of the contract shall be resolved through arbitration.

assisted negotiation   Negotiation where the negotiation function is delegated to another person, such as a lawyer or a social service worker, who negotiates on the person's behalf.

attorney   A representative, usually a friend or relative, who is formally appointed by a person to make decisions on his or her behalf.

attorney for personal care   Someone who manages health and personal care decisions for a person incapable of doing so for himself or herself.

attorney for property   Someone who manages the financial affairs of a person incapable of doing so for himself or herself.

balance of probabilities   The standard of proof in a civil trial; requires the party making a claim to prove that the claim is more likely to be true than not true.

best interests of the child   The requirement that legislation such as the *Child and Family Services Act* and family law statutes be applied so that the interests of the child are paramount and supersede the wishes of the child and the interests of others, such as the parents or the children's aid society.

beyond a reasonable doubt   The standard of proof in criminal trials; requires that the sum of all the facts pointing to guilt must be so convincing that no reasonable person would question that conclusion.

bona fide job qualifications   Specific skills or training that an employee must have to be able to perform a job.

burden of proof   The responsibility of proving something; for example, under Canadian criminal law, the state has the burden of proving an accused's guilt; *see also* onus.

bylaw   A rule created by a municipality, county, or other level of government smaller than a province; also, a rule created by a corporation to guide the way in which it will function.

capable   In the mental health context, able to understand the information required for making a decision regarding treatment or admission to a facility, and able to understand the consequences of the decision.

capacity   In the mental health context (under the *Health Care Consent Act*), being able to understand the information that is relevant to a treatment, admission, or service delivery decision, and being able to understand the reasonably foreseeable consequences of the decision.

caution   In the criminal law context, a formal warning, delivered by a police officer or a Crown attorney, to a suspect or an accused as part of a diversion initiative.

charity   A not-for-profit corporation that has been granted charitable status by the Canada Revenue Agency.

child support   Money ordered by a court to be paid by one parent to another for the economic support of the children, when the parents are living apart.

Children's Lawyer   A lawyer from the Office of the Children's Lawyer, a government agency, who may represent children in certain kinds of legal matters, including child protection proceedings and some family law matters.

citizen   In Canada, an individual who was either born in Canada or who, after arriving in Canada as an immigrant, completed the process of applying for citizenship and was granted full rights to participate in Canadian society.

civil law   A term usually used to describe all non-criminal law; sometimes used in reference to the law made under the *Civil Code* of Quebec (in contrast to judge-made common law).

code of ethics   A system of moral principles designed to guide the conduct of a person or identifiable group (for example, a profession).

cohabitation agreement   An agreement similar to a marriage contract, but made by a couple who are cohabiting or who intend to cohabit.

collective agreement   An employment contract, formally negotiated by a union and management, that governs the terms of service for all members of that union within a workplace.

common law   A body of legal principles, established through the decisions made in court cases, that binds future decisions in cases with similar facts.

community or contemporary policing   A philosophy of police services delivery that is based on connections to and partnerships with non-police members of the community.

community treatment order   An order that provides for the treatment, in the community, of a mentally ill person who meets the criteria for involuntary commitment to hospital.

conditional discharge   A sentencing order that includes no penalty other than probation.

conditional release   Any release of a prisoner from custody before the last day of his or her full sentence. All early releases are subject to conditions—for example, good behaviour, participation in a rehabilitation program, and reporting to a parole officer.

conditional sentence of imprisonment   A sentence served in the community, such as house arrest, that includes the imposition of restrictions on liberty which, if violated, can lead to serving the sentence in a custodial facility.

consecutive order   An order of society wardship followed by an order of supervision (in the care of parents or guardians) for a total period not exceeding 12 months.

consensual   Something that is consented to, agreed to, and permitted by the party to whom it is done or who participates in it.

consent   (n.) Sometimes called a waiver; a legal document by which a person gives up a right or privilege that he or she would normally have—for example, the right to confidentiality of personal information.

consent order   In the context of child protection, an agreed plan for the child's care, developed with input from the parents and/or the child, and consented to by them.

constitution   The statute that establishes the political structure of a nation and that sets out its fundamental laws.

constructive dismissal   A situation in which a person is not actually dismissed directly, but leaves employment because of unbearable conditions—for example, harassment that is perpetrated or tolerated by the employer. The court in such cases *construes* the situation as a dismissal.

contingency fee   A lawyer's fee for service that is calculated as a percentage of recovery. For example, a fee agreement may prescribe that the lawyer, if successful in winning a settlement or award of damages for the client, is entitled to 15 percent of the total settlement or award.

contraband   Goods illegally or unlawfully possessed.

contract   A binding agreement between two parties, which may be written but is not required to be in most cases.

convention   In the context of international law, an agreement between two or more nations.

Convention refugee   In reference to the *United Nations Convention Relating to the Status of Refugees*, a person who has a well-founded fear of persecution for reasons of race, religion, nationality, membership in a particular social group, or political opinion, and who is unable or afraid to seek protection from his country of nationality or residence.

co-operative housing   A housing arrangement by which members of a co-operative own (as opposed to rent) a share of a co-operatively owned residential complex or neighbourhood, and participate in the maintenance and administration of the complex.

coordinated access centre   In Ontario, a local or regional centre dedicated to processing applications for access to subsidized housing.

corporation   A business or non-profit organization that is registered as a corporation in its operating jurisdiction, and as a result is a legal entity separate from the people who run it.

counterclaim   A claim filed by a defendant against the plaintiff (the person who initiated a legal action).

criminal harassment   Harassment that causes the victim to fear for his or her safety, and a criminal offence under the *Criminal Code*.

criminal responsibility   In Canada, anyone who is aged 12 or older and who is mentally capable at the time of the commission of a crime may be tried, convicted, and punished for that crime.

criminogenic   Tending to lead to crime; for example, widespread poverty and lack of recreation programs in a community may be criminogenic.

cross-examination   Questioning, including leading questions, by one party of the other side's witnesses.

Crown wardship   The situation where, by court order, a children's aid society permanently assumes the role of parent with respect to a child or young person, and the child or young person may be adopted by a new family.

custodian   A person or organization, such as a hospital or long-term care residence, that is regulated by the *Personal Health Information Protection Act* and who is authorized to collect, use, and disclose personal health information.

custody   In the family law context, the legal arrangement for decision making with respect to the care of a child.

cyber-bullying   Harassment or abuse of others by means of electronic media, such as e-mail, text messaging, or the posting of comments and/or pictures on the Internet.

damages   Monetary compensation for harm suffered, paid by the person responsible pursuant to a judgment or an out-of-court settlement.

day parole   A form of parole that permits an offender to be absent from a custodial facility in the daytime, usually to go to work, and return in the evening.

defence   In criminal or civil law, the accused or the party who is responding to a lawsuit launched by another party; also, the arguments put forth by an accused or a defendant; also, in criminal law, a theory proposed by an accused that attempts to excuse the commission of the offence, such as self-defence.

defendant   In a criminal matter, the person accused of a charge, usually used with respect to summary conviction offences; in a civil matter, the person opposing a plaintiff's claim.

deliberation   In the criminal law context, any thinking about, planning, or consideration of the consequences of a crime that the accused undertakes before committing the crime.

demand urinalysis   A compulsory urine test for restricted substances, such as is carried out in a prison environment.

denunciation   Public or formal criticism of wrongdoing.

deterrence   The effect that punishment has to discourage future wrongdoing, either relating to an individual specifically or generally to the population at large.

direct discrimination   Discrimination that is blatant and obvious.

director   In the corporate context, a person who, along with the other directors, controls a corporation and makes corporate decisions.

disbursements   A lawyer's out-of-pocket expenses that he or she charges back to the client—for example, courier costs or a charge for conducting a database search.

disciplinary offence   A serious or recurrent breach of penitentiary rules, which are developed by penitentiary staff in accordance with the *Corrections and Conditional Release Act* to govern inmate behaviour.

disclosure   In law, the formal sharing of one party's information with the other party in preparation for a hearing.

disclosure by consent   Disclosure of confidential information made with the permission of the person to whom the information pertains.

disclosure required by law   Disclosure of confidential information, prescribed by law or ordered by a court.

discretion   In law, the power of a decision maker to exercise judgment based on the particular circumstances.

disposition   The court's resolution of a matter before it, such as a conviction or an award of damages.

diversion   In the context of criminal law, alternatives to the formal court process, such as the exercise of police discretion to give a warning to a suspect rather than arrest him or her.

division of powers   The plan for the sharing of legislative jurisdiction over specified subject areas between the federal and the provincial governments, as set out in the constitution.

domestic contract   A contract negotiated by spouses or partners to govern legal aspects of their union.

downsize   A reduction in the size of a workforce for business or economic reasons, resulting in layoffs.

dual relationship   A relationship between a social service worker and a client where there is both a professional relationship and a personal relationship.

duty counsel   A legal aid lawyer who works shifts at court assisting unrepresented litigants in need.

duty of care   Obligation to take care not to harm others who are so closely and directly affected by a person's actions that the person ought reasonably to have those others in contemplation.

duty to accommodate   The duty imposed on employers, landlords, and goods and services providers to accommodate the special needs of employees, tenants, and customers and clients.

earned release/supervised release/parole Terms used to describe early release from prison after serving a portion of a custodial sentence, but requiring the prisoner to comply with supervision terms, such as regular reporting to a parole officer.

election In criminal law, the choice between two procedures, such as a trial before a judge alone or a trial before a judge and jury.

elements of the offence The *actus reus*, or physical act or omission involved in committing the offence, and the *mens rea*, or state of mind or level of intent attributed to the accused that establishes fault in so acting or failing to act.

entitlement A right to receive a benefit, based on objective criteria; a person can be said to have an entitlement to a benefit whether or not he or she is actually receiving the benefit.

equalization payment In the family law context, a payment made by one spouse to the other in order to equalize the family property upon dissolution of the relationship.

evidence Proof of the truth of an allegation; usually witness testimony, or documentary or other physical object.

examination-in-chief Questioning of a party's own witness, limited to open-ended (not leading) questions.

exclusive possession In the family law context, one party may, by agreement or court order, be entitled to live in the matrimonial home without the other spouse.

exculpatory evidence Evidence that tends to suggest that the accused is not guilty.

extradition The process of delivering a fugitive to another country to face charges there.

extrajudicial measures or sanctions A referral or "penalty"—for example, community service—that is imposed on a criminal suspect with his or her consent. Compliance with the measure or sanction generally makes it possible for the suspect to avoid criminal prosecution or a criminal sentence.

extraordinary measures In the context of residential mental health services or criminal custody, intrusive steps taken to physically control a subject—for example, the use of mechanical restraints (straps, belts, handcuffs, etc.) or the administration of psychotropic drugs.

family support worker A person designated under the *Social Housing Reform Act, 2000* to assist anyone eligible for a rent-geared-to-income (RGI) subsidy in pursuing financial support from persons with a legal obligation to provide it.

federal system of government A division of law-making powers between the national (or federal) government and the provincial governments, according to subject matter.

fraud Obtaining money or benefits by deceit.

harassment Engaging in a course of vexatious comment or conduct that is known or ought reasonably to be known to be unwelcome.

hard-to-house individual A person who has encountered barriers to housing or has had trouble remaining in housing because of personal obstacles, such as chronic unemployment, disability or addictions, a personality disorder, or mental health problems.

hearing A formal opportunity for a party to a dispute to present evidence and arguments before a neutral decision maker.

homemaker Under the *Child and Family Services Act*, a person who works in the home of a vulnerable child in an effort either to support a struggling parent or to care for the child during the parent's temporary absence.

home-schooling A practice by which parents undertake to educate their children at home.

human rights Rights that many societies recognize as belonging to all individuals based simply on their status as human beings—for example, the right to be free from torture.

human smuggling The facilitation of illegal immigration for the purpose of collecting payments from people who are desperate to immigrate.

human trafficking The facilitation of immigration for the purpose of exploiting the immigrants in the new country, such as by using them as slave labour.

hybrid offence An offence that can be charged either as a summary conviction offence or as an indictable offence, according to the Crown's election.

imbalance of power A situation where one party in a dispute is vulnerable to relinquishing legal rights for reasons such as fewer financial resources, less education, or a history of intimidation by the other party; the imbalance of power between the parties may make it impossible for negotiations or mediation to lead to a fair result.

immigration   Relocating to a new country with the intention of making a permanent home there. Emigration, by contrast, describes the act of leaving one's country.

impartiality   Neutrality with respect to a dispute; having no bias or personal interest in the outcome.

inculpatory evidence   Evidence that tends to suggest that an accused is guilty.

indictable offence   A serious offence that attracts a significant penalty and that is tried through a more complex criminal procedure than summary conviction offences, which are less serious offences.

indictment   A type of charging process or document that is used to begin a prosecution, usually of an indictable offence.

indirect discrimination   Discrimination that is subtle and often unintentional, which results from discrimination that is not otherwise based on a prohibited ground.

information   A type of charging process or document that is used to begin a prosecution of a summary conviction offence.

intentional tort   A category of tort that involves causing harm on purpose rather than through negligence.

internal review   The review of an administrative decision by a different decision maker within the institution, rather than by an independent third party.

intervenor   A party who has no direct interest in a legal proceeding but who may be significantly affected by the precedent-setting significance of the outcome of the dispute, and is therefore granted permission by the court to make submissions or arguments for reasons of public policy.

involuntary admission or commitment   In the mental health context, requiring a patient to stay in a hospital without the patient's consent.

judicial interim release   Also called bail; release from custody pending a trial or appeal, sometimes with conditions, such as posting of a bond.

judicial review   A legal challenge to a tribunal decision on procedural grounds, such as whether the tribunal acted within its jurisdiction, and brought by a party by application to the Divisional Court.

jurisdiction   The scope of authority to make, interpret, or enforce laws.

jury   A group of people who examine the evidence and determine what facts and evidence are believable, and then apply the law, as explained to them by the judge, to the proven facts of the case.

"just cause" dismissal   The termination of a worker's employment for reasons that are significant enough to relieve the employer of its obligation to provide notice or pay in lieu of notice.

juvenile delinquent   A historical term for a young offender; no longer used.

kinship care   Placement of an at-risk child in the care of someone with a relationship or connection to the child, such as a relative or family friend or, if applicable, a member of the child's First Nations band.

labelling   The theory that by branding a person a criminal, the person may become more psychologically disposed to live up to that reputation and re-offend.

layoff   Temporary termination of employment for business reasons, such as economic downturn, with the expectation that the employee will be called back to work at some time in the future.

legal advice   Direction given to a person to take a particular course of action, with legal consequences, based on an application of the law to the circumstances of the person's situation.

legal aid   A subsidy regulated and partly funded by the government to assist low-income clients with part or all of the financial cost of certain kinds of legal services.

legal capacity   The right and ability of a person to exercise legal rights.

legal information   General information about the law, without reference to the particulars of an individual's circumstances.

legal person   An entity—either a person or a corporation—that is recognized by the law as able to bring or defend a lawsuit on his, her, or its own behalf.

legislature   The elected arm of government, which creates statutes and which is accountable to voters.

liability   The legal responsibility to fulfill an obligation, such as paying compensation for harm done to another party, or paying a debt owed pursuant to a contract.

litigation guardian   An adult who represents a child under the age of majority in litigation.

malpractice   Failure of a professional to perform in compliance with one's professional duty, such as by acting illegally, unethically, or negligently.

marginalization   The concept that people who are disadvantaged, such as by poverty, lack of education, poor language skills, addictions, or abuse, are less able to access the information and services that they need or to assert their rights.

marriage breakdown   The only ground for divorce under Canadian law; can be established based on evidence of cruelty or adultery, but is usually established by proving that the couple have lived separate and apart for at least one year.

marriage contract   A contract between two people who are married to each other or intend to marry each other, which may address most issues of ownership or division of property, spousal support obligations, and the right to direct the education of children, but may not address custody or access with respect to children.

matrimonial home   In the family law context, the home that served as a primary residence for a couple at the time that they separated.

means testing   Assessing a person's eligibility for a program by analyzing his or her financial situation (assets, income, benefits already being received, future entitlements, etc.).

mediation   An alternative dispute resolution approach in which a neutral third party attempts to support the parties in their efforts to resolve the dispute without resort to court.

mens rea   The "mental element" of a crime; the intent required to satisfy the description of an offence.

mitigating circumstances   In a criminal law context, a factor that tends to support the imposition of a lighter penalty—for example, a demonstration of sincere remorse on the part of the convicted person.

motion   A hearing on an individual legal issue within the context of a broader legal case—for example, a hearing to decide whether certain evidence should be excluded.

multidisciplinary approach   An approach to a problem or issue that involves the participation and collaboration of professionals and experts from different disciplines—for example, a social worker, a lawyer, and a psychiatrist.

municipal bylaws   Rules passed by municipal councils, governing local matters such as sewage and water supply, public health, public transit, and libraries.

natural justice   The right to a hearing with the submission of evidence and argument.

needs testing   Assessing someone's situation on the basis of his or her needs—for example, by asking how much the individual spends on rent, food, and medically necessary drugs.

negotiation   Communication for the purpose of resolving a dispute by agreement.

net family property   In the family law context, the class of property that is subject to division between the spouses after a marriage ends.

neutral   (n.) An impartial third party, hired by parties to a dispute, to assist them in resolving the conflict, either by mediating an agreement or by imposing a binding decision upon them after hearing both sides.

non-refoulement   A principle of international law denouncing any attempt by a country to send displaced people who are at risk of serious harm or persecution back into the nation in which they are at risk.

norm   A pattern of behaviour that is typical or usual for a particular culture, society, or community.

not-for-profit corporation   A corporation that is operated for a purpose other than making a profit, whether or not it is registered as a charity.

notice   In the context of legal procedure, the formal process of informing the opposing party of every procedural step taken, such as filing a claim.

notice of termination   In the context of employment law, and specifically with respect to wrongful dismissal, the length of time prior to actual termination of employment to which an employee is entitled to be informed of the pending termination.

offence   A wrongdoing that is identified or created by a statute and that can attract the imposition of a penalty.

onus   The burden of proof in a legal proceeding.

open custody   Imprisonment with less restriction on inmates' freedom of movement than secure custody.

oral evidence   Testimony, provided by witnesses.

overhoused tenant   A term used by subsidized housing administrators to indicate that a tenant is occupying a unit that exceeds his or her needs.

paralegal   A person with some legal training who is not a lawyer but who may provide a limited scope of legal services to clients.

paramountcy   The principle by which the federal government has jurisdiction in situations where a law does not fit squarely under either federal or provincial jurisdiction.

parens patriae   The doctrine by which the government takes on a parental role with respect to children removed from their homes.

parole   The release of an offender who is deemed not to pose an undue risk of reoffending within the term of his full sentence.

partnership   An unincorporated business that is owned by two or more partners.

pay in lieu of notice   In the context of employment law, payment to an employee given instead of notice of termination, equalling the salary or wages the employee would have earned during the period of notice to which he or she was entitled.

permanent resident   A non-citizen who has complied with Canada's immigration law and policy and has the right to stay in Canada indefinitely.

permanent resident status   The right of an individual to remain in Canada indefinitely.

person in need of protection   A person in Canada whose removal to his or her country of nationality or former residence might subject him or her to torture, death, or cruel and unusual treatment or punishment.

physical evidence   Objects or documents that are filed with the court as evidence in a crime (for example, a suspected murder weapon or a lab report).

plaintiff   The party in a civil lawsuit who initiated the lawsuit.

plan of care   In the context of the *Child and Family Services Act*, a plan that describes a children's aid society's recommendations with respect to services that should be offered to a child in need of protection.

plea   In criminal law, the accused's formal response to the charges against him—for example, "guilty" or "not guilty."

plea bargain   A negotiation between a prosecutor and an accused that results in a guilty plea to a lesser charge.

policy   An administrative procedure or rule, not specifically prescribed by law, that is adopted and followed by an organization.

power of attorney   The legal act that appoints someone as another person's attorney for property or attorney for personal care.

precedent   The principle that requires courts to follow the legal rulings made by superior courts in decisions based on similar facts.

preliminary hearing   A hearing held before a trial for the purpose of assessing the adequacy of the evidence or to narrow the issues for trial.

pre-trial motion/application   A hearing held before a trial begins to resolve a collateral issue, such as an issue of procedure, the admissibility of evidence, or whether or not the accused is fit to stand trial.

pre-trial release   Also called bail or judicial interim release; release from custody pending a trial or appeal, sometimes with conditions, such as posting of a bond.

privilege   An enhanced protection of the confidentiality of communications based on the relationship of the parties, such as solicitor–client privilege.

pro bono legal work   Legal services for which a lawyer waives all or part of the fee for professional or altruistic reasons.

probation   A sentence that includes the imposition of terms, such as reporting to a probation officer on a regular basis, that, if breached, may result in a more severe penalty.

procedural fairness   Fairness that is provided through the application of objective and consistent procedures.

procedural law   Law that prescribes the manner in which something is to be done; often designed to promote fairness or administrative efficiency.

proclamation   The method by which a statute is brought into force some time after it is passed into law, on a future unspecified date. This is different from royal assent, which brings a statute into force at the same time as it is passed into law.

professional misconduct   Practising a profession in a manner that is deemed, by the governing body of the profession, to be contrary to the standards of ethics, quality, or competence of the profession.

professional standards   Benchmarks for service quality against which the performance of a professional is measured.

prosecution   The process of presenting the case for convicting and sentencing a person accused of an offence, undertaken by the Crown attorney; also, the Crown attorney prosecuting a case.

prosecutor   The Crown attorney prosecuting a case.

quiet enjoyment   The right to occupy and use rented premises free from unexpected intrusions by the landlord.

real property   Land and buildings, also called real estate.

recidivism   Repeat offending after a conviction.

refugee   Generally, a person who has fled a nation or state in which he or she suffered or was at risk of harm or unjust persecution. A more specific statutory definition of "refugee" applies for the purpose of determining the validity of applications for immigration and protection.

regulation   A rule made by authority provided in a statute, which helps guide the application of the statute, often by prescribing how it is administered or by providing technical detail.

rehabilitation   In the criminal law context, the process of promoting positive changes in a convicted person that will support successful reintegration into society and reduce the risk of further offences.

remission   In the context of incarceration, time credits for good behaviour that support eligibility for early release.

rent control   Legislated restrictions on rent increases on rental properties under certain circumstances (typically, while the same tenant remains in the unit).

rent geared to income   A subsidy that allows a low-income tenant of non-profit housing to pay less than market rent.

reparation   A payment made to compensate for harm; may be ordered in individual criminal cases or by a government, such as to victims of war crimes.

reprisal   In the context of employment law, a consequence imposed on an employee by an employer, to punish him or her for having exercised rights.

respondent   The person opposing an applicant in a legal process.

restorative justice   An approach to justice that places an emphasis not on punishment of the offender, but on taking responsibility for actions, compensating for harm done to victims, and repairing relationships.

restraining order   A court order that prohibits an individual from some particular action—for example, selling an asset or approaching a specified person.

revoke   To terminate a privilege, permission, licence, or other extension of rights.

rights adviser   In the mental health context, a person who is available to speak with patients about their legal rights with respect to involuntary admission to hospital, including the right to appeal the admission.

sanction   An officially imposed consequence, such as a fine, the suspension of a licence, or the loss of a privilege that follows misconduct or the failure to meet compulsory standards of performance or quality.

search warrant   An order issued by a justice of the peace or a judge that allows a peace officer to search a location or person.

secure custody   Imprisonment with strict physical control of inmates.

sentencing circle   An alternative sentencing procedure in which the penalty for a crime is decided through a consultative process that involves the offender, the victim, and community stakeholders.

separation agreement   An agreement made between two people who are married or cohabiting with the intention of separating, or who are already separated; the agreement may include provisions governing each party's rights and obligations after separation, including ownership or division of property, support obligations, the right to direct the education of children, and custody and access with respect to children.

severance pay   A payment under the *Employment Standards Act* that an employer must pay to an employee upon termination of employment, in addition to notice of termination or termination pay in lieu of notice, if the employee qualifies as described in the statute.

sexual harassment   Harassment because of sex, and defined broadly to include jokes, staring, and unwanted touching.

shareholder   A person who, by investing in a corporation, has an ownership interest in the corporation that is represented by a "share."

signatory   A party who has signed a document, such as a contract or a treaty.

Small Claims Court   A court with a simplified procedure that hears trials in which the damages claimed fall below a prescribed monetary cutoff.

society wardship   The status of a child in care who is considered to be under the temporary care of a society and who is expected to eventually return to his or her parent(s).

sole proprietorship   A business that is owned by a single individual and that is not incorporated.

solicitor–client privilege   A rule of confidentiality protecting communications between lawyer and client.

sponsorship   In the context of immigration, an arrangement where a citizen or permanent resident takes on the financial responsibility of supporting a new immigrant, usually a relative.

spousal support   Money ordered by a court to be paid by one ex-spouse to the other after the breakdown of a marriage or common-law union.

standard of care   The degree of care that the law requires be taken to avoid harm to others—namely, the care that a "reasonable person" would exercise in the circumstances.

standard of proof   The level or degree of proof that a party must meet to be successful at trial.

status immigrant   An immigrant legally entitled to stay in Canada indefinitely, either as a refugee or as a permanent resident.

statute   A law that is passed by either the federal or a provincial legislature.

statutory release   The early release of a prisoner based on operation of statute and after the prisoner has served at least two-thirds of his or her sentence.

stay of proceedings   A court order that stops proceedings against an accused, often because of excessive delay.

strict-discipline program   An educational program outside the general public education stream that is designed to provide a setting for educating students who have been expelled for violating a school's code of conduct.

sublet   To lease a property, such as an apartment, by the first tenant to a new tenant, called the subtenant.

subpoena   A legal instrument that compels a witness's appearance in court by force of law.

subsidy   A monetary grant that is designed to defray an expense in whole or in part; usually not available except for the purpose of offsetting the targeted expense.

subsistence needs   A person's very basic living requirements, such as food and shelter.

substantive law   Legal rules and principles relating to various subject areas, such as employment law or criminal law, as opposed to procedural law, which governs legal process.

substitute decision maker   A person who makes decisions about legal, financial, or health matters on behalf of a person who is incapable of making these decisions.

subtenant   A tenant who leases property from another tenant.

summary conviction offence   Usually, a less serious offence that is tried by means of a simplified procedure and that attracts less serious penalties than does an indictable offence.

supervised access   In the family law context, access between a parent and a child that is supervised by another adult.

supervision order   Under the *Child and Family Services Act*, a court order requiring that certain activities, such as the child's return to the family home after a period of society care, will be monitored by a third party, usually a government employee.

survivor benefit   A benefit paid to the dependants of the benefit recipient after his or her death.

suspect   A person who is under investigation for a crime but who has not yet been charged under the *Criminal Code* in relation to that crime.

suspended sentence   The release of an offender into society subject to certain conditions set out in a probation order. If the conditions are breached, the offender may be required to serve a sentence.

systemic discrimination   Discrimination that permeates or is incorporated into policies and practices.

temporary care agreement   Under the *Child and Family Services Act*, a contract between a parent, a children's aid society, and sometimes a child that governs a plan of action to help a child in need of society intervention.

test case   A legal case undertaken in pursuit of a legal ruling with broader implications—beyond the effect on the particular litigants and potentially of benefit to others.

testimony   Oral evidence given in court by a witness or the accused.

tort   A wrongful act or an infringement of a right (other than under contract) leading to legal liability.

treaty   A formal, multiparty contract, often between nations.

trial court   Usually, the first level of court at which a legal matter is heard.

trier of fact   The party who makes findings of fact in a trial; in a jury trial, the jury; in a trial by judge alone, the judge.

trier of law   The party who decides how the law must be applied to a particular set of facts; in both jury and non-jury trials, the judge.

uncontested divorce   A divorce in which the parties settled all issues without resort to litigation, and apply jointly for a divorce.

undertaking   A promise.

undue hardship   The point at which an employer is not required to accommodate an employee's special needs. What this point is varies depending on the employer's resources and the employee's particular needs.

verdict   In a criminal trial, the judge's or jury's decision about whether the accused is guilty or innocent.

vicarious liability   A legal doctrine under which one party is held liable for harm caused by another.

waiver   Sometimes called a release or a consent; a legal document by which a person gives up a right or privilege—for example, the right to confidentiality of personal information.

wilful blindness   In tort law or criminal law, a state of mind in which the accused actively chooses not to think about the potential negative consequences of an act before doing it.

will say   A written summary of a witness's expected evidence—what the witness "will say" in court.

"without prejudice" statement   A statement made during negotiation that may not be used as evidence of the statement maker's intention to waive legal rights.

witness   A person who gives evidence in the course of an investigation, a trial, or a hearing.

written submission   A document that is prepared and filed with a court or administrative decision-making body to provide information relevant to a decision, often in lieu of oral testimony.

wrongful dismissal   Dismissal from employment without just cause or proper notice of termination.

young offender   An offender who was aged 12 to 17 at the time of the alleged offence.

youth worker   A person designated under the *Youth Criminal Justice Act* who assists young people in accomplishing a goal—for example, reintegration into the community after a custodial sentence.

Index